Custodians
of the Land
Ecology & Culture
in the History of Tanzania

Eastern African Studies

Custodians of the Land

Ecology & Culture
in the History of Tanzania

Edited by
GREGORY MADDOX, JAMES L. GIBLIN
&
ISARIA N. KIMAMBO

James Currey
LONDON

Mkuki na Nyota
DAR ES SALAAM

E.A.E.P
NAIROBI

Ohio University Press
ATHENS

James Currey Ltd
54b Thornhill Square
Islington
London N1 1BE

Mkuki na Nyota
PO Box 4246
Dar es Salaam

East African Educational Publishers
PO Box 45314
Nairobi

Ohio University Press
Scott Quadrangle
Athens, Ohio 45701

First published 1996
1 2 3 4 5 00 99 98 97 96

British Library Cataloguing in Publication Data

Custodians of the Land: Ecology and
Culture in the History of Tanzania. —
(Eastern African Studies)
I. Maddox, Gregory II. Series
967.8

ISBN 0-85255-725-6 (cased)
0-85255-724-8 (paper)

Library of Congress Cataloging-in-Publication Data

Custodians of the land : ecology & culture in the history of Tanzania
/ edited by Gregory Maddox, James L. Giblin & Isaria N. Kimambo.
    p.   cm. — (Eastern African studies)
Includes bibliographical references and index.
    ISBN 0-8214-1133-0 (cloth). — ISBN 0-8214-1134-9 (pbk.)
    1. Human ecology—Tanzania—History. 2. Environmental policy—
Tanzania. 3. Environmental protection—Tanzania. 4. Tanzania—
Social conditions. 5. Tanzania—Economic conditions. 6. Tanzania—
Politics and government. I. Maddox, Gregory. II. Giblin, James
Leonard. III. Kimambo, Isaria N. IV. Series: Eastern African
studies.
GF729.C87   1995   95-22932
363.7'009678—dc20   CIP

Typeset in 10/11 Baskerville by Colset Pte Ltd, Singapore
Printed in Britain by Villiers Publications, London N3

Contents

Introduction

Part One

Environmental & Demographic Change

v

Contents

Part Two

Environmental Change & Economic History
In Tanzania's Northern Highlands

Part Three

Politics & Environmental Change

Contents

Part Four

Environment & Morality

Maps, Figures
& Tables

Maps

Figures

Tables

viii

Photographs

ix

Abbreviations

AHD	*African Historical Demography*
AHT	Arusha Historical Traditions
AO/AD	Agricultural Officer, Arusha District
BArchP	Bundesarchiv Potsdam
BRALUP	Bureau of Resource Assessment and Land Use Planning, University of Dar es Salaam
CS/DSM	Chief Secretary, Dar es Salaam
DC/AD	District Commissioner, Arusha District
DKB	*Deutsches Kolonialblatt*
ELMB	*Evangelisch-Lutherisches Missionsblatt*
Jahresbericht	*Jahresbericht über die Entwicklung der Deutsches Schutzgebiete*
LDO	Land Development Officer
LF	Lushoto Department of Natural Resources
LO	Land Officer
MHT	Meru Historical Traditions
MIT	Mbugu Interview Transcripts
PC/NP	Provincial Commissioner, Northern Province
PDR	*Population and Development Review*
Sr. AO	Senior Agricultural Officer
TANU	Tanganyika African National Union
TNA	Tanzania National Archives
RKolA	Reichskolonialamt
UDSM	University of Dar es Salaam
ULUS	Uluguru Land Usage Scheme

Contributors

Christopher Conte is a doctoral student specializing in African history at Michigan State University. He has recently carried out fieldwork in Tanzania and is currently writing his dissertation on changes in human and environmental relations in the Usambara Mountains.

James L. Giblin is an Associate Professor in the Department of History and the African-American World Studies Program at the University of Iowa. He is the author of *The Politics of Environmental Control in Northeastern Tanzania, 1840–1940* (Philadelphia: University of Pennsylvania Press, 1993). Currently he is working on a history of Njombe District in southern Tanzania since the 1940s.

Isaria N. Kimambo is a specialist in East African history. He has authored several works on the precolonial history of Tanzanian peoples, including most recently *Penetration and Protest in Tanzania: The Impact of the World Economy on the Pare, 1860–1960* (London: James Currey 1991). He was formerly Chief Academic Officer and is currently Professor, Department of History, at the University of Dar es Salaam.

Juhani Koponen is a senior lecturer at the Institute of Development Studies at the University of Helsinki. His publications include *People and Production in Late Precolonial Tanzania: History and Structures* (Uppsala, 1988) and *German Colonial Policies in Mainland Tanzania, 1890–1914: Development for Exploitation* (Hamburg, 1994). Currently he is working on Tanzanian population history and development thinking in historical perspective.

Pamela A. Maack received her Ph.D. in Anthropology from Northwestern University in June 1992. She is currently teaching at San Jacinto College in Houston, Texas, and is working on future publications following a return trip to Tanzania in 1993–4.

Gregory Maddox is the author of several works on the history of central

Tanzania. He has taught at the University of Dar es Salaam and is currently at Texas Southern University in Houston, Texas.

Jamie Monson is an Assistant Professor of History at Carleton and St Olaf Colleges in Minnesota. Her research and publications focus on the social history of agricultural and ecological change in southern Tanzania. She is currently writing a monograph on boundary-making and the production of space in colonial Tanganyika.

Thomas Spear has written histories of *Zwangendaba's Ngoni*, the Mijikenda (*The Kaya Complex*), eastern and central Kenya (*Kenya's Past*) and *The Swahili* (with Derek Nurse), as well as editing (with Richard Waller) *Being Maasai* (London: James Currey Publishers, 1992). He is currently completing a social and economic history of the Arusha and Meru peoples of northern Tanzania. Formerly at La Trobe University and Williams College, he is now Professor of History at the University of Wisconsin-Madison.

Michele Wagner is an Assistant Professor in the Department of History, Williams College, Williamstown, MA. She received her doctorate from the University of Wisconsin-Madison. She has performed extensive research in both Burundi and Tanzania, and is writing a book on precolonial Burundi.

Acknowledgements

The editors would first like to thank the Mickey Leland Center on World Hunger and Peace Studies at Texas Southern University for its support for this project. The Center provided resources and helped arrange for Professor I.N. Kimambo to spend a year at Texas Southern as a Fulbright Scholar in Residence when much of the work of the project was done. In particular Dotie Atkins, Associate Director of the Center, has provided invaluable support.

The editors and contributors – particularly those of us who come from Europe and North America – also wish to express our gratitude to the Tanzania Commission for Science and Technology, the staff of the Tanzania National Archives, and the members of the Department of History, University of Dar es Salaam. Without their support and cooperation, our research would have been impossible. We also wish to thank Saidi Kilindo, Archaeology Unit, Department of History, University of Dar es Salaam, and David Guttenfelder, University of Iowa, for their kind assistance in preparing maps. We hope that this volume will be of some assistance to the Tanzanian teachers and scholars who, despite innumerable hardships, struggle to keep alive the study of history in Tanzania's primary schools, secondary schools and institutions of higher learning.

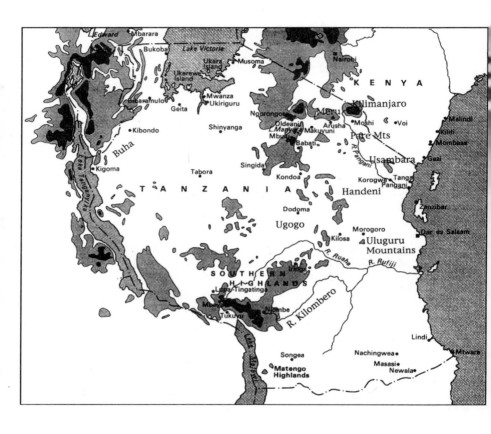

Map 1 *Tanzania (areas discussed in the chapters are indicated in large type).*

Introduction

Custodians
of the Land
Ecology & Culture
in the History of Tanzania

JAMES GIBLIN & GREGORY MADDOX

Environmental history and the scholarly and popular understanding of the Tanzanian past

In the essay which concludes this volume, one of the 'founding fathers' of Tanzanian history, Isaria Kimambo, reflects on the efforts of successive generations of historians to strike a balance between external causes of change and local initiative in their interpretations of Tanzanian history. He shows that nationalist and Marxist historians of Tanzania, understandably preoccupied through the first quarter-century of its postcolonial history with the impact of imperialism and capitalism on East Africa, tended to overlook the initiatives taken by rural societies to transform themselves.[1] Yet there is good reason for historians to think about the causes of change and innovation in the rural communities of Tanzania, because farming and pastoral peoples have constantly changed as they adjusted to shifting environmental conditions. Short- and long-term climate change, calamitous droughts and excessive rains, exhaustion of soils and grazing, outbreaks of disease and infestations of crop pests have prompted East African communities to change their patterns of cropping, settlement and trans-humance, their selection of seeds and cultigens, their management of vegetation and wildlife, their treatments of illness and their ways of thinking about good and evil. 'If we avoid assumptions about environmental equilibrium,' writes William Cronon, a historian of American environmental change, in a similar vein, 'the *instability* of human relations with the environment can be used to explain both cultural and ecological transformations.'[2] In other words, once we begin to think about farming and pastoral societies inhabiting ever-changing environments, we are led to consider how economic institutions, political and gender relations, intellectual leadership and moral imperatives may have been involved in the process of environmental adaptation. This relationship between environment and rural culture, politics and economy is the subject of this volume.

Our interest in exploring the initiatives taken by rural communities in response to environmental change immediately brings us face to face with problems which surface not only in the narrowly academic domain of East African environmental and demographic history, but also in the modern political life of Tanzania. Debate among historians about environment and demography has swung between two extremes: the 'Merrie Africa' approach, which sees stable precolonial communities as having lived in harmony with nature before suffering depopulation, ecological disasters and economic exploitation under colonial rule, and the 'Primitive Africa' approach, which depicts precolonial Tanzanians as having inhabited a hostile environment in perilous proximity to famine, epidemic and demographic reversals before achieving somewhat greater security in the colonial period.[3] Aside from other objections to these approaches, which are discussed below, both the 'Merrie Africa' and 'Primitive Africa' perspectives can be faulted for failing to consider sufficiently how rural societies change and develop. This tendency would seem to be more pronounced in the 'Primitive Africa' approach, but in fact the 'Merrie Africa' perspective also underestimates the capability for constructive transformation in rural communities. Its proponents tend to prefer images of stability over those of development, and place such heavy emphasis on the damage suffered by Tanzanians under colonial rule that their adaptability, innovativeness and occasionally successful struggles to achieve progress during the colonial period are obscured.

The historians' stress on precolonial harmony destroyed by colonialism and their tendency to neglect the detail of rural efforts to innovate and achieve development are reflected both in Tanzanian nationalist ideology and in the views of many social scientists who study Tanzania. Furthermore, these elements of historical interpretation have perhaps played a small part in encouraging a disturbing feature of modern Tanzanian political culture – the deep-seated scepticism held by many Tanzanians about the ability of their rural societies to endure change and achieve progress. In the political discussions which take place in rural homesteads, markets and schools, not to mention in the bars and offices of the cities, one often encounters an implicit distinction between national institutions, which are assumed to be able to effect change and improvement, and the villages, 'clans' or 'tribes' of the countryside, which are regarded as obstacles to development and progress. The widely held view of rural cultures as being incapable of transformation would seem to spring in part from a popular interpretation of the precolonial past. This interpretation holds that precolonial societies were held together not by institutions which were the products of political wisdom and ingenuity, but rather by natural bonds of affinity among members of extensive groups of kin. Political institutions, assume many Tanzanians, emerged only under colonial rule, and were bequeathed by colonialism to the independent Tanzanian nation. An interpretation such as this, which regards kinship rather than political institutions as the glue which held together precolonial communities and which attributes the creation of modern political institutions solely to the intervention of colonialism, leaves many Tanzanians doubtful that their own cultures can sustain material and political development.

Such doubts are perhaps more frequently expressed in the current period because, as the verities of Ujamaa and one-party rule have been swept away since the mid-1980s, Tanzanians in all walks of life have begun to face an unfamiliar future, a future that they expect to be dominated by the uncertainties of novel interparty debate and market-driven private enterprise. Thus they have entered a period of worry and vigorous debate about the future, a debate to which historians can contribute by bringing alive a sense of options and alternatives and by questioning interpretations about the past which might, however inadvertently, foreclose discussion about certain possibilities for the future. We believe that historical studies which situate farming and pastoral societies within their ecological contexts can be particularly effective in restoring confidence that rural cultures can develop, because, if they avoid the 'Merrie Africa' and 'Primitive Africa' extremes, they can demonstrate that communities have continually used their economic, political, cultural and moral resources to prosper in ever-changing ecological circumstances.

Historical research which emphasizes rural initiative and innovation inevitably challenges a rather simplified view of the Tanzanian past that has taken hold in scholarship which concerns itself more with questions of development than with history. In a number of studies of national development and current political issues, one finds precolonial societies portrayed as having been small in scale, relatively homogeneous and, to a great extent, self-enclosed. These studies tend to regard trade and other economic relations with the outside world, whether they be the nineteenth-century slave trade or cash crop production in the colonial period, as influences which corroded precolonial cultures.[4] The tendencies to overlook the complexity of political relations and conflicts in precolonial societies and to see trade and economic change as destructive forces have led a good many observers of Tanzania to ignore the agency of Tanzanians in economic change. Rather than identifying individuals, groups and social classes that might have welcomed economic and social transformation,[5] they have tended to regard Tanzanian communities as being on the defensive. Certainly the most influential example of this tendency is Goran Hyden's work on the 'economy of affection'. Along with a number of other studies, including some which modify or reject Hyden's theses outright, it sees Tanzanians as struggling to resist the influences of colonialism, commodity production, markets and modernity.[6]

The seductiveness of this kind of work (and, indeed, of the ideology of Ujamaa as well) lies in the fact that it counterposes certain indigenous cultural values and institutions against the influence of Western imperialism and capitalism. Like Ujamaa thought itself, however, it fails to examine the social, economic and political relationships within what it takes to be 'traditional' culture. As a result, studies which proceed from assumptions about the 'economy of affection' or about a Tanzanian predilection for avoiding market relations are less critical of state policies and ruling ideology than their authors probably intend. Like Ujamaa ideology, this approach precludes from the outset enquiry about a range of alternatives, including the historical role that capitalism and market relations might play in development. Rather than looking for the sources of agency and entrepreneurship which might shape economic transformation, a good deal of literature which is intended to be critical of the Tanzanian state finds only 'traditional' homogeneous societies united in defence of their values and way of life. Thus the fundamental weakness of the historical perspectives manifested both in much scholarship and in Ujamaa ideology is that Tanzanian societies are assumed to have been composed of small, egalitarian, non-political communities which, because they were organized primarily by kinship, developed a high degree of solidarity through constant interpersonal contacts. Both ideologues and scholars presume that Tanzanian societies were not divided by political conflicts in the past and did not produce groups and classes which were likely to seize opportunities for transformation.

While recent historical studies of Tanzania have often questioned these views, they nevertheless contain some implicit elements which may inadvertently contribute to such interpretations. An example of a study whose implicit assumptions are somewhat at odds with explicit intentions is the most comprehensive history of Tanzania, John Iliffe's *A Modern History of Tanganyika*,[7] a work which is deeply concerned with political history and with African innovation and adaptation. Throughout *A Modern History*, one encounters Tanzanians of the colonial period struggling through what Iliffe had earlier termed 'the age of improvement'[8] to come to terms with the new world of imperial politics, science and capitalism. Iliffe, like other nationalist historians of the 1960s who borrowed the concept of 'enlargement of scale' (see

Kimambo, 'Concluding Essay,' in this volume), was strongly influenced by the social anthropologists Godfrey and Monica Wilson. The Wilsons believed that when African societies were integrated into colonial systems they underwent 'expansion of historical scale', a process which exposed them to the stimulus of outside influences. The arrival of outsider innovators such as missionaries and colonial administrators, argued the Wilsons, broke down 'the conservatism of the African' and encouraged rapid social change.[9] Thus Iliffe was taking a viewpoint that was already well established in studies of Tanzania when he emphasized the innovating role of certain individuals, such as early Christian converts, who stand on the margins between two societies. For, like the Wilsons, Iliffe regarded contact between different societies, rather than the internal dynamics of Tanzanian societies themselves, as the sources of innovation and adaptation. Moreover, his interpretation was not intended merely to explain developments resulting from the clash of African and European cultures during the colonial period. Instead, it is integral to Iliffe's view of the entire sweep of Tanzanian history, for even in precolonial history, asserts *A Modern History*, the migrating ancestors of modern Tanzanians who converged on present-day Tanzania from various directions experienced 'dynamic autochthonous change which came from the mingling of diverse colonists'.[10]

Thus, although historians have often rejected the idea that precolonial Tanzanian societies were self-enclosed and isolated, little concerned with trade, organized by kinship rather than politics and unchanging, some of the implicit aspects of historians' interpretations may nevertheless remain compatible with views of the past found both in development-orientated scholarship and in the ideology of Ujamaa. The challenge for historians now is to restore a sense of the possibilities of change by showing, first, that transformation does not occur solely as a consequence of culture contact; secondly, that in the past Tanzanian societies were dynamic and capable of transformation; and thirdly, that it is far from certain that historical experience, culture and harshness of climate have left Tanzanians ill-equipped or little inclined to enter markets, accumulate wealth and pursue other paths towards development. The emphasis on rural initiative which informs studies of Tanzanian ecological history can carry us far towards these goals, but we must beware of difficulties which have emerged in an earlier generation of historical work on the Tanzanian environment.

The continuing tradition of environmental history in Tanzania

The studies presented in this volume build upon one of the strongest traditions of ecological studies for any African nation, a body of literature on history and environment in Tanzania that includes not only numerous impressive local studies conducted by ecologists during the colonial period, but also the work of Steven Feierman, John Ford, Helge Kjekshus and Meredith Turshen.[11] Indeed, these studies are a distinct extension of this tradition, because, while they share with these earlier works the view that human societies and nature cannot be regarded dualistically as separate systems,[12] they move beyond the debates which dominated some of the earlier work about whether precolonial Tanzanians exercised control over the environment. Instead, they examine the complex relations which link environmental concerns, political and economic structures and systems of belief. These studies take up some themes which have always been important elements of the environmental tradition – particularly demography – but at the same time they also treat other issues which have not often been studied in the context of ecological change, such as the morality of resource use and the interrelationship between environment and politics.

These essays also try to overcome problems in the environmental tradition created by time and space. Like most work on Tanzanian environmental history, they deal with the nineteenth and twentieth centuries, the period when Tanzania entered the capitalist world economy. During the nineteenth century, almost all of Tanzania became part of an international division of labour, initially by trading with caravans from the coast which sought ivory and slaves. The subsequent imposition of colonial rule gradually transformed some regions into producers of agricultural commodities and others into providers of migrant labour. New forms of political authority, new crops and agronomic practices and new patterns of mobility all affected the use of the Tanzanian environment.

The overwhelming importance of the passage from precolonial to colonial society has encouraged starkly dichotomous views of this era. Both the 'Merrie Africa' and 'Primitive Africa' approaches to Tanzanian history have found great differences and abrupt discontinuities between precolonial and colonial periods. In the Tanzanian environmental tradition, however, no one has seen greater contrast between these two periods than Helge Kjekshus, who, in *Ecology Control and Economic Development in East African History*, argued that the imposition of colonial rule destroyed the ability of Tanzanian societies to control their environments. He blamed the spread of tsetse fly and human and bovine trypanosomiases, as well as the breakdown of indigenous systems of production and redistribution, on the violence of colonialism and the colonial restructuring of local economies.[13] Moreover, Kjekshus's book has been shown to exemplify not only the problem of chronology in Tanzanian environmental history, but also a problem of space. This difficulty has been discussed by James McCann, a latecomer to the legion of Kjekshus critics, who has asserted that his 'wooden, two-dimensional image of precolonial African agriculture' resulted from his failure to do careful empirical study of 'agronomy, crop repertories, disease, and climate patterns'.[14] The lack of careful 'empiricism' which McCann decries seems to arise in studies which, like Kjekshus's book, attempt to achieve nationwide coverage. In contrast with Kjekshus and some other studies of the environmental tradition, however, the research presented in this volume attempts to show that the transition from precolonial to colonial society involved continuity as well as change, and that histories of environmental change must be rooted in close examination of specific and often highly localized ecological circumstances.

Despite its flaws, including the ahistorical and romanticized view of precolonial conditions which has drawn persistent criticism,[15] Kjekshus's widely read book has been influential and has done an important service by inspiring debate and much additional research about environmental history in East Africa. His argument has been refined by Juhani Koponen, who in *People and Production in Late Precolonial Tanzania*[16] sides with neither the 'Primitive Africa' nor the 'Merrie Africa' approaches. Although Koponen rejects Iliffe's characterization of nineteenth-century Tanzania as a hostile frontier zone where agriculturalists struggled for survival,[17] he also opposes Kjekshus's claim for Tanzania-wide precolonial environmental control and instead argues that 'environmental and social control and, ultimately, survival in precolonial Tanzania was not a "national" achievement but essentially a local affair. . . . What the Tanzanian productive and reproductive systems were adapted to was their local micro-environments.'[18] In this way, Koponen avoids the difficulties of time and space which have arisen in the environmental tradition.

Koponen's insistence on the need to understand how agronomic systems work within specific micro-environments is shared by McCann, the critic of Kjekshus who has called for increased attention to the detail of agricultural attention. Indeed, McCann has gone further in suggesting that agrarian studies in Africa have erred by concentrating on the political economy of agriculture at the expense of agricultural history. We would argue, however, in favour of a combination of agricultural history and political economy, because it provides a way of escaping the dilemma which confronts studies of Tanzanian environmental history. The dilemma is posed, of course, by the contradictory and equally unsatisfying 'Merrie Africa' and 'Primitive Africa' approaches. It can be overcome by recognizing that, in both precolonial and colonial societies, ecological relationships have been shaped by a complex set of constantly changing variables, which include agronomic technique and knowledge, political authority, relations of production, gender and morality. When we understand that rural Tanzanian societies have always witnessed conflict over control of labour and resources and that both political and ecological relationships were moulded by such conflict, we are then able to avoid both the 'Merrie Africa' and the 'Primitive Africa' tendencies. We need neither depict precolonial societies in overly romantic hues by making untenable assertions about political harmony and demographic and environmental stability, nor place so much stress upon the precariousness of precolonial life that we suggest inability to overcome environmental adversity. Of course, speaking of the difficulty caused by the 'Primitive Africa' tendency in a national historiography which has been dominated since the early 1960s by nationalist and Marxist interpretations might appear to be building a straw man, but, in fact, images of precolonial vulnerability in the face of environmental vagaries continue to influence thinking about Tanzanian history. For, aside from the insistence on precolonial insecurity found in the recent and brutally pessimistic book by Ronald Seavoy,[19] the same tendency is also evident in the incomparably more subtle and sensitive writing of Iliffe, who, as he describes early nineteenth-century Tanzanian communities in the memorable opening passage of *A Modern History*, borrows his central image of a 'vast and empty land' directly from H.M. Stanley.[20] Thus Iliffe seeks less to challenge descriptions of precolonial insecurity than to explain them by arguing that early nineteenth-century Tanzania was still a thinly settled frontier.

Another way to describe the way out of the 'Merrie Africa'/'Primitive Africa' dilemma is to say simply that we need to develop a truly historical perspective on environment and ecology. One need accept neither the view that precolonial societies were unaffected by demographic and subsistence crises nor the idea of primitive scarcity if, as McCann urges, one adopts an approach that embraces both the possibilities of progress and stability and the likelihood of reversals and crises. The causes of setbacks and failures in agriculture and environment control are all the more comprehensible, moreover, when we realize that, as Jan Vansina has long argued,[21] changes in agricultural productivity, division of labour, cropping patterns, selection of cultigens and vegetation management are all intimately related to political relations and structural transformation. Historians of Africa have come to realize not only that precolonial Africa developed an extraordinary diversity of political institutions, but also that those institutions were constantly changing.[22] What historians of environmental and agricultural change have to bear in mind is that structural changes have always affected productivity, the likelihood of adopting or resisting agronomic innovations and the scale and effectiveness of control over vegetation, disease, wildlife and crop pests. Thus what we should do is not so much to emphasize agricultural history in place of political economy, but instead to achieve greater awareness of the interdependence between social and political structures and the course of agricultural change in African history. When we speak here of political economy, however, we have in mind a theory and method which do not limit themselves merely to economic and political relations. Instead, we envisage an approach which, in so far as it considers culture, ideology, language, religion and morality to be integral dimensions of an economic or political system, is somewhat akin to the more sophisticated conceptions of a mode of production. Hence we are advocating an approach which is somewhat similar to that of the Indian historians Madhav Gadgil and Ramachandra Guha, for their concept of a 'mode of resource use' encompasses technology, economy, social organization and ideology, without neglecting 'the nature of the ecological impact itself'.[23]

In the African past, the ability of societies to achieve development and avoid crises depended largely upon the ability of social and political systems to promote production and ensure redistribution. If historical research on the African environment succeeds in combining an understanding of dynamic change in the spheres of both political economy and ecology, it may help to avoid the gravest danger in the current discussion of the African environment, the danger that such discussion may become a substitute for, or a way of evading, debate about the political and economic structures which shape the lives of modern Africans.

Assumptions underlying colonial views of conservation and demography

Because several of the essays in this volume discuss the impact of conservation policies and demographic change in the colonial period, it is useful to consider some of the assumptions which influenced colonial thinking about these matters from the time they began to attract considerable official attention in the 1930s. British colonial administrators of the period confronted environmental conditions that had worsened dramatically during the preceding thirty years of colonial rule as a result of population decline and diversion of labour to an export sector which provided little return to workers. Population reversals had many causes, including a series of devastating famines and epidemics and the violence of colonial conquest and rebellion. The consequence of demographic decline was the loss of control over vegetation across wide areas and the spread of disease-bearing wildlife and insects.[24] By the 1930s, colonial officials had also begun to perceive a great threat from soil erosion.[25] From then until the end of the colonial era the colonial government made a great many efforts at both conservation and maintenance of agricultural and pastoral productivity. The great majority of their efforts failed, partly because of almost universal opposition from African producers. In the last colonial decade, moreover, conservationist efforts were complicated by rapid population growth.

Colonial efforts to promote conservation floundered because of two assumptions which were shared by most colonial bureaucrats. First, administrative and technical staff assumed a duality between humans and nature. The goal of their conservation schemes was either to preserve nature in its 'pristine' state or to protect resources for exploitation as exportable commodities. Jamie Monson's essay in this volume describes this second situation, for she shows that, in order to establish control over valuable exportable timber, the British created forest reserves in the Kilombero Valley even though they disrupted a sustainable and productive agronomic system.

Colonial conservationists also assumed that African labour was a free resource, a view which sprang from the belief that there was a division in African societies between necessary and surplus labour.[26] Colonial policy assumed that Africans living a life of 'barbarous plenty'[27] had ample surplus labour which could be utilized by the state and foreign capital. Partly for this same reason, moreover, colonial conservationists made little investment in agricultural productivity, for, although the Department of Agriculture maintained a large staff, its efforts concentrated on exhortation and marketing.[28] Consequently, in a region such as the Uluguru Mountains, which is described in this volume by Pamela Maack, colonial bureaucrats expected Africans to build terraces, dig up crop stubble and plant trees, and to do so without receiving monetary compensation or any other appreciable benefit. In lowland pastoral areas, in contrast, conservationists often concentrated on destocking to maintain a balance between land and carrying capacity. Cattle owners stoutly resisted efforts to reduce their herds, although they were willing to pay for measures such as improvements in water supply that increased carrying capacity.[29] Indeed, measures such as bush clearing which brought benefits were often organized by the communities themselves.

Although some colonial officials began to see a link between population growth and environmental deterioration as early as the 1920s, demographic expansion became a much more pressing issue in the 1950s, when population began to grow at an even faster rate. Indeed, whereas Tanganyika Territory contained about 7 million inhabitants in 1948, Tanzania's population today exceeds 20 million. Colonial thinking about population tended to rely upon the classic Malthusian equation between resource base and population, a perspective which resembled the dualistic colonial view of society and nature. This perspective has been challenged by recent work on African demography which argues that colonial demand for labour called forth population growth in much of Africa. Recent studies also show that greater mobility and the creation of a market and transport infrastructure capable of moving large quantities of crops and famine relief removed the brake on population growth imposed by periodic famine.[30] In addition, this work suggests that constraints on fertility disappeared as households and communities faced demands for increased production, which could be met only through increased labour. As Iliffe has argued, however, the cost of removing famine and other checks on population growth was the emergence of structural poverty among the large portions of African populations which were denied access to various resources, including land.[31]

The organization of this volume

This volume is divided into: Part I, which consists of essays by Juhani Koponen and Gregory Maddox on demographic history; Part II, which presents studies of northern Tanzanian mountain regions by Isaria Kimambo and Christopher Conte; Part III, which explores the connections between environmental change and politics in essays by James Giblin and Pamela Maack; Part IV, which contains contributions by Michelle Wagner, Jamie Monson and Thomas Spear on institutions and moral thought which affect resource use; and a concluding chapter by Isaria Kimambo which considers the significance of environmental studies within the wider body of historical literature on Tanzania.

Each group of essays is preceded by introductory comments which identify important themes and show how they develop throughout the book. The essays build an argument in this way. In Part I, Koponen and Maddox establish a link between environment and political economy by showing that demographic change, which has an enormous impact on ecological conditions, is heavily influenced by economic and political structures. Moreover, their essays find a relationship between culture and demographic trends, for culture affects fertility as well as possibilities for easing the pressure of population growth through migration. In Part II, Kimambo and Conte consider the relationship between environment and political economy in a portion of Tanzania where the precolonial history is particularly well understood – the northern highlands. They discuss the precolonial initiatives taken by farming and pastoral highlanders to achieve security, and show that there was a dynamic interrelationship between innovation in political and economic life and environmental transformation. In Part III, Giblin and Maack carry forward the theme of rural initiative by examining the relationship between political life and environmental change. Political structures, they show, were the basis of environmental control in the precolonial period. In the colonial period, however, the dominance of environmentally harmful political authority led impoverished farmers to protest and enter the nationalist movement. In Part IV, Wagner, Monson and Spear examine the institutions and modes of thought which governed the use of natural resources in precolonial societies, and which clashed with the very different views of conservation introduced by the Europeans. In their view, ecological relations possessed a moral dimension in precolonial society. Hence the violation of the morality of resource use by colonial governments provided a powerful incentive to join in anticolonial protest.

Thus each group of essays explores a different dimension of the relationship between environmental change and society, and finds different ways of demonstrating that rural societies constantly make agronomic, political and ideological innovations as they learn to preserve natural resources and overcome the risks imposed by their environments. Taken together, they present a complex view of ecological relations which encompasses not only agronomy, land use and population growth, but also the economic activities, political institutions and forms of religious and moral thought which inspire innovation.

They do so, moreover, while also reflecting Tanzania's impressive environmental diversity. No book of this length, of course, could do complete justice to the range of climatic, topographical and environmental conditions which exist across the nation. Nevertheless, the contributors to this volume describe a wide variety of ecological conditions, from the high forested plateaux of Usambara to the vast savannahs of Buha, from the lush banana-and-coffee farms of Arusha and Kilimanjaro to the hot, tsetse-infested *miombo* woodland of Handeni, and from the plains of Ugogo and eroded hillsides of Uluguru to the marshes and waterways of Kilombero. The great variety of environments in Tanzania has of course been one of the factors which has impeded the writing of Tanzanian environmental history on a nationwide scale. Yet this diversity is more appealing than daunting, for certainly no aspect of Tanzanian history is more compelling than the story of how its rural communities have adapted to and benefited from a great variety of natural surroundings.

Notes

1. See also the somewhat different comments in Steven Feierman, *Peasant Intellectuals: Anthropology and History in Tanzania* (Madison, 1990), pp. 13–17.

2. William Cronon, *Changes in the Land: Indians, Colonists, and the Ecology of New England* (New York, 1983), pp. 1–16, quote from p. 14, emphasis in original.

3. Juhani Koponen, 'War, Famine and Pestilence in Late Precolonial Tanzania: A Case for a Heightened Mortality', *International Journal of African Historical Studies* 21, 4 (1988): 638, borrowing the terms used by A.G. Hopkins in *An Economic History of West Africa* (London, 1973).

4. 'Contact with the world outside undermined and then reversed most of the achievements of the tribal societies of the interior.' Andrew Coulson, *Tanzania: A Political Economy* (Oxford, 1982), p. 27.

5. 'Capitalist relations in Tanzania were not part of the process of organic development of the Tanzanian society. They were introduced as a result of imperialist invasion and subsequent colonization of the country. Finance capital partially destroyed the natural economy, introduced commodity production and integrated the Tanzanian social economy in the world capitalist market.' Issa G. Shivji, *Law, State and the Working Class in Tanzania, 1920–1984* (London, Portsmouth, NH, and Dar es Salaam, 1986), p. 239.

6. Goran Hyden, *Beyond Ujamaa in Tanzania: Underdevelopment and an Uncaptured Peasantry* (London, 1980); Deborah Fahy Bryceson, *Food Insecurity and the Social Division of Labour in Tanzania, 1919–1985* (New York, 1990); and John Sender and Sheila Smith, *Poverty, Class and Gender in Rural Africa: A Tanzanian Case Study* (London, 1990). A recent restatement of Hyden's perspective is Tony Waters, 'A Cultural Analysis of the Economy of Affection and the Uncaptured Peasantry in Tanzania', *Journal of Modern African Studies* 30, 1 (1992): 163–75.

7. John Iliffe, *A Modern History of Tanganyika* (Cambridge, 1979).

8. The title of Chapter 8 of John Iliffe, *Tanganyika Under German Rule, 1905–1912* (Cambridge, 1969).

9. Godfrey and Monica Wilson, *The Analysis of Social Change* (Cambridge, 1945), quotes from p. 163; Monica Wilson elaborated the theory presented in this work in a number of publications, including *Communal Rituals of the Nyakyusa* (London, 1959), *Religion and the Transformation of Society: A Study of Social Change in Africa* (Cambridge, 1971), and *For Men and Elders: Change in the Relations of Generations and of Men and Women among the Nyakyusa-Ngonde People, 1875–1971* (London, 1977).

10. John Iliffe, *A Modern History of Tanganyika* (Cambridge, 1979), p. 25.

11. Steven Feierman, *The Shambaa Kingdom: A History* (Madison, 1974) and *Peasant Intellectuals*; John Ford, *The Role of the Trypanosomiases in African Ecology: A Study of the Tsetse Fly Problem* (Oxford, 1971); Helge Kjekshus, *Ecology Control and Economic Development in East African History: The Case of Tanganyika, 1850–1950* (London, 1977); Meredeth Turshen, *The Political Ecology of Disease in Tanzania* (New Brunswick, NJ, 1984), and 'Population Growth and the Deterioration of Health: Mainland Tanzania, 1920–1960', in Dennis Cordell and Joel Gregory, eds, *African Population and Capitalism: Historical Perspectives* (Boulder, 1987), pp. 187–200. There is also a wealth of more specialized studies on vegetation patterns and epidemiology of human and bovine diseases.

12. See Elias C. Mandala, *Work and Control in a Peasant Economy: A History of the Lower Tchiri Valley in Malawi, 1859–1960* (Madison, 1990), pp. 1–22, for a sustained critique of this dualistic approach in the literature on African peasantries in general.

13. Kjekshus, *Ecology Control*.

14. James C. McCann, 'Agriculture and African History', *Journal of African History* 32, 3 (1991): 508–9.

15. See Michael Watts, *Silent Violence: Food, Famine and Peasantry in Northern Nigeria* (Berkeley, 1983) and John Iliffe, 'Review of *Ecology Control and East African History*', *Journal of African History*, 19 (1978): 139–40.

16. Juhani Koponen, *People and Production in Late Precolonial Tanzania: History and Structures* (Uppsala, 1988).

17. Iliffe, *Modern History*.

18. Koponen, *People and Production*, p. 367.

19. Ronald E. Seavoy, *Famine in East Africa: Food Production and Food Policies* (New York, Westport, CT, and London, 1989), especially Chapter 2.

20. Iliffe, *Modern History*, pp. 12, 75–6.

21. Jan Vansina, *The Children of Woot: A History of the Kuba Peoples* (Madison, 1978), Chapter 10, especially pp. 179ff.

22. I.N. Kimambo, *A Political History of the Pare of Tanzania, c.* 1500–1900 (Nairobi, 1969) and Jan Vansina, *Paths in the Rainforests: Toward a History of Political Tradition in Equatorial Africa* (Madison, 1990).

23. Madhav Gadgil and Ramachandra Guha, *This Fissured Land: An Ecological History of India* (Berkeley and Los Angeles, 1992), p. 14.

24. Ford, *Role of Trypanosomiases*; Kjekshus, *Ecology Control*; and James L. Giblin, *The Politics of Environmental Control in Northeastern Tanzania, 1840–1940* (Philadelphia, 1993).

25. Pamela A. Maack, 'The Waluguru Are Not Sleeping': Poverty, Culture, and Social Differentiation in Morogoro, Tanzania' (Ph.D. dissertation, Northwestern University, Evanston, 1992); Feierman, *Peasant Intellectuals*; and David Anderson, 'Depression, Dust Bowl, Demography, and Drought: The Colonial State and Soil Conservation in East Africa during the 1930s', *African Affairs* 83 (1984): 321–43.

26. Allen Isaacman, 'Peasants and Rural Social Protest in Africa', *African Studies Review* 33, 2 (1990): 1–120.

27. The term is Richard Burton's; it is quoted in Koponen, *People and Production*, p. 372.

28. D.M.P. McCarthy, *Colonial Bureaucracy and Creating Underdevelopment: Tanganyika, 1919–1940* (Ames, IA, 1982).

29. Wilhelm Östberg, *The Kondoa Transformation: Coming to Grips with Soil Erosion in Central Tanzania*, Scandinavian Institute of African Studies, Research Report no. 76 (Uppsala, 1986).

30. Michelle McAlpin, *Subject to Famine: Food Crises and Economic Change in Western India, 1860–1920* (Princeton, 1983) makes a similar argument for India.

31. John Iliffe, *The African Poor: A History* (Cambridge, 1987).

Part One

Environmental
&
Demographic Change

Demography provides one of the most important connections between environmental change and political economy. In this part, Juhani Koponen and Gregory Maddox argue that demographic conditions are closely related to economic structures. In later parts, several essays complete the chain of causation which links political and economic with environmental change. For example, James Giblin's study of Handeni shows that highly localized increases in population density allowed improvement in control of the disease environment, but that demographic reversals meant a worsening of the disease situation. Similarly, the essays on mountain regions by Pamela Maack and Thomas Spear describe the consequences of population growth in highland environments, which in some places included soil erosion, soil exhaustion, parcelling of land and overgrazing. They also demonstrate that environmental deterioration intensified political tensions both between highlanders and the colonial government and within highland communities themselves. However, Jamie Monson finds a much more direct connection between political economy and environmental degradation in the Kilombero Valley, for she shows that forest conservation policies, which forced farmers to overwork soils in areas which remained outside forest reserves, grew out of a complex set of political and economic considerations.

Thus by investigating the causes of demographic growth in the colonial period, Koponen and Maddox contribute to an understanding of the close connection between environmental change and political economy, which is the chief concern of this volume. In so doing, however, they find it necessary to revise the conventional chronology which takes the colonial conquest to have been the decisive turning-point in Tanzanian history. In particular, they challenge the chronology of demographic change presented by Helge Kjekshus, who regarded the beginning of the colonial period as the point of transition between two demographic regimes. Kjekshus argued that, whereas the precolonial period had witnessed gradual population increase, colonial conquest brought dramatic population decline. In contrast, Juhani Koponen, in a chapter which surveys an extensive body of demographic evidence from the entire territory of mainland Tanzania, argues here that a prolonged period of population decline spanned both the final pre-colonial decades and the early colonial period. The critical transition to demographic recovery occurred, he believes, between the First and Second World Wars. Maddox attempts to identify the moment of demographic transition even more precisely in a chapter which focuses upon the region of Dodoma. He contends that Dodoma experienced sustained population growth only from the mid-1950s.

Koponen and Maddox not only advance similar ideas about period-ization, but also give similar explanations for demographic transition, because both of them attribute population growth to changes in the colonial economy which ended catastrophic famines and increased demand for labour. Furthermore, because both Koponen and Maddox make comparisons with demographic patterns in other regions of the world, they encourage us to consider how the political and economic conditions associated with peripheral capitalism have produced the demographic regime (and also the environmental problems) charac-teristic of modern Africa. Koponen addresses this point directly. European demographic history, he notes, has persuaded demo-graphers that modernizing societies usually experience a combination of declining mortality and declining or stable fertility. In Tanzania, however, remarkable population growth has occurred, he argues, because declining mortality has been coupled with increased fertility (see also the comments on fertility by Conte in this volume). Thus the evidence of demographic change suggests that Tanzania is not following the same path taken by industrializing economies, but instead is experiencing a pattern of population growth (and associated environ-mental problems) which must be attributed to its peripheral location within a global capitalist economy. Maddox reminds us that the pattern of demographic growth characteristic of postcolonial Africa is at least partially responsible for some of its more obvious social problems. Increased colonial demand for labour and more effective provision of famine relief, he says, allowed population growth in Dodoma, a drought-prone region which, although it has long supported Gogo-speaking villagers who rely heavily on livestock-keeping, is poorly endowed for agriculture. As population increase pushed villagers on to Dodoma's more marginal lands, structural poverty (see also the

Introduction to this volume) took hold across the countryside. Meanwhile, many destitute Gogo people migrated to the cities, helping to create the stereotypical notion that all of Dar es Salaam's homeless beggars are Gogo.

Finally, both Koponen and Maddox show that demography is influenced by culture as well as by economic structures. Rates of fertility, of course, are affected by norms of sexual behaviour, methods of child rearing and gender relations. Similarly, as Maddox points out, rapid integration of newcomers through adoption of new cultural identities, through joking relationships and through fictive kinship can also encourage population growth, because it facilitates the movement of migrants from densely populated areas where there are obstacles to use of land such as tsetse flies into sparsely populated regions. Maddox suggests that Dodoma has long absorbed migrants from growing populations on its borders, and has been able to do so because Gogo culture has quickly absorbed newcomers.

One

~~~~~~

Population

A Dependent Variable

JUHANI KOPONEN

The intricate interrelations between population and economic and social development continue to cause controversy in Tanzania as elsewhere in Africa.[1] Perceptions about them have also changed. Indeed, like population growth itself, the present preoccupation with rapid population growth and the concomitant environmental stress caused by human activity is a relatively recent phenomenon in Africa. Under colonial rule, because little population increase appeared to take place, the major worry of colonial governments was underpopulation and inefficient exploitation of the environment, for small populations were regarded as being unable to gain ascendancy over nature. Thus, when population growth became evident in the late colonial period, it was welcomed and taken as a proof of the benefits conferred by European rule and Western civilization. In the present, the view that population growth fosters development has not completely withered away, but it has largely been superseded by the view that population growth causes poverty and environmental degradation.

Underlying these changing perceptions of the developmental role of population growth are more diffuse opinions concerning its basic causes and mechanism. Few people would continue to argue that European colonialism 'saved' 'the lives of millions of men who under the old conditions would have died early in childhood, or in later life, of famine, disease and violence'.[2] Yet many people continue to assume that population growth should indeed be credited to the intervention of development efforts during and after colonial rule. The disagreement is about how such intervention actually influenced demographic change. One influential view claims that development merely did away with

19

physical and biological constraints which were impeding population growth. Here, population is understood in Malthusian fashion as an 'independent variable', a biologically grounded 'ecological' factor which creates its own momentum once the physical shackles restraining its growth have been cut by biomedical or other development intervention. An alternative perspective, however, sees development intervention producing a profound restructuring of economic and social relations which is conducive to demographic growth. Here, demographic variables are seen as 'dependent', and population growth emerges as a consequence of the workings of other social, economic and cultural forces.[3]

In this chapter I examine population trends in mainland Tanzania, or Tanganyika,[4] concentrating on the late precolonial and colonial periods. Although my research on the historical transformation of Tanzanian social structures and population dynamics is still in progress, I have gathered enough data to put forward several theses. The problem of sources is obvious in a study of this kind, but I believe that the rough outline of Tanganyika's population trends can now be sketched out with a fair degree of probability, the factors affecting them can be discussed meaningfully and the main gaps in our knowledge can be located. On this basis, I wish to argue that population is more a dependent than an independent variable.

Because Tanzania's present population growth process began during the colonial period, it is reasonable to assume that colonial intervention had something to do with it. But I think that questions about when and how this growth began are more complex than the standard neo-Malthusian position allows. The mechanisms of population growth were more complicated, and the effects of colonialism were mediated through several mechanisms that remain imperfectly known. In particular, I strongly question the view that growth occurred because mortality decreased while fertility remained at its previous level. On the contrary, the death rate actually increased in the early colonial period and only began to decrease in the period between the world wars. In fact, I would argue that a major cause of population growth was an increase in fertility.

Moreover, I think that explanations of demographic change should not place too much emphasis on the beginnings of European colonization, for there were many forms of continuity between the late precolonial and early colonial times. Indeed, the whole period from 1850 to 1930 should be regarded as a historical divide. Although our knowledge of this period is fairly limited, it appears to have been a time when outside influences disturbed indigenous population dynamics, which had probably maintained long-term population growth. Only after this prolonged transitional phase of stagnating or even declining population, which spanned the period of late precolonial commercial expansion as well as the early turbulent decades of colonialism, did a long-term trend towards population growth set in.

Colonial development and population

It is sometimes alleged that the colonialists were not interested in developing their dependencies and did not care about the condition of the indigenous populations in them. The historical record for Tanzania shows otherwise. It is fair to say that colonialism had two faces: the exploitative and the developmental. However exploitative the motives of the colonialists and whatever they desired to achieve through their conquest, they inevitably ended up developing a colonial economy.[5] For this they needed some cooperation from the local people. Thus the number of indigenous inhabitants became a pivotal factor in colonial economic policy. Indeed, it was with the advent of colonialism that indigenous peoples began to be conceived of as a 'population' and a demographic discourse began.

The Germans, the first colonizers of Tanzania, were particularly concerned with the small size of the population. From the outset of German rule[6] until its end, they expressed strong interest in increasing the population.[7] In this task, the interests of the various groups that participated in the colonial occupation intersected. On the one hand, population increase was desired 'on moral, ethical grounds' and out of 'sentimental concern for our "black brothers"'. Fortunately, humanitarian concerns coincided with those of a 'healthy self-interest' and the 'purely practical interest which the colonial power inevitably has in the development of its dependencies'.[8] This interest was grounded in the need for labour-power, for exploitation of the 'dormant treasures of the colony' required, besides the 'energetic contribution of the European component', the 'labour-power of the negro'.[9] Settlers and plantation managers pursuing narrow interests, officials protecting the overall interests of the colonial power, doctors motivated by ethical considerations and missionaries preaching love of one's neighbour – all of them would concur with Bernhard Dernburg, Germany's ablest Colonial Secretary, that 'the native is Africa's most important asset'.[10]

The need for labour-power by no means diminished during the period of British rule. The British understood 'population' in terms of 'labour-power', just as the Germans did. However, they were not as concerned about population trends. They noted the small size of Tanzania's population and showed concern over signs of local population decline, but in some ways they thought that a small indigenous population was an advantage, above all from the standpoint of settler colonization. British colonial administration was guided by the concept of 'dual policy', an East African application of the 'dual mandate' systematized by Lord Lugard.[11] Colonial production, thought British administrators in East Africa, should be undertaken by both non-Africans and Africans.[12] There was no shortage of Africans capable of working, thought the British, especially from the late 1930s onwards.[13]

The differences in emphasis laid on the population question partly reflected differences in German and British colonial policies and partly reflected perceived differences between the actual and ideal population. German East Africa was at the outset sparsely inhabited and colonization further depleted the population.[14] According to German statistics, Tanganyika's population grew from about 3 million to 4 million between 1899 and 1913.[15] Such an estimate has to be rejected, however, particularly because not even all Germans officials agreed that the population had actually grown.[16] The figures are obviously vague estimates; it is probable that the figure for 1899 was an underestimation and that the population remained stable or perhaps diminished.

But there is little doubt that the Tanganyikan population started to grow during the interwar period. It is uncertain whether this growth began in the 1920s – as suggested by those who estimated the 1931 population – or later.[17] The rising trend was apparent from the census of 1948, and after that the upward curve became ever steeper. Even though it must be stressed that the figures presented in Table 1.1 are to be regarded with great caution and that population sizes prior to 1948 as well as all the mortality and fertility figures are rough estimates, it seems possible that when colonial rule ended in 1961 there were twice as many Tanganyikans as when it began in 1884.

African historiography, however warns against overestimating the effectiveness and impact of colonial policy. It is becoming increasingly evident that what happended in Africa during the colonial period often did not correspond to what the colonialists desired; rather, change resulted from the ways in which Africans themselves acted to control the colonial situation. Indeed, later in this chapter I will try to show that population trends in colonial Tanzania stemmed from African processes of adaptation and control.

Mortality trends

The pioneering work of Helge Kjekshus has shown that the 1890s was a decade of population disasters. The great rinderpest panzootic destroyed most of the cattle and perhaps half of the game in Tanzania, while epidemics and famines probably killed hundreds of thousands of people. However, there is little reason to accept the part of the Kjekshusian argument which posits a 'man-controlled ecological system' sustaining a growing and prospering population until the colonial conquest. On the contrary, it appears that the decades preceding

Table 1.1 Selected estimates of population, fertility and mortality in mainland Tanzania, 1913–1988

Year	Population (thousands)	Total fertility rate	Crude death-rate	Infant mortality
1913	4 063	–	–	230
1921	4 107	–	–	–
1931	5 023	–	–	–
1948	7 410	5.0–5.1	30–35	170
1957	8 655	5.6–6.4	24–25	190
1967	11 959	6.6–7.3	21–23	145–160
1978	17 040	6.9	19	137
1988	22 490	6.2	15	115

NB Figures up to 1957 are for the African population and, after that, for the total population.

The estimates in question are rough, gathered from several different sources and made by different methods; they are presented here only as an indication of the order of magnitude and the trends. The figures for 1988 are from Tanzania, *1988 Population Census. National Profile. Summary* (Dar es Salam, 1991). For the estimates and sources for 1913–1978, see Juhani Koponen, 'Population Growth in Historical Perspective: The Key Role of Changing Fertility', in Jannik Boesen, Kjell J. Havnevik, Juhani Koponen and Rie Odgaard (eds), *Tanzania: Crisis and Struggle for Survival* (Uppsala, 1986), pp. 33, 39–42.

colonization were extremely turbulent times which witnessed an increase of famine, pestilence and death. There is ample evidence of greatly heightened mortality and loss of population in that period. Thus, rather than being an abrupt watershed, the 1890s climaxed a long process which loosened the grip of the people over their environment, a process which accompanied the integration of East Africa into a global economic system.

Heightened mortality 1850–1920

I have presented evidence for late precolonial disease and famine elsewhere, and here shall only sum up the relevant parts of the argument.[18] It appears that war, pestilence and famine all increased in Tanzania towards the end of the precolonial period. An obvious factor was the slave trade, for East Africa's most important slave routes passed through Tanzania. The slave trade taxed the population of the area, though perhaps not as much as the most enthusiastic opponents of that trade claimed. Several hundred thousand people became victims of the slave trade during the nineteenth century. The majority of them, however, were probably settled as slaves on coastal plantations or elsewhere in East Africa.

23

Considerably more destructive in demographic terms were epidemics. The 'opening up' of the interior in the latter half of the nineteenth century through long-distance trade in slaves and ivory spread diseases which had been unknown – or known only in parts of Tanzania – and killed in large numbers. Among the most devastating diseases were cholera and smallpox. Whereas cholera may have been a new disease, or a disease returning after a long absence, smallpox was an old scourge. Although it had been found raging on the East African coast in the late eighteenth century, it appears to have spread with unprecedented vigour in the interior during the next century, probably as a result of increased caravan trade.

Colonial conquest gradually ended the slave trade, but brought wars, which increased mortality. To be sure, Africans had waged war among themselves, but precolonial 'means of destruction' had been as simple as means of production, and losses of human life in precolonial 'wars' were usually of a modest order.[19] The breechloaders and machine-guns of the colonial troops made battles during the colonial occupation much bloodier. According to a semi-official German military history, the colonial troops carried out some ten or so 'fairly extensive military operations' per year in the 1890s, after which the frequency of such operations decreased. The term 'operations' referred to skirmishes in which African losses varied from a few men to several hundred.[20] Critics of German colonial policy claimed in the Reichstag, the German parliament, that 26 200 Africans were shot dead in East African colonial wars between 1889 and 1910.[21] Even colonial officials sometimes considered the violence excessive. Military expeditions in which 'entire tribes [were] attacked with superior weapons for trivial reasons' damaged the economic development of the areas, complained the acting governor Franz Stuhlmann in 1903. He demanded that the expeditions be restricted, as did Dernburg somewhat later.[22]

Direct war casualties were few, however, in comparison with the loss of life due to disease and hunger which often accompanied war. 'Macroparasites', or the colonial conquerors, were followed by 'microparasites', disease-causing microorganisms, and 'mesoparasites', the vectors of disease.[23] That is, the spread of diseases continued during and was often exacerbated by colonial invasion. Their combination made a devastating impact. Three major phases of disaster can be discerned: (i) the 1890s; (ii) the great Maji Maji rebellion and its suppression in 1905–7; and (iii) the intra-imperialist conflict of 1914–18 known as the First World War and its aftermath.

The catastrophes of the 1890s began with the great rinderpest panzootic in 1890. Spreading southward from the Horn of Africa, rinderpest swept over the country like a bushfire, killing cattle and game. The estimate first put forward by a German lieutenant, who said that 90 per cent of Tanganyika's cattle and half of its wild animals

Brought by cattle imported

perished from rinderpest, may well be roughly accurate.[24] Famine and smallpox followed, especially among peoples who depended on cattle. While the endemicity of smallpox was no doubt maintained by caravan traffic, which had grown with the establishment of colonialism, another factor also involved in the smallpox epidemics of the 1890s was the increased mobility of people who were searching for food and security.[25] The pastoral Maasai, of whom perhaps two-thirds died, suffered the worst. Northwestern Tanzania was also hit by smallpox, particularly Karagwe.[26] In the mid-1890s German doctors claimed that 'every second' African had a pock-marked face.[27]

After rinderpest and smallpox came drought and locusts. In 1892–3, the rains were sparser than usual on the coast and in some parts of the interior and, in three successive years from 1897 to 1899 the rains were particularly poor. The locust plagues coincided with the years of drought. In 1893–5, they destroyed the harvest in the greater part of the country and in 1897–9 the same thing happened again, particularly in the northeast and in Sukumaland. In consequence, famines occurred in 1893–5 along the coast and in its immediate vicinity, as well as in central and northern parts of the country.[28] The second drought and wave of locusts brought catastrophe. In Bondei, it was remembered later (by men) as a time when 'mothers lost love and pity for the children they were suckling, left them to their men and fled'.[29] The first places to suffer were the coast and its environs, as well as Ugogo, Usandawe and Uhehe in the central parts of the country, but soon the famine reached the south and Sukumaland.[30] 'Great is the number of natives who have become victims of hunger,' the official annual report stated baldly.[31]

Overall losses are impossible to quantify. The district of Tanga may have lost some 60 000 people, or half of its inhabitants, in the famine of 1898. German East Africa's highest medical official, Dr Alexander Becker, claimed that 750 000 people died of hunger from 1894 to 1899.[32] That figure was of course a guess, and in all probability was exaggerated, for it was publicized as part of a propaganda campaign in favour of railway construction, but Becker, who had worked for ten years in East Africa, was not entirely out of touch with the actual situation. Surely the severity of the catastrophes during the 1890s was extraordinary.

The next demographic catastrophe was the suppression of the Maji Maji rebellion in 1905–7 in the southern parts of the country. The rebellion broke out in July 1905 in the Matumbi highlands in Kilwa District.[33] In two months, it spread over an area of 150 000 square kilometres which had become integrated into the colonial economy through the rubber trade and taxation. By the following spring, the rebellion had been crushed everywhere except in Ungoni, where sporadic guerrilla warfare continued until 1907. Initially, trusting in the power of magic water (*maji*), the rebels advanced boldly towards the colonial troops, but they saw the effectiveness of machine-guns[34] and changed over to guerrilla warfare. Famine proved more destructive than the actual war operations, as dwellings, fields and grain stores were destroyed, occasionally by the rebels and more systematically by colonial troops.[35]

The number of people who died in the rebellion remains a mystery. The official German estimate was 75 000, but that was certainly too small, for it covered only the period from July 1906 to June 1907. Similarly, a figure of 120 000 put forward later was probably also an underestimation. G.C.K. Gwassa, who studied the origins of the rebellion, estimated the number of victims to have been 250 000 to 300 000, a figure which John Iliffe accepted as realistic.[36]

A third disaster was the First World War and its aftermath. This war – called the Great War for Civilization by Europeans – was, as Iliffe has cuttingly remarked, the culmination of colonial exploitation, for Africa was reduced to being a mere battlefield.[37] In four years, armies with tens of thousands of soldiers tramped all over Tanzania. The Germans, whose purpose was to tie up as many opposing troops as possible in Africa, far from the main theatres of war, employed mobile delaying tactics and avoided big, open confrontations. The price was paid by the Africans of Tanzania and Kenya. Food supplies for the combat forces were extorted from them, and men were conscripted as porters.

The Germans lost, according to different estimates, 2500 to 5000 soldiers, of whom about 750 were white. The Allied forces lost at least 10 000 soldiers. These figures were small in comparison to the number of porters who died. Fewer porters fell in battle, but undernutrition, fatigue and disease made their ugly mark among them. An official British estimate was that 44 911 porters died, but the real figure was probably at least 100 000 and possibly even more.[38]

The war was followed by famine and disease. The influenza pandemic was officially estimated to have killed 50 000 to 80 000 people in Tanganyika in 1919–20. In Ugogo alone, 30 000 people were reported to have perished in the pandemic, as well as 15 000 to 20 000 in Tukuyu.[39] Once more, it is impossible to say exactly how many people died as a result of the war and subsequent epidemics, but there is every reason to concur with official British estimates that mortality was 'extremely great'.[40]

Reversing the trend towards increased mortality

The obvious implication of the preceding discussion is that, until after the First War, crude death rates in colonial Tanzania must have been

Photo 1 *A Cause of Declining Mortality? A Vaccination Campaign on the Usambara Railroad during the German Colonial Period.* (Bundesarchiv Koblenz)

27

at an exceptionally high level and must have been increasing. Thereafter, however, the trend was reversed. Local famines indeed continued and, in some places, probably became more frequent, but elsewhere the improvement of transport led to their decline. Diseases were still rife, but mass deaths ceased, partly because of the development of health care facilities. However, the impact of the colonial medical system, which initially was intended to serve whites, should not be overestimated.

A more important factor in the decline of epidemics may have been that human immunological defences were strengthened through exposure to disease. The worst killer disease of the late precolonial and early colonial periods, smallpox, was already brought under control in the German period. An extensive vaccination campaign involving probably the majority of Tanganyikans contributed to the control of smallpox.[41] Yet it is possible that, for the most part, smallpox was beaten by the phenomenon that German doctors termed *Durchseuchung*, a thorough saturation of the population by the disease, for, when the majority of the people had been exposed to the disease, the survivors acquired immunity.[42] Cholera was held in check, as was sleeping sickness. A combination of medication, directed and spontaneous resettlement, bush clearing and biological adjustment of the people prevented catastrophes like the severe sleeping sickness epidemic that broke out in Uganda at the beginning of the 1900s.[43]

The elimination of catastrophe mortality and the development of health care were reflected in a decline of infant and child mortality. Even though colonial officials did not compile statistics for infant and child mortality across the territory, there is evidence of an appalling situation in the early colonial years. The death rate was particularly severe among infants in the first year of life. In studies of small sample populations during the first two decades of the twentieth century, the lowest levels of child mortality were about 20 to 30 per cent, and the highest levels were as great as 70 to 80 per cent.[44] The extreme figures are probably unrepresentative, but a more reliable estimate may be offered by a study made at the end of the German colonial period on the basis of data gathered from over 46 000 African women. According to this study, 23 per cent of their children had died during their first year of life and 18 per cent died later; in other words, only 59 per cent of their children survived.[45] Although it is clear that all the figures must be regarded with a great deal of scepticism, these data lead one to suspect that nearly half the children born in early colonial Tanganyika died.[46]

What caused great mortality among children? Many German doctors and missionaries believed that African nutritional habits and unhygienic living conditions were responsible. Other German doctors believed that the nutritional problems were not crucial and that the basic cause of high child mortality was widespread diseases.[47] Recalling the population catastrophes discussed above, one can hardly refrain from asking, however, whether it was not inevitable that child mortality in the early twentieth century should have been very heavy. As the well-known missionary anthropologist of Kilimanjaro, Bruno Gutmann, argued, the alarming child mortality figures 'bear witness for the most part to the damage done in the new era, and they cannot as such be used as evidence of the people's standard of living in the recent past'.[48]

Infant and child mortality appear to have decreased, however, as the colonial period progressed. From the 1948 census onwards, recorded mortality was clearly at a lower level than that indicated by evidence from the German period and the early years of British rule. Whereas, according to scattered studies made at the beginning of the British period, it would seem that as many as half the African children born in Tanganyika died in childhood,[49] in both the 1948 and the 1957 population censuses, child mortality was said to have fallen to about a third. Both censuses stated that infant mortality (among children under 1 year) had dropped to below one-fifth.[50] Higher-than-average mortality figures were found only for women over 45 both in the 1948 census[51] and later in case-studies made in famine situations.[52] It seems evident, therefore, that infant and child mortality from the late 1940s onwards was at a lower level than before, and there is every reason to believe that this was due mainly to the fact that demographic catastrophes had ceased. The decline of child and infant mortality seems to have continued into the 1960s. While infant mortality, according to the 1957 census, was about 190 per 1000, in 1967 the figure was clearly lower – 160 at the most. On the other hand, it must be remembered that the death rate among 1- to 4-year-olds in 1967 was still high. All in all, even at that time, a quarter of Tanzanian children still appeared to be dying before their fifth birthday.[53]

Thus mortality, whether measured in crude death rates (number of deaths per 1000 population) or infant and child mortality rates, seems to have decreased between the late 1920s and the late 1940s; this obviously resulted mainly from the elimination of catastrophe mortality. After the late 1940s, death rates appear to have declined more slowly. According to estimates made on the basis of censuses, the decline was considerably less between 1957 and 1967 than it had been between 1948 and 1957. Nevertheless, despite the unrealiability of demographic data, the general belief was that the death rate was following a continuing downward trend.[54] The new mortality level cannot, however, be called low in absolute terms. Moreover, the interpretation of mortality figures is complicated by the fact that a part of the apparently falling death rates should be attributed to the statistical effect of a rise in fertility and growth of population at large.

Neither can the state of health of the African population be described as good. While the advance of smallpox and sleeping sickness was stopped, other diseases remained rampant, particularly endemic malaria, which caused 'a great deal of suffering in childhood and [was] responsible for much of the grossly excessive mortality rate'.[55] A majority of Tanzanians suffered from malaria. Neither had the spread of hookworm been halted. Colonial officials believed that hookworm, together with malaria, was responsible for a great amount of ill health and inability to work.[56]

The key role of changing fertility

The interpretation of mortality presented above contains three main propositions. First, mortality amongst Tanganyika's African population fell between the mid-1920s and the late 1940s. Secondly, this decrease was due primarily to the elimination of mortality peaks arising from catastrophes. Thirdly, after the elimination of catastrophe mortality, mortality remained at a new level, which was indeed gradually declining but still fairly high on an absolute scale.

Now, if this interpretation is correct, a major implication follows. The accelerated population growth of the late colonial period is difficult to explain solely – or even mainly – on the basis of the decrease in mortality. The population did begin to increase during the same period when mortality fell, that is, sometime between 1925 and 1945, but, as was shown above, the moment at which mortality began to decrease and the extent of its decrease are uncertain. Moreover, population growth seems to have accelerated towards the end of the colonial period more rapidly than would be supposed from the indicators of mortality decrease alone. This observation leads directly to the question of a possible increase in fertility, because in Tanganyika migration had no impact on the total population. Indeed, the more closely one goes into subject, the more probable a rise in the birth rate appears to be.

By far the best study of population trends in colonial Africa is R.R. Kuczynski's monumental *Demographic Survey of the British Colonial Empire*. Kuczynski held that the idea of traditionally high fertility among African women was a myth. He assumed that the birth rate in Africa must have been at roughly the same level as it had been in Britain at the end of the nineteenth century.[57] This line of approach has not subsequently been followed up, presumably because the first reliable population censuses of the colonial period, taken at about the time Kuczynski's work appeared, revealed the birth rate to have been at a higher level than Kuczynski supposed.[58] Yet it is possible that Kuczynski was not so far off track as it seems. The difference between his conceptions and census results could be explained by the fact that he did his research during a transitory period when fertility was beginning to rise. Kuczynski, however, would have had to use data from the period preceding that turning-point. Many pieces of evidence support the notion of such a transition to an increased birth rate. Separately, they would not perhaps be very convincing, but, together, they make it possible to argue that an increase in the birth rate must have been an important factor in the population growth that began during the colonial period.

During the German period, there had been much concern about the low birth rate. The annual colonial government report for 1912–13 argued that, when peace prevailed and epidemic diseases like smallpox were kept in check, the population should increase, but this did not seem to be happening.[59] A basic reason for the failure of population to increase was low fertility. German doctors who counted childbirths among African women obtained very modest figures. In general, it appeared that an average of three to four births were occurring per sexually mature woman. The regional differences were great, for, while there was extremely low fertility – even below one birth per woman – on parts of the coast, there were clearly more births in the interior. For each woman under 40 there were generally two to three births, and women over 40 years averaged four to five births. Another estimate, which included miscarriages and abortions, placed the average number of pregnancies at about four to five per woman.[60] In a report by medical officials in 1913, it was stated that 'from child statistics, it [could] be concluded that the population [was] increasing very slowly. In certain scattered areas such as central Ujiji, Bukoba and many coastal areas, by contrast, a marked decrease in population [could] be noted.'[61] However, the study also revealed small, scattered areas with high birth rates, where seven to nine – and, in extreme cases like Tukuyu, as many as twelve – pregnancies per woman were counted.[62]

Whether this state of affairs was 'traditional' is a moot point. In precolonial African societies, contrary to what is often supposed, fertility was by no means without restraint; in fact, many mechanisms, cultural as well as biological, regulated it.[63] It can be regarded as 'natural' fertility only in the sense that it was not restricted with a deliberate view to reducing the number of offspring. Its level was evidently not uniform either, but varied from one society to another.[64] However, although there had been regional differences in fertility even in precolonial times, it is possible that during the German colonial period the differences became more marked. In other words, while the birth rate may have been failing generally, in some areas it may have increased.

Nevertheless, there is a reason to suspect that the population catastrophes of the early colonial period caused a fall in fertility. Certainly they had repercussions on following generations, because women who endured these disasters gave birth less often than those who escaped them. For example, a thorough case-study of Ulanga in the 1930s observed that the Maji Maji famine lowered the fertility of its survivors by over 25 per cent, 'so that a quarter of what should have been the next generation was in fact never born at all'.[65] On the other hand, women who found some degree of security by living near mission stations enjoyed higher birth rates (one more birth of pregnancy per woman on average) than those who remained outside the sphere of influence of missions.[66]

In the late colonial period, however, fertility increased. Comparison of the censuses of 1948 and 1957 shows increased birth rates for all age-groups. The observed change was so small that census-takers initially thought it might be attributable to a sampling error, but the increases in birth rates were confirmed both by re-evaluations of the data and by the next census of 1967.[67]

Owing to the weakness of the statistical base, it is of course hazardous to make too much of the census figures, but the idea of a rise in fertility is further supported by a different type of quantitative material, the 1973 National Demographic Survey of Tanzania. In this survey, the data showing increased birth rates came from fertility histories of about 65 000 women. Interviews with these women found that the younger cohorts bore more children than had older women at the same age. The increase in birth rates was gradual up until the early 1960s, but became more marked thereafter.[68]

The rise in the birth rate is also shown by the change in the age struc-ture of the population, which is reflected in several population estimates and censuses, towards a greater proportion of children and young peo-ple. In the 1948 and 1957 censuses, the proportion of children under 16 was considerably larger than that found by the population estimate of 1931. However, the extent of the change in the age structure which took place between 1948 and 1957 is uncertain, although the proportion of children under 6 grew somewhat.[69]

Because the data from population censuses and other statistical sources are unreliable, they alone are not sufficient to confirm an increase of fertility. Thus additional evidence must be sought, perhaps by reconstructing family histories from parish records or other such documents, although it is uncertain whether the source material available in Tanzania and elsewhere in Africa would allow the sorts of analytical procedures which have proved fruitful in European demo-graphic history. Therefore, for the moment we must be content with existing local studies, although unfortunately very few local studies have concentrated on population trends. The best-known such study was the report on Ulanga written in the 1930s by two liberal colonial officials, A.T. and G.M. Culwick. It supports the hypothesis concerning the direct link between increased fertility and the cessation of catastrophe mortality. The Culwicks stated that, although child mortality had not decreased until just before the end of the period when they were conducting their study, the birth rate in Ulanga had been increasing since the early 1920s.[70] But this was, of course, only one small area.

Nevertheless, further support for the thesis of an increase in the birth rate can be gained from anthropological data. The relevant anthropological findings consistently indicate that, towards the end of the colonial period, intervals between births were growing shorter because the customs which, by enjoining sexual abstinence after births, had encouraged longer intervals between births had been transformed during the colonial period.[71]

The final piece of evidence for an increase in fertility comes from comparative research. The view presented above concerning a rise in birth rate is not widely shared among students of African population history.[72] It is not, however, entirely pioneering and revolutionary.[73] nor is it completely at variance with experiences elsewhere in Africa and in the rest of the world. As Ansley Coale has recently argued, the 'widely accepted thesis that traditional societies developed customs that promoted high fertility . . . should . . . be amended to say that traditional societies developed customs that kept fertility at *moderate* levels because it was most advantageous to their collective survival'.[74] Empirical evidence in favour of the fertility-rise thesis is also beginning to emerge in European and Third World demographic history.[75]

Fertility mechanisms

In order to make a convincing case for an increase in the birth rate, it is not enough merely to substantiate and document the increase, for it must also be explained. That task is demanding and far beyond the confines of this chapter. Here, I must be content with presenting a few theses and hypotheses, along with some data supporting them. In doing this, it is important to make a distinction between, on the one hand, background factors which promoted or made possible a rise in fertility and, on the other, the concrete mechanisms through which that increase took place.

The background factors must surely be sought in the context of colonialism. It is not difficult to imagine that the colonial need for labour-power created pressures for an increased population. If labour-power is understood broadly to include household labour, colonialism could certainly be seen to have created pressure to have more children. Such pressure was increased, moreover, by the fact that colonialism drew some children out of household labour and into schools, even though parents were often reluctant to let their children attend school because their labour was needed at home. For this reason, it was rare for all the children in a given family to be allowed to attend school.[76]

However, the demographic history of both Europe and the Third

World teaches us to beware of overly mechanistic socio-economic explanations. Background factors do not influence fertility directly. Instead, their impact is filtered through many biological, cultural and other kinds of mechanisms which have come to be known in demography as proximate determinants. These include the incidence of marriage, the age of marriage, various customs regulating frequency of sexual intercourse and use of contraceptives, and practices which cause temporary or permanent sterility. In Tanzania, two fertility-reducing proximate determinants dominated. One was childlessness, which was considerably more common in Tanzania than in Europe, and which was noticeably more common in certain regions, such as the coast, than in others. The causes of and trends in childlessness require further research, although they were probably connected with women's health. However, there is reason to think that childlessness may have decreased during the course of the colonial period.[77]

The other major proximate determinant causing reduced fertility was what demographers call 'post-partum non-susceptibility'. This is related to long periods of breast-feeding and is due to the combined effect of lactational amenorrhoea and post-partum abstinence during breast-feeding. Amenorrhoea is a physiological mechanism, for breast-feeding defers the onset of ovulation, whereas abstinence is culturally sanctioned, for women are forbidden to have sexual intercourse while breast-feeding. If precolonial breast-feeding periods were, as it appears, as long as several years, 'post-partum non-susceptibility' left African women with intervals of several years between births. In populations in which marriage was nearly universal and the marriage age for women was low, this was the major proximate determinant of fertility.[78]

Anthropological evidence from the 1950s to the 1970s strongly suggests that these fertility-inhibiting mechanisms were severely eroded during and after the colonial period. Neither cultural sanctions nor the spirits of the ancestors could have retained their authority intact in colonial society. Indeed, both initiation rites, with their teachings on sexuality, and various customs affecting sexual behaviour and pregnancy lost much of their vitality. The result was that, because pregnancy more and more often interrupted breast-feeding, intervals between births grew shorter than they had been even during the German period.[79] If a Sukuma married couple, for example, did not have a new child at regular intervals of about two years, then rumours started flying.[80] Chagga women, who had once left at least three years between births, now gave birth nearly every year.[81] In Bunyakyusa, the interval between births was reduced from four or five years to about two years.[82] In Ubena, the interval seems to have been shortened to somewhat over two years, or to half of what the interval had once been.[83] Amont the Maasai, the average number of children per woman appears to have grown from 6.5 to 8.[84] A relaxation of sanctions against pregnancy soon after births was also reported among matrilineal peoples of the east, although there is no information concerning the effect of this change on the number of children.[85]

The only anthropological evidence of a falling birth rate comes from a study of the Sonjo, a small Bantu group who live in the middle of Maasailand in northern Tanzania.[86] Also deviating from the general trend were the Haya of Bukoba, whose families remained small throughout the colonial period, although it is unlikely that their birth rate fell.[87] Even in Buhaya, any fear that the population was decreasing dissipated after the Second World War.[88]

If birth rates increased because of colonialism, we might assume that the birth rate rose more rapidly in those areas of the country which were more closely integrated into the colonial system. Although a definitive regional analysis would require that patterns of migration be taken into account, let us have a look at birth rates in different regions. Tanzania has always been a country of great internal variation, and it is clear that the regional population dynamics very considerably. The 1973 National Demographic Survey revealed that birth rates varied substantially, from around seven on Kilimanjaro and in Mbeya to about five in coastal regions.[89] What is uncertain is how these differences developed in the colonial period, for, while the National Demographic Survey shows increased birth rates in many areas in the 1960s, fertility appears to have increased much more slowly in certain coastal and central areas.[90]

Regional variations might also be studied by examining age distributions given for 'tribes' in population estimates and censuses. In both 1931 and 1957, the category containing the greatest relative proportion of children (about half the total population) included the Chagga and the Nyakyusa,[91] whereas the category with the smallest proportion of children (about a third) included the Haya, some eastern and southeastern matrilineal peoples such as the Zaramo and the Yao, and also the Nyamwezi.[92] There is need for further research with this material, although it is not easy to use for purposes of comparison.

One additional factor which must be considered is the impact of Christianity on the number of children. Christianity appears to have had a substantial influence on both rising birth rates and declining death rates. Already during the German period, the families of Christians appeared larger than those of 'pagans'. This was partly due to a fall in mortality caused by the dissemination by missionaries of information on hygiene and nutrition to Christian mothers.[93]

In addition, among Christians the birth rate increased and childlessness decreased in the course of the colonial period.[94] Many studies made in the 1950s and 1960s confirm that the families of Christians were larger than those of 'traditionalists'. In Sukumaland, one report calculated that Christian mothers had 6.4 children on average, while non-Christian mothers had an average of 4.5 children. Moreover,

Christian women were known to give birth more frequently.[95] From Kilimanjaro came reports that Christian families considered many pregnancies to be desirable.[96] In Bunyakyusa, where the average interval between children decreased to two-and-a-half years, Christians, who 'fear[ed] much less', had even shorter intervals.[97]

The increase in fertility among Christians does not seem difficult to explain. Missionaries attacked the old customs which had controlled fertility. They thought initiation rites were indecent; indeed, even the more liberal among them were horrified by 'their strongly exaggerated sexual side'.[98] There was an attempt by missionaries, therefore, either to eradicate the rites completely or to make them more acceptable.[99] Polygamy, which possibly reduced fertility,[100] was naturally shunned by most missionaries.[101] The rule that an African mother should not maintain her marital sexual life and become pregnant again during the course of a long breast-breeding period was held by many missionaries to be a superstition which encouraged polygyny and extra-marital relations by men. Thus missionaries, to set a good example, had children after intervals which, from the African viewpoint, were scandalously short. The Nyakyusa, for example, made 'many caustic comments on the irresponsibility of European missionaries in this matter'.[102]

Yet neither colonial policy nor missionaries were solely responsible for increased birth rates. Indeed, the evidence of increased fertility suggests that birth rates rose among non-Christians as well as Christians, though at a slower pace. If this was so, we should concentrate on the factors which eroded old customs. One such factor may have been the increase of infant and child mortality in the late precolonial and early colonial periods. Although the population catastrophes for a time caused abnormally low birth rates, eventually they may have encouraged increased fertility as communities recovered from the disasters. African families may have compensated for unusually frequent childhood deaths, and for the preceding period when few birth occurred, by having more children. Although child mortality later decreased, fertility may have remained at this high level. This would explain the coincidence of high fertility and falling mortality.

Concluding Reflections

In this chapter, I have traced some changes in Tanganyika's population dynamics during the last 150 years. I have suggested that the late precolonial and early colonial periods form a demographic phase of their own, marked by an increase in mortality and possibly a temporary fall in fertility due to devastating catastrophes. In the interwar period began a new phase which was characterized by a fall in mortality (at first comparatively rapid, and then slower) and a rise in fertility (at first hesitant, but accelerating with the approach of independence). In this phase, therefore, the change in birth rate must be taken seriously as a factor explaining population growth.

I have also briefly touched upon the background factors behind the increase in fertility. I have proposed that they must be sought in colonial history, primarily in the demand for surplus labour imposed by colonialism. The most important mechanisms directly affecting the birth rate, however, were the shortening of the intervals between births and probably also a decrease in childlessness. Regional and religious factors have also been dealt with briefly, but my main argument is that the basic demographic processes outlined were common to the whole of Tanzania, although in different places they proceeded at different rates.

Although the chapter has presented estimates of the order of magnitude of the changes in mortality and fertility, I have not attempted to estimate their exact extent or, accordingly, the extent to which they explain population growth. This task must be left to further research, particularly because Tanzania is such a large and heterogeneous country. But, if the basic pattern outlined above can be proved correct, at least two points follow. First, population growth cannot to be taken as an irresistible and biologically grounded force. Discerning the social, economic and cultural factors which affect population change leads to the conclusions that population trends change when social and cultural conditions change and that population trends can be influenced through policy measures.

Secondly, this does not mean that population trends in Tanzania will automatically follow any known pattern or that they can be manipulated at will. It is possible that Tanzania, like Africa in general, is not in an intermediate stage between 'traditional' and 'modern' society and is not undergoing a 'transition to capitalism'. Instead, Africa may be in the midst of a very different kind of social transformation whose distinguishing feature is an unprecedented pattern of human reproduction. In such a situation, historical research can hardly give simple prescriptions about what should be done; it can only show the complexity of the situation and give some idea of the feasibility of various policy options.

Notes

1. I have benefited from comments by the editors of this volume, James Giblin and Gregory Maddox. I am also indebted to Christine Mann for translating into English an earlier paper on which this chapter draws.

2. William Allan, *The African Husbandman* (Edinburgh and London, 1965) p. 338.

3. These are broadly similar to what other writers have called neo-Malthusian and anti-Malthusian perspectives. See the discussion by Gregory Maddox in Chapter 2.

4. All the factual information in this chapter is restricted to Tanganyika, unless otherwise mentioned. The inclusion of Zanzibar, however, would not alter the basic thrust of the agrument.

5. These claims are developed in Juhani Koponen, *German Colonial Policies in Mainland Tanzania, 1890-1914: Development for Exploitation* (forthcoming, Hamburg, 1994).

6. E.G. Oscar Baumann, *Usambara und seine Nachbargebiete* (Berlin, 1891), p. 292; Franz Stuhlmann, *Mit Emin Pascha ins Herz von Afrika* (Berlin, 1894), p. 866; Georg Volkens, *Der Kilimandscharo* (Berlin, 1897), p. 375; Hans Meyer, *Der Kilimandjaro* (Berlin, 1900), p. 277.

7. E.g. Karl Supf, 'Zur Baumwollfrage', in Karl Supf, *Deutsche Kolonial-Baumwolle* (Berlin, n.d.), p. 8; Otto Peiper, 'Geburtenhäufigkeit, Säuglings- und Kinder-Sterblichkeit und Säuglings und Kinder-Sterblichkeit und Säuglingsernährung im früheren Deutsch-Ostafrika', *Veröffentlichungen aus dem Gebiete der Medizinalverwaltung* 6, 9 (1902): 3.

8. The quotation are from Oscar Baumann, *Durch Massailand zur Nilquelle* (Berlin, 1894), p. 259; and Peiper, 'Geburtenhäufigkeit,' p. 3.

9. Carl Ittameier, 'Die Erhaltung und Vermehrung der Eingeborenen-Bevoölkerung,' *Hamburgische Universität, Abhandlungen aus dem Gebiet der Auslandskunde* 13, D/1 (1923): 62.

10. Dernburg to Reichstag Budget Commission, 18 February 1908, printed in the *DKB* (1908), p. 218.

11. Lord Lugard, *The Dual Mandate in British Tropical Africa* (London, 1922).

12. See, for example, 'Conference of Governors of the East African Dependencies, 1926, Summary of Proceedings', extract printed in Raymond Leslie Buell, *The Native Problem in Africa*, vol. I (New York, 1928), p. 552.

13. See, for example, Tanganyika, *Report of the Committee on Supply and Welfare of Native Labour in the Tanganyika Territory* (Dar es Salaam, 1938), p. 11; Tanganyika, *A Ten-Year Development and Welfare Plan for Tanganyika Territory* (Dar es Salaam, 1946), p. 11.

14. Besides Tanganyika, German East Africa also included the present Rwanda and Burundi. These were the most heavily populated areas of the territory, but for the most part, due to their remote location and powerful traditional political institutions, they remained outside the colonial economy and direct colonial administration throughout the German period.

15. I.e. taking the total growth for German East Africa (from over 6 million in 1899 to 7.6 million in 1913) and subtracting the figures for Burundi and Rwanda (which show growth from 3 million to 3.5 million). *Jahresbericht* (1899/1900), p. 203, and (1912/13), A, p. 36.

16. See e.g. *Jahresbericht* (1912/13), p. 10.

17. Cf. Tanganyika, *Census of the Native Population of Tanganyika Territory, 1931* (Dar es Salaam, 1932); and A.T. Culwick, 'The Population Trend', *Tanganyika Notes and Records*, 11 (1941): 13-17.

18. This passage draws on Juhani Koponen *People and Production in Late Precolonial Tanzania: History and Structures* (Uppsala, 1988). Precolonial famine and pestilence are discussed in chapter 4 and pp. 362-4. For the East African slave trade, see pp. 83-95.

19. Koponen, *People and Production*, pp. 142-3, 147-8. The term 'means of destruction' comes from Jack Goody, *Technology, Tradition and the State in Africa* (London, 1971), chapter 3.

20. Ernst Nigmann, *Geschichte der Kaiserlichen Schutztruppe für Deutsch-Ostafrika* (Berlin, 1911), pp. 149-57 and *passim*.

21. Matthias Erzberger to Reichstag, 6 March 1913, *Stenographische Berichte über die Verhandlungen des Reichstags*, vol. 288, p. 4307. The precise grounds for the estimate are not known, but its order of magnitude appears realistic. Erzberger announced as his source 'information obtained from the [Colonial] Minister'. The figure also included casualties of Maji Maji (see below).

22. Stuhlmann to Colonial Department of Foreign Office, 17 January 1903, as well as an undated typed copy of the same to all local administrative stations (appendix to the

Population: A Dependent Variable

above), BArchP, RKolA 699, 142–9 (quotations 146, 143); Dernburg, 'Bericht über eine vom 13. Juli bis 30. Oktober 1907 nach Ostafrika ausgeführte Dienstreise, Geheim', BArchP, RKolA 300, exp. 37.

23. 'Micro-' and 'macroparasites' are William McNeill's terms: *Plagues and People* (Garden City, NY, 1976), pp. 13–14.

24. Prince, 'Verwertung Uhehes', BarchP, RKolA 10, 108; Koponen, *People and Production*, pp. 146–8.

25. This is analogous to the Kenyan area, see Marc H. Dawson, 'Smallpox in Kenya, 1880–1920', *Social Science and Medicine*, 13B (1979): 245–50.

26. Baumann, *Durch Massailand*, p. 165; Moritz Merker, *Die Masai*, 2nd edn (Berlin, 1910), pp. 347–8; R.R. Kuczynski, *Demographic Survey of the British Colonial Empire*, vol. II (London, 1949), p. 122, fn. 5.

27. Becker, *Arbeiten aus dem Kaiserlichen Gesundheits-Amt*, 13 (1897): 19.

28. *Central Africa* (1899), pp. 69–71, 85–7; Eduard Kremer, 'Die unperiodischen Schwankungen der Niederschläge und die Hungersnöte in Deutsch-Ost-Afrika', *Aus dem Archiv der Deutschen Seewarte* 33 (1910): 29, 35–6, 38; Helge Kjekshus, *Ecology Control and Economic Development in East African History: The Case of Tanganyika, 1850–1950* (Berkeley and Los Angeles, 1977), pp. 138–9.

29. Samuel Sehoza, *Central Africa*, March 1933, according to John Iliffe, *A Modern History of Tanganyika* (Cambridge, 1979), p. 125.

30. *Jahresbericht* (1898/99), pp. 209, 264–5, 274, 279; D.W. Malcolm, *Sukumaland* (London, 1953), pp. 12–13; Walter Busse, 'Forschungsreise durch den südlichen Teil von Deutsch-Ostafrika', *Beihefte zum Tropenpflanzer* 3, 3 (1902): 111–12.

31. *Jahresbericht* (1898/99), p. 203.

32. *Jahresbericht* (1898/99), p. 238; Alexander Becker, 'Über Bahnbau in Deutsch-Ostafrika', *DKB* (1899): 761.

33. On the Maji Maji in general, see Iliffe, *Modern History*, chapter 6.

34. Oral tradition includes numerous descriptions of unequal confrontations, for example in G.C.K. Gwassa and John Iliffe, eds, *Records of the Maji Maji Rising* (Nairobi, 1968), pp. 21–2.

35. Mohoro District (Grass) to Government, 4 October 1905, TNA G3/90, 271; Adolf von Götzen, *Deutsch-Ostafrika im Aufstand* (Berlin, 1909), pp. 149, 248; Detlef Bald, 'Afrikanischer Kampf gegen Koloniale Herrschaft. Der Maji-Maji Aufstand in Ostafrika', *Militärgeschichtliche Mitteilungen* 1 (1976): 39–41.

36. Iliffe, *Modern History*, p. 200. C.J. Martin has put forward an even higher estimate, half a million, but without giving documentation for it. C.J. Martin, 'Estimates on Population Growth in East Africa, with Special Reference to Tanganyika and Zanzibar', in K.M. Barbour and R.M. Prothero, eds, *Essays on African Population* (London, 1961), p. 50.

37. Iliffe, *Modern History*, p. 241.

38. Concerning the figures, see Ludwig Boell, *Die Operationen in Ost-Afrika* (Hamburg, 1951), pp. 427–9; K. Moesta, 'Die Einwirkung des Krieges auf die Eingeborenenbevölkerung in Deutsch-Ostafrika', *Koloniale Rundschau* (1919): 6–11, 22; and Iliffe, *Modern History*, pp. 249–50.

39. Tanganyika, *Medical Report*, 1921, p. 80; Peter Rigby, *Cattle and Kinship Among the Gogo* (Ithaca, NY, 1967), p. 22, fn. 17; Iliffe, *Modern History*, p. 270.

40. 'Papers relating to the health of Native Populations', p. 53; quoted by Kuczynski, *Demographic Survey*, p. 396. Cf. Moesta, 'Einwirkung', p. 22, which suggests the total number who died to have been as many as 740 000.

41. Emil Steudel, 'Das Gesundheitswesen in Deutsch-Ostafrika', in W. Arning, ed., *Deutsch-Ostafrika* (Berlin, 1936), p. 185.

42. *Medizinal-Bericht über die Deutschen Schutzgebiete* (1903/4): 15

43. Emil Steudel, 'Die Schlafkrankheit in Deutsch-Ostafrika vom Beginn bis Gegenwart', *Mitteilungen aus den Deutschen Schutzgebieten* 28 (1928): 61–79; F.K. Kleine, 'Die

Juhani Koponen

Schlafkrankheitsbekämpfung in Deutsch-Ostafrika vor und nach dem Krieg', *Deutsche Tropenmedizinische Zeitschrift* 45 (1941): 23-9; David F. Clyde, *History of the Medical Services of Tanganyika* (Dar es Salaam, 1962), pp. 28-32, 122-6, 184-6; John Ford, *The Role of the Trypanosomiases in African Ecology: A Study of the Tsetse Fly Problem* (London, 1971), esp. chapters 12 and 13.

44. E.g. Ittameier, 'Erhaltung', pp. 37-40; and Peiper, 'Genurtenhäufigkeit', pp. 8-19. On the latter figures for Upare, see also J.J. Dannholz, 'Säuglingssterblichkeit in Mbaga', *Die ärztliche Mission* 9 (1914): 125.

45. L. Külz, 'Zur Biologie und Pathologie des Nachwuchses bei den Naturvölkern der deutschen Schutzgebiete', *Beihefte zum Archiv für Schiffs- und Tropenhygiene* 3 (1919): 866 ff; L. Külz, 'Familien-Nachwuchsstatistik über die Eingeborenen von Deutsch-Ostafrika', *DKB* (1914): 440-57.

46. German doctors spoke vaguely of children who were 'over 1 year of age' or 'older'. Officially, the age limit for a 'child' was defined as 14 years: Peiper, 'Geburtenhäufigkeit', p. 16.

47. For the differing opinions, see Peiper, 'Geburtenhäufigkeit', pp. 6, 10, 26-34, 37-42; Ittameier, 'Erhaltung', pp. 40-4, 47-50.

48. Bruno Gutmann, *Das Recht der Dschagga* (Munich, 1926), p. 144.

49. Tanganyika, *Medical Report*, 1921, pp. 82-3 (the limit of childhood was taken here as the commencement of the tenth year).

50. Martin, 'Estimates'; Tanganyika, *African Census Report 1957* (Dar es Salaam, 1963), p. 91. These figures are not, of course, directly comparable with earlier ones, but they indicate the downward trend.

51. United Nations, *Additional Information on the Population of Tanganyika* (New York, 1953), p. 5.

52. E.g. M.C. Latham, 'A Clinical Nutrition Survey of Certain Areas of the Dodoma and Kondoa Districts of Tanganyika', *East African Medical Journal* 41 (1964): 76.

53. Bertil Egerö and Roushdi Henin, *The Population of Tanzania: An Analysis of the 1967 Population Census* (Dar es Salaam, 1973), pp. 184-5.

54. United Nations, *Additional Information*, p. 5; Tanganyika, *African Census Report 1957*, p. 91; Egerö and Henin, *Population*, pp. 184-5. For figures, see Table 1.1 above.

55. David F. Clyde, *Malaria in Tanzania* (London, 1967), p. 18.

56. J.F.R. Hill and J.P. Moffett, eds, *Tanganyika: A Review of Its Resources and Their Development* (Dar es Salaam, 1955), pp. 99-100.

57. Kuczynski, *Demographic Survey*, pp. 117-18.

58. The 'gross reproduction index', that is, the average number of female children born to a woman living through to the end of her reproductive cycle, was 2.3 in Britain at the end of the nineteenth century (Kuczynski, *Demographic Survey*, p. 118). In Tanganyika, according to estimates made on the basis of the 1957 population census, the figure was 2.7 (Tanganyika, *African Census Report 1957*, p. 95); and according to the 1967 population census, it was at least 3.1 (Egerö and Henin, *Population*, p. 194).

59. *Jahresbericht* (1912/13): 10.

60. Peiper, 'Geburtenhäufigkeit', pp. 4-14; Ittameier, 'Erhaltung', pp. 5-8.

61. Familien-Nachwuchsstatistik, *DKB* (1914): 440-1.

62. Ittameier, 'Erhaltung', p. 6. He does not speak of 'pregnancies', but rather of 'total numbers of children' (*Gesamtkinderzahl*).

63. When Richard Burton became the first European to travel through Tanganyika in 1857, he was assured that 'the women are not prolific': Richard Burton, 'The Lake Regions of Central Equatorial Africa', *Journal of the Royal Geographical Society* 29 (1859): 311.

64. Koponen, *People and Production*, pp. 323-32.

65. A.T. Culwick and G.M. Culwick, 'A Study of Population in Ulanga, Tanganyika Territory: I', *The Sociological Review* 30 (1938): 375.

66. Ittameier, 'Erhaltung', pp. 6-7; Peiper, 'Geburtenhäufigkeit', pp. 13-14.

Population: A Dependent Variable

67. Cf. Tanganyika, *African Census Report 1957*, p. 87, and Egerö and Henin, *Population*, p. 201. For these and other numerical estimates, see Table 1.1 above.

68. Douglas C. Ewbank, 'Fertility Estimation', in Roushdi A. Henin, ed., *The Demography of Tanzania: An Analysis of the 1973 National Demographic Survey of Tanzania*, vol. VI (Dar es Salaam, n.d.), p. 92; Roushdi A., Henin, Douglas C., Ewbank and Nicholas E. Oyo, 'Fertility Trends: Analysis of Fertility Histories', in *idem*, pp. 94–109.

69. In the 1931 population count, which was still on an estimate basis, the proportion of 'non-adults' in the population was 37.5 per cent (sexual maturity was used as the defining factor): Tanganyika, *Census of the Native Population 1931*, p. 5. The 'general census' of 1948 gave the proportion of under-16s to be 44.9 per cent, and the 'sample census' gave a figure of 42.2 per cent. The corresponding figures for 1957 were 44.3 and 43.9. The proportion of under-6s had risen according to both counts, being in 1957 23.8 per cent (general census) and 21.2 per cent (sample census): Tanganyika, *African Census Report 1957*, p. 31. See also C.J. Martin, 'Some Estimates of the General Age Distribution, Fertility, and the Rate of Natural Increase of the African Population of British East Africa', *Population Studies* 7 (1953): 185–6.

70. Culwick and Culwick, 'Ulanga, I', pp. 375–6, and 'A Study of Population in Ulanga, Tanganyika Territory: II', *Sociological Review* 31 (1939): 31–9. .

71. This is discussed in the next section below.

72. AHD and *African Historical Demography, II. Proceedings of a seminar held in the Centre of African Studies, University of Edinburgh*, 24–25 April 1981 (Edinburgh, 1981), *passim*. See esp. AHD, p. 12 (J. Caldwell on Africa in general) and p. 438 (K. David Patterson on Ghana); and the review by C.C. Wrigley, *Journal of African History* 20 (1979): esp. 129–30. See also John C. Caldwell and Pat Caldwell, 'The Cultural Context of High Fertility in Sub-Saharan Africa,' *PDR* 13 (1987): esp. 411.

73. For Tanzania, Meredeth Turshen has suggested the idea of a fertility increase, but without thorough documentation: *The Political Ecology of Disease in Tanzania* (New Burnswick, 1984), pp. 47–9, 126–7, and 'Population Growth and the Deterioration of Health, Mainland Tanzania, 1920–1960', in Dennis D. Cordell and Joel W. Gregory, eds, *African Population and Capitalism* (Boulder, 1987), pp. 187–200. For Kenya, there is a considerably better documented case-study: Marc H. Dawson, 'Health, Nutrition and Population in Central Kenya, 1890–1945', in *idem*, pp. 201–17.

74. Ansley Coale, 'Fertility in Prerevolutionary China: Defence of a Reassessment', *PDR* 10 (1984): 478 (emphasis in original).

75. For an introduction to the subject and the sources, see Tim Dyson and Mike Murphy, 'The Onset of Fertility Transition', *PDR* 11 (1985): 339–440.

76. See e.g. Edward H. Winter and T.O Beidelman, 'Tanganyika: A Study of an African Society at National and Local Levels', in Julian H. Steward, ed., *Contemporary Change in Traditional Societies*, vol. 1 (Urbana, Chicago and London, 1967), p. 88.

77. For a more detailed discussion on proximate determinants and childlessness, see Juhani Koponen, 'Population Growth in Historical Perspective: The Key Role of Changing Fertility', in Jannik Boesen, Kjell J. Havnevik, Juhani Koponen and Rie Odgaard, eds, *Tanzania: Crisis and Struggle for Survival* (Uppsala, 1986), pp. 48–9.

78. For further discussion, see John Bongaarts, Odile Frank and Ron Lesthaege, 'The Proximate Determinants of Fertility in Sub-Saharan Africa', *PDR* 10 (1984): 522–4.

79. On the precolonial period, see Koponen, *People and Production*, p. 323; and on the German period, Peiper, 'Geburtenhäufigkeit', esp. p. 26.

80. Corlien Varkevisser, in Angela Molnos, ed., *Cultural Source Materials for Population Planning in East Africa*, vol. III (Nairobi, 1973), p. 241.

81. Sally Falk Moore and Paul Puritt, *The Chagga and Meru of Tanzania* (London, 1977), p. 2.

82. Monica Wilson, *Communal Rituals of the Nyakyusa* (London, 1959), p. 205 and Varkevisser in Molnos, *Cultural Source Materials*, vol. III, p. 249; M. Hauvast-Mertens, in *idem*, p. 255.

83. Marc J. Swartz, 'Some Cultural Influences on Family Size in Three East African Societies', *Anthropological Quarterly* 42 (1969): 79–80.

84. Cf. Merker, *Masai*, p. 199, and Angela Molnos, ed., *Cultural Source Materials for Population Planning in East Africa*, vol. I (Nairobi, 1973), p. 241.

85. E.g. Marja-Liisa Swantz, *Ritual and Symbol in Transitional Zaramo Society With Special Reference to Women* (Uppsala, 1970), p. 304; Lloyd W. Swantz, 'The Role of the Medicine Man among the Zaramo of Dar es Salaam' (Ph.D. Dissertation, University of Dar es Salaam, 1974), p. 133.

86. Robert F. Gray, *The Sonjo of Tanganyika* (London, 1963), pp. 62–3.

87. See note 59 above; Audrey Richards and Priscilla Reining, 'Report on Fertility Surveys in Buganda and Buhaya, 1952,' in Frank Lorimer, ed., *Culture and Human Fertility* (Paris, 1954), pp. 365, 378.

88. See Culwick, 'The Population Trend'.

89. Ewbank, 'Fertility Estimation', p. 91. A noticeable exception on the coast was Tanga, whose total fertility figure was the same as that for Kilimanjaro, 7.0.

90. Sylvester A.M.M. Ngallaba, 'Fertility Differentials in Tanzania with Special Reference to Four Regions' (MA Thesis, University of Dar es Salaam, 1972), esp. pp. 53, 81; Ewbank, 'Fertility Estimation', pp. 104–7.

91. According to the 1957 population census, the greatest proportion of children was observed among the 'Rundi' living on the Tanganyikan side of the Burundi border (59.1 per cent under 16), but the census-takers suspected the figure to be erroneous. In the 1931 estimates, the Rundi are not mentioned as a separate group. For sources, see note 92 below.

92. Tanganyika, *Census of the Native Population 1931*, p. 7; Tanganyika, *African Census Report 1957*, p. 46.

93. Ittameier, 'Erhaltung', pp. 56–8; Peiper, 'Geburtenhäufigkeit', exp. p. 13; Elise Kootz-Kretschmer, 'Abriss einer Landesgeschichte von Usafwa in Ostafrika', *Koloniale Rundschau* (1929): 127.

94. Note 66 above.

95. Corlien Varkevisser, in Molnos, *Cultural Source Materials*, vol. II, p. 224, and vol. III, p. 236.

96. O.F. Raum, *Chaga Childhood* (London, 1940), p. 107.

97. Hauvast-Mertens, in Molnos, *Cultural Source Materials*, vol. III, p. 255. See also M. Wilson, in *idem*, pp. 249–50. Quotation is from Monica Wilson, *Rituals of Kinship Among the Nyakyusa* (London, 1957), p. 232.

98. E.g. Lyndon Harries, 'Bishop Lucas and the Masasi Experiment', *International Review of Missions* 34 (1945): 392.

99. On the latter attempts, see Inkeri Peltola, *Uzaramu* (Helsinki, 1950), pp. 67–73; Klaus Fiedler, *Christentum und afrikanische Kultur: Konservative deutsche Missionare in Tanzania 1900–1940* (Gütersloh, 1983); Harries, 'Bishop Lucas'; and Terence Ranger, 'Missionary Adaptation of African Religious Institutions: The Masasi Case', in Terence Ranger and Isaria N. Kimambo, eds, *The Historical Study of African Religion* (London, 1972), pp. 221–51.

100. The effect of polygamy on fertility is in fact open to dispute. Ittameier, 'Erhaltung', p. 11, and Culwick and Culwick, 'Ulanga, I', pp. 376–9, did not observe that it reduced fertility.

101. The exceptions were certain 'traditionalist' missionaries, like the Moravian Traugott Bachmann in Unyiha. Traugott Bachmann, *Ich gab manchen Anstoss*, ed. Hans-Windekilde Jannasch (Hamburg, n.d. but *c.* 1956), pp. 147 ff.; and Marcia Wright, *German Missions in Tanganyika 1891–1941* (London, 1971), pp. 131–2.

102. Monica Wilson, *Religion and the Transformation of Society* (Cambridge, 1971), p. 80.

Two

~~~~~~

Environment
& Population Growth

In Ugogo
Central Tanzania

GREGORY MADDOX

Ugogo, in central Tanzania, has throughout the twentieth century been regarded as the most famine-prone region of the country. Today, Ugogo, the land of the Gogo people, covers most of Dodoma and Mpwapwa Districts in Dodoma Region and Manyoni District in Singida Region. It occupies the southern portion of the central plateau of Tanzania from the Rift Valley in the west to the Ruhebo Mountains in the east and from the northern border of Dodoma District south to the Ruha River. Generally it lies about 1000 metres above sea level and rainfall averages about 500 millimetres a year, right on the borderline that will support agriculture. Adaptation for survival, which stresses agropastoralism and social and geographic mobility in the face of the variability of agricultural production in this environment, defines the Gogo people more than anything else.[1]

Over the course of the late nineteenth and the twentieth centuries famine struck the region repeatedly. The people of the region remember by name numerous famines and food shortages. From the *Mtunya* ('The Scramble') of 1916–20 to the *Nzala ya Merika* ('Famine of America', referring to relief grain from America) of 1961, from the *Sabatele* (named after a measure of grain given as relief) of 1905 to the *MauMau* (which occurred concurrently with the uprising in Kenya, although it involved an outbreak of violence in Ugogo also) of 1954, drought, war, disease and infestation all struck the region. Yet during the British colonial era, from 1916 to 1961, population in the region and the number of people called 'Gogo' by the colonial government grew quite substantially (see Table 2.1). However, a closer examination of this population growth reveals that population did not grow uniformly during the

43

Table 2.1 *Population of Ugogo*

	Gogo	Ugogo	Dodoma	Manyoni	Mpwapwa	Old Dodoma
1913	124 814					299 400
1921	118 500					270 890
1928	166 233	211 687	128 126	44 912	38 649	
1931	182 114	211 322	130 349	43 563	*37 380	
1948	278 755	369 522	*218 800*	*52 600*	100 673	268 849
1953		*371 300*	*221 200*	*55 500*	*94 600*	
1957	299 417	409 766	236 152	58 829	114 785	
1967	360 131	553 371	297 180	80 157	176 034	

* 5400 people shifted from Manyoni District to Tabora between 1928 and 1931.
Italic indicates estimates. In 1948 Dodoma and Manyoni were combined into
one district; estimates of each division's population are from the District Books.
Sources: Census of Tanganyika and Tanzania; Gogo Development Scheme.

British colonial era, but instead grew most rapidly between 1920 and
1930 and after 1955. In between, and especially in the period between
1942 and 1954, famine acted as a demographic brake on population
growth.

The two periods of population growth mark changes in the demographic regime that accompanied changes in the relations between local
communities and the broader colonial world. In turn, these changes
reflect both changes in the social organization of production and the
interaction between local communities and their environment. Population growth between 1920 and 1930 occurred as local communities
absorbed immigrants and returning refugees after the depopulation of
the preceding four decades. Cattle owners absorbed immigrants as
workers in their fields and increased production of agricultural commodities for markets. However, economic and demographic growth
slowed after 1930 as the Depression reduced returns to agriculture and
the colonial state became more efficient at draining surplus from local
producers. Indeed, the famines after 1942 revealed that this growth had
been extensive, not intensive. New demands on individual producers
and communities in general resulted in over a decade of demographic
stagnation. Only after 1954 did colonial famine relief efforts and the
expansion of employment opportunities result in a decline in famine
mortality and renewal of population growth.

Problems of demographic analysis in Tanzania

Although demographic historians of Europe have developed quite
sophisticated models of population change based on records such as

parish registers, caution must be used in applying these models to Dodoma.[2] The first problem is that, in Dodoma, no records comparable to the parish registers of early modern Europe exist at all. Demographic reconstruction must be based on censuses and qualitative evidence, but, as will be shown below, the censuses in Tanganyika (and throughout Africa during the colonial era) present their own problems.[3]

More important than these technical problems are the structural differences between early modern European villages and African communities under colonial rule.[4] The European communities on which the most research has been carried out were part of national economies which sought domestic economic growth. In Africa under colonial rule, however, local communities were incorporated into externally orientated systems where demand for surplus was initially imposed without regard for level of productivity. This circumstance affected the ability of local communities to continue meeting their own subsistence needs while meeting the demands of long-distance traders and colonial rulers.

Studies of demographic circumstances in colonial Africa have developed two general perspectives, although most scholars agree that, during the two decades before and after 1900, the population of Africa stagnated, if it did not decline.[5] Kjekshus has argued, for instance, that population in some regions of Africa declined by about 50 per cent by 1920 while others see a smaller reduction. Views diverge sharply, however, concerning the growth in population that began in the 1920s and has continued to the present. One perspective is neo-Malthusian and natalist. In particular, C.C. Wrigley has argued that population began to grow because health care and sanitation improved under colonial regimes.[6] John Iliffe has modified Wrigley's analysis by stressing that Western health care of any sort did not become available in rural areas until at least the 1950s in most of Africa. Relying on McAlpin's[7] analysis from India, he argues that mortality declined in Africa as transport and markets evened out variations in food supply. In his analysis, 'feast and famine waned' together as periodic crises in subsistence, the so-called *ancien régime* crises, were replaced by permanent poverty and malnutrition for many in African societies.[8] These analyses all depict African societies caught within high-fertility-high-mortality equilibriums before the twentieth century, and assume that population grew once mortality was reduced during the colonial era. Some scholars argue that this growth has outstripped the ability of African environments to support it, leading in turn to repeated famine and increasing dependence on food imports and food aid. Deborah Fahy Bryceson and Jane Guyer, among others, have suggested that agricultural innovation in the face of population pressure (as modelled by Boserup) has resulted in increased productivity, but productivity gains have not been distributed evenly throughout African societies and have lagged behind population growth.[9]

Over the last few years, however, a new anti-Malthusian analysis has developed that attacks the notion of a high-fertility–high-mortality equilibrium in pre-colonial Africa which gives way to rapid growth in the colonial era with reduction of mortality. Several scholars have developed this approach out of case-studies and have marshalled some convincing evidence. Much of their work builds upon Kjekshus's argument for massive demographic decline in the late nineteenth and early twentieth centuries and resulting loss of ability by African societies to control the environment. The second major contention of the anti-Malthusians is that population growth in the twentieth century results not from a reduction of mortality but from an increase in fertility. Thus they assume that many precolonial African societies had achieved a low-fertility–low-mortality equilibrium. After this equilibrium was destroyed, the resulting destruction of social controls coupled with a demand for surplus production and labour by colonial states led to a rise in fertility.

The evidence for rise in fertility is, as is all demographic evidence for Africa, impressionistic and episodic. Various authors have suggested that a decline in polygamy and a lower marriage age for men are key factors in the rise in fertility.[10] However, as E.A. Wrigley and R.S. Schofield have argued, the marriage age for males generally has little effect on fertility rates.[11] Likewise, while a decline in polygamy does lead to reduced birth spacing for individual women, and hence increased fertility over a woman's lifetime, there is no evidence of a decrease in the incidence of polygamy so great as to lead to a large increase in fertility.[12]

For this argument the critical elements are marriage age for women and birth spacing, and some evidence does support the contention that marriage age for women declined during the colonial era. Several examples exist of breakdowns in female age grades that might have resulted in lower marriage ages for women. In one case in eastern Tanzania, a system of ritual confinement for women from puberty lasting several years gradually disappeared.[13] Finally, although studies in European demographic history have found birth spacing within marriage to be one of the least variable factors in demographic regimes, ethnographic accounts often emphasize this factor as a positive means of fertility control.[14]

Taken together, all of these factors would support the contention that fertility did increase, although perhaps not by as much as some of the staunchest anti-Malthusians insist. Moreover, the strength of any one of these factors varied across regions. Abstraction is difficult and, indeed, dangerous for just as demographic regimes in African societies differed those of Europe, they also differed greatly from one another. Ugogo, as the evidence will show, experienced both increased fertility and decreased mortality in the twentieth century, but these conclusions are not automatically adaptable to other regions even in Tanzania.

The population history of Ugogo over the twentieth century provides a clear example of the different determinants of a demographic regime, including the cycle of famine and recovery. The population of Ugogo clearly declined between the last decades of the nineteenth century and 1920. Between 1920 and 1930 it grew very rapidly. Between 1930 and about 1955 it grew moderately. After the mid–1950s rapid growth returned. The major questions about these patterns concern their scale and causes.

Late precolonial demography in Ugogo

Reconstructing precolonial African population changes is a notoriously difficult task. In East Africa it is made especially difficult by the obvious but difficult task of quantifying demographic decline before 1920.[15] Helge Kjekshus attempted to do so for Tanzania based on the assumption that the decline was dramatic. His 'maximum population disruption thesis' implied a population loss of up to 50 per cent for parts of the interior. Some of the loss came due to war and slave raiding, but most came from the more rapid spread of disease, loss of cattle and famine associated with that loss, and colonial conquest. Some loss in the interior represented a shift in population from the interior to plantations along the coast. In some regions population decline continued into the colonial era as 'pacification' continued and demands for surplus production affected already destabilized production systems.[16] In Ugogo, Carol Sissons estimated the pre-1850 population of Ugogo at 300 000. She based her estimate on the maximum disruption thesis, worked backwards from a German estimate of 160 000 in 1913 and a British census total of 118 500 in 1921, and then developed estimates of population densities based on European travellers' accounts of the late nineteenth century.[17] While her assumptions are not supported by oral traditions in the region, which downplay the severity of famines before the *Mtunya* of 1917-20, there were great losses, although they may have been concentrated around the First World War rather than spread more evenly over the previous decades.[18]

The availability of food for purchase by caravans is the starting-point for Sissons' analysis; caravans moving between the coast and Tabora, Lake Tanganyika and Ujiji seldom had difficulty in buying food. She even computes an estimated annual average grain sale of about 2000 tons, a total which is strikingly similar to total grain exports from the region during the early part of the colonial era.[19] Such evidence does not necessarily prove the existence of a more productive agricultural system before the 1880s, but it proves that individuals could control

47

enough surplus for trade. Most trade appears to have occurred at caravanserai controlled by 'chiefs'. Payments of *hongo*, taxes levied on passing caravans, always accompanied it, although individuals appear to have had the opportunity to sell to the caravans.[20] Stanley's comment that 'one would think there was a school somewhere in Ugogo to teach low cunning and vicious malice to the chiefs, who are masters in foxy-craft' indicates the degree to which trade had become important in the region.[21] However, as the link between political authority, 'chiefs' and trade shows, production for this trade seems to have remained subservient to exchanges of cattle, grain and labour. Not only did trade during the nineteenth century give owners of large herds the opportunity to use some surplus to acquire trade goods, but at least two of the most common items imported into the region also figured in the cattle, grain and labour nexus. Iron became more common, and possibly increased agricultural productivity because it was used especially for agricultural implements such as hoes.[22]

Labour was also imported in the form of slaves. Informants recounted few traditions of slave raiding in the nineteenth century and instead stressed the importance of dependants in building the wealth of *watemi* (ritual leaders whose authority was based on control of the rains) and clan leaders. Travellers' accounts also mention leaders in the region who purchased slaves with ivory. Although such transfers perhaps did not occur on a large scale, they indicate both the ability of Gogo leaders to turn trade in their favour due to their control over water and the importance of labour in agriculture. L.E.Y. Mbogoni argues that the cultivated area in the region increased before 1880 as a result of better implements and increased labour.[23]

Colonial demography and environmental adversity in Ugogo

The difficulties in identifying population changes become only slightly easier during the twentieth century. Early colonial population figures, even if presented as part of formal censuses, often contained more guesswork than counting. The German census of 1913 was more of an estimate than a census, while the British census of 1931 repudiated the British census of 1921. Only after the Second World War did the colonial government establish a more professional census process. Finally, administrative divisions did not become regularized until the 1930s, making comparisons at local and district levels very difficult before the post-Second World War period.[24]

The figures recorded in Tables 2.1 and 2.2 merit some explanation. They come from the census reports of 1921, 1928, 1931, 1948, 1957 and 1967. The figures for 1913 and 1921 reflect German administrative boundaries, which combine what became Dodoma, Mpwapwa, Kilimantinde (which became Manyoni when its administrative headquarters moved in the 1920s) and Singida Districts into a greater Dodoma District. Neither the census of 1921 nor the District Books gave any further geographical breakdown of those figures, although they did give ethnic breakdowns. The 1913 census was regarded as highly inaccurate, and the first British administrators relied on other records and tax rolls when in 1916 they estimated the number of Gogo to be 160 000. Between 1921 and 1928 the implementation of Indirect Rule brought some stability to district and 'chiefdom' boundaries and more direct knowledge by British colonial officials of the population. Hence some of the increase in population between 1921 and 1928 is due to more accuracy in estimation. By 1931, when another census was taken, in part because of questions about the veracity of many of the estimates in 1928, a territory containing 5400 people had been transferred from Manyoni to Tabora District (making any percentage change computations from 1928 for Manyoni pointless). In 1948 Manyoni and Dodoma Districts were combined; the estimates in italics come from figures recorded in the District Books by colonial officers. The 1953 figures come from a detailed development plan.[25]

Several important circumstances become apparent when comparing the census data with more qualitative evidence provided by informants and colonial records. Given the shifting nature of administrative boundaries it is more realistic during the early decades of British rule to concentrate on 'tribal' breakdowns provided in the 1921 and 1931 censuses. The increase in the number of people labelled Gogo by colonial administrators reflects more accurate estimation, demographic increase, return migration and changes in ethnic identity. For Ugogo, the latter two factors are extremely important for the population changes in the region, especially in the 1920s.[26] Between those censuses the number of people counted as Gogo increased from 118 400 to 182 114, an increase of 53.7 per cent or an annual rate of increase of 4.3 per cent. In contrast, between the census of 1948 and 1957, the number of people identified as Gogo increased from 278 755 to 299 417, an increase of 7.4 per cent in total or an annual rate of increase of only 0.80 per cent (see Table 2.2 overleaf).

The increase between 1921 and 1931 of people counted as Gogo represents both an undercount in 1921 and an increase in the number of Gogo. The undercount of 1921 reflects both the inability to carry out a census, and the absence of many people from the region as a result of the *Mtunya*.[27] However, the increase also represents a real increase in population. Hugh Hignell, a British officer who had served in the region since 1918, noted in 1927:

Table 2.2 *Population of Ugogo – rates of growth (%)*

Gogo				Dodoma	Manyoni	Mpwapwa
1921–1928	4.95	1928–1931		0.58	n/a	1.11
1921–1931	4.39	1931–1948		3.09	1.12	6.00
1931–1948	2.54	1948–1957		1.62	2.24	2.98
1948–1957	0.80	1957–1967		2.33	3.14	4.37
1957–1967	1.86					
		1928–1967		2.13%	2.66%	4.54%
1921–1967	2.45%					

Rates of growth computed using the compound interest formula, log $(N1/N0)/T$ where $N1$ = ending population, $N0$ = beginning population and T = years. Manyoni growth rates computed from 1931.

> In the Aniramba, Wanyaturu and Wagogo, we have, I suppose, the three most fecund tribes in the Territory. In spite of infantile mortality these, and in fact, all the tribes of the Central Province, are increasing rapidly.

Hignell went on to note that both return migration of Gogo and new migration continued. He wrote:

> Whilst the tribesmen who fled the country during the great famine [the *Mtunya*] are still returning to all parts of the Province, immigration has been most marked on the north western border into Mkalama, and from the east into the Mpwapwa area. The Wagogo tribe, formerly regarded as 'the most degraded tribe in the whole of Africa – not excluding the Pygmies', have always cut no small figures in their own eyes, and Stanley commented almost as bitterly on their 'almost unbelievable arrogance' as he railed against their unbounded rapacity. If imitation be the sincerest form of flattery, the Wagogo have been fortified in their superb self conceit by the coming of immigrants from other tribes who seek and accept Gogo citizenship as no mean thing. These immigrants may resist the lure of the pigtail and the tribal markings but their children are just as fed polled [*sic*] and just as ridiculously mutilated as those of the most fanatical Wagogo.[28]

While the 1921 census undercounted the number of people in Ugogo, the substantial increase recorded between 1921 and 1931 represents a real increase in population from both migration and natural increase. The rate of growth is substantially larger than any other rate of growth during the colonial era, including that after 1955. The census of 1931 records an increase of 22 per cent in population (which probably represents more accurate enumeration as much as natural increase) for the whole territory since 1921 while the number of people recorded as Gogo increased by 53.7 per cent.[29] Even if the census estimates in Ugogo of 1921 were especially inaccurate because of the massive disruption caused by the *Mtunya*, the more rapid increase in people enumerated still represents a rapid increase in the population of the region.

Table 2.3 *Changes in ethnic distribution of population - Mpwapwa*

	Total	Gogo	Kaguru	Hehe	Sagara	% Gogo
1931	38 649	26 724				69.15
1948	100 673	47 659	14 178	14 573		47.34
1957	114 785	45 727	29 735	20 421	6 581	39.84
1967	170 282	60 375	41 209	33 466	12 042	35.46

NB The 1921 census combines what became Mpwapwa, Dodoma, Manyoni and Singida into Dodoma District. That district had a population of 270 890 of which 122 993 were Gogo, 13 355 were Hehe, and any Sagara and Kaguru were recorded as part of the 1927 listed as miscellaneous.

Table 2.4 *Changes in ethnic distribution of population - Manyoni*

	Total	Gogo	Hehe	Turu	Other	% Gogo
1931	43 563	19 678				45.17
1957	58 829	22 757				38.68
1967	75 535	28 198	7 753	12 270	47 337	37.33

NB The 1921 census combines what became Mpwapwa, Dodoma, Manyoni and Singida into Dodoma District. That district had a population of 270 890, of which 122 993 were Gogo and 13 355 Hehe. In 1948 Manyoni was a part of a larger Dodoma District.

Although Hignell emphasized the integration of immigrants into local communities, not all immigrants became Gogo. In the eastern parts of Mpwapwa, substantial numbers of Kaguru founded settlements and in southern Dodoma and Mpwapwa Hehe settlements, present since the nineteenth century, expanded greatly. During the 1920s not only did people return after seeking refuge elsewhere during the *Mtunya* but many individuals either moved to Ugogo or came with their parents. In the western and northern regions of Ugogo most recent immigrants came from Ukimbu, Unyamwezi or Usukuma.[30] In southern and eastern Ugogo many spoke of origins in Uhehe and in some cases, such as Kibakwe and Wotta in the far southern Mpwapwa District, separate Gogo and Hehe communities lived in the same region.[31] The migration into Mpwapwa continued throughout the colonial era, with its population growing more rapidly than that of Dodoma and Manyoni, and becoming much more diverse.[32] The population of Manyoni, in particular, grew much less rapidly than that of the other two districts that made up Ugogo (see Tables 2.3 and 2.4).

The depopulation of Ugogo during the East Africa Campaign, of course, explains the rapid growth; however, both the sources of it and the integration of newcomers into local communities within Ugogo bear examination. First, the immigration occurred into an area prone to drought. The 1920s saw droughts and food shortages in 1924–5 and 1928.[33] Secondly, given the decline in population in many areas of Tanganyika, general land shortage for agriculture cannot serve as an explanation for the migration. The migration occurred because Ugogo, except for its far western reaches in the Rift Valley, remained free of tsetse fly and, as a result, of trypanosomiasis.[34] Manyoni District, which included the Rift Valley, did not grow as rapidly as Dodoma and Mpwapwa.

People came to Ugogo because they could keep or get cattle. Many became Gogo and 'adopted [the Gogo] cult as regards cattle, dress and personal disfigurement',[35] because it represented the only way to survive and gain cattle within the arid lands of Ugogo.[36]

Demographic change, patronage and fluctuating demands for labour

Of course what it meant to be Gogo changed as communities within Ugogo reconfigured themselves within the context of colonialism. The expansion of markets for grain and groundnuts after the war presented cattle owners with the opportunity to expand production by utilizing the labour of those needing cattle. This opportunity allowed them to integrate the providers of this labour into local communities. Although I have no statistical evidence on this point, I interviewed several elders who had migrated to Ugogo from Unyamwezi, an area where tsetse spread during the early twentieth century. Because they shared several important cultural elements, including a similar conception of local political authority, people who moved from areas losing cattle integrated more readily than those, like the Hehe and the matrilineal Kaguru, who had fewer cattle initially. However, as one elder from southern Mpwapwa said when asked why many Hehe had moved into his village, 'They came for cattle.'[37]

The movement of people into Ugogo in search of safe grazing for cattle or as a means of acquiring cattle began even before the First World War. Rinderpest, bovine pleuropneumonia and trypanosomiasis all reduced the ability of surrounding areas to support cattle. The founder of one of the most prominent families in the region moved these during the era of German rule. Malecela came to Mvumi, just east of Dodoma, from the Nguu region of Handeni. He became known as a rain-maker attached to the *Mtemi* of Mvumi. One Mawala of the clan Wasemwali, with reputed origins both in western Ugogo and among the Hehe, created this settlement by conquest sometime in the nineteenth century. His successor, Chalula, held the office when German administration began. Chalula, not being a 'first settler', apparently felt the need of outside help in controlling the rains. Malecela became his rain-maker and a wealthy man. In 1905, during the *Sabatele* or *Sotoka Pili* (Rinderpest Again) famine, Malecela had to go to work for the Anglican Mission (an option open to him because he knew Swahili) in Mpwapwa and converted to Christianity, taking the name Yohana. In the words of one of his grandsons, Malecela, his sons and his grandsons (and presumably his daughters and granddaughters) had become Gogo.[38]

The rate of growth of population slowed during the 1930s, 1940s and early 1950s. During the 1930s, however, this slowing of growth cannot be attributed to demographic crises associated with famine or disease. Although drought struck several times during the 1930s and between 1929 and 1931 a major invasion of locusts destroyed crops all over eastern Africa, neither oral testimonies nor colonial records indicate that the resulting food shortages escalated into major famines.[39] What did happen was that the possibilities for growth, both economic and demographic, closed during the Depression of the 1930s. The demographic increase of the 1920s resulted from economic growth within a 'vent for surplus' situation. The railway and extension of marketing operations after the war meant that a demand existed for agricultural produce. Land was readily available both physically and institutionally. Cattle, more than money in this era, could mobilize labour not just within the region but also from outside it to put these resources to work. During the 1920s district officers marvelled at the number of lorries brought in by mostly Asian businessmen to transport exports and worried about the influence of opportunities in business on tribal solidarity.[40]

The figures in Tables 2.2, 2.3 and 2.4 reveal another important element of demographic change in Ugogo during the colonial era. While the growth in the numbers of individuals counted as Gogo slowed after 1928, the population of all three districts increased much faster. Tables 2.3 and 2.4 show that for Manyoni and especially Mpwapwa the proportion of people counted as Gogo in those districts declined sharply over the colonial era. This partly represents more careful use of ethnonyms by colonial officials. Especially in eastern and southern Mpwapwa, colonial officials, both European and African, more accurately recorded how people identified themselves rather than how *Watemi* identified them. However, from Hignell's time on, district officers commented on the movement of people into the region from Iringa and Kilosa.[41] The population of Mpwapwa also grew from 1948 to 1952 and shrank afterwards as a result of the ill-fated Groundnut Scheme at Kongwa.[42]

Demographic and economic growth in Ugogo remained extensive rather than intensive because production remained organized through ties of dependency. While wealthy cattle owners could mobilize large amounts of labour for agricultural production through the manipulation of cattle, they could not accumulate in a capitalist sense because they owed subsistence to their dependants in years of drought. Likewise the wide availability of land within Ugogo gave dependants some negotiating position.[43]

Agricultural production for market expanded greatly in Ugogo in the 1920s, reaching peaks in exports of groundnuts, millet and maize never officially equalled during the colonial era.[44] Marketed production stagnated during the 1930s, but during the years of the Second World War there were almost no exports recorded given the nature of the serious famines in the region and the lack of administrative ability to monitor the trade that did occur. Exports of agricultural produce increased after 1955. By 1960, groundnut exports almost equalled their previous high in 1927, both years in which rains were good. Yet in 1960, despite a much larger nominal population, improved varieties of crops (especially maize) and improved transportation, agricultural exports of grain were much lower than in the 1920s. Agricultural production recovered after the *Mtunya* because cattle owners saw ways to increase their wealth through the sale of agricultural commodities and those without cattle saw the opportunity to acquire cattle.[45]

The men most in a position to benefit from the use of cattle to control labour were those who were acclaimed *mtemi*, or chief, under the system of indirect rule. In particular, Mazengo, the son of Chalula of Mvumi east of Dodoma, became both the most powerful *mtemi* under the British and the man best known as an employer of labour. In Veulla, west of Dodoma, several elders vehemently denied that the colonial government had ever helped the people during famines before the Second World War and insisted that only Mazengo had provided food in return for work.[46]

Colonial officials had little doubt as to the source of the exports of the 1920s and 1930s. Much was made of the ability of cattle owners to mobilize the labour of neighbours through payment in cattle, loans of cattle, payments by the day in grain and communal beer drinks. In stark contrast to Mbogoni's assertion that each family cultivated only an average of three acres, colonial agricultural officers before the Second World War argued that the cultivation in Ugogo was too extensive for the available labour. R.R. Staples noted in 1939:

> The Native tribes in the Central Province tend to plant up (one can hardly say cultivate) unusually large shambas [fields] mainly because of the inadequacy of the rainfall. The average would appear to be in the region of six acres per family but numerous instances can be found where this figure has been greatly exceeded. Frequently the shambas are so large that the greatest difficulty is experienced in protecting them from the depredations of baboons, pig etc.[47]

In 1941 Staples asserted that: 'Gogo families have been noted to plant up as much as fifteen acres'.[48]

As Staples correctly noted the question of labour was the critical one for agricultural production. Both informants and colonial officials noted the ability of wealthy households to mobilize labour. In 1926 A.V. Hartnoll the District Officer in Dodoma asserted that most people in the region were recent immigrants working in the fields of the *mtemi*'s family or other cattle owners.[49] In 1925 High Hignell wrote to the administrative officer in Manyoni concerning a food shortage in Unyangwira that:

> As the trouble in Mombo's [the *mtemi*] country arguably arose because the men now with big surplus stocks of grain were allowed last year to exploit the labour of their less fortunate neighbours I instructed Mombo to bring pressure on these men at the planting season to make them help by loans of grain on a basis of recovery of two tins for one at the harvest.[50]

One elder, when asked about the ways people cooperated in times of hunger, joked that cattle owners became better cooperators when they could sell surplus crops. Other informants emphasized the increase in the price of cattle in terms of labour and the increasing formalization of ties of dependency. Over the course of the twentieth century, instead of becoming a dependant when short of food and receiving *songeleta*, loans of food to be repaid on a one-to-one basis, food came in return for specific amounts of work and loans had to be repaid, as Hignell urged, with an implicit interest.[51]

But this is not a simple case of a new economic and demographic equilibrium developing after a massive disaster. The role of the colonial state proved decisive. Prices for agricultural commodities dropped dramatically during the 1930s in Tanganyika but demands from the state on Africans remained constant. The drainage of surplus through taxes in the case of Ugogo overwhelmed both the economic growth of the 1920s and the investment in infrastructure. After 1930 conditions in Ugogo steadily worsened. Local communities became less and less able to meet subsistence needs through redistribution and dependency. Assimilation seems to have stopped and population growth slowed.

Prices for agricultural commodities dropped starting in 1928, and as a direct result, every year from then until 1935 some sort of relief works became necessary somewhere in Ugogo. Funding for such relief works came from local resources. Hignell claimed in 1934:

> The Central Province is the potential famine area in Tanganyika, but, since 1920, it has never cost the Central Government one penny in famine relief. No year has passed without some shortage of food in one part or another of the province but, in every case, it has been possible to give quick and adequate relief by local measures, controlling the sale of grain on the markets, prohibiting the manufacture of pombe [beer], etc. etc.[52]

While locusts and typical annual fluctuations in the rains were the proximate cause of the food shortages in the 1930s, one District Officer in Manyoni noted the structural problems when he wrote that the region suffered from 'an acute money famine' in 1931.[53] Both decades had three years with substantially below-average rainfall, and yet administrative reports make much greater comment on the shortages of the 1930s than of the 1920s.[54]

The collapse in prices, more than climatic variation and infestation, explains both the changes in marketed output and the underlying structural changes. Exports of groundnuts and grain never in the 1930s equalled the highs of the 1920s, coming closest in 1937. Cattle prices did not fall as far as agricultural prices, and hence cattle owners began to sell more stock for cash in order to meet needs for tax. Cattle sales increased dramatically after 1928, rising from a suspiciously low figure of 1200 head in 1927 for Dodoma and Mpwapwa to over 15 000 head. Cattle sales never fell below 13 000 head again for Dodoma District alone after 1927 as opposed to common estimates of between 1000 and 5000 a year before.[55] This change began the process of destroying the patron and client links that cattle had helped build. Likewise, during years of food shortage, cash, not cattle, became the means to acquire food. In 1934 another food shortage in Unyangwira in Manyoni became severe as the Sandawe living to the north refused to take cattle in exchange for grain from the Gogo of the area. The Sandawe insisted on cash for their surplus food.[56] As a result, many people from Manyoni moved to Singida District to work for food.[57]

The demographic impact of labour migration

The Second World War then marks a new stage in the demographic history of the region. The decade of famine that began with the war braked demographic growth and caused population declines during the worst of the years (for example, 1949 and 1950) as migration and mortality increased dramatically.[58] The famines that began in 1942 showed that after fifty years of colonial rule and despite the presence of the Central Line railway through the region, the communities of Ugogo still faced the risk of 'conjunctural poverty', of killing famine. These famines cannot just be laid at the door of the war effort, for, in terms of mortality, the famines of 1946, 1949, and 1952–5 were worse than that of 1942–4.

If there is a single factor which explains this transition it is the beginning of regular labour migration by men from the region. Several scholars have noted the rise in importance of people from Ugogo in Tanganyikan labour markets during and after the Second World War. The process began with conscription of young men during the war, mostly for civilian labour on sisal and rubber estates. Concurrent with labour conscription came forced cattle sales for the war effort. By 1942 the increased demands on producers in Ugogo created an extreme vulnerability, one in which the slightest disruption of agricultural activity could lead to widespread famine. A slightly below-average rainy season set off a cycle of famine that lasted three years. The colonial government did arrange for the import of large amounts of food at various times, but insisted as far as possible that recipients pay for the food either at the time, in repayment or through local tax revenues. As a result households often faced debts to the government in cash along with taxes far in excess of annual earnings, and local government had little money to spend on education, health care or infrastructure. Indeed, the major plan developed by the colonial government for systematic development in the region died because of the expense of famine relief. Before the Second World War, the obverse of cattle owners' ability to control labour was the entitlements to food they provided for labourers. During the Second World War the colonial regime moved decisively to destroy these relationships in favour of direct exploitation of the labour of the people of Ugogo. The result was the decade of famine and demographic instability.[59]

Labour migration by young men continued after the war. The age grade initiated during the war took the name *al Manamba* after number, the name given to labour contracts. During relief operations from the 1940s onwards colonial agents often commented on the extremely high proportion of 'abandoned' women with children in need of relief. Even during years of adequate rainfall, migration remained at levels of up to 20 per cent of all adult men according to one report.[60]

The loss of this labour reduced production in agriculture in the region and caused many households to shift to less labour-intensive crops. For most households, the labour lost locally brought little in return. It paid debts and taxes, for a fortunate few it paid for health care or education, but mostly it paid for food.[61] Labour migration coincided with an increase in cattle sales by cattle owners and declines in the wage, in terms of cattle, paid by cattle owners for work in their fields. Labour conscription and government demands for cash to repay famine debts catalysed these changes. For cattle owners, cattle became more of a commodity and less a means to control labour. Cattle prices rose during and after the war, faster than either crop prices or cash wages. Average prices for cattle on the Dodoma market rose from Shs 10/- in the 1930s to Shs 48/- in 1947 to Shs 141/- in 1952.[62] Cattle owners thus forced down the demands dependants could place upon them in favour of selling cattle. For cattle-poor households, and especially young men, the only way to gain access to cattle came through wage labour, not labour as dependants.

As a result of the changing local value of labour, bridewealth also began to decline. Most informants claimed that in the past bridewealth should have totalled twenty-eight head of cattle and twenty-eight small stock. In the early 1960s Rigby recorded an average of less than twenty.[63] Ernest Kongola, in his clan history, recorded that he and his elder brother both paid over twenty-five head in each category in the 1930s.[64] Mzee Kongola and all other informants confirmed that bridewealth today seldom totals more than five or six head of each type. This decline reflects the declining importance of agricultural production, and hence labour, in economic relations in the region.

For the shrinking proportion of the population that owned cattle, only 35 per cent of all taxpaying adult men in 1942,[65] cattle sales still allowed them to survive. Households without cattle pursued more risky strategies. Exports of new crops, often less labour-intensive than groundnuts, increased dramatically during the 1940s and 1950s. At various times sunflower seed, castor seed, sesame, onions and even tomatoes for urban markets all enjoyed small booms. Maize became the only grain exported in large amounts as a result of changing market preferences, and in only three years after 1947 did exports exceed 200 tons. The disappearance of sorghum and millet exports and the shift to maize reflect the more risky strategy adopted by farmers. Sorghum and millet remained the basic stable in most parts of Ugogo but maize, especially after 1952, became increasingly important. Even though improved varieties of maize (some informants claimed that they were developed locally from yellow maize brought in as famine relief from the United States) had improved drought resistance, it still failed more often than sorghum and millet.

Despite these initiatives, labour migration caused a large decline in crop acreage in the region. Where up to the Second World War, colonial officials had often commented on the large fields in the region, especially after 1944, charges that the Gogo cultivated only small fields became common in colonial reports. In 1944 the Provincial Commissioner claimed that the average field cultivated by a household totalled only 1.14 acres compared to Staples' estimate of six acres only two years earlier.[66] In 1946, Acting Provincial Commissioner G.A.R.W. Ansdell described more bluntly the nature of the transformation:

> The moral effect of continual food difficulties cannot help having a depressing effect on the mentality of the people. In short, many are 'famine minded' and, with the passing of the years they have become apathetic both in making an effort to provide for themselves and even in preserving their supplies for use during the months of shortage.[67]

Ansdell's comments reflect a perverse 'blame the victim' attitude common to colonial officials. The people of Ugogo had not become famine-minded but had become impoverished by labour migration.

The crisis caused by this transformation of Ugogo into a labour reserve can be seen not just in the repeated famines and the thousands of deaths, not just in the stagnant population growth, but in amazingly high observed infant mortality. A visiting doctor, Cicely Williams, in 1954 and 1955 reported that in several rural areas she interviewed 325 women who had 464 living young children and 503 deceased ones. In a survey of a few local government dispensaries over an eight-week period in early 1954 she recorded 194 stillbirths and miscarriages and, of 967 births, 503 infants died.[68] She made her survey during one of the worst famines of the entire colonial era, but, as she also noted, respondents claimed that child deaths were only slightly above normal. During this famine, poor nutrition caused most of these deaths, but higher infant and childhood mortality could be linked to decline in the proportion of households that owned cattle.[69] The young administrative officer in charge of famine relief in the region glossed over the chronic problems when he wrote of that famine:

> It is quite impossible to give any figures [on deaths caused by famine] since no hard and fast line can be drawn between the various factors that caused death even in individual cases, but if it is true that a second year of famine hastened the death of the aged, of those suffering from chronic disease, and of a few babies for whom medical aid was sought too late, it is also true that in no case could a coroner's verdict be other than that of 'death by natural causes'.[70]

Despite reports such as that of Williams, the colonial government totally ignored the problems caused by the structural changes within Ugogo.[71]

A moment of demographic transition

A single year, 1954, marks the point when famine mortality ceases to be a demographic brake. The benefits McAlpin sees flowing from the improvements in transportation infrastructure, the expansion of markets for agricultural surplus and for surplus labour, and the institutional ability of the colonial government to identify famine and bring in food finally became the norm in Ugogo.[72] Increased staff levels led to improved information. Fear of outside scrutiny, especially from the United Nations, led the central government to emphasize ensuring that few people starved rather than maintaining control over expenses. In 1954, the territorial government even asked for and received a large shipment of dried milk from UNICEF for distribution in Ugogo. However, as Iliffe argues, this decline in mortality had its costs because poverty replaced famine. Indeed, there is precious little evidence that points to a decline in the general level of mortality over the colonial era, only to a decline in crisis mortality.[72]

Between 1955 and 1960 not only did population begin to grow rapidly, but agricultural production increased and cattle sales declined somewhat. However, labour migration remained heavy and some colonial officials reported a labour shortage as cattle owners had difficulty finding labour to harvest their crops. Wage-labour relationships had replaced the implicit wage of patronage and access to cattle and, as such, cattle owners had difficulty in meeting the cash wage for young males who could find employment elsewhere. They could still, however, draw on women and others with more limited opportunities. For households without cattle, and especially young men, rising cattle prices made it increasingly difficult to purchase cattle, even with cash from migrant labour. In essence, the pattern after 1955 resembled that of the 1920s in Ugogo. Production expanded extensively; however, the region still continued to send young men off as labour migrants.

Implicit in the foregoing is a model of production that remains labour-intensive throughout the colonial era. This explains why fertility did not fall in Ugogo after 1955 as crisis mortality did, and indeed has not fallen in much of Africa. E.A. Wrigley has indicated that lack of a 'living', of opportunity, exerted strong negative pressure in early modern Europe, especially England, on fertility rates.[74] In Ugogo, that exact opposite was the case. The more labour within a household, the better off it was. Hence the reduction in crisis mortality after 1955 allowed population to grow rapidly.

The reduction in mortality proved real, not just transitory, despite a major drought in 1960–61 which caused widespread crop failures. Extensive relief efforts, including the importation of relief aid from the United States (hence the name *Nzala ya Merika*), kept mortality from rising. Population growth continued apace and, as migration continued, the stereotype that the Gogo made up most of the beggars and casual labourers took hold in the towns of Tanzania.

Demography and Gogo identity

The demographic history of Ugogo over the twentieth century reflects more than just the response of local communities to the changing economic conditions brought by colonialism. The cycles of expansion and contraction continue a pattern from the era before colonialism, albeit one that alternates around an ever-increasing mean. Because of the uncertainty of agriculture in the region, it is likely that population in the region fluctuated. Many clans in Ugogo claim origins in neighbouring areas, and many maintain links across the cultural boundaries drawn during the colonial era.[75] Linguistically, Cigogo is marked by strong dialectical variation. It is closely related both to Kaguru and

Sagara and shares much vocabulary with Kimbu and Hehe, languages that are classified as parts of different branches of eastern Bantu. Yet it is not closely related to the languages to which neighbouring languages are related. This rather odd situation results from strong and probably long-term interaction within the region.[76] Ugogo seems to be a permanent frontier, surrounded on the west, south and east by better-watered lands where cattle keeping was problematic, and bordered on the north by arid lands where agriculture was not possible. Population expanded into the region during better years and then receded during the bad ones. Over the long term this process created a layering effect seen in the multiple origins of Gogo clans and in the linguistic complexity of the language. That a plurality of clans holding the *Utemi* and controlling the rains claimed origins in Uhehe shows the most recent layering occurred as the prestige and authority of the Hehe state expanded in the nineteenth century.[77]

During the twentieth century, this process continued, although on a scale perhaps unmatched before. The catastrophe of the *Mtunya*, coming on the heels of two decades of disasters, opened up Ugogo, and people flooded in. In the 1920s, many adopted *Cigogo* – not just the language but the way of the *Gogo* – as the only means of survival in the region. After the 1920s, however, the attraction of Ugogo declined, and even those who moved into the region retained more of the identity of their homes as a result of the hardening of tribal identities under indirect rule.

These cultural processes interacted with economic ones to guide the demographic structure of the region. The demographic disaster around the turn of the century resulted in increased fertility (and immigration) to meet the demands of the colonial state for production and to occupy abandoned lands. Mortality declined much more slowly, but, even with mortality in decline, the labour-intensive nature of production prevented decline in fertility. Ugogo, like Tanzania generally, seems locked in a cycle of population growth caused by low productivity.

Notes

1. See Michael Patton, *Dodoma Region, 1929–1959: A History of Famine*, BRALUP Research Report, no. 44 (UDSM, 1971); Gregory H. Maddox, '*Mtunya*: Famine in Central Tanzania, 1917–1920', *Journal of African History*, 31, 2 (1990): 181–198 and ' "Leave, Wagogo! You Have No Food!": Famine and Survival in Ugogo, Central Tanzania 1916–1961' (Ph.D. Dissertation, Northwestern University, Evanston, IL, 1988); Peter Rigby, *Cattle and Kinship Among the Gogo: A Semi-pastoral Society of Central Tanzania* (Ithaca, NY, 1967); Carol Jane Sissons, 'Economic Prosperity in Ugogo, East Africa, 1860–1890' (Ph.D. Dissertation, University of Toronto, 1984); L.E.Y. Mbogoni, 'Food Production and Ecological Crisis in Dodoma – 1920–1960: Colonial Efforts at Developing the Productive Forces in Peasant Agriculture' (MA Thesis, University of Dar

es Salaam, 1981); and Clarke Brooke, 'The Heritage of Famine in Central Tanzania', *Tanzania Notes and Records*, 67 (1967): 15-22.

2. E.A. Wrigley and R.S. Schofield, *The Population History of England, 1541-1871: A Reconstruction* (Cambridge, MA, 1981); and Michael W. Flinn, *The European Demographic System, 1500-1820* (Baltimore, 1981).

3. Bruce Fetter, 'Demography in the Reconstruction of African Colonial History', in Bruce Fetter, ed., *Demography from Scanty Evidence: Central Africa in the Colonial Era*, (Boulder, 1990), pp. 1-24; Dennis D. Cordell and Joel W. Gregory, 'Historical Demography and Demographic History in Africa', *Canadian Journal of African Studies* 14, 3 (1980): 389-416. Some missions did keep registers of baptisms, marriages, and deaths. Such records have not been used to the extent that they could be for the reconstruction of African demographic regimes. The records cover only mission adherents and require careful analysis to determine whether demographic patterns of mission adherents differ from those of the rest of the population (see Chapter 1 by Juhani Koponen for a discussion of possible differences). Despite these limitations they are a critical source and deserve much greater attention. See Reginald P.A.N. Mihanjo, 'Social and Biological Reproduction during Capitalist Transformation: The Historical Demography of the Lake Nyasa Region', Paper presented to the Department of History Research Seminar, University of Dar es Salaam, 11 November 1993, for one attempt to use these records.

4. Dennis D. Cordell, Joel W. Gregory, and Victor Piché, 'African Historical Demography: The Search for a Theoretical Framework', in Dennis Cordell and Joel W. Gregory, eds, *African Population and Capitalism: Historical Perspectives* (Boulder, 1987), pp. 14-34.

5. R.R. Kuczynski, *Demographic Survey of the British Colonial Empire*, Vol. II: *East Africa etc.* (Oxford, 1949); Charles Ambler, *Kenyan Communities in the Age of Imperialism: The Central Region in the Late Nineteenth Century* (New Haven, 1988); and Helge Kjekshus, *Ecology Control and Economic Development in East African History: The Case of Tanganyika, 1850-1950* (London, 1977).

6. C.C. Wrigley, 'Aspects of Economic History', in A.D. Roberts, ed., *The Colonial Moment in Africa: Essays on the Movement of Minds and Materials 1900-1940* (Cambridge, 1990), pp. 77-139.

7. Michelle McAlpin, *Subject to Famine: Food Crisis and Economic Change in Western India, 1860-1920* (Princeton, 1983).

8. John Iliffe, *The African Poor: A History* (Cambridge, 1987).

9. Deborah Fahy Bryceson, *Food Insecurity and the Social Division of Labor in Tanzania, 1919-1985* (New York, 1990) and Sara S. Berry, 'The Food Crisis and Agrarian Change in Africa: A Review Essay', *African Studies Review*, 27 (1984): 59-112. Ester Boserup, *The Conditions of Agricultural Growth* (New York, 1965), Jane Guyer, 'Household and Community in African Studies', *African Studies Review*, 24 (1981), pp. 87-137.

10. Meredeth Turshen, 'Population Growth and the Deterioration of Health: Mainland Tanzania, 1920-1960', in Cordell and Gregory, eds, *African Population*, pp. 187-200.

11. Wrigley and Schofield, *Population History*.

12. Patrick O. Ohadike, 'Social and Organization Variables Affecting Central Africa Demography', in Fetter, ed., *Demography from Scanty Evidence*, pp. 252-4.

13. Personal communication from Pamela Maack.

14. See for example S.I. Nyagava, 'History of the Bena to 1906' (Ph.D. Dissertation, University of Dar es Salaam, 1988), pp. 106-9. In addition, it is possible that viable births increased in some regions as various forms of infanticide, a form of positive check of population growth found in early modern Europe also, died out. However, the evidence for substantial infanticide, in both Africa and Europe, has been greatly exaggerated. I.N. Kimambo, *Penetration and Protest in Tanzania: The Impact of the World Economy on the Pare, 1860-1960* (London, 1991), pp. 60-1. For charges of exaggeration, see James L. Giblin, *The Politics of Environmental Control in Northeastern Tanzania, 1840-1940* (Philadelphia, 1993),

pp. 107-11, and John Boswell, *The Kindness of Strangers: The Abandonment of Children in Western Europe From Late Antiquity to the Renaissance* (New York, 1988).

15. Kuczynski, *Demographic Survey*, pp. 118-22.

16. Kjekshus, *Ecology Control*, pp. 10-25.

17. Sissons, 'Economic Prosperity', pp. 44-6.

18. See Maddox, 'Leave Wagogo', Chapter 2 for a more detailed discussion.

19. Sissons, 'Economic Prosperity', p. 91, and Maddox, 'Leave Wagogo', pp. 136, 178.

20. Walter Hutley, *The Central African Diaries of Walter Hutley, 1877-1881*, ed. James B. Wolf (Boston, 1976), pp. 34-5; and Abdul Sheriff, *Slaves, Spices and Ivory in Zanzibar* (London, 1987), pp. 169, 177.

21. Henry M. Stanley, *In Darkest Africa*, Vol. 2 (New York, 1890), p. 446.

22. Mbogoni, 'Food Production and Ecological Crisis', pp. 13-14.

23. I/8/5B Mlundi; I/38/87A-95A Magagi; John Iliffe, *A Modern History of Tanganyika* (Cambridge, 1979), pp. 73-4; and Mbogoni, 'Food Production and Ecological Crisis', pp. 18-20.

24. I.B. Jaeuber, *The Population of Tanganyika* (New York, 1949); and Tanganyika, *Census of the Native Population 1931* (Dar es Salaam, 1932), p. 3.

25. TNA 42245/1, H.S. Senior, 'Gogo Development Plan', June 1953.

26. Gregory Maddox and Robert H. Jackson, 'The Creation of Identity: Colonial Society in Bolivia and Tanzania', *Comparative Studies in Society and History* 35, 2 (1993): 273-84.

27. Fetter, 'Demography in the Reconstruction of African Colonial History', pp. 1-24.

28. TNA 967.825, Provincial Commissioner's Reports Central Province, H. Hignell, Annual report for 1927, 18 January 1928.

29. Tanganyika, *Census* pp. 10, 16.

30. I/37/82A-86A Ali etc. (Meia Meia); I/39/96A-101A Luangi etc. (Bahi); I/41/107A-112A Mnyambwa etc. (Mwitikira); and I/45/114A-117A Kaloli etc. (Chipanga).

31. I/49/124A Nyalingo etc. (Kibakwe); and I/50/130A-142A Abdallah Mnyama etc. (Ipera).

32. Tanganyika, *Census*, 1921, 1931, 1957.

33. Maddox, 'Leave Wagogo', Chapter 4.

34. John Ford, *The Role of Trypanosomiases in African Ecology: A Study of the Tsetse Fly Problem* (Oxford, 1971), p. 613 and James L. Giblin, 'Trypanosomiasis Control in African History: An Evaded Issue?', *Journal of African History* 31, 1 (1990): 69.

35. Dodoma Provincial Book, H. Hignell, 'Report on the Wagogo', 18 June 1927.

36. Maddox and Jackson, 'Creation of Identity' for a fuller discussion.

37. For a discussion of the integration of outsiders into Gogo communities see interview I/5/5A Mlundi. See also I/36/61A-73A Mapalasha etc. and I/49/124A-129A Nyaulingo etc.

38. I/4/4A Canon Lusinde, I/46/118A Job Lusinde, and Mathais Mnyampala, *The Gogo: History, Customs and Traditions*, trans. and ed. Gregory H. Maddox (Armonk, NY, 1995), pp. 53-5.

39. Maddox, 'Leave Wagogo', Chapter 5.

40. TNA 967.825, H. Hignell, Provincial Commissioner's Report for the Central Province 1927, where he notes: 'Like the millet grown under similar arid conditions in Balochistan, this uwele stands export overseas. And whenever there is a food shortage in India or Somaliland, the grain specials begin to run from Dodoma to the coast'.

41. TNA 967.825, Provincial Commissioner's Annual Reports.

42. See Maddox, 'Leave Wagogo', pp. 322-5 and Jan S. Hogendorn and K. M. Scott, 'Very Large-Scale Agricultural Projects: The Lessons of the East African Groundnut Scheme', in Robert I. Rotberg, ed., *Imperialism, Colonialism, and Hunger: East and Central Africa* (Lexington, MA, 1983), pp. 167-98.

43. Kimambo, *Penetration and Protest*, pp. 19-28; and Bryceson, *Food Insecurity*, p. 64.

44. TNA 967.825, Provincial Commissioner's Annual Reports.

45. In 1927 marketed production of groundnuts in the three districts was 3575 tons and marketed production of sorghum, millet and maize was 3793 tons. In 1960, Dodoma District alone recorded production of 2444 tons of groundnuts and 778 of castor seed with no recorded marketed production of grains. Manyoni and Mpwapwa also reported good years and Mpwapwa reported some grain, mostly maize, exports. See Maddox, 'Leave Wagogo', pp. 136, 178, 321, 403.

46. I/36/74A–81A Mapalasha etc.

47. TNA 26298/Vol. II, Draft Provincial Programmes for Increased Production of Agricultural Export Crops for the 1939/40 Season, Wakefield, 1 Dec. 39 (quoting a report prepared by Staples).

48. TNA 46/20/31, R.R. Staples, Monthly Report 14 Jan. 1941.

49. TNA 967.828, A.V. Hartnoll, Annual Report, Dodoma District, 1926.

50. TNA 146/A20/1/Vol. I, Hignell to Lawrence, 15 Aug. 1925.

51. I/6/6A–7A Lyacho; and I/5/5A Mlundi.

52. TNA 146/A20/1/Vol. II, Hignell to Chief Secretary, 6 Oct. 1934.

53. TNA 967.823, G.K. Whitlamsmith, Annual Report, Manyoni, 1931.

54. See Maddox, 'Leave, Wagogo', Chapters 3 and 4.

55. TNA 967.828, Annual Reports.

56. TNA 146/A20/1/Vol. II, E.J.W. Carlton to Provincial Commissioner, 7 Dec. 1934.

57. Dodoma District Book, C.B. Wilkins, Agriculture.

58. TNA 435/2/Vol. I, Dodoma District Annual Report, 1950, J.T.A. Pearce, 9 Jan. 1950.

59. See Gregory Maddox, 'Famine, Impoverishment and the Creation of a Labor Reserve in Central Tanzania', *Disasters* 15, 1 (1991): 35–41 for a fuller discussion. Mbogoni, 'Ecological Crisis', p. 80; Majorie Mbilinyi, 'Agribusiness and Casual Labor in Tanzania', *African Economic History* 15 (1986): 107–24; Bryceson, *Food Insecurity*, p. 49; Walter Rodney, *Second World War and the Tanzanian Economy* (Ithaca, NY, 1976); and Amartya Sen, *Poverty and Famines: An Essay on Entitlement and Deprivation* (Oxford, 1981).

60. Public Record Office, Colonial Office 736 Vol. XXXVI, *Annual Report of the Labour Department 1953* (Dar es Salaam, 1954), p. 5.

61. Informants showed major differences according to gender in their views of the results of labour migration. Several women charged that men abandoned women with families and never sent or brought money back, causing hardship and death. Men who had worked outside Ugogo claimed that extended families and the government took care of those in need, and that the money which they earned was used for 'important matters' such as tax or bridewealth. See I/39/96A–101A Luangi etc.

62. TNA 42245/1, H.S. Senior, 'Gogo Development Plan', June 1953. 1952 was a famine year, and prices had declined from a high of Shs 164/- in 1951.

63. Rigby, *Cattle and Kinship*, pp. 225–35.

64. *Historia Mbeya ya toka 1688 mpaka 1986: 'Mbukwa Muhindi wa Cimambi'* (Dodoma, 1986).

65. TNA 42245/1, H.S. Senior, 'Gogo Development Plan', June 1953.

66. 'Central Province', *Annual Report of the Provincial Commissioners for 1944* (Dar es Salaam, 1945), p. 2.

67. G.A.R.W. Ansdell, Acting P.C., 'Central Province', *Annual Report of the Provincial Commissioners for 1946* (Dar es Salaam, 1947), p. 1.

68. TNA 184/A3/31/1954–55/II. Draft of the Report by Dr Cicely Williams on progress of food shortage and relief measures undertaken.

69. Alexander de Waal, *Famine that Kills: Darfur, Sudan, 1984–1985* (Oxford, 1989), pp. 172–94, finds that childhood mortality was slightly lower in households with cattle because they had milk for children who had been weaned.

70. TNA 184/A3/42/1954–55. R.O.H. Porch, 13 May 1955, Dodoma District Report on the Food Shortage, September 1954 to April 1955.

71. Brigitta Larsson, *Conversion to Greater Freedom?: Women, Church and Social Change in North-western Tanzania Under Colonial Rule* (Stockholm, 1991).

72. McAlpin, *Subject to Famine*, pp. 15–17.

73. Iliffe, *African Poor*, pp. 156–60.

74. Wrigley and Schofield, *Population History*.

75. Rigby, *Cattle and Kinship*, pp. 63–81; and Maddox and Jackson, 'Creation of Identity', pp. 274–5.

76. Thomas H. Hinnebusch, Derek Nurse and Martin Mould, *Studies in the Classification of Eastern Bantu Languages* (Hamburg, 1981), pp. 60-2, 107–8. Christopher Ehert is working on the relationship between language and population as evidenced by Cigogo; see Dennis D. Cordell and Joel W. Gregory, 'Earlier African Historical Demographies', *Canadian Journal of African Studies* 23, 1 (1989): 16.

77. According to Mnyampala's *The Gogo*, seven of the clans holding government-recognized Native Authority positions in Dodoma and Manyoni came from Uhehe, three from Ukimbu, two from Nyaturu, two claimed indigenous origins among the Ng'movia, a group speaking a Cushitic language, and one each came from Usukuma, Unguu and Usangu. See Rigby, *Cattle and Kinship*, p. 67.

Part Two

/\/\/\/\/\/\/\/\/\/\/\/\/\/\/\/\

Environmental Change
&
Economic History
In Tanzania's Northern Highlands

The northern highlands of Tanzania have an extraordinarily interesting ecology and history. The snow-capped peaks and the volcanic soils which nourish prolific coffee plots and banana groves on Kilimanjaro are world-famous, of course, but even the less well-known Usambara Mountains boast uncommonly diverse communities of unusual flora and fauna. The human history of the highlands is no less intriguing than their natural history. Precolonial political and ideological creativity was so conspicuous in this region that Steven Feierman and Isaria Kimambo, writing in the 1960s about Usambara and the Pare Mountains respectively, were able to demonstrate that the richness and originality of indigenous political thought and institutions disproved diffusionist theories of African state-building.[1] More recently, the research of Thomas Spear has shown that Mount Meru has also been the site of noteworthy historical development. As his contribution to this volume tells us, the convergence of migrating farmers and pastoralists on Mount Meru produced a culturally diverse and agronomically sophisticated society. In the twentieth century, the farming communities of the highlands would become remarkably innovative. Even a government as strongly committed to preventing rural accumulation as the British colonial regime would have only very limited success in frustrating the efforts of mountain farmers to prosper through market production.

The chapters this section by Isaria Kimambo and Christopher Conte examine the relationship between environmental change and human history in the northern highlands. Kimambo presents a broad survey of precolonial developments in the Usambara and Pare Mountains and on Kilimanjaro. Thus he establishes the context in which Wambugu pastoralists, the subject of Conte's closely focused case study, settled in Usambara and transformed the forests of its high plateaux.

Isaria Kimambo's chapter is principally concerned with the sources of precolonial economic innovation. Hence it seeks to understand the precolonial precursors of the impulses towards improvement and entrepreneurship which are so prominent in Spear's discussion of Mount Meru during the colonial period. Although Kimambo considers that population increase and political structures may have stimulated agricultural intensification, the utilization of diverse microenvironments and the adoption of American cultigens, he is ultimately more interested in how trade provides incentives for innovation. Implicitly challenging views of the Tanzanian past which regard commerce as having been an alien innovation (see the Introduction to this volume), he argues that highland markets are old institutions where villagers acquired food and other goods which were necessary for survival. Much trade occurred between highlands and lowlands, he writes, and the development of trade networks linking mountains with surrounding plains facilitated the penetration of the Zanzibari-based commercial system in the nineteenth century. In commenting that precolonial rulers were expected to ensure the smooth functioning of markets, Kimambo leads us to contrast precolonial political authority with the British colonial state, which, as the chapters by Giblin, Maack, Spear and Monson show, discouraged trade.

Yet, while Kimambo concludes that it would be incorrect to regard precolonial African economies 'as being static and incapable of transformation to a market orientation', he is no more inclined to adopt the 'Merrie Africa' approach than the 'Primitive Africa' viewpoint. Instead, he argues that late nineteenth-century trade in ivory and slaves reduced both security against famine and environmental control. Thus he finds an explanation for the late precolonial decline in population discussed in Part I by Koponen and Maddox, which is consistent with his insistence on the capability of precolonial societies to make important improvements in agriculture, trade and environmental control.

Christopher Conte places similar emphasis on precolonial capacity for adaptation to new environmental and economic conditions in his history of the Wambugu of Usambara. He shows that the Wambugu have passed through successive stages of adjustment to new conditions. The first Wambugu settlers in Usambara had to adjust to highland forest surroundings that were unlike the plains from which they had migrated. They developed close relations of cooperation and trade with Washambaa farmers, only to have those relations broken during the extended period of severe cattle epidemics, slave trading and civil war in Usambara during the second half of the nineteenth century. Once again, however, the Wambugu adapted, this time by relinquishing their heavy reliance on pastoralism as they took up farming. Under colonial rule, the Wambugu saw much of their land enclosed in forest reserves, but here again they adjusted, argues Conte, by learning to use European conceptions of land ownership as the basis of their own claims to land.

Conte shows that at each stage in this process of continual adaptation, the activities of the Wambugu (and, in the colonial period, of European foresters as well) modified the forests of the highland plateaux. Each stage of land use changed the flora, although the most dramatic transformation may have occurred in the colonial period, when forestry policy caused drastic reduction of species diversity and brought permanent environmental damage in the forms of deforestation, a drier microclimate and soil erosion. Like Wagner, Spear, Monson and Maack in this volume, Conte identifies a precolonial ethic of conservation as well as techniques of resource preservation. However, Conte, who is as wary of 'Merrie Africa'/'Primitive Africa' approaches as Kimambo, argues that the precolonial Wambugu were not always successful conservationists, and sometimes caused deforestation. Thus by acknowledging the possibility that precolonial societies could have harmed their environments, Conte's study implicitly re-emphasizes the significance of the institutions and thought which imposed a morality of resource use on precolonial communities. This morality, which is discussed in different ways by Wagner, Spear and Monson in Part IV, must have constrained those who wished to waste natural resources, but at the same time it must have required the sanction of political leadership. Hence one can see why a close association between political authority and environmental knowledge, which Wagner discusses with particular clarity in her history of Ha earth priests, and which is also touched upon by Giblin and Maack in this volume, should have developed.

Note

1. Steven Feierman, *The Shambaa Kingdom: A History* (Madison, 1974) and Isaria Kimambo, *A Political History of the Pare of Tanzania*, c. 1500–1900 (Nairobi, 1969).

Three

Environmental Control
& Hunger

*In the Mountains & Plains
of Nineteenth-Century Northeastern Tanzania*

ISARIA N. KIMAMBO

Introduction

In the Usambara, Upare and Kilimanjaro highlands of northeastern Tanzania, as in many other African societies, the same term covers a range of meanings from hunger to life-threatening famine.[2] The cognates which expressed these meanings in the northeastern highlands were *njaa* in Chagga, *dhaa* in Pare and *saa* in Shambaa. In the sense of famine, they denoted a phenomenon which was rare in the highlands. In the sense of chronic hunger or impoverishment, however, they denoted factors which drove the communities of the region to search for ways of controlling their environments. Their effort to achieve control of their environment led highland communities to interact with one another and with neighbouring groups in the surrounding lowlands.

Usambara and Upare are ranges of mountains, the Shambaa block being higher and more consolidated than the Pare mountains, which are broken into three separate blocks. Kilimanjaro, on the other hand, is a volcanic mountain rising to 19 140 feet above sea level, an altitude which makes it the tallest mountain in Africa. The inhabitants of these mountains (the Shambaa of Usambara, the Pare of Upare and the Chagga of Kilimanjaro) generally preferred to live on the high ground at altitudes of 3 500 to 6 000 feet, far above the lowlands called *nyika* which they considered unsuitable for residence. The Pare preferred the high plateaux of their mountain blocks, except the Shengena mountain in the south Pare block which rises to 8 000 feet above sea level. The Shengena area above 6 000 feet remained forested, as did similar areas on the Usambara block and also the area between 6 000 and 10 000 feet on Kilimanjaro.

Preference for high-altitude residence, therefore, is the first element which the inhabitants of these environments had in common before the nineteenth century. Many explanations can be given for this preference. In contrast to the surrounding *nyika*, there was more rain, more water and there were therefore better possibilities for producing food on the mountains. Life there was also healthier. Highlanders recognized the danger of living in the *nyika*, where one could become sick with *mkunguru* (Pare) or *iseng'u* (Chagga), that is, fever. Hence for centuries, people have migrated from the lowlands to the mountains in pursuit of these environmental advantages.[3] Indeed, migrants often cite famine in the lowlands as the cause of their movements.

The second common element among highlanders was their crops. Bananas were the main staple on all these mountains. As a perennial plant which grows well in cool, fertile and well-watered mountain regions, the banana provided a dependable food supply. At the same time, mountain farming allowed planting of numerous annual crops which were suitable for different highland ecological zones. Some annuals were grown at various altitudes to minimize the possibility of crop failure. Grains, such as finger millet (eleusine) and sorghum, and a number of legumes thrived despite the different lengths of time which they required to reach maturity. During the eighteenth and nineteenth centuries, new crops were introduced into the region and were quickly integrated into existing farming systems.

There were three main farming zones in the mountains. The first was the main residential zone, where buildings as well as banana groves were located. Some annual crops could be grown under banana trees. The second farming zone, located at lower altitudes, brought cultivation towards the base of the mountain and to the *nyika* in the foothills. With the introduction of maize, *nyika* cultivation expanded rapidly in the nineteenth century, initially without altering the residential pattern. The same thing happened in the third and highest zone, the plots near the mountain forests, where a cool climate allowed a third cropping season after the *nyika* cultivation cycle was completed. Although other grains could also be grown, maize and varieties of beans came to dominate this zone.

The third common element was the application of 'specialized' field techniques,[4] including irrigation, manuring and terracing. These are forms of 'agricultural intensification', but as Thomas Hakansson has shown, they were not necessarily the result of population increase.[5] Because there were dry seasons on the mountains (although they were not as severe as in the lowlands), irrigation could ensure the growth of bananas and two or three harvests of annual crops. Furthermore, the mountain environment contained a great variety of small ecological zones which demanded intensive methods of utilization. The ridges and valleys on a single slope might contain a variety of soils and different amounts of rainfall. In the same way, a plateau might contain a number of valleys and slopes which received varying amounts of rain. Irrigation ensured a harvest where rain would have been insufficient or at a season when rain was usually insufficient for farming. Manuring allowed continuous use of the same land generation after generation, while terracing helped to minimize soil erosion. Thus these specialized techniques made possible the planting of numerous crops in different zones on the mountains. When new crops were introduced they were quickly tried in different locations and in different seasons.

. But to what extent was agricultural intensification influenced by factors beyond the need to satisfy daily subsistence requirements? Hakansson mentions commercial, political and religious factors.[6] Clearly, political and religious factors would be related to demands created by political centralization. Once state structures were established over lineage communities new demands began to be placed on the cultivators. However, irrigation systems may be older in this region than political centralization itself. After examining accounts by various nineteenth-century European travellers and missionaries who asserted that the Kilindi rulers of their state in Usambara were responsible for the construction and maintenance of the irrigation system, P.C. Fleuret discounted the role of political centralization. 'I suspect', he concluded, 'that such practical affairs were in the past, as they are today, largely the business of local communities'.[7] Indeed, from Usambara to Meru, each irrigation furrow was identified with a lineage which had first planned or constructed it. The lineage continued each irrigation season to perform the rituals required before repairs were undertaken, and repair work and development of irrigation schedules were done by all those who used the water. Ruling groups did not control the irrigation systems, except those of the new *marombo* type which were constructed by the Ugweno kings in the lowlands of Upare after the introduction of maize.[8]

The demand for tribute may have been a strong catalyst for agricultural intensification. However, in South Pare at the beginning of the nineteenth century, even though rain-making and other ritual functions allowed the ruling lineages of the small, loosely centralized states of the region to obtain tribute irregularly, it had little effect on the production process. Where the political system was more centralized, as in Usambara, Ugweno and Kilimanjaro, more regular tribute collection may have encouraged intensification of agricultural production.

Commercial incentives for intensification are more complicated. Two important elements in this connection are to be borne in mind. The first one is the existence of market-places in all these mountain communities. However, development of market-places does not necessarily mean that the societies involved had market economies. At the same time the non-existence of market-places does not signify absence of market economies either. Our present knowledge of African economies would make categorisation of all precolonial African economies as 'subsistence economies' incorrect. In fact, even prior to the nineteenth century there was enough specialization in production and distribution in some societies to justify saying that commodities were already produced specifically for their exchange value. Yet there were other societies, particularly in western Tanzania, where the production of goods for exchange existed without market-places because goods were carried by peddlers from household to household.[9]

In the mountains of northeastern Tanzania, however, market-places seem to have been old institutions. Even before political centralization, almost every local community had a market-place. It would appear, therefore, that the development of the market-place was connected with the efforts of communities to ensure food security and keep away hunger. The concentration of population in the highlands made trade in market-places more convenient than reliance on peddlers.

Another factor encouraging exchange was regional cooperation involving mountain communities and neighbouring groups in the lowlands. The main impetus for this cooperation was the sharing of scarce resources needed by all communities. The Pare were most fortunate in having iron ore in their territory, for ironsmiths in mountain and lowland communities across the region depended on products made by Pare smelters. Salt, on the other hand, was a resource found only in the lowlands. Lack of clay on Kilimanjaro also made its people dependent on the Pare and the Kahe of the lowlands for their pots.

Similarly, the old historical ties between different mountain regions must have encouraged trade. Indeed, the original language of the Pare people in Ugweno is considered to be related to the dialects of Kichagga spoken on Kilimanjaro.[10] In his ongoing study of the history of Kilimanjaro, Dr J.C. Winter of the University of Bayreuth in Germany has highlighted the connections between the two regions. In a lecture in February 1991 at the University of Dar es Salaam on the Kilimanjaro age-set structure he showed that Ugweno acted together with the rest of Kichagga speaking areas of Kilimanjaro in the organization of initiation rites; the cycles always started in Ugweno and then were taken up by the Kilimanjaro states in turns.[11]

Thus the patterns of regional exchange among highlanders and between mountains and lowlands probably represented the beginning of the market process that Harold K. Schneider defines as 'people engage[ing] in producing things in order to obtain other goods in exchange'.[12] Members of communities which needed scarce items such as salt would travel, often in groups, to areas where they could obtain them. By the nineteenth century people were specializing in producing and carrying the scarce items to regional markets so that others could more easily obtain them closer to home. Thus when the region became integrated into a wider network of exchange in the nineteenth century, the regional network had already prepared the ground. By the end of the century, however, integration into the wider network of exchange had come into conflict with the local imperative of defeating hunger.

The local focus

In the introduction we referred to three mountain environments with three separate population groups. But it is necessary to bear in mind that at the beginning of the nineteenth century the communities of at least two of these three population groups were not identified in the way that they came to be known during the colonial period. In Usambara, having become a centralized state under the Kilindi ruling family some time in the eighteenth century, the Shambaa were all part of one territorial structure long before Kimweri ye Nyumbai came into power in 1815.[13] Therefore, politically and to some extent culturally, the Shambaa could act as one group, although, economically, the productive units (the households) tended to function in the same way as those of the other, less unified mountain areas.

In Pare and Kilimanjaro, however, there was no single political unit. Even though the whole of the north Pare block had come under the Ugweno kingdom,[14] by the beginning of the nineteenth century a small independent state had emerged in Usangi on the southern side of the block with the intrusion of migrants from south Pare. In the south Pare and middle Pare ranges there were a number of small competing states and at least one lineage-based federation at Vudee on the western side of the south Pare range.[15] The name Pare was probably used more by outsiders than by the Pare themselves. Although Chasu, the Pare language, may have already become common all over the Pare mountains, culturally the Ugweno kingdom was still distinct. Indeed, the people who immigrated into Usangi from south Pare were not allowed to participate in Ugweno initiation rites and had to return to south Pare for such rites.

Similarly, on Kilimanjaro there were more than thirty small states on the ridges of the mountain. The communities were identified more by their geographical locations than by the ethnic name applied to them later. Like 'Pare', the name 'Chagga' may have been used by outsiders more than by the Kilimanjaro inhabitants themselves. It became a 'tribal' name during the German colonial period. In contrast, Pare 'tribal' identity was not created until the British period. Indeed, the persistence of highly localized identities was encouraged on both

Kilimanjaro and Pare by the diverse responses of households to varying ecological circumstances.

Modes of residence varied considerably both within and between the three mountain zones. Shambaa chiefdoms, as shown by Steven Feierman, were located at the edge of the mountain escarpment. Each chiefdom had a town as its capital, and each capital was surrounded by villages whose people worked plots scattered over distances of about five miles. Villagers would go to work daily on their plots, or on those of the capital, and return in the evening. Banana groves were located near the villages in Shambaai, the zone near the residences, while other crops were scattered in different ecological zones extending up to the forests at higher altitudes and down to the *nyika* of the plains.[16]

This pattern of residence was quite different from that found in other mountain zones. In both Upare and Kilimanjaro, residences were spread out amongst agricultural holdings that were normally held by lineages. A household would build its residence and cultivate annual crops within or near its banana grove. Additional plots for annual crops would be located far away from the banana area on higher and lower elevations to take advantage of different ecological conditions. It is not easy to explain this difference in residential patterns. P.C. Fleuret argues that the Shambaa congregated in villages to defend themselves against raids by the Maasai, Taita and other neighbouring people.[17] But it is difficult to see why this factor would apply to the Shambaa alone, particularly because defence was a growing concern for the whole region during the second half of the nineteenth century. Feierman stresses that compact small chiefdoms facilitated Kilindi collection of tribute in labour or kind, but it is certain that the Kilindi found the pattern already established and exploited it. The main explanation for the concentration of population along the edges of the escarpment seems to be the convenience of residing in a highland location where one could utilize not only the Shambaai zone, but also the *nyika* as well as the cool areas at higher altitudes.[18]

The Shambaa in western Usambara occupied basically one mountain range and could more easily arrange their exploitation of the environment in the pattern described. On the other hand, the Pare and the Chagga occupied much more diversified mountain environments: in Pare, the mountain ranges and their varying elevations, plateaux and valley; and on Kilimanjaro, the different sides on the slopes of the mountain and its different altitudes, including its ridges and ravines. Despite all these variations, however, the inhabitants of the three mountain environments continuously refined methods of controlling their mountain surroundings so as to ensure availability of food within their communities throughout the year.

Agricultural production depended on the activities of each household.

Evidence from all these mountain environments indicates that no household depended on crops from only one ecological zone. In Usambara, for example, a cultivator had to take advantage of three different rainy seasons: March–May, November–December and August. He or she had to decide which crops to plant in the *nyika*, which in Shambaai and which in the higher zone near the forest. Although it was possible to plant most grains and beans in all seasons and in all zones, it was better to plant in the *nyika* and in south Shambaai (Vugha and Bumbuli) in the longer rainy season (March–May), in north Shambaai (Mlalo and Mlola) in November–December and in higher Shambaai in August. Secondly, the cultivator would have to take into consideration the arrangements or alliances which would enable him/her to obtain irrigation water to save the crop in case rain was not sufficient. All this was possible because the irrigation system was controlled by the people who used it.

In Upare the system was similar, except that the cooler zone was smaller. Planting was done in the *nyika* as well as in the fertile valleys and ridges above the foothills. The foothills only became crucial when new crops were introduced and demanded further expansion of cultivation.[19] Similarly on Kilimanjaro, the cultivator had to consider crops and suitable times for planting in the three cropping seasons, which were even more clearly demarcated than in Usambara. On Kilimanjaro, the cooler ecological zone and the forest belt were bigger than in Usambara and Upare because of the higher elevation of the mountain.[20]

By the nineteenth century, new crops provided cultivators with a wider variety of strategies in their struggle against hunger. At least four new crops – sweet potatoes, tobacco, maize and cassava – were introduced into this region in the eighteenth and nineteenth centuries and adopted by innovative cultivators. No study of the spread of sweet potatoes into the interior of East Africa is known to this writer, but there is hardly any place in this region where this crop is not grown. It grows in many types of soils and serves as a famine security crop between harvest seasons. Many East African peasants would not recognize it as a new crop since it seems to have been there all the time. It spread into the interior much faster than the other new crops, undoubtedly because of its palatability. In 1985 this writer conducted a survey in the Pare mountains which indicated that sweet potatoes were already grown in all parts of the mountains before maize. They added to the variety of root crops without displacing the yams and other mountain tubers which were already grown.

Tobacco seems to have spread almost as rapidly as sweet potatoes, even though it requires manuring, special tending, curing and packing. In the 1940s I watched my grandmother process it. I asked why she knew how to handle it while my mother did not. The answer was that

Photo 2 *A Sign of Agricultural Achievement on Kilimanjaro: a Precolonial Chagga Granary.* (H.H. Johnston, *The Kilimanjaro Expedition* [London, 1866], p. 158.)

one's knowledge of tobacco depended not only upon whether one consumed it, but also on whether one had an opportunity to learn how to grow it. Tobacco was grown in small quantities, especially around residences, mainly for personal consumption. Any surplus could easily be exchanged in a local market-place if properly cured and packed. All markets between Usambara and Kilimanjaro carried this item by the middle of the nineteenth century. Preparation of snuff was its main local use, although smoking was also known among elderly men. Because the cultivation of tobacco was quite limited, its introduction did not much alter the land-use habits of households; it only added an additional item to be looked after near some residences. In Usambara, coastal demand for tobacco may have made its production more popular in the nineteenth century, although most of it remained within local markets.[21]

The spread of maize made an ultimately greater, though more gradual, impact in the whole region. In Usambara and Pare it probably began to be grown before the beginning of the nineteenth century and by the middle of the century it was widespread.[22] By the end of the century maize had overtaken bananas as the most important food in Usambara and Pare.[23] On Kilimanjaro maize also became popular, but could not compete with bananas and finger millet, both because bananas grew much better in the wetter climate and more fertile soils of Kilimanjaro than in Usambara and Pare, and also because finger millet was required for banana beer brewing. Nevertheless, maize grew well in all three ecological zones of Kilimanjaro and was popular because it could be eaten green. Storage was a problem, however, for, while there were well-established methods of storing finger millet for several years, no such method was known for maize.[24] My grandmother explained to me that, until Indian shops opened and began to buy dry maize, people wanted to do all they could to finish their maize harvest while it was still green. Nevertheless, maize cultivation increased the area under crops in two zones on Kilimanjaro, the *nyika* and the higher area near the forest, because in both zones maize could be grown with finger millet and beans.

Expansion of landholding on the upper part of the slope was not difficult because lineages simply expanded their holdings. Many lineages had plots near the forest or towards river valleys. But in the *nyika* landholding was controlled by rulers of the states which had access to *nyika*. Plots were normally given annually, although once allocated the households continued to use them. Expansion required new allocation and normally tribute was collected in return for these allocations.[25] I remember that when homesteads needed new *kihamba* in the 1950s, it was easy to convert plots near the forest without permission from the chiefs. In contrast, however, chiefs had the right to allocate plots in the *nyika* even if families had been cultivating them for several generations.

In north Pare, the dramatic change in land tenure reveals why rulers took control of the *nyika*. Because maize made land at the foothills much more attractive for cultivation, the ruling class of the centralized Ugweno kingdom increased its power by claiming 'ownership' of unused land. They appointed land allocators to distribute plots and collect tribute. The state also controlled irrigation works in the foothills which 'consisted of larger reservoirs known as *marombo* made by blocking rivers and making irrigation channels leading the water to cultivated land'.[26]

In south Pare, however, maize-growing did not reach the foothills until the caravan trade led to the opening of residential stations in the plains. Thus there was no change in the relationship between rulers and cultivators. The rulers continued to perform rituals required to ensure agricultural success and in return they collected a portion of harvests as tribute. One has the impression that a similar kind of situation also existed in Usambara, where *nyika* cultivation was so well integrated into the agricultural system that maize only gradually displaced sorghum without changing the system itself.[27]

The spread of cassava came even later. Available evidence indicates that by the 1850s it was already grown in Usambara and south Pare and was traded in local food markets, including the Gonja market.[28] The author's 1985 survey indicated, however, that cassava did not spread as rapidly into north Pare, where as late as the 1930s it was still not very well accepted. On Kilimanjaro its acceptance was even slower. I can remember how difficult it was in the 1950s to convince people living high up on the mountain to grow cassava because they thought it was dangerous and capable of killing people.[29] Thus cassava could not compete with bananas and maize in areas of high rainfall and fertility, but it was more attractive for people who had settled in the *nyika*, for here the arrival of cassava in the nineteenth century brought reinforcements in the war against hunger.

With all the diversity in crops, possibilities for cultivation in different ecological zones and irrigation, why was it necessary to institute markets? The answer is that the market-place was part of the subsistence structure throughout the whole region. In Usambara, where villages were groups of residences, markets, such as the ring of market-places around Mbuguland described by Fleuret, were located in areas where they facilitated exchange of needed items.[30] The Mbugu provided the products of animal husbandry in exchange for grain and other products of the field. The agriculturalists also needed products of the *nyika*, especially honey, which reached them through the exchange system. Within Shambaa villages exchange went on continuously in order to satisfy needs of individual households.

In both Upare and Kilimanjaro, each political unit had at least one market-place, and sometimes several.[31] As in Usambara, markets were normally held every fifth day. The extreme diversity of ecological zones encouraged marketing. Certain areas on the same mountain could harvest at different times, not only because of differences in elevation, but also because the winds brought more rain to some areas than to others. The South Pare range, for example, was generally in the rain shadow of the Usambara mountains. The eastern side of the north Pare range and the eastern side of Kilimanjaro received their main rains in the November–December season while the other sides depended on the main rainy season of March–May. Crops planted on the lower slopes of Kilimanjaro could mature several weeks earlier than those planted higher up on the mountain. Markets not only allowed the distribution of crops which were harvested at different times, but also provided access to medicines, building materials, game, honey and salt from forests and *nyika*. Because nearby markets enabled women to walk to a market-place daily, market-places were dominated by women.

Market-places served many neighbouring communities. Indeed, even if there was hostility between two communities, the market cycle was protected, partly because the market-place perpetuated economic alliances between individuals and households. For example, Sally Falk Moore describes the alliance between households which enabled cattle-rich individuals in one state on Kilimanjaro to keep cattle with another household in another state. If a borrower decided not to honour his debt, the owner had two options: either appeal to his ruler to negotiate on his behalf, or go to the market-place of the borrower and curse him. If the curses were repeated on several market days he would certainly have to do something about it.[32] Rulers not only helped preserve alliances, but also spared markets from taxation by appointing destitute persons to clean the markets for a small fee paid by women traders. Later, however, as a result of expansion of caravan trade, market levies seem to have been introduced, especially in the new types of markets which are discussed below.[33]

The regional focus

So far we have looked at the internal dynamics of interaction between people and their environment in the mountain communities. However, such an internal focus is incomplete because it does not include the relationships between the mountain communities themselves and their neighbours on the plains. As we pointed out in the introduction, the green mountain environment constantly attracted population from the neighbouring plains, especially in times of drought. But even in normal times there was exchange of products between the two ecological zones.

Such exchange was necessitated not only by drought, but also by uneven distribution of natural resources such as iron, clay and salt

Photo 3 *A Modern Regional Market at Kwamakame in Usambara. On Fridays, the Kwamakame Market Attracts Hundreds of Buyers and Sellers.* (Sabine Barcatta).

which were needed by the people of the whole region. Iron was required by all communities on the mountain and plains for making hoes, axes, machetes, knives, spears, arrowheads and swords. As already pointed out, iron ore was available only in the Pare mountains. Pare smelters, the Wafinanga, produced iron ingots, which were forged into iron products by smiths all over the region. Even among the Pare themselves, Washana lineages specialized in forging. Similar lineages of smiths existed in different states in Kilimanjaro, in Usambara and among their lowland neighbours, such as the Zigua and the Maasai. Although the Zigua had separate sources of the iron which they traded with the Shambaa,[34] iron tools were scarce items in their country throughout the nineteenth century.[35] Thus the whole region was heavily dependent on the Pare smelters.

The second scarce resource was clay for making pots. This was mainly a problem on Kilimanjaro where sources of good clay did not exist except at two places in Narumu and Nshara at Machame and

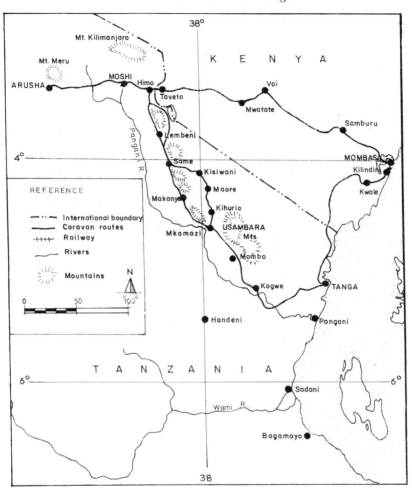

Map 2 *Mountains and Plains in Northeastern Tanzania in the Nineteenth Century.*

Usseri. Otherwise, the whole of Kilimanjaro depended on Upare and Kahe. In the 1950s, as a middle school teacher and agricultural teacher, I had an opportunity to live for three years at Lyamungo (near Narumu) and two years in Usseri. While at Lyamungo I learned that pot-making at Narumu and Nshara did not flourish after the improvement of transportation in the colonial era because the pots were not as good as those of Upare. Because the clay was of poor quality, the pots had to have thick walls, which made them too heavy for carrying water and too slow in cooking. A similar kind of explanation was given in Usseri. Thus no good clay was available in Kilimanjaro.

Salt, the third scarce item, was found in three areas of this region: Kahe on the Kilimanjaro plains, Kileo on the north Pare plains near Kahe, and the Shambaa plains in what came to be part of the Zigua country. It was also possible to obtain salt from the Indian Ocean. Kahe and Kileo salt was in fact a salt substitute, a kind of soda called *magadi* in Kiswahili. Before the nineteenth century it was customary for parties from mountain communities to travel to the source of salt and collect as much as they could carry home. They could exchange some of it in the local markets, as they did any other food item. As regional markets developed, it became easier to obtain salt, especially in the Pare and Shambaa areas. Chagga parties travelled to Kahe throughout the nineteenth century, since Kahe itself was inhabited by people related to the Chagga who wanted mountain products. Although not as conveniently located as Taveta, Kahe was a regional market.

How did these regional markets begin? In Kahe, the market originated at the point of extraction of salt. In Usambara, a string of market-places lay between Shambaai and the *nyika*. On the eastern side, for example, Mbaramo and Kitivo were Kamba stations. Further south and west, Matarowanda was a Maasai station, while Makuyuni and Mazinde were Zigua villages. The political centralization of Shambaai in the eighteenth century expanded to East Usambara and the Bondei country, and by the time of Kimweri ye Nyumbai political control had reached the two coastal towns of Tanga and Pangani, where although the Sultan of Zanzibar controlled trade, the king of Usambara was sovereign. The king could collect tribute but could not trade directly with the towns.[36]

The Shambaa political system depended more on tribute collection than on trade. The string of market-places inhabited by foreigners was within territory which could have been controlled by the king of Usambara, but as the land was barren the stations were not considered important to the Shambaa political authorities. Yet, to the Shambaa cultivators, these were important points of exchange. Makuyuni, for example, was located on the southern tip of Shambaai. Here the Shambaa and the Zigua exchanged food and seeds because their agricultural seasons were different, although each group had its own specialities. The Zigua had iron implements, game meat and salt, while the Shambaa could offer bananas and tobacco. Visitors from the coast also came to the Makuyuni market, bringing cowrie shells and beads to exchange for *samli* (ghee) and tobacco from Shambaai. A similar kind of trade with the Maasai involved the exchange of livestock and livestock products for agricultural items.

Regional market-places in the Pare mountains attracted people from the plains. Iron and iron products had an important place in these markets, although the Pare also offered other items, including antelope skins, which were sold at the Gonja market for ritual use in Usambara, and pots and iron ingots which were sold for Chagga' consumption at .the Mruma market. On Kilimanjaro, markets facilitated trade between the Chagga and the Maasai. Helge Kjekshus mentions two such markets, one in Kibongoto, which attracted the Maasai of West Kilimanjaro, and another in Usseri, which served the Maasai of Laitokitoki on the eastern side. It appears that some regional markets, such as Kibongoto and Usseri, met on a ten-day cycle, while others met once a month with the appearance of a new moon.[37]

What were the consequences of this regional trading system? First, certain standards of exchange developed. Secondly, some items exchanged over a large area became commodities. Thirdly, some groups of people specialized as traders. In Pare, many items could serve as standards of exchange. Food could be measured in terms of maize units (*vivale*), with each *kivale* consisting of four large maize ears or six small ones tied together. Iron pieces cut to standard sizes by the smelters could also be used in local and regional trade, as were livestock. On Kilimanjaro, livestock were probably the most common standard of exchange, although hoes and other iron products provided smaller units. Fine finished iron articles which were the speciality of Chagga smiths, such as iron wire and chains, became popular for this purpose along with hoes and other implements.

Clearly there was no single common standard. The Shambaa seem to have had more firmly established standards to facilitate exchange with the plains and the coast. The smallest unit was 'the round, hard cake of tobacco. Forty of these packed together were called an *mzungu* (pl. *mizungu*)'. Larger equivalent units were: six *mizungu* for one billy goat, twelve *mizungu* for one nanny goat, three billy goats for one bull and six billy goats for one cow.[38] Although it is difficult to compare standards for the whole region, it appears that goods may have been cheaper on Kilimanjaro and more expensive towards the coast. For example, while six goats were exchanged for a cow in Usambara, on Kilimanjaro four goats were exchanged for a calf.[39] Later in the nineteenth century, European travellers found food to be cheaper on Kilimanjaro than in other areas.[40]

The second consequence of regional trade was commodity production, or the production of items for exchange. Iron and salt were commodities in regional trade as well as necessities of daily life in a subsistence economy. Some people specialized in their production and distribution in order to make them available at market-places. So the process of commodity production was already beginning, even though some theorists would call it 'primitive'.[41] A similar argument can be made concerning the trade in pottery and tobacco.

The third consequence of regional trade was specialization by traders, but this is a much more controversial topic. Was there a class of traders in this region prior to the expansion of caravan trade from the coast? There is no doubt that people travelled from one village to another in search of what they needed, either on market days or at other times. Chagga groups journeyed to Kahe to get salt, although we are not yet aware of groups that specialized in selling salt on the mountain. The Shambaa were in a better position to develop a class of traders because of their proximity to the coastal towns. Feierman mentions small groups of Shambaa who would make trips to Pare villages to get *samli* for sale in Pangani. However, even in this case, it is unlikely that a class of Shambaa traders had developed. Occasionally, individual Shambaa cultivators would take certain items to the coast, but, even though Tanga and Pangani were paying tribute to Kimweri ye Nyumbai, the fact that the kingdom was not supposed to engage in trade with the towns discouraged the development of trade between the Shambaa and the coast. Of course, this situation would have changed if Kimweri and his chiefs had been interested in trade, but their reliance on tribute left them uninterested in trade until near the end of Kimweri's time.

Two groups who resided in the lowlands near Shambaai, the Kamba and the Zigua, seem to have specialized more in trade. Feierman has presented evidence of Kamba colonies along the rim of Shambaai, at Kitivo and Mbaramo on the northeastern side, which existed before the end of the eighteenth century when Kamba trade is believed to have expanded.[42] The Kamba colonies are known to have been involved in elephant hunting and in the trade of tusks to the coast. Their proximity to Shambaai enabled them to exchange meat for other items, thus making their colonies part of the string of regional markets connecting Shambaai with the *nyika*. Shambaa kings did not control them, as we have already pointed out, because trade was not important in their political system in the early nineteenth century. There is also evidence of similar trade relations between the Kamba and Rombo on the eastern side of Kilimanjaro going back to the eighteenth century, although in this case the Kamba did not form colonies.[43] The early political prominence of one of the rulers of eastern Kilimanjaro, Orombo, is attributed to his ability to control trade with the Kamba. Kamba groups in Pare were also relied upon by political leaders because of their hunting expertise, although it is impossible to tell whether they played any major trading role. For eastern Kilimanjaro and Usambara, however, it is clear that the Kamba were already established as traders of ivory before the major expansion of caravan trade into the Pangani Valley.

The Zigua case has been ably discussed by James Giblin in his study of Handeni District. The Zigua lived in a 'drought-prone' environment where cultivators had to concentrate their work in lowland valleys, around hills and along watercourses, where the soils retained moisture. There were periods of severe food shortages in the early years of the nineteenth century 'which were survived through the barter of captives for foodstuffs or by accepting captivity with persons who were able to provide food'. They developed wide-ranging trade relations, including trade with Maasai pastoralists, with whom they exchanged grain and crafts for cattle and cattle products. They also developed trade with the coastal towns, especially Pangani and Sadani. Some trade items, such as tobacco, ghee, sesame and honey they produced themselves, but over time they trained themselves to become middlemen. Iron from the Nguu mountains could be taken for exchange with the Shambaa. We have also seen how they controlled the trade in salt, which was obtained from the coast as well as from sources on the Shambaa plains.[44] In this way the Zigua established themselves in foothill villages that controlled regional markets, such as Makuyuni and Mazinde. These were to become important stopping stations for caravans later in the nineteenth century. But, before that happened, the Zigua had already begun to specialize in trade by acting as suppliers of grain and *samli* to the coastal towns.

Thus, in this and other ways, the regional trading network prepared the way for the penetration of a wider trading system. Before the creation of a new trading network based on the coast, the system of market-places had maintained food security for the whole region. Mountain communities depended on one another, while lowlanders and highlanders were also interdependent. The new, wider network of trade, however, would gravely affect this established system of food security.

Integration with the coast

The east coast of Africa has for centuries been integrated into a worldwide network of trade through the Indian Ocean. In the eighteenth century, the Omani Arabs, after helping the East African city-states to drive away the Portuguese, built their own network. By the beginning of the nineteenth century, Omani presence on the coast was evident at three main places: Zanzibar, Mombasa and Kilwa.[45] But, until

Seyyid Said became the Sultan of Oman in 1806, there was no strong centralized control of the evolving system of trade. The Mazrui governor of the Omanis in Mombasa, for example, developed his own autonomous system of trade with the Miji Kenda people. It was Seyyid Said who started to build up Zanzibar as the entrepôt of trade controlled by himself and connected with other parts of the Indian Ocean, Europe and America. In Zanzibar he encouraged development of plantation production of cloves and coconuts, which was controlled by Arab immigrants from his home country. Gradually Seyyid Said consolidated his control of the coast. By the time he transferred his capital from Muscat to Zanzibar in 1840, the East African trade was firmly under his control.

In the Pangani Valley region, the nineteenth-century process of integration with the coastal trade network can be divided into three periods. The first was the period up to 1837 when Seyyid Said was able to break the Mazrui power in Mombasa. The second is the period between the 1830s and the 1850s, when the Pangani Valley routes into the interior developed, while the third period between the 1860s and the imposition of colonial rule in the 1890s witnessed the strong impact of coastal trade on the societies of the area.

In the first period, the coastal network built its own connections with the industrialized world. European and American merchant houses established their trading centres in Zanzibar, while Seyyid Said used Indian financiers to establish a commercial system which could handle the expanding trade. Until the Mazrui were ousted, however, Mombasa seemed to be a separate point of connection with the outside world.[46] South of Mombasa, coastal towns such as Vanga, Tanga, Pangani and Sadani began to make financial connections with Indian financiers in Zanzibar. In this way the Pangani Valley regional trading network came to be connected with the coastal system. The Kamba and the Zigua, as specialists in trade, provided links with the interior. During this time, ivory was the main attraction for coastal merchants, although slave trading may also have been involved.

As we have already noted, the Kamba were middlemen in the ivory trade with Kilimanjaro. The eastern side of the mountain had a corridor from the *nyika* to the mountain forest, with a high concentration of elephants. It was in this region that Orombo, the first strong ruler, arose. By the beginning of the nineteenth century he had consolidated the small states of Rombo into one unit, although after his death they broke apart once again. His rise to power seems to have involved two strategies. The first involved organizing a reliable supply of iron and iron weapons by allying himself with Mamba, another small state further southwest which had special arrangements with Ugweno in north Pare.[47] Secondly, Orombo controlled the trade with the Kamba, for unlike the Shambaa area where the Kamba were elephant hunters, on Kilimanjaro they bought the ivory from Chagga who specialized in hunting and trapping elephants.

Orombo may also have introduced the system which came to be embraced by other rulers on the mountain, that of centralizing all trade with foreigners. All ivory obtained from his territory was taken to him to be exchanged for other items such as iron and livestock, although later coastal items such as cotton cloth, beads, brass, iron wire and eventually firearms may have dominated. The accumulated goods 'traded with outsiders' were shared with his leading men. 'Thus the chief and his men had a strong interest in enlarging the area of his monopoly'.[48] This was consonant with the tribute collection system in which the ruler was not only the collector of wealth but also its distributor to his people. After the fall of the Mazrui in Mombasa, Kamba connections with the Rombo area seem to have weakened and trade contacts with other Kilimanjaro states in the southwest were enhanced. Further south from Mombasa, the Miji Kenda people of Vumba-Digo started to organize caravans directly from Vanga to Kilimanjaro through Taveta in the 1830s and 1840s.[49]

In the Usambara region, proximity to the coast and the existence of trading groups connecting the mountains with the coastal commercial centres facilitated faster integration of the regional market system with the coastal trade. Soon the regional market-places on the plains became stopping places for caravans going further into the interior or returning to the coast. Coastal commerce met the demand for good-quality ivory, and, as plantation ventures succeeded in Zanzibar and Pemba, demand for slaves also increased. The Zigua were so successful in transforming themselves into effective controllers of trade on the lowlands of the Pangani Valley that their power eventually seemed to overshadow that of the Shambaa kingdom. The more arid environment of Uzigua induced the Zigua to search widely for exchange connections which would enable them to survive in difficult years. The establishment of such connections led to the creation of Zigua chieftaincies. Because the chieftains controlled the main trading stations, they became important allies of the Zanzibar agents in the coastal towns, through whom they obtained international trade goods, including guns.[50] In this way, besides supplying grain and other local items, they became chief suppliers of ivory and slaves.

In the second period, between 1837 and the 1850s, one sees the consolidation of power of the leading Zigua chieftains. Those of northern Uzigua, like Kivuma (near Mazinde) and Mamba (near Korogwe), were openly a threat to Shambaai itself. Feierman tells us that, when Kimweri ye Nyumbai came to power in 1815, 'guns of any kind were unknown in the Pangani Valley region'.[51] After the Zigua became powerful because they obtained guns, however, Kimweri also tried to acquire firearms, but by then the Zigua leaders were far ahead of him. By 1852 Krapf estimated that Kimweri had about 400 guns, 'while one of the important Zigua chiefs had 600'.[52]

Shambaai was in the front line of the expanding coastal trade into the Pangani Valley. The impact of the trade was beginning to be noticed even before Kimweri ye Nyumbai died in 1862. One of his sons, Semboja, grasped the shift in balance of power between Shambaai and the *nyika* caused by the expansion of trade and moved the capital of his chiefdom from the mountains to the Zigua colony at Mazinde, thereby transforming himself into a Zigua chieftain by creating a commercial centre in the *nyika*. When his father died in 1862, it was Semboja (a descendant of an unimportant house in the royal line) who was able to shape events in Vugha, the capital of the Shambaa kingdom.

At the time of expansion of long-distance trade, the system of Zigua villages on the plains served two important functions to the caravan trade. First, they provided security for traders who maintained trade relations or blood-brotherhood alliances with the Zigua chieftains. Secondly, such settlements became important market centres. It should not be surprising, therefore, that the regional market-places on the Shambaa *nyika* would become major long-distance trade stations. Until the early years of the 1860s the system of Zigua-style chieftaincies on the plains had not gone beyond Mazinde. But caravans were already using the Pangani Valley route through the Pare plains to Kilimanjaro, and, as we have already mentioned, Taveta had already become a station for caravans originating from Mombasa and the ports of Vanga, Tanga and Pangani. Although some slaves may have been brought to the coast, the main commercial drive was the search for ivory. By the 1850s, the sources of ivory near the coast must have been exhausted and the remaining elephants were driven more and more towards Mount Kilimanjaro.[53]

All this led some cultivators to become elephant hunters in order to obtain imports in exchange for ivory, as Baron C.C. von der Decken learned in 1862. While approaching the Pare plains from the coast, he met a caravan from Vanga led by a Swahili by the name of Msuskuma, who called himself an elephant hunter. The Baron discovered that the caravan was going to Ugweno, where Msuskuma had enjoyed connections for some years. He also discovered that Msuskuma was an ivory trader rather than a hunter, and that he depended on people in Ugweno who had specialised in elephant hunting in the area surrounding Lake Jipe.[54] This was an important development in the trade of European and American industrial commodities for Pare rural products. The search for ivory among the Pare themselves was not limited to Ugweno, for on the same journey von der Decken met two Pare men at Kisiwani who had been searching for ivory in Mbaga, a state in south Pare.[55]

The search for ivory must have begun even earlier on Kilimanjaro, which had been visited by Kamba traders since the days of Mazrui power in Mombasa. However, as Swahili traders from the Pangani Valley coast made direct contact with various states on the southern and western sides of Kilimanjaro, the number of leaders competing to control the ivory trade increased. Within each state elephant hunting and trapping must have been encouraged, especially higher up on the mountain, but there is also evidence that Chagga rulers obtained elephant tusks by purchasing them from neighbouring people in the lowlands.[56] Indicative of the high value placed on trade with the coast was the reported willingness of Chagga leaders to pay as much as forty cows and forty goats for only one tusk.[57]

In this second phase of the expansion of caravan trade into the Pangani Valley, the general population became involved since each passing caravan needed food supplies. The provisioning of caravans became a special business involving cultivators who could get foodstuffs to the stations of the Shambaa and Pare foothills. As soon as a caravan arrived at a station, the leader would fire a few shots to announce their arrival. The cultivators on the mountains would carry their produce to the station, where a market would be held. At Gonja in south Pare, for example, von der Decken's caravan bought beans, yams, cassava, pumpkins, *kweme* (an oil nut), sugar cane, chickens, goats and baskets in exchange for cotton cloth, brass and iron wire and beads of many kinds.[58] Because of the distance between the mountain villages and the lowland stations, the rulers of Upare could hardly control the new type of markets. The commodities from the coast therefore accrued in different hands; however, the rulers could send their own foodstuffs to market and also send representatives to collect tolls and market fees.

On Kilimanjaro rulers controlled trade more effectively, particularly because their capitals were situated toward the lower end of the inhabited slope. Foreigners coming from the plains had to report at the capital, where they were given a camping ground near the court and supplied with grains, bananas, milk, banana beer and livestock. The rulers succeeded in increasing food production to meet this demand by using tribute labour and by increasing tribute collection. This meant that the cultivators had to increase production in order to meet this demand as caravans became larger and their visits more frequent. There was also 'a considerable petty trade between the women of ordinary households and the ordinary bearers. The women flocked to the grounds where many dozens of caravan porters camped and there conducted their own exchange directly with the coastal visitors'.[59]

Towards the end of the 1860s the third phase began, for what had already happened in the front line where Zigua chieftains were challenging the leaders of Shambaai in the previous phase, began to happen in the rest of the Pangani Valley. Raiding for slaves gradually became more prominent than the ivory trade. In the Pare Mountains coastal traders became allies, not only of states, but of any small territorial unit. Competition for control of the coastal trade involved many autonomous petty leaders. By the 1880s the situation was quite different from what it was in the 1860s, because even normal trade between the communities could not be guaranteed. In Usambara, there was competition between various Kilindi leaders after the death of Kimweri ye Nyumbai. The kingdom fell apart as Zigua-style settlements, established by both supporters and opponents of Semboja, began to spread beyond Mazinde into the Pare plains. Most of these settlements were established at caravan stations such as Kihurio, Gonja, Kisiwani, Hedaru, Makanya, Mwembe and Same. By the 1880s the expansion of settlements had reached Lembeni in north Pare.[60]

The presence of trading settlements on the Pare plains increased slave raiding on the mountains and the availability of guns. On Kilimanjaro, such proliferation was slowed by centralizing trading activities at the court, but competition among the states, particularly in the form of livestock raiding, was eventually intensified by the need to obtain more livestock to provision caravans. With the increase in raiding, communities constructed defence ditches and stockaded areas with 'earthworks and wooden fences'.[61]

All over the Pangani Valley, the caravan trade required alliances with leaders on the plains and mountains. As the caravans became larger (perhaps for defence as well as for economic reasons), the provisioning business, as well as slave and ivory trading, became part of the economic endeavours of all these communities. In the concluding section we shall examine how this expansion of coastal trade affected the main economic goal of conquering hunger and ensuring that food was available to each household from day to day.

Conclusion

The story of environmental control and economic development in the three mountain areas has given us the opportunity to challenge the incorrect picture of precolonial African economies as being static and incapable of transformation to a market orientation. Throughout the nineteenth century (and even before) a number of agricultural innovations increased food security. New crops were fitted into the multiplicity of ecological zones, new irrigation patterns came into use even where, as in the case of Ugweno, cultivation had not been practised before, and the institution of the market-place integrated redistribution in both mountains and plains.

The expansion of exchange which integrated the region into world markets passed through three different phases during the nineteenth century. Gradually communities began to participate in the new trade and, by provisioning caravans as well as by trading ivory and slaves, they obtained a variety of new commodities, including cotton cloth, brass and iron wire, beads and guns. Although individual cultivators often participated directly in trade, in many cases community leaders organized labour and controlled trade. On the Pare plains, a new innovation was introduced during the final phase of this expansion: the establishment of settlements in the foothills of the south Pare range which introduced agriculture, particularly the growing of rice, an important economic crop in the twentieth century.[62] Thus cultivators in this region expanded their participation in the market-oriented system throughout the nineteenth century. Obviously the process of 'peasantization', that is, making subsistence-orientated cultivators produce for the market, did not begin with the introduction of the colonial economy.

Yet other changes, including the slave trade and the reorganization of labour for non-productive activities, had a harmful impact on food security. Whatever new imports may have been brought in by trade, as long as this involved the exchange of able-bodied human beings previously engaged in production, production was weakened. When one adds to this the unrest created by slave raiding, one can see how agricultural production and innovation were impaired. Similarly, leaders mobilised warriors and other able-bodied men for activities other than agricultural production, such as the construction of fortifications, for stockaded villages on the plains and big defence tunnels and ditches on the mountains became common by the 1880s. Of course, the leaders who mobilized warriors exchanged the booty taken in raids for imported commodities, but these imports were not food.

Thus, while it can be argued that 'agricultural production must have been increased',[63] when one takes into account the greater need to provision caravans and to feed the people who were taken out of production to defend the system, one will see that perhaps there was no substantial improvement in food security. In fact, by the 1880s the agricultural system designed to ensure food security was no longer working properly in both Upare and Usambara. Because unrest interfered with agricultural production, famine threatened society. Certainly life had become extremely insecure when armed Pare men had to escort their wives to markets.[64]

Notes

1. The author would like to acknowledge with thanks financial assistance from the Fulbright Program of the USA and the Mickey Leland Center at Texas Southern University which enabled him to write up this study while he was a Scholar in Residence at Texas Southern University in the 1991–2 academic year.

2. Alexander de Waal, *Famine That Kills: Darfur, Sudan, 1984-1985* (Oxford, 1989), p. 12.

3. See Steven Feierman, *The Shambaa Kingdom: A History* (Madison, 1974); I.N. Kimambo, *A Political History of the Pare of Tanzania, c. 1500-1900* (Nairobi, 1969); and Kathleen Stahl, *History of the Chagga People of Kilimanjaro* (London, 1964).

4. James C. McCann, 'Agriculture and African History', *Journal of African History*, 32, 3 (1991): 511.

5. Thomas Hakansson, 'Social and Political Aspects of Intensive Agriculture in East Africa: Some Models from Cultural Anthropology', *Azania* 24 (1989): 12.

6. Hakansson, 'Intensive Agriculture', p. 18.

7. P.C. Fleuret, 'Farm and Market: A Study of Society and Agriculture in Tanzania' (Ph.D. Dissertation, University of California, Santa Barbara, 1978), p. 32.

8. Steven Feierman, *Peasant Intellectuals: Anthropology and History in Tanzania* (Madison, 1990), p. 65; I.N. Kimambo, *Penetration and Protest in Tanzania: The Impact of the World Economy on the Pare, 1860-1960* (London, 1991), p. 22; and Sally Falk Moore, *Social Facts and Fabrications: 'Customary' Law on Kilimanjaro, 1880-1980* (Cambridge, 1986), p. 23.

9. Kimambo, *Penetration and Protest*, p. 24.

10. Derek Nurse, *Classification of Chaga Dialects* (Hamburg, 1979).

11. The results of Dr Winter's study should provide dramatic new insights into the history of the region.

12. Harold K. Schneider, 'Traditional African Economics', in Phyllis M. Martin and Patrick O'Meara, eds, *Africa*, 2nd ed (Bloomington, 1986), p. 181.

13. Feierman, *Peasant Intellectuals*, p. 87.

14. See Kimambo, *Political History*.

15. Kimambo, *Penetration and Protest*, Chapter 2.

16. Feierman, *Shambaa Kingdom*, p. 29.

17. Fleuret, 'Farm and Market', p. 38.

18. Feierman, *Shambaa Kingdom*, p. 122; see also Steven Feierman, 'Concepts of Sovereignty Among the Shambaa and Their Relation to Political Action' (D.Phil. Thesis, Oxford University, 1972).

19. Feierman informs me that similar places also existed in some parts of Shambaai such as Bumbuli.

20. Sally Falk Moore and Paul Puritt, *The Chagga and the Meru of Tanzania* (London, 1977), pp. 4-5.

21. Feierman, *Shambaa Kingdom*, pp. 131-2.

22. Feierman, *Shambaa Kingdom*, p. 25; Kimambo, *Penetration and Protest*, p. 21.

23. Kimambo, *Penetration and Protest*; Fleuret, 'Farm and Market', p. 93.

24. In the region maize ears were tied together in units of four or six for ease of handling. In Upare these became units of exchange. In Kilimanjaro the tied units were packed on a tree near the residence, where they could be safe for a season or two before being attacked by insects.

25. Moore and Puritt, *Chagga and Meru*, p. 22.

26. Kimambo, *Penetration and Protest*, p. 22.

27. Feierman, *Shambaa Kingdom*, p. 27.

28. Kimambo, *Penetration and Protest*, p. 21.

29. This writer happens to have been an agricultural teacher on the eastern side of Kilimanjaro at that time.

30. Fleuret, 'Farm and Market', p. 176.

31. Some states in Kilimanjaro had more than one; the Ugweno kingdom had at least one for each district. See Moore, *Social Facts*, p. 23; Kimambo, *Penetration and Protest*, pp. 24-6.

32. Moore, *Social Facts*, pp. 24-6.

33. Fleuret, 'Farm and Market', pp. 173-5.

34. Feierman, *Shambaa Kingdom*, p. 131.

35. James Giblin, 'Famine, Authority and the Impact of Foreign Capital in Handeni District, Tanzania, 1840-1940' (Ph.D. Dissertation, University of Wisconsin-Madison, 1986), pp. 73-4.

36. Feierman, *Shambaa Kingdom*, p. 124.

37. Kimambo, *Penetration and Protest*, p. 25; Fleuret, 'Farm and Market', pp. 167, 179; Helge Kjekshus, *Ecology Control and Economic Development in East African History: The Case of Tanganyika, 1850-1950* (London, 1977), pp. 114-15.

38. Feierman, *Shambaa Kingdom*, p. 132.

39. Moore, *Social Facts*, p. 28.

40. H.H. Johnston, for example says: 'Food could scarcely have been cheaper anywhere in the world than in Chaga'. *The Kilimanjaro Expedition* (London, 1886), p. 215.

41. Kimambo, *Penetration and Protest*, p. 27.

42. Feierman, *Shambaa Kingdom*, p. 125. See John Lamphear, 'The Kamba and the Northern Mrima Coast'; in Richard Gray and David Birmingham, eds, *Pre-Colonial African Trade* (London, 1970), pp. 75-101.

43. Moore, *Social Facts*, p. 30. Feierman quotes a tradition told to Krapf by Kivui Mwenda in 1849 that the Kamba originated from the area near Mount Kilimanjaro and that trade connections with the region had continued ever since. *Shambaa Kingdom*, pp. 127-8.

44. Giblin, 'Famine, Authority', Chapters 1 and 2; quote on p. 80.

45. A.I. Salim, 'The East African Coast and Hinterland, 1800-45', in J.F.Ade Ajayi, ed., *UNESCO General History of Africa*, vol. VI: *Africa in the Nineteenth Century Until the 1880s* (Paris and Berkeley, 1989), p. 211.

46. Salim, 'East African Coast', p. 220.

47. See Kimambo, *Political History*, p. 139.

48. Moore, *Social Facts*, p. 30.

49. Salim, 'East African Coast', p. 223.

50. Giblin, 'Famine, Authority', p. 127.

51. Feierman, *Shambaa Kingdom*, pp. 140-1.

52. Feierman, *Shambaa Kingdom*, pp. 140-1.

53. Stahl, *Chagga People*, p. 50.

54. C.C. von der Decken, *Reisen in Ost-Afrika*, vol. 2 (Leipzig and Heidelberg, 1869), p. 13.

55. von der Decken, *Reisen*, vol. 2, p. 15. See also Kimambo, *Political History*, p. 127.

56. Stahl, *Chagga People*, p. 173; Moore, *Social Facts*, p. 28.

57. Moore, *Social Facts*, p. 28.

58. Kimambo, *Penetration and Protest*, p. 39.

59. Moore, *Social Facts*, p. 32.

60. See Kimambo, *Political History*, chapter 10.

61. Moore, *Social Facts*, p. 32.

62. See Kimambo, *Political History*, p. 66.

63. Moore, *Social Facts*, p. 37.

64. See Kimambo, *Political History*, pp. 164-5.

Four

~~~~~~

Nature Reorganized

Ecological History in the Plateau Forests of the West Usambara Mountains 1850–1935

CHRISTOPHER CONTE

This chapter examines ecological change on northeastern Tanzania's Usambara mountain massif.[1] It focuses on the central plateau forest region of West Usambara, where, between the mid-nineteenth century and the late 1930s, social and economic changes among herding communities, known locally as the Wambugu, led to a marked change in their relationship with nature. Ecological change began with the breakdown in complementary social and economic relations between the Wambugu, who occupied the upland forests, and their neighbours, the Washambaa, who farmed the slopes and basins lower on the elevation gradient and nearer to the massif edge.

The Wambugu settled in Usambara's mountain forests sometime during the early eighteenth century.[2] By the mid-nineteenth century, they had managed to carve out a well-defined territorial niche for themselves as pastoralists. Their adaptation depended on a well-spring of environmental knowledge, careful resource management and complex social relations among various Mbugu communities. However, what Mbugu oral histories now interpret as a precolonial ethic of pastoralism and forest conservation in an isolated society was only possible so long as the Mbugu communities maintained social and economic ties with their Shambaa neighbours. When these relations broke down completely during the 1880s and 1890s, the Wambugu were forced to shift from raising cattle, sheep and goats to growing crops. This transformation, when coupled with the problems created by colonial policies, had long-term consequences for both the forest environment of central Usambara and Mbugu culture.

This study's approach to ecological change stresses a diachronic analysis of the interactions among social relations, local and regional economy and the environment. The first section outlines the natural history of Usambara and explains how Mbugu precolonial socio-economic relations and pastoral production operated in this environmental context. The second section shows how disease and the slave trade, which brought violence and disorder to the Usambara Mountains and the Pangani Valley, disrupted the nineteenth century Mbugu economy and altered the ecology of central Usambara. Finally, the discussion turns to the colonial economy and argues that German and British colonial policies, which precluded the re-establishment of precolonial arrangements, further undermined the viability of Mbugu pastoralism and resulted, by the 1930s, in contentious land disputes.

Natural and human histories converge: social and economic relations in a precolonial mountain environment

The Usambara Mountains rise from the dry savannah, forming an island of climatic regularity. From the standpoint of natural history, the massif's proximity to the stable Indian Ocean rainfall regime, its geology and soils, and its physical isolation from the drier, hotter plains surrounding the massif have allowed the evolution of an unparalleled diversity of flora and fauna.[3] Variations in topography and aspect have created several microclimates, soil complexes and related forest communities on the massif itself. An example of the great differences between microclimates can be seen by comparing the relatively dry rain shadow climate of the central plateau, where the Wambugu settled, with Mazumbai, which is only about 30 kilometres to the southeast (see Figures 4.1 and 4.2). Distinct communities of forest flora and fauna now correspond to the various microclimatic zones, just as they would have before human settlement, when forest covered most of the massif.[4]

Without doubt, forested islands of stable rainfall such as Usambara have attracted farming communities for millennia, but just how the forests were transformed by human occupation remains largely unknown.[5] European visitors to Usambara between 1848 and 1879 were concerned with political and social conditions and did not record forest conditions except for vague references to the variety of flora and the availability of valuable timber.[6] However, German scientists who entered the area in the 1890s began to grasp the scientific importance of species diversity and endemism in Usambara's forests.[7] Their inventories of mountain flora usually described the vegetation of climax forest communities (Urwald), that is, ancient forest stands which existed in a state of undisturbed ecological equilibrium. However, most of these

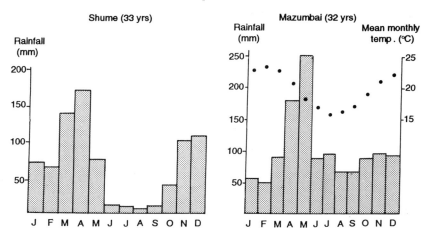

Figure 4.1 *Annual Rainfall in Usambara.*

From: Bjorn Lundgren, 'Soil Conditions and Nutrient Cycling under Natural and Plantation Forests in the Tanzania Highlands', *Reports in Forest Ecology and Forest Soils* 31 (Uppsala: Swedish University of Agricultural Sciences, 1978), pp. 35 and 41.

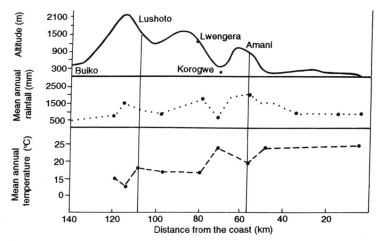

Figure 4.2 *Usambara: Relationship Between Altitude, Climate and Distance from the Coast.*

From: W.A. Rodgers and K.M. Homewood, 'Species Richness and Endemism in the Usambara Mountains Forests, Tanzania', *Biological Journal of the Linnean Society* 18 (1982), p. 202.

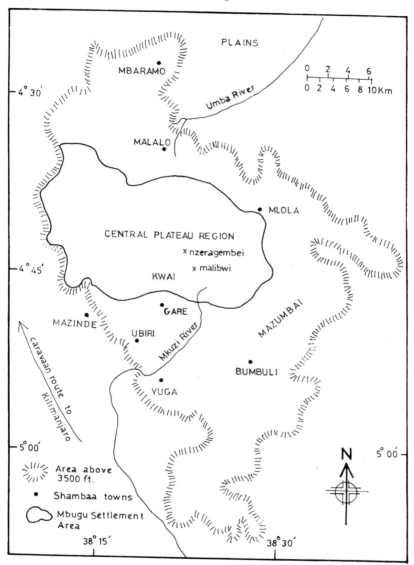

Map 3 *West Usambara*

Adapted from Steven Feierman, *The Shambaa Kingdom*
(Madison: University of Wisconsin Press 1974), p. 24.

early scientific studies tended to gloss over regions used by farmers and herders.[8]

R.E. Moreau has provided the clearest description of two major Usambara forest communities where Mbugu pastoralism functioned.[9] In the relatively wet and warm areas of West Usambara's central plateau, where average rainfall is above 1000 mm, he described what he called a 'highland evergreen forest community', a closed canopy forest dominated by podo (*Podocarpus* spp., Kishambaa *Msee*) and camphor (*Ocotea usambarensis*, Kishambaa *Mkulo*) and numerous codominants. In areas where annual rainfall drops below 1000 mm, the 'cedar forest community' dominated. In the cedar forest a tangled mass of scrub vegetation about 15 feet high dominated the landscape, although some individual cedars (*Juniperus procera*, Kishambaa *Muangati*) more than 100 feet tall thrust up through it.[10]

What appears in the literature as a series of forest types none the less provides clues to the effects of Mbugu pastoralism on the landscape. That human communities used these forests is manifest in Engler's mention of the presence of meadows and Moreau's description of the 'short grassland community' which he found dispersed throughout the 'cedar forest community'. 'This short grassland,' he commented, 'supports numerous stock to which it must owe in part its beautiful lawn-like texture.'[11] Moreau's statement suggests that the forests had been altered to suit the needs of the Mbugu herders, who by the 1930s had grazed their stock in West Usambara's forests for about two centuries.

Moreau saw deforestation as the consequence of colonialism, increased settlement and the market economy.[12] He was partly right, but Moreau failed to account for the antiquity of human/environmental interaction in Usambara's forest communities and the social relations among farmers and herders which permitted deforestation in some areas and conservation in others. Indeed, to comprehend change in East Africa's forest communities, one must reconstruct the changing circumstances of human history over the long term, for in Usambara, as in the nearby highlands of Taita, Pare and Uluguru, Iron Age peoples had long ago simplified the environment's biological diversity.[13] Archaeological and linguistic evidence for precolonial Usambara suggests that, for at least the past two thousand years, the humid forests which ring the massif below 1400 metres have been periodically burned, cut and cultivated by Bantu-speaking communities.[14] Perhaps because of their inaccessibility, aridity and colder temperatures, however, the central plateau forests above 1600 metres proved less attractive to these cultivators, but humans have altered them none the less. However, as will be argued below, sudden and dramatic human-induced ecological change is a more recent occurrence.

Precolonial Usambara's highland forest people, the Wambugu

Mbugu informants refer to their ancestors as the Vamaa, who in centuries past occupied Kenya's Laikipia plateau until a series of conflicts with Maa-speaking pastoralists caused them to flee southward and eastward across the Rift Valley.[15] These movements were punctuated by stays with Cushitic- and Bantu-speaking farmers in what is today northern Tanzania. This history may explain the historically close social and cultural ties which the present-day Wambugu maintain with the Pare people and the ritual importance of certain places in the Pare Mountains.[16] Some accounts also recall a time of residence among Zigua farmers in the region immediately to the south of Usambara.[17]

A pattern emerges from the traditions which argues for a series of conflicts and accommodations between the Vamaa and their neighbours and a high degree of adaptability to a variety of environmental, social and political contexts. Vamaa residence in Usambara fits this model of contact. In fact, eighteenth-century Usambara would have presented immigrant herders with an especially advantageous social, political and ecological situation.

Mbugu oral histories recount Vamaa settlement in Usambara as a series of movements by groups into the mountains from the southern and western sides of the massif.[18] The groups are now recalled as specific lineages, although their identities as lineages might well have been constructed after settlement. In any event, the migrants, whatever their affiliation, ended up occupying the driest and coldest of the massif's microclimates. Naturally these areas were not favoured by the resident cultivators, the Washambaa, because they preferred to remain within reach of the plains below the massif in order to exploit the region's warmest and wettest microclimates. Occupation of central Usambara coincided with a period in Shambaa history when farming communities lived in locally centralized neighbourhoods under the auspices of certain lineage heads, but did not exhibit any degree of political unity across the massif. By introducing their livestock into the mountains, the Vamaa offered individual Shambaa leaders in the neighbourhoods of Ubiri, Gare, Vuga, Bumbuli and Mlalo easy access to an important source of wealth.[19] In fact, Steven Feierman argues that Mbugu migrations into Usambara helped precipitate a political revolution which resulted in the unification of Shambaa communities under the Kilindi dynasty.[20]

Although the Wambugu had entered the mountains in separate groups, they came to occupy a contiguous region, but one whose rainfall varied with aspect and elevation. They also shared a common myth of origin in Laikipia. In addition, their tradition of residence in Upare fostered a powerful cultural unity, which was renewed regularly when

Mbugu initiates and elders met in the forests of the south Pare hills for *mshitu*, or adolescent male initiation ceremonies. Moreover, their Cushitic language, their pastoral economy and their forest enclave clearly separated them from their Shambaa neighbours who had developed their own complex system of agricultural production.

The ecological transition from plains savannah to highland forest marked the beginning of an economic and cognitive shift. The Wambugu remained pastoralists, but retooled their land-use practices and their social relations to fit the forest environment. From a psychological perspective, the forested uplands of central Usambara represented a sanctuary, an ideal place to practise pastoralism far removed from the disorder of the Rift Valley which they had traversed throughout their history.

Mbugu culture and economy in Usambara

If the forest offered less immediately available pasture than the plains, its rain and mists meant higher precipitation. Oral accounts note that, upon arrival in the Usambara forests at Shume and Magamba, the Wambugu found large open glades (*viringo*) suitable for grazing.[21] Such testimony is contradictory on the subject of pasture creation, although the most likely scenario would have Mbugu herders firing the edges of these glades and other suitable areas to expand the amount of pasture.[22] Councils of Mbugu elders regulated the use of these pastures in their respective settlement regions, although it seems that access to them was easily negotiated, especially during droughts.[23]

The Wambugu lived in dispersed homesteads. Each small settlement maintained exclusive rights to an area close to its houses (*mvera*), where animals could be herded in the early morning and evening.[24] The houses themselves were built among the trees and were large enough for the livestock to sleep indoors, although sturdily built, fenced, outdoor cattle enclosures (*boma*) also dotted the landscape. Mbugu leaders also sanctioned the construction of large defensible enclosures called *heiboma*, which, hidden in the forest, served as animal sanctuaries and hideaways during wars.[25]

In addition to pasture, the forest provided fuel and building materials. Mbugu women foraged the ground litter for dead trees and shrubs of *mihaghio* (*Maba buxifolia*), *ngiti*, *mziragembe* (wild olive, *Olea chrysophylla*), and *muandala* (*Ptaeroxylon obliquum*) to make cooking fires.[26] Just what effect this had on the nineteenth-century forest ecology is difficult to determine, but because collection was carried out fairly close to the homestead, the lack of ground litter and decrease in nutrient cycling may have impoverished nearby stands of forest. The Wambugu also stripped cedar bark for use as roofing material and as a medicine.[27]

Human and animal population densities would have affected forest ecology, but the size of these populations in the eighteenth and early nineteenth centuries is impossible to determine. None the less, Mbugu premarital sex prohibitions, child spacing and delayed marriage probably slowed population increase.[28] Control of herd size, essential to the maintenance of the pastoral economy, was regulated through regular ritual slaughter of animals and exchanges between the Wambugu and the Washambaa.[29] The Wambugu also exchanged livestock, hides and dried meat for vegetable produce and iron implements from the neighbouring Shambaa cultivators.[30] After the advent of Kilindi rule in Shambaa neighbourhoods, the Wambugu cultivated relations with the chiefs by paying regular tribute in livestock, labour and women.[31]

In addition to exchanges outside Mbugu territory, herders could spread their animals across several Mbugu-controlled localities by marrying several times and distributing their livestock among their wives' sons. These marriage patterns fostered Mbugu unity across the plateau, while the dispersal of livestock limited overgrazing and mitigated the effects of localized rainfall failure.[32] Thus the Wambugu built a network of social relations which allowed movements of livestock and people within Mbugu territory in times of localized drought:[33]

> We'd hear that there grazing was abundant and here was a desert . . . there would be a cousin there who would take the animals. In fact all over the Usambaras we had relatives with animals. People sometimes moved with their families, sometimes not if they expected to return. People had their clan areas, so that when they came back they had their place that they own.

Such movements could be temporary or permanent, but only as a last resort did they mean leaving Mbugu territory altogether.

Temporary movements (*urang'a*) usually involved a day's walk from the home camp.[34] At such short distances from home, the herders could be visited regularly by family members, who brought them food and news of home. During severe droughts, entire Mbugu families might migrate permanently to be closer to food. Utilizing their ties with Shambaa farmers, they sought out areas on the edges of farmlands where agricultural produce was readily available in exchange for labour or for the livestock, which became an important marker of wealth for the Kilindi and the Washambaa.[35] The Wambugu have sometimes been depicted as a reclusive people, but in fact their economic history in Usambara is closely tied to that of their farming and herding neighbours downslope.[36]

The relationship linking the Wambugu with honey and the forest environment deepens the paradox created by images of reclusiveness and the reality of close ties with neighbouring farmers. Honey had cultural importance for the Wambugu, since it served as the main ingredient for the beer brewed at all ritual and social occasions. Furthermore, bridewealth required partial payment in honey. One informant went so far as to claim that the Wambugu had a 'honey culture'.[37] Since forest flora greatly facilitated Mbugu honey production, informants saw a clear relationship between their identity as forest dwellers, honey production, honey's cultural significance and their cultural separation from the Washambaa.[38] Honey, however, had much more than cultural significance for the Wambugu. Informants recall honey's importance as a dietary supplement, especially during seasons of hunger. Honey's regional economic value was manifest in its importance as a medium of exchange in transactions with Maasai pastoralists, who also used honey ritually. Moreover, Mbugu honey gatherers purchased their hives from the Washambaa.[39] Thus honey production tied the Wambugu economy to that of their neighbours, but reinforced cultural separateness.

Over the course of about a century and a half, Usambara's Cushitic-speaking communities transformed themselves into the Wambugu. They shifted from their tenuous existence as clients and refugees on the plains to a much less risky forest-based pastoralism in the Usambara Mountains. This situation in some ways repeated earlier patterns of complementary interaction with farmers, for Mbugu pastoralism always depended on reciprocal relations with their neighbours. However, their security would be eroded by the introduction into the Pangani Valley of a merchant economy based on the East African coast and Zanzibar. This economic shift, along with the ecological disasters which affected East Africans during the 1880s and 1890s, transformed Mbugu relations with their neighbours and with their environment.

Transitions in mountain agriculture, pastoralism and trade, 1870–1914

Informants throughout the mountains remember the late nineteenth century as the time of *Njaa ya Pato* ('the hunger of greed'). For the Washambaa and the Wambugu, civil war and the growth of the slave trade during the two decades before German conquest brought a period of violence and political chaos which reorientated economic life in the mountains.[40] Increasing numbers of coastal caravans moved up the Pangani Valley, bringing new trade opportunities to plains towns such as Mazinde, where caravans sought provisions in exchange for Western goods. The orientation of trade toward the plains increased the values of slaves, ivory, arms and cloth, and decreased the value of livestock.[41] As demand for slaves grew, making the mountain people the targets of raiders, agricultural and pastoral production suffered, and trade between mountain communities became more difficult. Slave raiders occasionally kidnapped Mbugu men and women, and at least one Mbugu lineage reportedly participated in slave raiding.[42] The crisis intensified during the early 1890s, when the Wambugu experienced the spate of animal diseases which threatened pastoralists (especially the Maasai) throughout East Africa.[43] Wambugu informants relate that the rinderpest (*kidei*) epidemic, which struck just before the Germans reached Mlalo in 1892, substantially reduced their herds.[44] The Wambugu sought to rebuild their herds, and although some of them obtained animals from the herders of the Pare Mountains, others raided their neighbours.[45] However, the Maasai were also desperate to restock, and so launched their own raids on the Wambugu.[46]

To escape the dangers, the Shume Mbugu fled away from the western edge of the Usambara escarpment to the more inaccessible areas around Malibwi, Kwai and Mshangai.[47] Here, in the centre of the massif, Mbugu families gathered together their remaining livestock and constructed stockades (*heiboma*), where young men of the warrior age-set could protect the community's wealth. Should lookouts detect a threat, herders quickly brought the livestock into these bomas, where they would be held until the raiders retreated from the area.[48] Others left the massif altogether, travelling as refugees to East Usambara and Bondei.[49] These circumstances weakened the web of relations between the Wambugu and the Shambaa farmers as the Wambugu migrated away from the danger zones.

At the same time, as Patrick Fleuret has argued, civil war and the region's increasing importance as a source of slaves interrupted the intensification of Shambaa agriculture, which had been occurring since the early nineteenth century. In Fleuret's view, slave raiding forced the Shambaa people to live in heavily fortified hilltop communities. Women who had previously cultivated their maize fields several miles from their villages either farmed closer to home on overused, less fertile fields, or were escorted to work by men who neglected their irrigated fields. Hence this dangerous situation disrupted the forms of agriculture which had supported population increases earlier in the nineteenth century.[50] Yet, as ivory- and slave-seeking coastal caravans passed below the Usambara massif with increasing regularity, those Shambaa communities still producing surpluses in the mountains responded by selling them in plains markets or by moving to new settlements on the plains.[51] Thus, as some villages ceased to produce grain surpluses and others sold their surpluses along the caravan routes, the Wambugu found it more difficult to obtain grain.

The uncertainties of the 1890s were summed up by the Wambugu lineage (*ombweji*) leader at Malibwi, Mlimahadala, in a conversation with Ernst Johanssen, a missionary who visited the Wambugu in 1897. The young chief spoke to Johanssen about his people's recent bad luck. He complained that the Mbugu elders had taught their young nothing about agriculture or medicinal herbs, for which they depended on the Washambaa. Dependence on livestock, he believed, had made them vulnerable to cattle diseases which destroyed their herds and threatened starvation.[52] Clearly, Mlimahadala understood that the Wambugu would have to adjust to the new epidemiological, economic and political forces entering the mountains. Perhaps this is why he repeatedly asked the German missionaries at Hohenfriedberg (Mlalo) for a teacher.

The movement of agricultural surplus out of the mountains, together with cattle disease and raiding, forced the Wambugu to become increasingly dependent on cultivation. Certainly by the mid-1890s, the Wambugu around Mshanghai and Malibwi had begun to cultivate maize and pumpkins.[53] To prepare their gardens, they burned forest underbrush, and then fenced and planted the area with maize for three or four years before moving on to cultivate a new plot. These cultivated areas were probably not very extensive, but a shift to mixed farming was in progress.[54] Evidence for the late nineteenth-century shift in production appears in a forest survey done during 1935 in Magamba, which had been a precolonial centre for Mbugu settlement but which by 1935 had been enclosed as a colonial forest reserve. In his report, the Assistant Conservator of Forests made reference to secondary growth on the eastern edge of the Magamba forest, about an hour's walk from Kwai:[55]

> About ten percent of the forest consists of secondary growth on land once (or sometimes twice) burnt and cleared for native cultivation . . . Although no records exist, it is fairly evident that the natives were evicted from these areas in German times [around 1900] when the forest was demarcated as a reserve. These areas of secondary growth are found at or fairly near the edges of the reserve, mainly on the eastern (Magamba) side, though some strips stretch for over a mile into the forest up one or two valleys. The fact that more or less the same stage (community) in the sere is to be found in most of these areas rather suggests that they were all left at about the same time.
>
> Unless grazed and browsed over, when grassland will develop, deserted fields are usually quickly colonized by a thick mass of herbs, of which a mauve flowered composite, *Erlangea* spp., is about the commonest . . . Some trees of *Pygeum africanum* (*Rosaceae*, Kishambaa, *Mkomohoyo*]) and the deciduous *Clausena melioides* (*Rutaceae*, Kishambaa, *Mkunguni*) are usually found in these areas of secondary forest. They may have been left when the original forest was cleared, but it is believed that the cultivation of the soil following clearing may have some favourable effect on their development.

The observations of the Assistant Conservator suggest that the Wambugu opened up some forest for cultivation during the 1890s, although other areas which had been twice burnt had been cultivated even earlier, for, as he noted, another portion of contiguous secondary

Photo 4 *Remnant of an Indigenous Forest in Usambara. This swath is being decimated by cultivators and by gatherers of timber and firewood. Eucalyptus marks the forest reserve boundary. Jacaranda and agave are planted along the roadbed.* (Christopher Conte)

Photo 5 *Clear Cutting of Japanese Camphor at Magamba Village, West Usambara. Japanese camphor was planted about 1940 as a faster-growing replacement for indigenous camphor, Ocotea usambarensis.* (Sabine Barcatta)

forest had been destroyed by fire two or three generations before 1934.[56] The Wambugu had probably burned the area in the 1880s to begin grazing and agriculture. Thus this evidence supports the argument that during the 1880s and 1890s, the Wambugu intensified land use at the expense of the forest.

Another observer, Eick, described the central Usambara landscape in the vicinity of Kwai and Malibwi in 1896:[57]

> Travelling in a northerly direction, I arrived at the highland plateau of Kwai, a true paradise for the German farmer. All of the vegetation and mountain formations were as if transformed. Between the hills there were large grassy plains, broken here and there by small or large stands of trees. On the mountains one sees in places, thick, beautiful primeval forest, which, as one climbs higher, loses its tropical character and at 1600 meters and above is mixed with numerous conifers, podocarpae, falcata and *Juniperus procera*. The plains are cut by many small streams, which, due to the slight gradient, have a swampy appearance and are surrounded by thick stands of reeds and rushes. The inhabitants of this land, as well as of the bordering regions with the same vegetation, are the Wambugu, exclusively cattle herders, who cultivate their luxuriant shambas [cultivated plots] only for their own needs.

Eick paints a wonderful bucolic portrait of pasture, forest and luxuriant gardens, but the Wambugu's survival as pastoralists depended upon recolonizing abandoned areas and rebuilding relations with their neighbours.

Even with the new patterns of land use, much of central Usambara's turn-of-the-century landscape remained the domain of high forest. Eick described a patchwork of forest and pasture which could only appear to be a paradise for German settlement. Hence, by the late 1890s, the attractiveness of this region brought Mbugu monopoly of forest use in central Usambara to an end. Decisions regarding Usambara's forests were now made in Dar es Salaam in the Department of Natural Resources and Surveying on the basis of reports by European forestry 'experts' who began to assess the commercial worth of Tanzania's forests. The first Usambara Forest Ordinance, which restricted forest use, was passed as early as 1895.[58]

Foresters, settlers and pastoralists: the clash over resources, 1900–1935

Colonial officials considered central Usambara to be a key region for economic development.[59] The German and British administrations passed extensive legislation which subordinated indigenous interests to commercial exploitation of the land by settlers and timber concessions. European forestry officials considered both the resident Mbugu pastoralists and the slow-growing camphor, podo and cedar trees of the forest to be hindrances to commerce. They sought, therefore, to remove the African population from potentially profitable forest reserves and to introduce faster growing exotic tree species. European settlement in Kwai, Mkuzi and Magamba further complicated the Mbugu situation, since settlers sought African labour for their plantations to clear the forest cover. Ultimately, settlers, foresters and the Wambugu clashed over the boundaries and uses of the land. In the face of these alien views of the forest, the Wambugu struggled to retain their rights to use the land and to preserve their pastoral economy.[60] However, because they were relegated to the edges of their former range, they increasingly depended on cultivation and livestock sales to pay colonial taxes. Nevertheless, by the early 1930s the Wambugu had developed a variety of strategies which slowed their transition from pastoralism to agriculture.

German settlers first gained access to the central Usambara plateau region in the late 1890s and carved out large estates in forested areas of Malindi, Kwai and Magamba before the colonial forest service could object.[61] In granting leases to settlers, German officials obviously did not consider Wambugu residency as an obstacle.[62] Several years later, the forestry service set up their Usambara station at Wilhelmstal (Lushoto), and by 1909 the foresters had managed to survey and reserve 50 590 hectares of the still predominantly forested regions of Shume and Magamba which were used by the Wambugu.[63]

Under the German reservation scheme, the Wambugu retained their usufruct rights to those forest glades which appeared to have been occupied continuously for long periods. However, in areas of recent occupation, indigenous peoples were required to leave immediately after harvesting their crops.[64] This meant the eviction from the Shume forest of those Wambugu who had fled during the difficulties of the 1880s and 1890s. Surveyors marked the pastures where the Wambugu remained with stone cairns and designated them 'free settlements'. Although literally ringed in, the Wambugu maintained an important foothold in their former range, which would prove useful when the Germans evacuated Usambara in 1916, for the *de jure* restrictions did not completely halt the movement of animals into the forest reserve. None the less, a clear cognitive boundary between public land (*raiya*), over which they had some control, and completely restricted government and private settler land, became part of Mbugu consciousness.

In addition to demarcating forest boundaries, the German government conducted numerous silvicultural experiments, granted a 3000-acre concession in the Shume/Magamba area to Wilkins and Wiese Co. for the construction of a sawmill, and subsidized commercial forestry by building a spectacular funicular railway between the western escarpment edge and the plains 1400 metres below. Nevertheless, German foresters never managed to exploit much of the central plateau forests.

Yet even the Wambugu residing on *raiya* land outside government reserves experienced German intrusion because the grants of large tracts of Mbugu territory to settlers at Kwai and Magamba played havoc with indigenous patterns of work and residence. Settlers desperately needed farm labourers, but could not always procure them locally because many Wambugu managed to evade corvées.[65] Unlucky Wambugu herded settler animals or provided settlers with milk in lieu of labour service,[66] but resistance to forced labour induced settlers to bring in workers from other regions. For example, Illich, owner of a large estate at Kwai, hired Nyamwezi labourers whose presence allowed European settlers to force the Wambugu away from the vicinity of their estates, confiscate Mbugu cattle and destroy their homes. The evictions created Mbugu diasporas on the plains at Mombo and Mazinde, in Shambaa agricultural areas at nearby Gare and at more remote Kinko and Mgwashi, far from effective German colonial control.[67]

German plans were never fully implemented, but, because they introduced their own conceptions of land use and the proper role of indigenous peoples, their twenty-year presence in central Usambara disrupted Mbugu land-use practices, settlement patterns and their notions of negotiated access to pasture. The colonial state saw land and timber as commodities, and gave settlers and the forest service the right to determine their use. Although the German 'free settlements' policy gave tacit recognition to the rights of some Mbugu families to pasture inside the forest reserve, commercial logging and settler agriculture explicitly restricted Mbugu usufruct rights to forest resources. Indeed, the economic viability of colonial forestry hinged on its successful alteration of the forest environment to produce marketable timber. Access to the forest came to be determined not by negotiation between local communities concerned about the health of a pastoral economy, but by global market forces. The German occupation thus marked the beginning of a process of dispossession, which would continue under British rule and would eventually sap the viability of Mbugu pastoralism.

The First World War provided a hiatus of sorts for the Wambugu, for between 1914 and 1921 many Wambugu returned to their pre-colonial settlement areas in forest reserves and settler areas. At Kwai and Magamba, several tracts alienated to settlers were reoccupied by the Wambugu. The postwar British administration duly noted how the Wambugu had faced restrictions under the Germans, and the new District Officer even suggested that a large German estate near Kwai be purchased and transferred to the Wambugu as public land.[68] However, this concession did not change the legal distinction between public, private and government land.

The British forestry service showed a decided preference for continuing German policy by maintaining the former forest boundaries and restricting access to reserves. A pattern of encroachment on the reserves by cultivators and livestock-keepers came to the notice of a forester, A.S. Adamson, when he toured the central plateau forests during 1921 and 1922. The Wambugu were attempting to reclaim the formerly evacuated areas of their range, under the assumption that clearing, bounding and planting crops on land implied ownership. Indeed, Adamson's report stated that the Wambugu around Mshangai, Ndabwa, Longoi, Rangwi, and Shume had successfully cleared large tracts for cultivation.[69] Growing crops became a strategy for claiming land, although the forest service did not consider such claims as legitimate. Adamson's agitation increased when he found that most of the boundary markers had either been destroyed or rotted away, and he immediately set about recutting the boundary lines and giving notice to indigenous cultivators and herders to clear out.[70]

Certainly by 1923 the brief respite from colonial forestry restrictions had ended for the Wambugu. In fact, as had its German predecessor, the British forest service sought to replant newly cleared areas with fast growing exotics rather than granting access to cultivators. Usambara timber was needed to meet colony-wide demand for fuel (especially for the railways), building materials and high-grade exports.[71] The Forest Department was charged, for example, with ensuring that Tanganyikan timber would be cheaper than imported Burmese teak.[72] Indeed, the British colonial government considered the management of valuable natural resources to be the exclusive domain of the state. R.S. Troup, Director of the Imperial Forestry Institute from 1924 to 1939, maintained that African forest use, which threatened the entire colony's timber supplies, was unjustifiable. Gaining control of forest land was not easy, however. In 1940, Troup discussed problems of forest reservation in his classic *Colonial Forest Administration*:[73]

> Forest reservation is usually unpopular with the local inhabitants as it imposes restrictions which are seldom understood. The process of reservation is considerably easier where the land belongs to Government than where it belongs to native communities . . . The difficulty of carrying it out varies directly with the density of the population and the demand for land. In sparsely populated tracts there is usually little difficulty in reserving forest to the extent considered necessary. Here timely reservation, before pressure on the land becomes acute, can be carried out with the minimum of hardship and friction, and at a much lower cost than after rights of user have been established. Where possible, therefore, reservation should proceed in advance of any immediate pressure on the land.

The policies based upon these views not only worked against the interests of Mbugu herders, but also attacked the integrity of the forest community itself. The health of Usambara's forest depended upon a complex association of trees, herbs, creeping vines, orchids and wild flowers, which could not be regenerated artificially. Nevertheless, in place of the natural forest, colonial foresters created tree plantations where one species of tree, usually an exotic, replaced hundreds of species.[74]

Such a dramatic transformation of nature required abundant labour in the reserves, but, when the Tanganyika Forests and Lumber Company, a government-subsidized timber concession, reopened the old German site at Hornrow, it immediately faced labour shortages. To meet demand, the Forest Service introduced a 'squatter system', which kept labour in the forest but allowed no permanent cultivation.[75] Under this plan, registered 'squatters' were permitted to cultivate in clear-felled areas which had recently been replanted with seedlings or in areas scheduled for replanting. The squatters moved on to other plots three or four years after seedlings had been planted. In return for permission to cultivate, 'squatters' became labourers for the forest service and received a modest monthly wage of Shs 11/- However, even after several years of operation, the 'squatter system' had not attracted a sufficient labour force.[76]

One problem with the squatter system was that only the poorest Wambugu chose to become squatters. Because of severe restrictions placed on the number of animals which squatters could possess, Wambugu with more than a few animals generally preferred to stay on *raiya* land close to reserves, where they were sometimes licensed to practise grazing. Moreover, they could also bribe forest guards to gain access to grazing in the government forest.[77] The squatters, on the other hand, experienced considerable hardship, for they farmed areas made marginal by cold temperatures and unreliable rainfall. Hence a series of crop failures drove squatter families to depend primarily on wages to meet subsistence needs.[78]

Throughout the 1920s and 1930s, the Wambugu continued to establish illegal pastures and farms inside the forest reserves, although the government attempted to restrict encroachment:[79]

> Within recent years there has been a large increase in the number of cattle, goats etc. permitted in the Reserve, and the available grazing is quite inadequate for the number allowed with the result that grazing has taken place in many parts of the forest and damage done e.g. trampling and extension of grass areas. This state of affairs cannot be allowed to continue and grazing must only be allowed in the open grass glades in charge of herdboys under strict supervision of the forest guards. Forest guards should be instructed to report any case of cattle found grazing in the forest and the owner and his cattle turned out of the reserve. In this way cattle will be reduced or they will starve. As an instance at Kwekangaga there are over 50 cattle and at the moment there is scarcely a blade of grass left in the open glade.

Such problems led the forestry department to prohibit all grazing in Forest Reserves in 1935.[80]

The boundary dispute in Kwambugu: new concepts of land ownership and use

One particular dispute at Nzeragembei, near Mshangai, highlights both the shift in Mbugu land use and the philosophical gulf between Mbugu and colonial notions of forest value. In August 1935, a forest guard showed the Forester D.A. Fletcher a portion of the outer reserve boundary where 'there is constant trouble with the residents over the boundary line'.[81] Upon further investigation Fletcher found that the dispute dated from at least 1931, when the last survey had been carried out in poor weather conditions with a 'misaligned compass'. Fletcher's own resurvey of September 1935 determined that sixty acres of maize gardens and pasture used by Mbugu 'squatters' actually belonged to the forest reserve. Land use in this so-called 'encroachment' area was very similar to that found outside the reserve boundary. Fletcher described it as a patchwork of pasture and both primary and secondary forest. He argued that the Wambugu, as 'excellent exponents of shifting cultivation', could be accommodated on adjacent 'public lands', but his supervisor in Lushoto believed this pattern of use was inimical to the interests of forest protection.[82]

However, the Wambugu of Nzeragembei had a very different viewpoint. Shortly after Fletcher's new survey, a delegation met with the Assistant District Officer at Malibwi, the headquarters of Jumbe Kidala. The Mbugu representatives stressed that the families at Nzeragembei believed they were within their rights as long-term users of the area in remaining on the reserve. Obviously concerned about the Mbugu land claims, the District Officer requested that the Assistant Conservator of Forests allow the Wambugu to remain. He reasoned that the Wambugu 'shifting cultivators' would eventually move out of the reserve if they were prevented from making any further encroachment.[83] But true to the conservationist doctrine of the Forest Service, the Assistant Conservator of Forests at Lushoto countered with a strident letter arguing that the Wambugu had been aware of the boundary since the German regime and had been reminded about it during the survey of May 1931, when Fletcher's predecessor had inspected Nzeragembei farms and pointed out the boundary to Jumbe Kidala:[84]

> To condone continued residence until present houses and shambas shall become untenable would, in my opinion, incur unwarrantable delay, whilst it might later be taken as strengthening the native claims by virtue of their still longer establishment. . .The forester has reported ample ground available on nearby Public Lands for the absorption of these families and I would therefore ask if you can please allow my proposals to be adopted, unopposed.

The Assistant Conservator ordered that Nzeragembei residents quit the reserve by the end of March 1936 after harvesting their crops, and as a concession offered free issues of timber to be used in building new houses elsewhere.

By claiming long-term use as the basis of their right to reside at Nzeragembei, the Mbugu contingent at Malibwi made their case in legal terms which were recognized by the colonial government. However, the Forestry Service would only entertain the land claims of those Wambugu who had been living on the same site or near it for more than seven years and who had kept the area under permanent cultivation. This decision set a disturbing precedent for the Wambugu, since their evolving system of pastoralism and shifting maize cultivation did not guarantee them usufruct rights under colonial law. Clearly, only permanently settled and cultivated land could remain inviolate, while landscapes featuring a patchwork of pastures, forest and impermanent gardens simply invited further reservation by the Forestry Service.

Ironically, forestry officials failed to recognize the role of forest conservation in Mbugu culture and economy, even though they sometimes heard expressions of a conservationist ethic:[85]

> When I asked one man who had been the most forward in cutting into the Reserve why the huge stretch [of forest] toward Majiwa was left he told me that it was the chief's portion and was left untouched so that the people could have refuge during the Masai invasion! It is a far cry to the Masai invasion and I relate these stories to show with what facts they back up their claims to this part of the Reserve.

That the Wambugu still feared a Maasai invasion seems highly unlikely, particularly because during the mid–1920s they had peacefully sold livestock and honey to them at the nearby Kwekanga livestock market.[86] However, the fact that the subchief Kidala, who controlled access to public land, refused to allocate a particular forested area for cultivation suggests that preserving forest cover still seemed important. Perhaps the forest was used as a hiding place from tax collectors and census takers, but it was also a place where important rituals and honey collection could continue. The Wambugu recognized the forest's ritual importance and its role as protector and keeper of secrets.

Nevertheless, despite their conservationism, Mbugu land-use practices had changed dramatically since the turn of the century. For in the same region where Eick, Baumann, Meyer and Johannsen had noted little or no cultivation in the 1890s, the government forester saw in 1935 a patchwork of primary- and secondary-growth forests, pastures, and cultivated fields. In his opinion, it was an underutilized agricultural area:[87]

> There are altogether __ families [number crossed out] and ten houses approx. in this disputed area. The natives are practically all Wambugu who are excellent exponents of shifting cultivation; the whole of the areas outside the Reserve is a chequered patchwork of pori [bush] and 'mbuga' [pasture]

with a few shambas scattered here and there. There is therefore plenty of room in my opinion for them on Public Lands and I ask that steps may be taken to have them removed from Forest Reserve.

The survival of pastures and secondary forest suggests that Mbugu pastoralism had not yet been completely subordinated to cultivation, but that a transition to a more intensive system of land use was in progress. Indeed, colonial land management actually encouraged this trend, even though it would cause deforestation of public lands. What Eick had identified as meadow and pasture, the British regarded as an underused farming area inhabited by shifting cultivators.

Conclusion

This survey of the natural and human history of West Usambara's central plateau shows that ecological change accelerated rapidly between the mid-nineteenth century and the 1930s. Both Africans and Europeans sought to transform the region's forests for the production of food and commodities. However, their attempts at environmental control were rooted in different notions of economic well-being, and their methods differed radically in scope and intensity. When Mbugu and European visions inevitably clashed, the Wambugu responded with a strategy which combined resistance and accommodation to the colonial situation.

This type of response fitted into a centuries-old pattern of adaptation to a variety of social, political and environmental situations. Leaving an old tradition of pastoralism in the Rift Valley, the founders of Mbugu communities changed their pastoral economy to accommodate a new environment. With their farming neighbours, they established complex social and economic ties which sustained their pastoral economy in the face of periodic drought and food shortage. When these ties were broken during the regional violence of the late nineteenth century, however, the Wambugu survived by pooling their resources in the less accessible central area of their range and by cultivating the land. Rebuilding their pastoral economy and reclaiming their former territory proved impossible under colonialism because the European administration denied them access to the western side of their range at Shume. The Wambugu reacted by adopting Western notions of rights in land and, when the opportunity arose, by laying claim to as much of their former range as possible.

For the central plateau forests of West Usambara, human habitation resulted in an irrevocable loss of species diversity. Of course, Mbugu pastoralists inevitably destroyed forest species by burning tree cover on the edges of forest glades. None the less, until the early twentieth century, the Wambugu fostered a philosophy of forest conservation

Photo 6 *Severe Soil Erosion near Mlalo, Usambara.* (Christopher Conte)

commensurate with their economy and culture. Even after about two centuries of residence, German observers of the 1890s found a great deal of biologically diverse forest, which, the colonial forestry service felt, merited reservation. But, once the colonial European conception of resource control took hold within forest reserves, the species diversity of the forest was quickly and deliberately impoverished. Unable to regenerate naturally occurring tree species, the Forestry Service sanctioned the clear-felling of camphor, podo and cedar and replanted with fast-growing exotic species such as eucalyptus, cypress and pine. The conversion of the forest to a source of commodities ultimately rendered it useless for grazing because clear felling and replanting eliminated forest glades. In addition, plantation forestry also reduced the variety of plant species and contributed to soil erosion and microclimatic drying.[88] The subsequent relegation of the Wambugu to public land on the margins of their former range forced them to begin a shift away from pastoralism which, by the end of the colonial period, would leave them completely dependent on agriculture. This transformation has left central Usambara with the chronic hydrological and meteorological problems of a deforested landscape.[89]

Nature Reorganized

Notes

1. This chapter would not have been possible without the assistance of Peter Mlimahadala, who helped arrange and conduct the interviews with Mbugu elders.
2. Approximate date based on Kilindi chronologies and account of Mbugu history in Steven Feierman, *The Shambaa Kingdom: A History* (Madison, 1974), chs 3 and 4; E.C. Green, 'The Wambugu of Usambara (With Notes on Kimbugu)', *Tanzania Notes and Records* 61 (1963): 177; and Mbugu Interview Transcripts (hereafter MIT) Francis Baharia and Seuya at Magamba 12/3/23, placing Mbugu entry into Usambara a generation or two before the arrival of Mbegha, founder of the Kilindi ruling dynasty. Traditions collected by B.D. Copland in Mlalo in 1933 place migration to Usambara in the mid-seventeenth century: B.D. Copland, 'A Note on the Origin of the Mbugu with a Text', *Zeitschrift für Eingeborenen-Sprachen* 24 (1933-34): 242.
3. Jonathan Kingdon, *Island Africa: The Evolution of Africa's Rare Animals and Plants* (Princeton, 1989), p. 130; W.A. Rodgers and K.M. Homewood, 'Species Richness and Endemism in the Usambara Mountain Forests, Tanzania', *Biological Journal of the Linnean Society* 18 (1982): 197-242.
4. Rodgers and Homewood 'Species Richness', p. 205.
5. Stanley Ambrose, 'Archaeological and Linguistic Reconstructions of History in East Africa', and Derek Nurse, 'Bantu Expansion into East Africa: Linguistic Evidence', in Christopher Ehret and Merrick Posnansky, eds, *The Archaeological and Linguistic Reconstruction of African History* (Berkeley, 1984), pp. 104-58, 199-223; Robert Soper, 'Iron Age Sites in Northeastern Tanzania', *Azania* 2 (1967): 31; David Phillip Collett, 'The Spread of Early Iron Producing Communities in Eastern and Southern Africa' (Ph.D. Dissertation, Cambridge University, 1985), vol. 1; Christopher Ehret and Derek Nurse, 'The Taita Cushites', *Sprache und Geschichte in Afrika* 3 (1981): 125-68.
6. J.L. Krapf, *Travels, Researches and Missionary Labours During Eighteen Years' Residence in Eastern Africa* (London, 1860), p. 277, and J.P. Farler, 'The Usambara Country in East Africa', *Proceedings of the Royal Geographic Society* 1 (1879): 91. Farler noted the variety of flora and suggested that a botanist accompany him on his next journey through Usambara.
7. See especially Adolph Engler, 'Uber die Flora des Gebirgslandes von Usambara, auf Grund der von Herrn Carl Holst daselbst gemachten Sammlungen', *Botanische Jahrbücher für Systematik, Pflanzengeschichte und Pflanzengeographie* 17 (1893): 156-68, 'Uber die Vegetationsformationen Ost-Afrikas auf Grund einer Reise durch Usambara zum Kilimandscharo', *Zeitschrift der Gesellschaft für Erdkunde zu Berlin* 38 (1903): 254-79, and 'Uber die Gliederung der Vegetation von Usambara und der angrenzenden Gebiete', *Abhandlungen der Koniglichen Akademie der Wissenschaften* (1894): 1-86; E. Eick, 'Berichte über meine Reise ins Kwai- und Masumbailand (Usambara) vom 12. bis 16. März 1896', *Mitteilungen aus dem Deutschen Schutzgebiet* 9 (1896): 184-8.
8. For a notable exception, see O. Warburg, 'Die Kulturpflanzen Usambaras', *Mitteilungen aus den Deutschen Schutzgebieten* 7 (1894): 131-99.
9. R.E. Moreau, 'A Synecological Study of Usambara, Tanganyika Territory, with Particular Reference to Birds', *Journal of Ecology* 23 (1935): 1-43.
10. For an earlier, but briefer, description of Usambara's cedar forest and grazing regions, see A. Engler, 'Uber die Gliederung', pp. 58-9 and 68.
11. Engler, 'Uber die Gliederung', p. 68; Moreau, 'Synecological Study', p. 29.
12. Moreau, 'Synecological Study', pp. 30-2. Also noted in German sources with the repetition of the term 'Urwald' to describe high closed canopy forest.
13. On the fallacy of the concept of climax communities, see William Cronon, 'Modes of Prophecy and Production: Placing Nature in History', *Journal of American History* 76, 4 (1990): 1128.
14. See note 4 above.
15. The Wambugu refer to themselves as Vama'a and speak a language which has been

117

Christopher Conte

classified as a branch of Southern Cushitic: Derek Nurse, 'Extinct Southern Cushitic Communities in East Africa', in Marianne Bechaus-Gerst and Fritz Serzisko, eds, *Cushitic-Omotic. Papers from the International Symposium on Cushitic and Omotic Languages, Cologne, 6–9 January, 1986* (Hamburg, 1988), pp. 93–104; see also A.N. Tucker and M.A. Bryan, 'The Mbugu Anomaly', *Bulletin of the School of Oriental and African Studies* 37 (1974): 188–207 and Morris Goodman, 'The Strange Case of Mbugu', in Dell Hymes, ed., *Pidginization and Creolization of Languages* (Cambridge, 1971), pp. 243–54.

16. For linguistic and historical ties to Upare, see Green, 'The Wambugu of Usambara', p. 176 (which describes a 'colony' of Wambugu still residing in north Pare and occasional Mshitu ceremonies in south Pare); Copland, 'Origin of the Mbugu' p. 243; Tucker and Bryan, 'The Mbugu Anomaly', p. 190; MIT, Seuya and Baharia, pp. 2–3 and 11, and T. Mganga, at Kwefingo 29/3/92, p. 13.

17. MIT, Dominque Ndala at Batai (Magamba), p. 21; Salim Kadala at Mshangai 27/4/92, p. 27.

18. MIT informants recall these lineage names as follows: the Londo (Ombweni), Ombeji, Gonja, Nkandu, Ngarito Ngarire and Kwangwana. Feierman, *Shambaa Kingdom*, ch. 3, and Green, 'The Wambugu', also note lineage names in their treatments of Mbugu history.

19. MIT, Seuya and Baharia, p. 2. Informants claimed that the Shambaa had no cattle at this time and that the Wambugu purchased their rights of residence with cattle.

20. Feierman, *Shambaa Kingdom*: for Shambaa agriculture see chapter 1 and for Mbugu–Shambaa relations during the eighteenth century see chapter 3.

21. MIT, Seuya and Baharia, p. 3, Dominique Ndala, at Batai, 42/2, p. 21, T. Mganga, p. 14. These glades may have been conditioned by buffalo, bushbuck and other ungulates common in central plateau forests until the 1940s.

22. For evidence of burning forest to create pasture, see Copland, 'Origin of the Mbugu' p. 244; MIT, Paulo Mwavoa and Mlango Msasu at Kinko 3/2/2, p. 39; MIT, T. Mganga, p. 14. Mzee Mganga claims that the Mbugu never cleared forest to create pasture.

23. MIT, Mkanda Shusha, at Mshangai, 2/92, p. 25.

24. O. Baumann, 'Usambara', *Petermann's Geographische Mitteilungen* 2 (1889): 47; MIT, T. Mganga, pp. 14 and 20; Seuya and F. Baharia, 1/92, p. 11.

25. MIT, T. Mganga, p. 16. This feature might have become more common during the late nineteenth century. Place names in central Usambara also indicate the former presence of large bomas, especially around Kwai, Mshangai, and Malibwi.

26. MIT, T. Mganga, p. 15. As far as I know, no extensive list of indigenous plant names exists for Mbugu forest areas.

27. MIT, D. Ndala, p. 22. Cedar bark for roofing was used exclusively by the Wambugu. The Shambaa thatched their roofs with grass gathered from the waterlogged basins (*dau*) near their neighbourhoods. Foraging for firewood in nearby forests was commonly practised by Shambaa women.

28. MIT, Seuya and Baharia, pp. 9–10.

29. Ibid., p. 11. Maddox also notes herd culling and availability of meat through regular ritual slaughter of animals in Ugogo. Gregory Maddox, personal communication.

30. MIT, Senya and Baharia, p. 7.

31. Steven Feierman, *Peasant Intellectuals: Anthropology and History in Tanzania* (Madison, 1990), p. 49, and *Shambaa Kingdom*, p. 55; MIT, T. Mganga, p. 20.

32. MIT, T. Mganga, p. 20.

33. MIT, M. Shusha, p. 25 (my translation from Swahili). This informant used the Swahili word 'jangwa', here translated as 'desert', to describe an area without adequate grazing.

34. MIT, Paulo Mwavoa and Mlango Msasu, at Kinko 3/92, p. 39.

35. MIT, T. Mganga, p. 14; P. Mwavoa and M. Msasu, p. 39.

36. For reclusiveness see E.C. Green, 'The Wambugu of Usambara', p. 175. For

another example of interactions between pastoralists and farmers in East Africa, see John Berntsen, 'The Maasai and their Neighbors: Variables of Interaction', *African Economic History* 2 (1976): 1–11.

37. MIT, T. Mganga, pp. 17–18, and 20.

38. MIT, T. Mganga, p. 19, D. Ndala, pp. 21–22, Mkanda Shusha, p. 27. For honey production in East African forest ecology see R.H. Blackburn, 'Honey in Okiek Personality, Culture and Society' (Ph.D. Dissertation, Michigan State University, 1971), chs 1 and 2.

39. MIT, T. Mganga, pp. 17–18, M. Shusha, p. 27. Once mixed with maize, honey could be stored for months until needed; see also Blackburn, 'Honey in Okiek Personality', Ch. 3, for honey-related economic relations between Okiek (highland forest) and Maasai (plains) people.

40. For a political history of this period, see Feierman, *Shambaa Kingdom*, chapters 6, 7 and 8.

41. Ibid., p. 172.

42. MIT, Seuya and Baharia, p. 3, Salim Kadala, p. 28.

43. Called alternatively *njaa ya pato* and *njaa ya mchele* depending on the informant. For effects on the Maasai, see Richard Waller, 'Emutai: Crisis and Response in Maasailand, 1883–1902', in Douglas Johnson and David Anderson, eds, *The Ecology of Survival: Case Studies from Northeast African History* (Boulder, 1988), pp. 73–112.

44. MIT, Salim Kadala, p. 29; Dr Neubaur, 'Die Besiedelungsfähigkeit von Westusambara', *Zeitschrift für Tropische Landwirtschaft* 6 (1902): 504.

45. MIT, Paulo Mwavoa and Mlango Msasu at Kinko 3/2/2, p. 39.

46. MIT, T. Mganga, p. 16; D. Ndala, p. 21; M. Shusha, p. 27; S. Kadala, p. 28; P. Mwavoa and M. Msasu, p. 39.

47. Eick, 'Bericht über meine Reise', p. 187; Copland, 'Origin of the Mbugu', p. 244; MIT, Salim Kadala at Mshangai 27/4/92, pp. 28–9.

48. MIT, T. Mganga, p. 16, P. Mwavoa and M. Msasu, p. 38.

49. Feierman, *Shambaa Kingdom*, p. 166.

50. Patrick C. Fleuret, 'Farm and Market: A Study of Society and Agriculture in Tanzania' (Ph.D. Dissertation, University of California, Santa Barbara, 1978), ch. 1. For illustrations of fortified settlements, see Oscar Baumann, *In Deutsch Ost-Afrika während des Aufstandes* (Vienna, 1890), pp. 85, 107 and 163.

51. See Feierman, *Shambaa Kingdom*, ch. 5; Isaria Kimambo, *Penetration and Protest in Tanzania: The Impact of the World Economy on the Pare, 1860–1960* (London and Athens, Ohio, 1991), ch. 3; and Abdul Sheriff, *Slaves, Spices and Ivory in Zanzibar* (London, 1987), ch. 5.

52. E. Johanssen, 'Missionsarbeit unter den Wambugu', *Nachrichten aus der ostafrikanischen Mission* 11 (1897): 126.

53. E. Johanssen, 'Die Mission unter den Wambugu', *Nachrichten aus der ostafrikanischen Mission* 8 (1894): 25; Brüder Becker, 'Die Wambugukinder', *Nachrichten aus der ostafrikanischen Mission* 8 (1894): 98.

54. Baumann, 'Usambara', p. 49.

55. C.J.W. Pitt-Schenkel, 'Some Important Communities of Warm Temperate Rain Forest at Magamba, West Usambara, Tanganyika Territory', *Journal of Ecology* 26 (1938): 60.

56. Ibid., p. 55. Pitt-Schenkel noted that, according to Wambugu elders, a large portion of the Magamba forest around Ndabwa was destroyed by fire between 1860 and 1885.

57. Eick, 'Berichte über meine Reise ins Kwai', p. 186.

58. Hans Schabel, 'Tanganyika Forestry under German Colonial Administration, 1891–1919', *Forest and Conservation History* 34, 3 (1990): 131.

59. For a discussion of Usambara settlement see: Neubaur, 'Die Besiedelungs-fähigkeit von Westusambara', pp. 496–513; Eick, 'Berichte über meine Reise', p. 186; Johannes

Christopher Conte

Buchwald, 'Westusambara, die Vegetation und der wirtschaftliche Werth des Landes', *Zeitschrift für Tropische Landwirtschaft* 1 (1897): 82–85; F. Wohltmann,'Die Aussichten des Kaffeebaues in den Usambara-Bergen', *Zeitschrift für Tropische Landwirtschaft* 1 (1897): 612–17.

60. For a view of the clash of Western and non-Western notions of land use and ownership in North America under European colonization, see William Cronon, *Changes in the Land: Indians, Colonists and the Ecology of New England* (New York, 1983), ch. 4.

61. D.K.S. Grant, 'Forestry in Tanganyika', *Empire Forestry Journal* 3, 1 (1924): 33. Grant believed that Usambara possessed the finest natural forests in the colony.

62. Schabel, citing Economy Director Eick to Dar es Salaam Government, 14 August 1899, TNA/GR/G8/526, says that German officials believed that area to be uninhabited, but see Eick, 'Berichte über meine Reise', pp. 186–8.

63. Th. Siebenlist, *Forstwirtschaft in Deutsch-Ostafrika* (Berlin, 1914), pp. 7–10.

64. Ibid., pp. 7–8.

65. MIT, D. Ndala, p. 23, and for Salim Kadala on Mlimahadala, see footnote 44.

66. MIT, Seuya and Baharia, p. 7. Mzee Seuya recalls that his father was expelled from Magamba by a German settler. He was accused of delivering 'dirty' milk and thus had to pay a fine in livestock. As the story goes, Nyamwezi herders slaughtered one of the animals, a young bull, and then accused the Magamba Wambugu of stealing it back. With this, Mzee Seuya and his family were expelled and their homes burnt.

67. MIT, T. Mganga, p. 13; F. Baharia and Seuya, p. 6; D. Ndala, p. 23.

68. TNA/72/21/1, A.D.O. Lushoto to Chief Secretary, Dar es Salaam, Feb. 8, 1921, no page number. The British administration designated former German estates as 'ex-enemy property' and resold them.

69. LF/11/B/1/3, A.S. Adamson, Safari Report for Shume Reserve 14/8/22 to 19/8/22, p. 3.

70. LF/11/B/1/3, A.S. Adamson, forester, Shume Station, Safari Reports for 19/22/21 to 23/12/21, 14/8/22 to 19/8/22, 13/7/21 to 18/7/21. Recutting the boundary line involved finding the German markers and clearing the underbrush between them. Sisal, aloe and eucalyptus were often planted as markers of the boundaries.

71. Tanganyika Territory, *Third Annual Report of the Forest Department*, 1923 (Dar es Salaam, Government Printer, 1923), p. 2.

72. Tanganyika Territory, *Fourth Annual Report of the Forest Department* (1924), p. 4.

73. R.S. Troup, *Colonial Forest Administration* (Oxford, 1940), p. 127.

74. Personal communication from A.J. Lubango, forester, Magamba forest station, and M. Mrecha, forester, Mazumbai forest research station, Mazumbai forest reserve; Björn Lundgren, 'Soil Conditions and Nutrient Cycling Under Natural and Plantation Forests in Tanzanian Highlands', *Reports in Forest Ecology and Forest Soils* 31 (Uppsala, 1978), ch. 2.

75. The 'squatter system' was an adaptation of the system popular with the British forestry service in India, called Juming or Taungyar.

76. Tanganyika Territory, *Fourth Annual Report of the Forest Department* (1927), p. 3.

77. MIT, M. Shusha, p. 24.

78. Tanganyika Territory, *Thirteenth Annual Report of the Forest Department* (1933), p. 8.

79. Quote from LF/11/B/1/3, Assistant Conservator of Forest to D.A. Fletcher, Forester, Shume, June 19, 1930. Also, LF/11/B/1/3, Conservator of Forests to the Assistant Conservator of Forests, Magamba, 27 May 1930, p. 15.

80. Tanganyika Territory, *Fifteenth Annual Report of the Forest Department* (1935) p. 4.

81. LF/11/B/1/3, D.A. Fletcher, Forester, Shume to Assistant Conservator of Forests, Lushoto, 30/8/35, p. 64.

82. LF/11/B/1,3, Forester, Shume to Assistant Conservator of Forests, Lushoto, 16/11/35, p. 69, and Assistant Conservator of Forests, Lushoto to District Officer, Lushoto, 17 October 1935, 'Boundary Dispute at Nzeragembe', p. 70.

83. LF/11/B/1/3, District Officer R.E. Seymour to Assistant Conservator of Forests,

Lushoto, 19/10/34. The DO had reason to support Mbugu claims in light of a difficult land dispute between a British settler and Wambugu at nearby Kwai.

84. LF/11/B/1,3, Assistant Conservator of Forests to D.O. Lushoto, 25/10/35.

85. LF/11/B/1/3, Forester Fletcher to Assistant Conservator of Forests, Lushoto, 28/10/35, p. 69.

86. MIT, M. Shusha, pp. 24 and 27; T. Mganga, p. 17. Mzee Mganga notes that the livestock market at Kwekanga, the main livestock market in Usambara until the 1970s, opened in 1928 at a time when the Wambugu were beginning to sell livestock for cash. The *mnada* (livestock market) was regularly attended by Maasai livestock buyers from the plains.

87. LF/11/B/1/3, Forester Fletcher to Assistant Conservator of Forests, Lushoto, 28/9/35. p. 69.

88. A.J. Lubango, 'Report on Forestry in the Usambara Mountains', unpublished, April 1992, p. 7. Mr Lubango, Chief Forester at Magamba Forest Station, notes the drying factor, especially in areas cropped with cypress.

89. MIT, Seuya and Baharia, January 1992, p. 8; S.Kidala, p. 30; P. Mwavoa and M. Msasu, p. 39; Musa Paulo, April 1992, at Magamba, p. 37. Anecdotal evidence suggests that this process has significantly altered the region's microclimate and watershed.

Part Three

∧∧∧∧∧∧∧∧∧∧∧∧∧∧∧∧∧∧∧∧∧∧∧∧∧∧

Politics
&
Environmental Change

This section includes two chapters on culturally similar areas of eastern Tanzania. James Giblin discusses Handeni District in the nineteenth and early twentieth centuries and Pamela Maack studies the Uluguru Mountains of Morogoro during the 1940s and 1950s. Both contributions find close connections between environmental change and political life. In the late precolonial farming communities of rain-poor Handeni, argues Giblin, political relationships with patrons provided many agriculturalists with access to sources of food during periods of shortage. Because stable communities did not disperse in search of food with the onset of each episode of dearth, they were able to control vegetation and wildlife and thus maintain cattle diseases in an endemic state. The breakdown of this form of environmental control can also be attributed to political conditions, for, when the power of Handeni's patrons was broken by colonial conquest, farmers lost their security against food shortage, famines provoked the flight of the destitute, and bush, wildlife and disease-bearing insects encroached upon the remaining villagers and their cattle. In Handeni, famines were both the cause and consequence of environmental deterioration, because the depopulation which followed famine hastened the worsening of the disease environment and the loss of cattle to disease made famine more likely. In at least two respects, conditions in Handeni seem to have resembled those found in other regions. For example, in both Handeni and the Dodoma instance discussed by Gregory Maddox, famine caused depopulation and led to environmental deterioration. Moreover, in several regions, the decline of patronage made villagers much more vulnerable to famine and destitution. However, there is a contrast between Handeni, where Giblin sees a steady decline in patronage after 1890, and Dodoma, where Maddox finds that the fortunes of Dodoma patrons waxed and waned depending upon wider conditions within the colonial economy. Nevertheless, it is clear that the British policies which prevented the reconstruction of patronage networks in Handeni during the interwar period had their counterparts in the Kilombero Valley where, as Monson shows, forest conservation and restrictions on trade created difficulties in maintaining cooperation among *walongo*, the mutual aid groups, which must certainly have included patrons and their clients.

Pamela Maack picks up the story of environmental decline and the politics of patronage during the post-Second World War years, and thereby explains the famous episode of defiance against conservationist policies which shook Uluguru in 1955. The major environmental problem, which as she shows can be traced back to the precolonial period, was hillside soil erosion. The colonial solution to erosion was labour-intensive terracing. Protest erupted over the imposition of forced terracing, but, as Maack shows, it widened into an expression of dissatisfaction with local administrative chiefs as well as with colonial government.

Both chapters are concerned with the conditions which allow or frustrate the pursuit of local initiative, and thus carry forward a central theme of both Kimambo and Conte in Part II. Giblin suggests that the nineteenth-century Zanzibari commercial system allowed communities to maintain political autonomy even though they were heavily involved in trade with the coast. Hence patrons remained responsive to the considerable pressure exerted on them by clients to make regular redistribution of food and other goods acquired through trade. Under these circumstances, control of the disease environment actually improved in the last precolonial decades despite widespread slave trading. (Thus Giblin believes that in Handeni the consequences of the slave trade were not as harmful to subsistence security and environmental control as they were, according to Koponen and Kimambo in Chapters 1 and 3 elsewhere in Tanzania.) However, under colonial rule independent political authority disappeared, and appointed chiefs depended upon colonial administrators. Under these new circumstances, patrons had little opportunity to accumulate wealth, clients had little influence over government-installed chiefs, and breakdown of food redistribution and reversal of the late nineteenth-century improvements in disease control were the results. In other words, the loss of autonomy deprived local political institutions of their ability to provide the demographic stability required for control of the disease environment.

Throughout her essay, Maack turns again and again to circumstances which deprived the Luguru people of initiative. She shows that although

Luguru farmers well understood techniques of erosion control, and indeed had used them in the precolonial era, they ceased to employ labour-intensive methods because the colonial economy gave them little chance to benefit from such efforts. They had few opportunities to sell food crops profitably, and came under heavy pressure from the government to grow the burdensome and unremunerative crop of cotton. These circumstances reduced opportunities for accumulation and made patronage much more difficult to obtain.

Both of these essays also show (and here they reiterate the point made so persuasively and with originality by Steven Feierman in his books on Usambara) that concepts of proper political authority were closely related to the obligations of leaders to preserve a beneficent environment. The Washambaa, says Feierman, believed that their rulers could 'harm' or 'heal' the land. Similarly, Wagner's essay in this volume shows that the kings of Buha associated closely with the earth priests, who held expert knowledge of the environment. In Handeni, precolonial leaders derived their authority both from their ability to provide the patronage which enabled farmers to keep disease at bay, and also from their ability to mediate with the ancestors, who bestowed blessings in the form of rain, soil fertility and freedom from illness. And, in Uluguru, these concepts of proper authority remained powerfully alive in the 1950s and, just as they did in Usambara, inspired support for TANU activists. For, as Maack tells us, the protests of 1955 erupted not simply because terracing was a detested duty, but more importantly because the appointed chiefs of Uluguru were perceived as having failed in their obligations to provide patronage and protect the fragile mountain environment. Indeed, Maack argues that in imposing the onerous task of terracing, they only worsened soil degradation, and did nothing to bring the promise of prosperity which would have made the investment of labour in terracing seem worthwhile.

Thus the studies of Giblin and Maack, like Feierman's histories of Usambara, reveal strong continuity in political culture across eastern Tanzania. In precolonial society, this culture maintained concepts of chiefly and patronal obligation, which provided the basis of environmental control. In the colonial era, this same political culture induced men and women who worried about the worsening of environmental conditions to join in nationalist opposition to colonial rule. As the essays by Wagner and Spear in this volume demonstrate, however, neither continuity of political culture spanning the precolonial and colonial periods nor a conservationist dimension to nationalist politics was limited to eastern Tanzania.

Five

The Precolonial Politics of Disease Control

In the Lowlands
of Northeastern Tanzania

JAMES L. GIBLIN

One day in 1983, Nyangasi Mohamedi Munga, an elderly resident of Kilwa Village in the northeastern Tanzanian district of Handeni, found himself drawn into discussion with a visiting researcher about local history and the problems of farming. A number of his neighbours gathered at his homestead to hear what he had to say, because they respected Munga for his knowledge of the past and for his diligence and expertise as a farmer. Everyone could see the results of his and his wives' farming abilities, for their intensively cultivated plots were in full view of the homestead. The talk quickly turned, as discussions in Handeni District often seemed to do during the early 1980s, to what Munga and others regarded as the signs of increasing environmental adversity. They spoke of diminished rains, soils grown tired, widespread tsetse flies, and the bush pigs, monkeys and birds that ravaged their crops. His neighbours listened attentively as Munga explained why he thought conditions had grown worse, and why farmers had lost control over the forces of nature. He said that, in the past, farmers had cultivated contiguous plots, where they coordinated planting and harvesting to make guarding crops from birds and bush pigs easier.[1] They did this rather than work independently, said Munga, because they were under the authority of settlement heads:

> The head person could compel others to do things. Now a person was not able to go off and cultivate by himself some place. He might be killed by people from there. That's why people cultivated together. It was because of the threat of war and violence, because at that time there was no central government. The only government was of the head person who rules others.

He was the ruler who protected people. That's why people cultivated together, not because they wanted to.

The last point took Munga to the heart of his argument: farmers obtained the benefits of a healthy, productive environment only when they submitted to the authority of patrons who controlled entire neighbourhoods and coordinated the labour of their dependants. Group cohesion was lost, however, in the colonial period: 'When colonial government was introduced, people dispersed . . . in other words, that form of government destroyed the old forms of unity.'

In suggesting that a particular kind of political authority was the basis of precolonial environmental control, Nyangasi Mohamedi Munga offered an insight that is too rarely found in studies of African environmental change, for even some of the finest such treatments neglect the politics of environmental control.[2] Indeed, they often appear to subscribe to the view that precolonial political relations were less important than kinship and affinity, even if they do not state explicitly, as does one of the more recent studies of environmental history in East Africa, that:[3]

> no power (the State) existed above [precolonial Ugandan producers] and estranged itself against the interest of the whole society. The clan community that existed was for the most part a result of communal cooperation and management of the resources.

This chapter will explore the historical circumstances which would lead Nyangasi Mohamedi Munga to conclude that politics and political authority were the foundation of precolonial environmental control. For even in a 'stateless' region such as Handeni District, control of the disease environment was affected by politics, although they were the small-scale politics of largely autonomous neighbourhoods. Political relations between patrons and clients allowed the growth of stable farming communities, which effectively managed vegetation and wildlife and thereby controlled insect-borne bovine diseases. Because many late precolonial farmers obtained food reserves by participating in the politics of patronage, they did not leave the region in search of food during famines, but instead remained on their farms, where they continued to manage vegetation and keep disease-bearing insects at bay. Hence this chapter begins by describing the role of patronage in precolonial cattle-keeping and agricultural production in nineteenth-century Uzigua, the region populated predominantly by Zigua-speaking farmers, which includes present-day Handeni District. Between 1840 and 1890, the most powerful patrons in Uzigua were chiefs, who integrated the region into Zanzibar's commercial empire by trading ivory and slaves for a variety of imports, including cloth and firearms.

The chapter will close by contrasting late precolonial circumstances in Handeni with the colonial period. Colonial rule undermined patronage by disrupting precolonial patterns of trade, introducing taxation and using military force to weaken the powerful chiefs and other patrons. Many residents of early colonial Handeni ceased to be the clients of patrons, who were obliged to provide famine relief, and instead came to rely on casual labour, which provided no guarantee of long-term access to food reserves. In periods of early colonial food shortages, therefore, many villagers had to abandon their farms to seek food in other regions. Their departure interrupted management of vegetation and wildlife and led to outbreaks of cattle diseases in the wake of each period of acute food shortage. Thus, just as Nyangasi Mohamedi Munga had asserted, political change during the colonial period rule caused environmental deterioration.

The politics of patronage in an idiom of kinship

Neither written sources nor oral testimony from Handeni provides information on social relations and environmental conditions in Uzigua before the early nineteenth century. However, after 1840 it is possible to trace the development of patterns of patronage which would permit demographic stability and control of insect-borne diseases despite frequent droughts and crop failures in Uzigua. Both oral traditions and written accounts show that, during the middle decades of the nineteenth century, settlement leaders throughout Uzigua entered the networks of long-distance trade which were expanding from towns of the *Mrima* coast such as Pangani, Sadani and Bagamoyo. From the merchants of these towns, who were closely connected with the major merchant houses of Zanzibar, the entrepreneurial leaders of Uzigua received cloth, firearms, grain and other imports, as well as credit which they used to replenish their supplies of imported goods. They paid for these goods by supplying slaves, ivory, grain and livestock to the coastal merchants.

Their participation in trade with the coast, together with their success in extracting tolls from the caravans which crossed Uzigua as they approached the *Mrima* ports, bringing slaves and ivory from western Tanzania, enriched the entrepreneurial chiefs and enabled them to create extensive patronage networks. The most powerful of these chiefs – men such as Mhelamwana of Manga and Sonyo of Magamba, who are still well remembered throughout Handeni – used their access to imports and credit to place less fortunate settlements in a state of dependence.[4] At the same time that they were creating a hierarchy of clientage between themselves and lesser patrons, who remained the heads of dependent settlements, the powerful chiefs were also gathering around them their own followers, who accepted various forms of dependence and servility. The slaves, clients, spouses and junior kin of the great chiefs cleared and farmed large areas around their leaders' settlements. In this way they created densely populated, intensively cultivated zones which, because they were free of disease-bearing tsetse flies and ticks which prevailed elsewhere in Uzigua's *miombo* woodland, provided healthy environments for livestock. Thus, despite the conditions of insecurity and violence created by the expanding trade in slaves, the rise of the entrepreneurial chiefs of Uzigua and their creation of patronage networks permitted an improvement of environmental control, diversified sources of food and enhanced the ability of their communities to cope with drought-induced crop failure.

Yet, in spite of the success of the trading chiefs, their entrepreneurship would not have guaranteed widespread access to famine reserves and made farming communities more stable had clients not possessed the political means to make claims upon the resources of their patrons. However, clients were able to use notions of reciprocal obligation, kinship and common genealogical origins in order to assert rights to the assistance of chiefs and lesser patrons. Patrons and clients articulated concepts of reciprocal rights and duties in an idiom of kinship, an idiom which not only allowed patrons to claim the labour required to accumulate through agricultural production, but also provided clients with ways of asserting that their work for patrons must be compensated with long-term guarantees of assistance. Thus the political disputes articulated within this idiom constitute the inner history of late nineteenth-century environmental control.

Among the primary sources of information about precolonial political conflict are traditions from Handeni which describe the original settlement of small territories called *si* in the Zigua language and *nchi* in Swahili. These stories show that political conflicts involved ambitious individuals who tried to overcome the restraint of reciprocal obligations, and dependants who tried to check ambition by constraining adherence to the norms of reciprocity.

The first settlers of *si*, who in the stories from Handeni are generally described as farmers searching for land, usually include a male leader and several women who are considered to be the founders of matrilineages.[5] These settlers are regarded as honoured ancestors by those who inherit the name of their *si* (individuals take the matrilineal *si* names, or *kolwa*,[6] of both parents). The *si* name bearers believe that they belong to a large group, sometimes referred to as '*lukolo*' in Zigua and '*ukoo*' in Swahili, which, they assume, comprises the matrilineages that descend from the female settlers.

The stories of *si* settlement, which usually remain silent about the social origins of *si* founders, portray the settlers as being free to establish autonomous communities because they are not involved in relationships that would have limited their independence. The stories rarely mention any prior membership in a *si* community[7] and often depict the founders as migrants from obscure, distant places such as the Lake Malawi region or Uhehe in southern Tanzania.[8] Traditions which recount short movements within Handeni or between Handeni and adjacent areas are more common, but here again *si* founders' origins are not specified.

One of the traditions involving short-distance migrations tells of newcomers from Ukaguru, a region southwest of Handeni, who moved to Kwa Dundwa in western Handeni District.[9] The first part of the story describes the lone wanderings of the original female settler and makes it clear that she was unrestricted by obligations that would have impinged upon the independence of her *si*.[10] As the story continues, however, it describes a kind of struggle for autonomous control of dependants, which recurs frequently in traditions of the *si* founders. The Kwa Dundwa *si*, relates the tradition, was established by Feda, a native of the mountains overlooking Kwa Dundwa Valley, who, while living temporarily in Ukaguru, married Chume, the wandering woman introduced at the beginning of the account. After assembling a group of dependants in Ukaguru, he and Chume moved to Kwa Dundwa and used their support to prevail over his brother in a contest for the valley. Thus the plots of this and other *si* traditions, which frequently recount the division of *si* and subsequent foundation of new *si*, intimate not only that rivalries frequently caused the breakup and formation of groups, but also that conflicts over scarce riverine and valley-bottom lands were common. Clearly, one purpose of the *si* traditions was to lay claims to land.

Although the traditions of *si* founders depict conflict and tensions, their descriptions of the origin of what might be thought of as clans composed of several matrilineages also explain a fundamental, unifying form of identity. Thus they use an idiom of kinship to convey a complex set of ideas about the obligations and rights, as well as the conflicts, which grow out of shared identity. Nevertheless, the identities associated with a particular *si* were not formed merely by kinship, but were moulded by political history. Certainly the precolonial bearers of a *si* name were not a corporate descent group. Indeed, few people actually live in the neighbourhoods where they believe their *si* ancestors settled, for, just as is the case now, most nineteenth-century Handeni villagers were tied to their *si* primarily by their names and some sketchy, perhaps apocryphal information about *si* locations.[11] The element of uncertainty, however, is what allowed *si* identities to play a part in consolidating loyalties grounded not in kinship, but in politics. Because everyone had an inherited relationship with at least two *si*, and because knowledge of *si* locations, relations among *si* and membership in *si* groups was imprecise, the possibilities for rediscovering forgotten genealogical relationships were endless. Hence neighbours who were connected primarily by proximity and subordination to a patron might well discover that they also shared with their leader descent from common *si* founders, and might therefore find reason to participate together in the rituals which he or she conducted to honour ancestors. *Si* identities were much less important, however, than political relationships, as the practice of naming settlements after incumbent village leaders, rather than according to *si* designations, indicates. Thus an individual's mental map of Handeni reflected knowledge of political relations rather than descent.[12] The primacy of politics is acknowledged, moreover, even by historical accounts which, in the idiom of kinship, portray a traditional precolonial society composed of discrete descent groups, for they must reconcile this image with their knowledge of political change. One such account, which was written in 1968 by Ernest L. Mkomwa and Godfrey Nkwileh, explains the origin of descent group leadership by invoking the political circumstances created by the slave trade with the *Mrima* ports.[13] Mkomwa and Nkwileh contend that in this period *si* groups vested authority in leaders (*wegazi*, sing. *mwigazi*) who knew the history of relations between *si*, so that they would not inadvertently marry off their women to old, vengeful enemies who would sell the women into slavery. Thus Mkomwa and Nkwileh situate their image of a kinship-based society in political history by explaining an institution associated with descent groups as a response to changing political conditions. Nevertheless, while political authority and loyalties held together communities, *si* identities played an important role in sanctioning political leadership and facilitating the assimilation of newcomers. Villagers gave captives and their children *si* names,[14] and altered *si* identities and associated traditions to confirm genealogical links with newcomers or to enhance a leader's legitimacy by showing that he descended from *si* founders. *Si* traditions continued to be modified for political purposes in the colonial period.[15]

One instance of political contest over *si* identity occurred in the 1880s in the central Handeni neighbourhood of Magamba. After the death in 1884 of Mani, the founder of a late precolonial chiefdom, the right of his son Sonyo to succeed him was challenged by dissidents who were united by the belief that they were descended from the original settlers of a *si* called Kwa Luguru. They argued that Mani had usurped control of Magamba from them, and went so far as to repudiate Mani by refusing to permit his burial (a form of posthumous condemnation also imposed upon other slave-trading chiefs of the period[16]) in what they considered to be the Kwa Luguru *si*. Thus they forced Sonyo to inter Mani a considerable distance outside Magamba. Sonyo responded to this challenge by forming a new *si* community in order to destroy the unity of the Kwa Luguru group. He began performing ancestor propitiation at his father's burial place,[17] knowing that, because people think of their own *si* as the place where they prefer to hold such ceremonies and interact with fellow *si* group members, participation by his subjects would hasten their acceptance of the *si* identity which Sonyo claimed through descent from Mani. Although most of his subjects presumably had no relationship with the *si* of Sonyo's father, traditions could be revised to accommodate newly discovered links with its founders.

Although a change in *si* identities helped Sonyo to build a new form of unity among his subjects, both his power and the new community identity at Magamba were rooted in political realities. Villagers accepted Sonyo's rule not merely because they respected him as a leader of ancestor veneration, but also because they understood the benefits of his patronage and the costs of exclusion from his protection. He and his father had accumulated considerable wealth over several decades of trading ivory and slaves to merchants of the *Mrima*, and had made Magamba an important market, a centre of cattle keeping and the largest village in central Handeni.[18] They were well equipped, therefore, to provide various forms of patronage, including food during seasonal shortages as well as protection from slave raiders. By the same token, exclusion from Sonyo's sphere of patronage during a period of intense slave dealing meant not only loss of access to his subsistence reserves, but also the likelihood of enslavement. These circumstances left most villagers with little alternative but to accept Sonyo's domination, and indeed gave them considerable incentive to accept his modification of *si* group identities, for as members of Sonyo's *si* group their claims to his assistance would carry great weight. The example of Magamba under Sonyo demonstrates that both rulers and their opponents modified *si* identities and traditions to cement loyalties, justify exclusion, legitimate power, challenge authority and assert claims to patronage. None the less, although the identities and associated traditions were cast in the idiom of kinship, villagers united or divided over issues and conflicts that arose from the politics of patronage.

The power and influence of patrons was so pervasive that men and women often had to share authority over their own children and kin with their patrons. Indeed, even within the confines of the household there were various cross-cutting and overlapping forms of control, for most individuals were subject to the authority of both matrilineal and patrilineal kin as well as of patrons and political leaders. For this reason, residential groups were not necessarily the focus of the most enduring loyalties and affections, because their members were tied as firmly to outside social networks as to co-residents. The diversity of overlapping relationships is reflected in many aspects of life, including the frequent movements by young men between the homes of their fathers and mother's brothers; the practice of all the women from a settlement or residential quarter gathering together to cook for their men, who similarly ate in large groups; and the preference of many wives for maintaining their own fields, granaries and homesteads, where they would live with their children apart from their husbands.[19] Indeed, the need to balance and resolve conflicting claims on individuals is a central theme in the account of precolonial society composed by Mkomwa and Nkwileh.

Patronal authority was probably the most powerful impingement on autonomous control of dependants, as an episode at a Catholic mission of the Spiritan Order demonstrated in 1883. A man approached the missionaries and pledged to become 'something like a vassal' if they would save his wife and children, who had been sold into captivity by their kin. They were about to be taken to the coast by caravan when the missionaries, acting as the man's patrons, reclaimed them by asserting their right to override the authority of his wife's and children's kin. This instance shows not only that the power of patrons took precedence over kinship in determining control of dependants, but also that overlapping claims concerning dependants could cost a household head his independence. The man had no recourse but to surrender his autonomy because his affines and the matrilineal kin of his children threatened to take away his family.[20] While not all household heads fell into such peril, few of them gained independence from interfering affines and siblings, and fewer still stood free of obligations to patrons.

Many villagers depended upon patrons for staple foods, because the output of their own farms could not satisfy their needs. Competition for scarce prime agricultural land near streams and in valleys probably prevented weaker villagers from attaining self-sufficiency. They would have had difficulty in gaining rights to the relatively few moist plots that reliably produced a second annual harvest during the short rains of December, and to the fallow whose bush and thicket were easier to clear than mature tree cover. Such competition contributed to significant inequalities in landholding. Records concerning land obtained by the Germans in the early years of colonial rule at several locations in Handeni District show that, although the average size of thirty-seven expropriated farms was 2.13 hectares, 57 per cent of them were smaller than 1 hectare, while 5 per cent of them were larger than 5.5 hectares. One-quarter of the dispossessed farmers held 60 per cent of the land for which the Germans paid compensation, while another one-quarter of them held only 8.5 per cent of the land. The size of expropriated holdings varied considerably, moreover, ranging between 0.75 and 6.25 hectares at Kwediboma in western Handeni District, for example.[21] It is not implausible to assume, in fact, that the majority of farmers worked less than 1 hectare, for this has also been true in Handeni during recent decades.[22] Thus the majority of farms could have supported only the smallest domestic groups, for farmers working less than 1 hectare would have had to achieve yields of sorghum and maize considerably higher than modern maize yields in order to produce the 900 kg consumed annually by three adults. (In modern Handeni, maize yields are about 766 kg per hectare.[23]) Of course, a wide variety of alternative foods were available, including wild vegetables and roots gathered by women, meat brought home by hunters, milk and various foodstuffs obtained in trade, but the most common source of subsistence reserves was patronage.

Thus clients commonly performed seasonal agricultural labour for their patrons. During hoeing seasons, when food stocks were low and the need for labour was greatest, village leaders and other affluent patrons engaged workers, whom they compensated with grain and root crops. They also distributed food during seasonal shortages, with the understanding that it would be repaid at the next harvest, and thereby ensured, wrote a Spiritan missionary in the 1880s, that no one would suffer excessively from food shortages.[24] Their dependants replenished grain reserves by performing labour service, making tributary contributions and repaying part of their own harvests to creditors. Throughout the region, missionaries in the 1880s saw that chiefs and patrons organized obligatory work parties, and observed that leaders distributed provisions in return for their subjects' labour and tribute. Food was most abundant, they found, in the villages of major chiefs.[25]

The French Catholic missionaries of the Spiritan Order, who built their first permanent station in Uzigua in 1878, engaged in the politics of patronage themselves. Always short of labour for farming, construction and other activities, the missionaries adopted arrangements which prevailed in neighbouring communities, and in effect became patrons. The missionaries put large fields under crops by entering into a variety of relationships with dependants in order to obtain labour. Like their fellow patrons in neighbouring villages, they organized day-long work parties at which they provided food and drink for groups from nearby settlements who performed field work, and they also employed neighbours who sought temporary employment on an individual basis to earn foodstuffs, cloth and currency. Indeed, the readiness of many villagers to work for hire indicates that agricultural labour outside the household was a common activity.

For some villagers, reliance on Spiritan patrons began during the famine of 1884–86, when they became indebted to the missionaries and repaid their debts by doing field work and paying part of their own harvests to the missionaries.[26] As the missionary communities became firmly established in the 1880s and 1890s, labour service for the missionaries and redistribution from the Spiritan granaries acquired a seasonal rhythm. [Clients worked in the mission fields during the hoeing and harvesting seasons, labouring particularly in the pre-harvest months of January, February and March for grain to carry them until the next harvest. At harvest-time, they sold their own maize and sorghum to the Spiritans for cloth.] '[They] have rendered us valuable service in the cultivation of our fields and vegetable gardens,' related a missionary in 1888, 'as well as in a great number of other necessary tasks . . . They also bring the products of the fields and their poultry which they sell to us at low prices. Likewise they come looking for work at the mission, in order to get something to wear.'[28] As the number of farmers who depended upon the missionaries increased during the 1890s, some of those who relied upon the mission for food and imports became permanently indebted to the Spiritans. In 1893, more than 500 farmers (including at least 200 women) were engaged in construction projects at the Spiritans' Mhonda mission, while at least 100 village heads sent subjects to do agricultural labour under the Spiritans. These patterns of employment and redistribution continued at Mhonda and other Spiritan missions throughout the German colonial period.[29]

Through these same relations of patronage which would serve as a model for the Spiritan missionaries, political leaders throughout Uzigua accumulated food reserves and became the principal sources of subsistence during pre-harvest scarcity in the last precolonial decades. During that period of extensive enslavement and slave trading, their ability to accumulate food stocks created both power and servility. 'If someone had food,' stated one Handeni farmer in the early 1980s, 'he would be the chief and would rule everyone. Many people were kept in servility by [the chiefs'] control of food. So when someone achieved mastery of farming ['*ushujaa wa jembe*'], his hoe brought him slaves.'[30]

Precolonial patronage, bovine disease control and security from famine

Just as Nyangasi Mohamedi Munga believed, the ability of patrons to coordinate field labour was the key to a productive agronomic system which provided a degree of security from famine. Moreover, because they were successful in developing well-populated, healthy villages surrounded by intensive cultivation and an outer ring of peripheral parklands whose vegetation was carefully tended, the patrons were able to accumulate a resource which played a crucial role in networks of patronage: livestock. Indeed, one of the outstanding achievements of the late precolonial chiefs and lesser patrons is that they created conditions which allowed the keeping of relatively large numbers of cattle despite the prevalence of disease-bearing ticks and tsetse flies in Uzigua's *miombo* woodland.

By using fire and bush clearing to create large areas of open parkland around their settlements and grazing grounds, farmers destroyed the bush, dense tree cover and long grasses which provide favourable habitats for tsetse flies, ticks and wild animals. Thus, by keeping most tsetse and ticks away from villages and pastures, they prevented them from frequently infecting domesticated livestock with the blood parasites that cause lethal forms of bovine trypanosomiasis and theileriosis (East Coast fever) when they are carried from antelope, buffalo and other wildlife. Although they neither eradicated disease-bearing tsetse and ticks nor prevented the transmission of these infections entirely, their control of vegetation limited contacts between disease-bearing insects and livestock to a level which permitted only intermittent trypanosomal and theilerial infection. Such mild and infrequent infections enabled cattle, goats and sheep to build immunological resistance. Thus vegetation management prevented deadly epizootics because resistant cattle were able to tolerate the relatively mild infections to which they were exposed.[31] Because drought and crop failures occurred commonly in Handeni, however, the achievement of control over bovine disease required that the majority of farmers have access to food reserves during seasons of shortage if they were to manage vegetation without interruption. Hence bovine disease control depended upon the ability of clients to make claims on patrons for the food stocks which would permit them to continue cultivating, clearing the land and burning away bush and grasses in spite of drought.

Control of the disease environment and the politics of patronage were inextricably connected, for, while accumulation and redistribution required an environment in which patrons could increase their wealth in cattle, an epizootic-free environment could be maintained only so long as patrons respected the norms which required them to provide for dependants. By redistributing food, patrons ensured that their dependants would obtain subsistence during droughts and hungry seasons, and would not be forced to migrate in search of provisions. Instead, they would be able to remain on their farms and continue the work of cultivation, clearing and burning that was vital to the maintenance of a favourable bovine disease environment. Because livestock, unlike perishable grain, could be kept for long periods in anticipation of scarcity, wealthy stock owners, who might have 100 to 200 cattle, attracted clients for whom a relationship with a cattle-holding patron was insurance against destitution. Thus as clients the majority of villagers who held at most a few animals gained some of the benefits of stock ownership, including milk from stock-owning patrons and manure from the animals which they penned on their farms.[32] 'Some people had no cattle,' explained one Handeni farmer, 'that's why livestock owners distributed cattle to be tended by others.'[33] This arrangement not only permitted clients to fertilize tobacco plots and other fields, but also gave them a chance to build small herds, since the norm was that every third calf born in the care of the borrower should become his or her property.[34] Because distribution of livestock in this manner often cemented relations between patrons and clients who lived

James L. Giblin

Photo 7 *The Late Amos Kazubi, a Skilled Farmer, at Kwediboma Village in Handeni District in 1983.* (James Giblin)

Photo 8 *Typical Cultivation in Handeni District: a complex crop association beneath a mountain watershed. Intercropped maize, cassava, sugar cane, beans, bananas, avocados and oranges in the field of the late Amos Kazubi (see Photo 7) beneath the rock face of Mount Njwila at Kwediboma.* (James Giblin)

in different micro-environments, clients also gained greater security against localized droughts and crop failures.

Both the effectiveness of patronage in providing subsistence to carry Handeni's farmers through periodic droughts and crops failures and the cost of submission to patronal authority are illustrated by the consequences of the severe famine of 1884–6. Early colonial Uzigua could remember no episode in at least fifty years preceding 1884–6 to compare with the famine, which became known as '*lugala*', or 'star', because it coincided with the appearance of a comet.[35] *Lugala* was a tragedy because, for the destitute, the cost of survival was servility or dependence upon patrons and chiefs. Yet it is important nevertheless to distinguish between its tragic social impact and its demographic and environmental consequences, for, in comparison with famines of the colonial period, the effects of *lugala* were limited. Whereas famines in the colonial period were followed by devastating cattle diseases because cultivation and vegetation management were interrupted when the hungry left their homes in large numbers, during 1884–6 most farmers obtained food reserves close to home and continued farming, clearing land and burning off bush.

The crop failures which caused the *lugala* famine began during a drought that lasted from late 1883 through the long-rains season of March and April 1884. Yet, despite widespread shortages, relatively little population movement occurred. Certainly there is no evidence of anything like the massive flight that took place during colonial famines. In many places, including Mandera, where the Spiritans had established a mission, cultivators generally stayed in their homes throughout the famine and relied on Zigua-speaking and missionary patrons, who, like other chiefs and patrons throughout the region, were prepared to claim new dependants because they had accumulated currency, food reserves and livestock through trade with the *Mrima* merchants during the 1870s and 1880s.[36] Relations with chiefs and other patrons determined the fate of many farmers, for, while the clients, kin and affines in the chiefs' closer circles of dependants received stored and imported foods, politically peripheral communities not only had no claim on the resources of chiefs, but might well find their grain reserves drained away as tribute. This was in fact the situation in much of the Nguu Mountains in western Handeni, where leaders such as the powerful chief Mtiga, having obtained grain from tributary farmers, distributed some of it to their core constituencies and sold the rest to caravans, merchant camps and the lowland residents who sought food in Nguu during the famine. Consequently, although food was available in the chiefs' settlements, hunger became so widespread in outlying areas that, even after an early harvest in May 1884 increased maize supplies, reduced prices by 60 per cent and attracted food purchasers from the lowlands, many highland farmers still lacked staples.[37]

Some tribute-paying highlanders survived *lugala* by leaving their homes for the chiefs' core territories. Their departure emptied villages in politically peripheral areas such as the portions of northern Nguu that were:[38]

> to a great extent depopulated by a famine two years ago, which drove away the people into Uzeguha [lowlands], and they have not yet returned. Where there used to be villages and shambas [cultivated plots] there is now nothing but jungle.

The refugees from northern Nguu moved no more than fifteen or twenty miles eastward, however, where they entered the domain of the powerful lowland chiefs who lived at Mbwego. Among the attractive places in which they settled was the valley beneath Kilindi Mountain that cheered the German visitor Franz Stuhlmann in 1888:[39]

> The enchantingly fertile valley has a nearly flat bottom with dark soils, through which flows the small Msiri creek . . . Numerous villages have been established at slight elevations in the valley and on the surrounding mountain slopes. From a single vantage point one can see six villages, which is a rare occurrence in Africa . . . The people appear to be fairly prosperous, for I saw very good cattle and many firearms. Often people from the coast stop here to buy food, tobacco, etc.

The newcomers, drawn to these areas by trading opportunities and a healthy cattle environment as well as by patronage, made this and other valleys east of Nguu some of the most densely settled localities in Handeni after *lugala*.[40]

The price of refuge in these favoured environments, however, was the status of client, pawn or slave. For this reason, residents of modern Handeni associate *lugala*, much more than subsequent famines of the early colonial period, with loss of autonomy by the powerless and predatory behaviour by the powerful:[41]

> If you went travelling on the road with your wife and your possessions you could be robbed of everything. . .If you were weak you would be robbed . . . that's the way the *lugala* famine was . . . The locust famine [of 1894–1896] did not cause this same type of chaos . . . the number of slaves increased [during 1884–86].

Yet, while *lugala* not only meant upheaval in personal fortunes but also environmental reversals in the areas which lost farmers, management of vegetation continued in many places and probably improved in the neighbourhoods where the chiefs attracted refugees, for the newcomers expanded the cleared, cultivated and tsetse- and tick-free areas where much of the region's livestock lived. Indeed, the movement of many farmers into the chiefdoms during *lugala* confirms Nyangasi Mohamedi Munga's belief that submission to political authority – the concession made by the newcomers to populous, more secure settlements – was the foundation of late precolonial environmental control.

Yet for all the powers of patrons, the constraints placed upon them by norms of reciprocal obligation remained a crucial element in the maintenance of a favourable disease environment, for, although disease control depended upon accumulation by patrons, it also required that the pursuit of individual advantage be tempered by acceptance of the obligation to redistribute wealth. As one modern Handeni resident put it, not only the rich, but also the poor, who 'push' ['*wanawasukumiza*'] their affluent neighbours to distribute resources, were responsible for prosperity.[42] Communities maintained control of bovine trypanosomiasis and theileriosis when most villagers were able to obtain subsistence reserves from patrons close to home rather than having to migrate in search of food. Ensuring access to reserves, however, was a political struggle conducted by dependants, who, in the idiom of kinship, pressed patrons to honour their claims to assistance.

The transformation of political and environmental conditions under colonial rule[43]

Between 1840 and 1890, the primary external influence in Handeni was Zanzibari merchant capital, which, through its mercantile agents in *Mrima* ports, extended credit and expanded long-distance trade in ivory, slaves, livestock and other goods. In the Zanzibari mercantile system, the patrons of Uzigua flourished. Indeed, coastal merchants encouraged their expansion of patronage networks, because the patrons provided several essential services for long-distance traders. Not only did they furnish ivory, slaves and livestock for sale to coastal merchants, they also made foods available for purchase to passing caravans and to the seasonal trading camps which were established by agents of the *Mrima* merchants in Handeni. In addition, the chiefs of Handeni who dealt with coastal merchants guaranteed the safety of their agents. Thus the expansion of mercantile influence from the *Mrima* allowed the incorporation of increasing numbers of clients into the patronage networks of the major chiefs, although of course it also exposed individuals who lacked the protection to powerful patrons to increased likelihood of enslavement.

In the early 1890s, however, a very different form of external inflence became predominant in Handeni, for at this time German colonialism began to establish control over the area. German (and, after 1916, British) colonial rule transformed both political authority and environmental conditions. It introduced a form of authority which, unlike precolonial mercantilism, had no interest in maintaining patronage. Moreover, once colonial administrators became aware that Handeni would have little importance in the colonial economy, they showed equally little interest in its environment. Hence colonial conquest replaced a form of foreign influence which had allowed the expansion of patronage and improvement of environmental control with a regime which, by depriving many cultivators of patronage, prevented them from maintaining control over the bovine disease environment.

Three factors were chiefly responsible for the decline of patronage during the first two decades of colonial rule: the disruption of pre-colonial commercial and credit networks, the imposition of colonial taxation and the use of military force to break independent political authority. The swift decline of trade with the *Mrima* ports during the 1890s was caused partly by the fact that Zanzibar and its Tanganyikan hinterland fell under different colonial regimes, partly by the European efforts to suppress slave trading and partly by railway construction and the increasing importance of Dar es Salaam as an entrepôt. These circumstances deprived Handeni's chiefs of credit and opportunities for profit. Their decline was hastened, moreover, by punitive raids and expropriations conducted frequently by the German military throughout the 1890s. Finally, the chiefs were overwhelmed by the conjunction of a terrible famine and the institution of colonial taxation from 1898 to 1900. Many patrons could neither provide famine relief for clients nor pay taxes for them, as they were expected to do by their dependants. Under these conditions, patrons often decided to sever their long-standing ties with clients. The Spiritan missionaries were among the patrons who were placed in straitened circumstances, and, although they did not entirely cease to extend patronage, like other patrons they too chose to grant access to their patronage much more selectively.

Colonial policies prevented the reconstruction of patronage networks throughout the entire pre-Second World War period. By choosing to install outsiders as village-level office holders, or Akidas, the Germans deprived local leaders of one avenue through which they might have re-established themselves. The British abolished the system of Akidas in the 1920s, but the men who were recognized as chiefs under indirect rule were entirely dependent on the British for their stipends, and thus were unresponsive to villagers who appealed for their patronage. A more important factor in preventing the chiefs of the indirect rule period from providing patronage, however, was that the government deprived them of all opportunities to accumulate through market production and trade. Indeed, British administrators frustrated all entrepreneurial initiatives in Handeni by Indians as well as Africans during the 1920s and 1930s.

The disappearance of patronage in Handeni would have a profound impact upon environmental conditions. A series of major famines afflicted Handeni between 1896 and the early 1940s. Famine conditions were certainly exacerbated by the decline of patronage, although they were caused by several other factors as well, including monetary taxation, which forced food sales, as well as locust plagues and perhaps a worsening of East African climatic conditions, which made droughts more frequent. Following each of the major famines, which occurred in 1894–6, 1898–1900, 1907–8, 1910, 1916–18, 1925 and 1932–5, terrible epizootics of bovine trypanosomiasis and theileriosis (East Coast fever) broke out. Neither German nor British colonial authorities acted to halt the deterioration of the bovine disease environment. Throughout the first four decades of the twentieth century, tsetse-fly belts steadily widened as tsetse spread into formerly cultivated areas from the waterless, uninhabited wooded zones (John Ford's so-called *Grenzwildnis*) to which they had been confined in the late precolonial period (Map 4). In addition, areas of heavy tick infestation became larger, wildlife populations increased, and occupied larger areas of Handeni District, livestock mortality increased, and the cattle population of the district diminished. Not until the late 1930s did colonial officials study the Handeni situation carefully, and they did so at that time only because dramatic expansion of tsetse infestation following the 1932–5 famine raised administrative fears that the thousands of migrant labourers from southern Tanzania who walked through Handeni *en route* to the sisal plantations of the Pangani Valley would be exposed to human trypanosomiasis.

British epidemiological studies conducted in the wake of the 1932–5 famine demonstrated that tsetse and tick infestations had become so widespread as to threaten the complete eradication of cattle populations in some parts of Handeni. The expansion of infestation by these disease vectors had occurred, researchers found, in areas which had been abandoned by cultivators during the great famine of the mid-1930s. Uncultivated fields and untended pastures and parklands around villages had been colonized by bush and long grasses which provided suitable habitats for tsetse and ticks. As cultivating communities grew smaller, moreover, the wildlife hosts of trypanosomal and theilerial infection, such as bush pigs and buffalo, moved closer to villages, bringing virulent strains of these infections into proximity with domesticated livestock.

The epidemiological researchers of the 1930s did not enquire into the reasons why so many farmers had abandoned homes and fields during the 1932–5 famine. They assumed that flight was an inevitable response to drought, crop failure and famine. Yet, as the example of the 1884–6 famine shows, when farmers had been integrated into effective systems of patronage, many of them had been able to remain at home despite serious food shortages. In the 1930s, in contrast, many villagers left home during the famine because, following the collapse of patronage networks, they could find no local sources of famine relief.

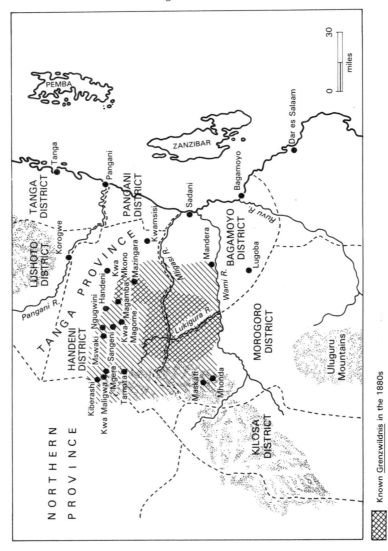

Map 4 *Handeni District, Showing the Expansion of Tsetse Fly during the British Colonial Period.*

Thus they abandoned farms, pastures and parklands to colonizing vegetation, roaming wildlife and disease-bearing insects.

Just as the epidemiological researchers of the 1930s did not ask why depopulation occurred during the famine of the mid 1930s, so too they did not investigate epidemiological conditions prior to the 1930s. A reconstruction of evidence from the 1890s through the 1930s shows, however, that the events of the mid-1930s had been preceded by similar sequences of dearth, flight and epizootic during each major famine of the period. The famines which occurred between the mid-1890s and the mid-1930s were quite different from their 1884–6 predecessor, for whereas population movement had been minimal during 1884–6, each of the subsequent famines provoked widespread migration away from Handeni as destitute villagers, lacking patronage, sought subsistence in other regions. Moreover, whereas the 1884–6 famine had led to a concentration of population and an improvement of environmental conditions in the neighbourhoods controlled by the major patrons, each famine of the pre-Second World War colonial period was followed by expansion of tsetse and tick infestation, encroachment of wildlife on pastures and settlements and deadly epizootics of trypanosomiasis and theileriosis. Thus the imposition of a form of colonial authority which was interested neither in the maintenance of patronage networks nor in environmental conditions in Handeni, together with the transformation of local political authority and the decline of patronage, caused the loss of control over the bovine disease environment.

Conclusion

This chapter began by contrasting the absence of attention to political life in the scholarly literature on African environmental history with the emphasis on political authority in the discussion of environmental deterioration by the Handeni farmer Nyangasi Mohamedi Munga. The lack of any connection between political and environmental history is one of the more striking qualities in what probably remains the best-known study of Tanzanian ecological history, Helge Kjekshus's *Ecology Control and Economic Development in East African History*. Kjekshus has been severely criticized, of course (and perhaps damned by neglect in this volume), and yet his work was more important than any other in inspiring the turn towards environmental change by historians of Tanzania. However, it is reflective of the infrequency with which connections are made between political and environmental change that while his critics have spotted some of the problems which stem from Kjekshus's neglect of political life – such as the tendency to depict changeless precolonial societies inhabiting an idyllic, tranquil 'Merrie Africa' – they have not actually drawn attention to the absence of political history.[44] Indeed, even critics of the 'Merrie Africa' approach have not always devoted sufficient attention to sources of political power, to political action and debate, to ideological representations of political authority and to the political relationships and conceptions which governed the control and distribution of labour and resources.

How the debate between the 'Merrie Africa' approach and its critics can neglect the specifics of political history is evident in important West African studies by Paul Richards and Michael Watts. Richards has often emphasized the importance of integrating an understanding of local initiative and local knowledge into discussions of ecological change, and in a review article which reiterated this point he carried his argument to the conclusion that knowledge of local environment had produced an 'idiom' and 'values' which were the basis of 'an African tradition of decentralized socialism'.[45] Such a conclusion would have met heavy resistance during the 1980s in the very Ujamaa villages which were the products of 'African socialism' in Handeni. Indeed, the implicit point of Nyangasi Mohamedi Munga and others was that Tanzanian socialism had produced worse environmental conditions than those which had existed under the hierarchical, sometimes exploitative and certainly non-socialist regime of the late precolonial chiefs. Watts criticized this article for its 'populism' and inadequate treatment of political, economic and social relations.[46] Yet, in his own work on famine, subsistence security and 'moral economy' in northern Nigeria, Watts touches only lightly on the detailed substance of political life and ideology in precolonial Hausaland, even though he affirms the importance of political relations and class conflict.

As these West African examples indicate, even scholars who understand that political and environmental history are intimately related may not give sufficient recognition to their interrelationship. Nevertheless, some East African studies have begun trying to integrate political history into narratives of environmental change, although as yet connections between the environmental and political have been examined in only a few instances, and only rarely in precolonial contexts. Among the first scholars to make the connection between environmental and political change was Meredeth Turshen, who, in a book tellingly entitled *The Political Ecology of Disease in Tanzania*, forcefully argued that tropical disease must be understood within the context of 'colonialism and underdevelopment'.[47] A more recent volume, edited by Anders Hjort af Ornäs and M.A. Mohamed Salih, has considered recent political conflicts as the causes of environmental degradation.[48] The strongest statements about the need to include politics in analyses of precolonial ecology have come from areas of East Africa which developed relatively centralized political systems. Johan Pottier has argued against the notion, implicit in the 'Merrie Africa' approach, that precolonial modes of famine prevention arose 'spontaneously'.

He shows instead that, in precolonial Rwanda, exchanges of food between food-surplus and food-deficit zones occurred because nobles used their authority over client labour to accumulate subsistence reserves, and because clients obtained food from patrons in return for work.[49] In their *Siaya*, David Cohen and E.S. Atieno Odhiambo reach a very similar conclusion, and at the same time adopt a perspective that is similar to that of Nyangasi Mohamedi Munga. They agree with Pottier that security from famine does not develop naturally; indeed, one of their most memorable vignettes shows that villagers who often go hungry may not know how to care for a child who has fainted from hunger. Moreover, having compared evidence of hunger in modern Siaya with images of plenty in the late precolonial states of the Lake Victoria region, they conclude that 'the generation of plenitude and the image of tropical abundance in the past rested not on nature but on prevalent political conditions . . . [and] was generated by elaborate forms of state coercion, which more recent struggle has made irreproducible'.[50] However, Cohen and Atieno Odhiambo only sketch out their argument. A fuller history, which once again comes from a region which was controlled by a precolonial state, is Steven Feierman's work on the Usambara Mountains of Tanzania. In his *Peasant Intellectuals*, Feierman demonstrates that the Shambaa people believed political conflict 'harmed the land' and proper political authority 'restored' or 'healed' the land.[51]

The evidence from Handeni District strengthens the connection between political and environmental history, for it shows that, even in a region of highly decentralized political authority, environmental conditions were influenced by political relationships. Indeed, although political thought and debate were expressed in an idiom of kinship, political relations between patrons and clients provided the primary ways of controlling labour and accumulating resources.[52] Moreover, while the Handeni evidence helps to restore the political dimension which is lacking in the studies of Kjekshus and others, it also shows that despite the scepticism of some historians, Kjekshus was correct in asserting that precolonial societies were capable of 'ecology control'. Nevertheless, as Koponen has argued,[53] 'control' of ecological conditions can be demonstrated only in very localized contexts, and only with regard to a limited set of environmental factors. In Handeni, precolonial communities exerted control over the bovine disease environment, but they did not necessarily possess a more general form of 'ecology control'.

Furthermore, the history of Handeni demonstrates that control of environmental factors depended upon specific political circumstances. In late precolonial Handeni, political relationships between patrons and clients and an ideology of reciprocal obligation allowed the accumulation of surpluses and made redistributed resources available to the majority of the farming population. Despite the predation caused by slave trading, the expansion of long-distance trade between 1840 and 1890 provided credit and opportunities for profit which allowed the expansion of patronage networks and further improvement of environmental conditions in some localities. Thus precolonial control of the bovine disease environment existed in political conditions which allowed accumulation of resources by patrons, and which gave common farmers the ideological and political means to make effective claims on the resources of patrons. Patronage was effective in improving environmental control because it existed within a commercial framework which did not threaten the patrons, but instead relied upon them to organize markets. Ultimately, late precolonial patronage and bovine disease control were interdependent, for, while patrons required cattle, a healthy bovine disease environment required the coordination of agricultural labour by patrons.

Colonial governments did not depend upon patrons, however, and had little interest in the environmental conditions of an economically unimportant district such as Handeni. Instead, they undermined the authority of patrons by reducing their opportunities for accumulation, and through the 1940s frustrated most attempts by would-be patrons to accumulate through trade and market-crop production. Clients who had relied upon long-term relationships with patrons found themselves transformed into casual labourers. Deprived of access to famine reserves, former clients fled their homes during the succession of famines which struck early colonial Handeni, and thereby interrupted the work of maintaining a tick- and tsetse-free environment. Thus colonialism disrupted political relations within farming communities and destroyed the most impressive achievement of the late precolonial trading chiefs: a healthy environment for cattle.

Notes

1. Nyangasi Mohamedi Munga (Kilwa, September 12, 1983). This last point is emphasized by others as well, for example Mzee Samgome (Kwediboma, 25 February 1983).

2. For example, John Ford, *The Role of the Trypanosomiases in African Ecology: A Study of the Tsetse Fly Problem* (Oxford, 1971), Michael Mortimore, *Adapting to Drought: Farmers, Famines and Desertification in West Africa* (Cambridge, 1989), and Helge Kjekshus, *Ecology Control and Economic Development in East African History: the Case of Tanganyika, 1850–1950* (Berkeley and Los Angeles, 1977).

3. Jonathan Musere, *African Sleeping Sickness: Political Ecology, Colonialism and Control in Uganda* (Lewiston, NY, 1990), p. 46.

4. See James L. Giblin, *The Politics of Environmental Control in Northeastern Tanzania, 1840–1940* (Philadelphia, 1993), chapter 3.

5. Ernest Mkomwa (Kwa Masaka, 29 September 1983); Paul Nkanyemka (Muheza-Hedigongo, 18 August 1983); Omali Gumbo (Kwinji, 5 May 1983); 'Historia ya

Wazigua' (Anon., n.d.), in Handeni District Book, vol 1, Tanzania National Archives [hereafter TNA]; Anthony Mochiwa, *Habari za Wazigua* (London, 1954), pp. 3–5. *Si* are discussed in Mwalumwambo A.O.M. Muya, 'A Political Economy of Zigua Utani', in Stephen A. Lucas, ed., *Utani* (Dar es Salaam, 1975), pp. 187–248.

6. Ernest L. Mkomwa and Godfrey Nkwileh, 'Jadi, Mila, Desturi na Historia ya Wazigua' (Handeni, 1968), pp. 55–6.

7. 'Historia ya Wazigua', p. 6.

8. Omali Gumbo (Kwinji, 5 May 1983) and Rashidi Mwenjuma Manyagala (Kilwa, 11 September 1983).

9. 'Historia ya Wazigua', pp. 5–6; Omali Maligwa Kidiza (Gombero, 20 September 1983).

10. Abdala Hamani Msede and Ali Omali Kipande (Kwa Dundwa, 12 September 1983).

11. Alexandre Le Roy, 'À la Découverte', *Les Missions Catholiques* 19 (1887): 309.

12. Cado Picarda, 'Autour de Mandera', *Les Missions Catholiques* 18 (1886): 246, and François Coulbois, 'Une Tournée dans le Vicariat Apostolique de Zanguebar, Oct.–Nov. 1884', *Les Missions Catholiques* 17 (1885): 513.

13. Mkomwa and Nkwileh, chapter 10.

14. Ali Mohamedi Masomo (Mgera, 19 August 1982); Father Strick, 'Organisation of the Tribe–Clan' (1935), Morogoro Province Book, TNA.

15. 'Historia ya Wazigua'; Elders of Magamba and their 'Asili ya Kwa Luguru' (30 September 1983); Abedi Juma (Manga, 10 October 1983); Ernest Mkomwa (Kwa Masaka, 29 September 1983).

16. Mani was buried at Mzimkuru, some distance from Magamba: BArchP, RKolA 217/7. Bungire, a ruler at Kilwa in northern Nguu who was reputed to be a rapacious slave dealer, was also refused burial: Abdala Hamani Msede and Ali Omali Kipande (Kwa Dundwa, 12 September 1983) and Rashidi Mwenjuma Manyagala (Kilwa, 11 September 1983).

17. RKolA 217/7.

18. Magamba under Sonyo is described in W.H. Kisbey, 'A Journey in Zigualand,' *Central Africa* 18 (1900): 174, and United Society for the Propagation of the Gospel, UMCA Archives, Letter of Bishop John Hine (Korogwe, 10 February 1907), Box A.1 (XIII), Folio 699.

19. Picarda, 'Autour de Mandera', pp. 236 and 296.

20. Mhonda Journal, 16–17 February 1883 (microfilmed copies of this and other Spiritan mission journals are in the Spiritan Archives USA, Bethel Park, PA). For similar cases involving the transfer of dependants, see Mhonda Journal, 7 June 1887 and 25 March 1892; Raoul de Courmont, 'Rapport', *Annales Apostoliques de la Congrégation du Saint-Esprit et du Saint Coeur de Marie* 9 (1894): 83; RKOLA 856/113–115.

21. TNA G8/773, G8/776, G23/205, G55/54, G55/55, G203/153.

22. Government reports show, for example, that twenty-six Handeni District villages cultivated only 0.9 hectares per able-bodied farmer in 1974: Handeni District File A.3/4/IX, 'Agriculture: Monthly Reports'. Another survey done in the same period showed that Handeni villages cultivated only three-quarters of a hectare per household: Suleman Alarakhia Sumra, 'An Analysis of Environmental and Social Problems Affecting Agricultural Development in Handeni District' (MA Thesis, University of Dar es Salaam, 1975), p. 130. Research done by Sumra and others in various villages produced similar results. See also Michaela Von Freyhold, *Rural Development Through Ujamaa*, vol. 2: *Case Studies From Handeni* (University of Dar es Salaam, 1971) and G. Tschannerl *et al*, *Handeni Water Supply: Preliminary Report and Design Criteria*, BRALUP paper no. 22 (University of Dar es Salaam, 1971).

23. Data on modern crop yields are from Sumra, 'Analysis of Environmental and Sosial Problems', pp. 130 and 135–6.

24. Picarda, 'Autour de Mandera', p. 246.

James L. Giblin

25. Étienne Baur, 'Dans l'Oudoé et l'Ouzigoua', in Étienne Baur and Alexandre Le Roy, À Travers le Zanguebar (Tours, 1893), pp. 84-8; Mandera Journal, 21 February 1882 and 16 January 1883; Anton Horner, 'L'Oukami (Afrique Orientale) I', Les Missions Catholiques 5 (1873): 585 and 'L'Oukami (Afrique Orientale) VI', Les Missions Catholiques 6 (1874): 21. Also, J. Kohler, 'Beantwortung des Fragebogens über die Rechte der Eingeborenen in der deutsche Kolonien', Rhodes House, Micr. Afr. 480.

26. Mhonda Journal, 1878-1879 and 19 January 1881, March-May 1884, 14 May, 19, 21 and 31 August, 1886; Mandera Journal, 21 July 1884 and April 1885.

27. Mandera Journal, 4 July, 8 and 12 August 1887, 18-20 February 1888; Picarda, 'Autour de Mandera', p. 249; Coulbois, 'Une Tournée' p. 498; Étienne Baur, 'Lettre', Annales de la Oeuvre de la Sainte-Enfance, Paris 35 (1884): 339.

28. Bulletin de la Congrégation du Saint-Esprit 14 (1887-1888): 640-1.

29. Mandera Journal, 16-20 September 1883, 21, 25 and 27 July 1884, April 1885; Mhonda Journal, 13 and 27 September and 15-19 October 1889, 1 January 1890, 15 December 1891, 9 June 1911, 16 February 1912, 9 November 1914; Maskati Journal, January 1910, May 1914, November 1915; Lugoba Journal, 9 June 1912, 26 June 1914; Bulletin de la Congrégation du Saint Esprit 16 (1889-1890): 723; RKA 6467/140.

30. M.A. Mavullah, speaking with Hasani Bakari and others (Balanga, 23 May 1983). Similar comments were made by Mohamedi Mjewe (Kwediboma, 27 September 1982).

31. See James L. Giblin, 'Trypanosomiasis Control in African History: An Evaded Issue?' Journal of African History 31, (1990): 59-80, and 'East Coast Fever in Socio-Historical Context: A Case Study from Tanzania', International Journal of African Historical Studies 23, 3 (1990): 401-21.

32. Rajabu Sudi (Manga, 10 October 1983); Mohamedi Semsambia (Kilwa, 11 September 1983); Mohamedi Mjewe (Kwediboma, 19 September 1982).

33. Salimu Kisailo (Kwa Maligwa, 19 May 1983). Also, Mdoe Nyange (Kiberashi, 17 May 1983); Mhonda Journal, 30 May 1883; E.B. Dobson, 'Land Tenure of the Wasambaa', Tanganyika Notes and Records 10 (1940): 19-20.

34. Mdoe Nyange (Kiberashi, 17 May 1983); Mohamedi Mjewe (Kwediboma, 19 September 1982).

35. Mandera Journal, 24 July 1898.

36. Mandera Journal, February, May, July (especially 28 July) 1884.

37. Mhonda Journal, various entries, 1884.

38. 'Letter' Church Missionary Intelligencer and Record 12 (1887): 693.

39. Mohamedi Lusingo (Mafisa, 1 July 1983); Omali Maligwa Kidiza (Gombero, 20 September 1983); Franz Stuhlmann, 'Bericht über eine Reise durch Usegua und Unguu', Mitteilungen der Geographischen Gesellschaft in Hamburg 10 (1887-8): 167-168.

40. For evidence of similar movements during 1884-6, see Carol Jane Sissons, 'Economic Prosperity in Ugogo, East Africa, 1860-1890' (Ph.D. dissertation, University of Toronto, 1984), p. 144.

41. Mzee Ndege (Mafisa, 1 July 1983).

42. Asumani Nyokka (Kwediboma, 11 May 1983).

43. Fuller discussion of the material discussed in this section is found in Giblin, The Politics of Environmental Control, Parts Three and Four, especially chapters 6, 8 and 10, 'Trypanosomiasis Control' and 'East Coast Fever'.

44. John Iliffe, 'Review of Ecology Control and Economic Development in East African History', Journal of African History 19 (1978): 139-141; Juhani Koponen, People and Production in Late Precolonial Tanzania: History and Structures (Uppsala, 1988), pp. 21-3; Michael Watts, Silent Violence: Food, Famine and Peasantry in Northern Nigeria (Berkeley, 1983), pp. 145-6.

45. Paul Richards, 'Ecological Change and the Politics of African Land Use,' African Studies Review 26,2 (June 1983): 55.

46. Michael Watts, ' "Good Try, Mr. Paul": Populism and the Politics of African Land Use', African Studies Review 26, 2 (1983): 78 and 80.

The Precolonial Politics of Disease Control

47. Meredeth Turshen, *The Political Ecology of Disease in Tanzania* (New Brunswick, NJ, 1984), p. 14.

48. Anders Hjort af Ornäs and M.A. Mohamed Salih, *Ecology and Politics: Environmental Stress and Security in Africa* (Uppsala, 1989).

49. Johan P. Pottier, 'The Politics of Famine Prevention: Ecology, Regional Production and Food Complementarity in Western Rwanda', *African Affairs* 85, 339 (April 1986): 207-37.

50. David William Cohen and E.S. Atieno Odhiambo, *Siaya: The Historical Anthropology of an African Landscape* (London, 1989), chapter 8 (quote from p. 75).

51. Steven Feierman, *Peasant Intellectuals: Anthropology and History in Tanzania* (Madison, 1990).

52. An anthropologist who has long argued that historians have exaggerated the importance of kinship in precolonial Africa is W.D. Hammond-Tooke. For an introduction to the debate, see his 'Kinship Authority and Political Authority in Precolonial South Africa', in Andrew D. Spiegel and Patrick A. McAllister, *Tradition and Transition in Southern Africa* (New Brunswick and London, 1991), pp. 185-99.

53. The term is discussed in Koponen, *People and Production*, pp. 366-7.

Six

~~~~~~

'We Don't
Want Terraces!'

Protest & Identity
under the Uluguru Land Usage Scheme

PAMELA A. MAACK

In 1955, an estimated 4000 inhabitants of the Uluguru Mountains of
Morogoro District in Tanzania, the Waluguru, began hurling insults,
sticks and stones at their native authority chief and British rulers.
The riot began at a meeting called by colonial officials in the Matombo
sub-area on the eastern side of the mountains to discuss the growing
resentment of the Waluguru with soil conservation measures introduced
in 1947. In the fracas which ensued an African demonstrator, John
Mahenge, was shot and bled to death while an angry company of
colonial police sought to control an even angrier body of Waluguru.
As the Waluguru chanted in Kiswahili, 'We don't want terraces,
give us back our old ways,' they were protesting against a way of
life in which increased hard work did not bring increased rewards.
The riots represent the cry of a people struggling to deal with colonial
policies which were based on erroneous assumptions about Waluguru
land ownership patterns and labour practices. These assumptions
threatened internal power relations within Morogoro while reminding
the Waluguru that in the last analysis power lay with the colonial
government. Moreover, these soil conservation measures strained not
only social relations but also the already fragile soils in the mountain,
thus posing a serious threat to the livelihood of the people. For a time,
therefore, the Waluguru found their disparate interests united in their
struggle against a common enemy: the colonial government.

During the Depression of the 1930s and the Second World War,
concern with soil conditions was subsumed by the perceived need
to increase production. But, following the war, colonial officials who
were creating the 'new colonialism' of the postwar period became

overwhelmingly concerned with the problem of soil erosion in Tanzania.[1] Colonial officials instigated five regional development schemes in Mbulu, Usukuma, Kondoa, Usambara[2] and Uluguru in the late 1940s. The purpose of these schemes was to address stagnation in agricultural production at local levels. In practice, all five schemes sought increased production in the long term through various soil conservation methods. Because these schemes required a great deal of African labour, their success was dependent on African cooperation. Initially, officials believed Africans would willingly contribute to 'help themselves'. In some areas, notably Mbulu and Usukuma, they did 'help themselves' because they obtained benefits immediately. The remaining three schemes were unquestionably failures. All three collapsed and were abandoned by colonial officials in the latter half of the 1950s. Iliffe summarizes the reasons for their failure:[3]

> Thus the Mbulu and Sukumaland schemes succeeded in so far as they coincided with African drives toward capitalism and colonisation. This conclusion is supported by the failure of the other three schemes, all in areas of agricultural involution . . . in such deprived regions government could not offer incentives to make worthwhile the drudgery involved in schemes which attacked only the symptoms and not the causes of deprivation. Successful schemes took place only in regions which were able to develop within the framework of the colonial economy.

In Uluguru, the Waluguru resisted efforts to combat soil erosion because they derived few benefits from their labour. Their complaints against the scheme echoed their wider struggles against the growing impoverishment and domination of their society and united them in a common purpose. In 1955, Waluguru resistance erupted into violence.

Morogoro District, in the eastern part of Tanzania, is a mountainous region inhabited by the Waluguru people. It is dominated in the north by the Uluguru Mountains, which gradually slope into plains in the north and east. Toward the west lies the arid central plateau. The presence of the mountains causes vast differences in soil quality and rainfall patterns between highly productive mountain slopes and valleys and the arid plains. The eastern side of the mountains receives heavy rainfall while the western side remains relatively dry. For this reason the east is a tsetse area while the west is fly-free. Crops grown in the east include hill rice and tropical fruits such as oranges, mangoes and coconuts. In the west, maize, kidney beans and vegetables, such as Irish potatoes, onions, carrots and cabbage, are grown. Cassava, yams and sweet potatoes are grown in both areas. Cotton was grown on the lower slopes and bordering plains, while at higher elevations people grew robusta coffee and plantains. The population in the district increased steadily from 155 000 in 1931, to 230 000 in 1948, 264 000 in 1957, and 337 023 in 1978.[4]

Pamela A. Maack

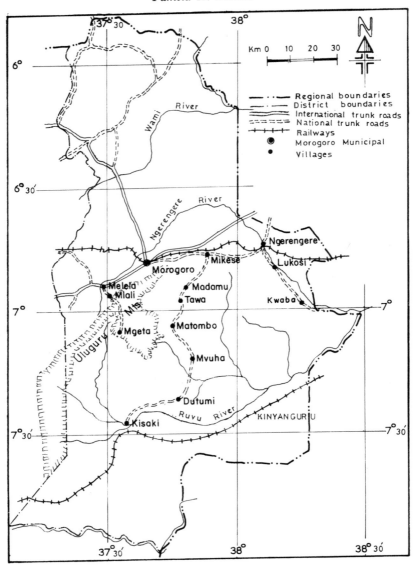

Map 5 *Uluguru*

154

'We Don't Want Terraces!'

The Uluguru Land Usage Scheme (ULUS) was initiated in 1947, following a report submitted by the Regional Assistant Director of Agriculture, A.H. Savile.[5] Savile's 1947 report raised an alarm which resounded through the colonial administration hierarchy. His report noted the increase in the amount of land under cultivation, the decrease in the amount of fallow time, depletion in soil fertility and deforestation, which led to rapid runoff and flooding in the major rivers which originated in Morogoro and supplied water for the nearby sisal estates and Dar es Salaam.

The Uluguru Mountains have suffered from severe overpopulation for as long as my informants could remember. At the turn of the century, they tell me, there was an acute famine caused by the decreasing fertility of the soil, which prompted many Waluguru to move down into the foothills and the plains in search of better land. Many of the older inhabitants in these areas told me they had moved down to the plains as small children just prior to and during the First World War. All speak of the severe land shortage which affected high mountain areas before the First World War. This land shortage caused overuse of land which resulted in severe soil erosion and, ultimately, famine. Thus, beginning in the German period, Waluguru began moving down from high mountain areas in search of land, a movement made possible because the arrival of the Germans curtailed the operation of the caravan trade in the area.

The family of Saidi Ramadhani Ming'walu, who estimated his age to be 93 in 1987, was one of the first to settle in the area of present day Melela on the plains below the Uluguru Mountains. During the time of the Germans, his parents moved down to the plains fleeing the famine which was consuming the highlands:[6]

> My parents were born in Lusungwi near Mgeta [high in the mountains]. My maternal uncle, Mkuya, owned land at Lusungwi. My parents moved to Magali near Mlali [in the foothills midway up the mountains] and then to Melela [on the plains], where I was born. My parents moved down as there were no more crops. The soil was not productive. The only crop doing well was cassava. Families were not well and they had to come down to the plains to get millet for beer for celebrations. It was a long way to come so they decided to move down. In the mountains plots were very small and they had to make terraces to get crops. There were too many people.

Mzee Ming'walu's story is not at all unusual. While his family may have led the way in the movement down to the plains, many others followed as land shortage, soil deterioration and famine persisted in the highlands.

The problem of soil erosion was noted consistently throughout the British colonial period. As early as 1927 the Provincial Commissioner of Morogoro described the growth of population in the mountains and its consequences:[7]

The natives are cultivating up to the forest reserve boundaries and in parts plantations on the steep hillsides seem to be on poor soil. All of which is subject to erosion.

However, it was not until after the Second World War, when the British government became more concerned with 'development' as colonial policy, that they addressed the problem.

From the beginning, the ULUS was poorly conceived and improperly implemented. ULUS was allotted ten years and £50 000 from agricultural development funds to redress the problems of a hundred years. Not surprisingly, in the first few years of the project there was much discussion and little action. Finally, as officials realized time was passing they made a hasty decision to spend the bulk of their money on staff salaries. They formulated goals for ULUS at a meeting attended on 25 March 1949 by the Secretary for Native Affairs, the Provincial Commissioner and the Conservator of Forests. The Member for Local Government and District Commissioner were also present.[8]

After discussing numerous anti-erosion measures, ULUS officials eventually decided to bench-terrace the majority of land on the mountain slopes and to do tree-planting at higher elevations. Initially, there was discussion of surveying the land to determine which lands would benefit from bench terraces, which should be ridged as in the Mgeta area, which should be tie-ridged, and which should be planted in permanent tree crops, but very little of this work was accomplished. Instead, implementation consisted of training the Waluguru in the construction of bench terraces, which involved wide terraces built step fashion into mountain slopes. On these areas, crops such as corn and rice were to be grown. However, there is no clear reason why bench terraces became the main erosion technique stressed under ULUS. In fact, initial tests in the area with bench terracing so disturbed the fragile topsoil that the terraces proved to be sterile. Throughout the history of the scheme the advisability of bench-terracing as a suitable method of soil preservation was questioned by officers in the field and, as we shall see, by the Waluguru themselves.

In the middle years of the scheme responsibility for its implementation was placed in the hands of a 'special' District Officer. Under the District Officer were three or four European Agricultural Officers, who supervised a large body of African Instructors, who came from both inside and outside the district. The job of the African Instructor was to educate the people on the importance of bench-terracing and to supervise its implementation. Similarly, on the higher slopes, instructors supervised the planting of trees. Trash burning and the burning of fields was forbidden and instructors working with the Native Authorities were responsible for enforcing these prohibitions. Terracing was declared mandatory by law in the pilot areas of

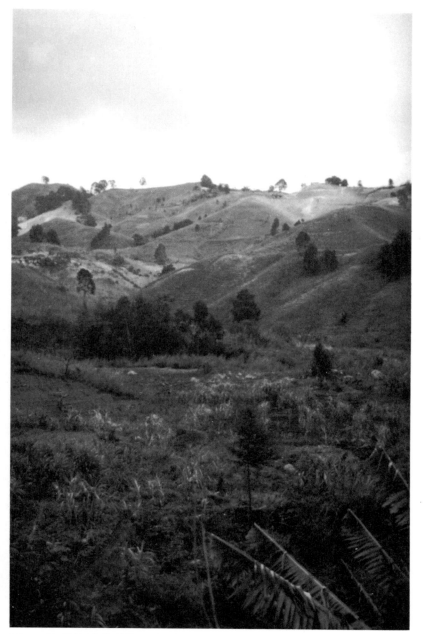

Photo 9 *Hillside Soil Terracing in the Uluguru Mountains.* (Gregory Maddox)

Matombo, on the eastern side of the mountains; Mgeta, on the western side; Tangeni, on the northern face; and later, Mkuyuni, also on the eastern side. This law was enforceable by the Native Authority in the native courts. African Instructors and Native Authorities could fine or imprison a person for failure to comply with these statutes.[9]

Because they could perceive no benefits in terracing, the Waluguru as a whole did not engage in this 'hard work' voluntarily. The British soon moved beyond the stages of building demonstration plots to active intervention in the production processes in the mountains. By using methods now familiar to scholars of peasant resistance in Africa, the Waluguru in the pilot areas protested against terracing by simply ignoring colonial dictates. Moreover, they continued to burn their fields in preparation for planting even though they were forbidden to do so. Protest became more active when houses which were being constructed for the new agricultural instructors were repeatedly burned in the night. Nevertheless, the British did not recognize these acts as signs of serious resistance.

As the scheme progressed, British officials at all levels became more and more discouraged by what they perceived as a lack of success. Responsibility for the scheme was returned to the hands of the District Commissioner, R.H. Gower, who, when he expressed dissatisfaction with the scheme and with the practice of universal terracing, was told by the Provincial Commissioner to 'get on with the job'.[10] Quotas of running yardage of terraces to be constructed were instituted and pressure from the top made African Instructors at the bottom rely on threats of coercion. Eventually, running yardage was given up as a measurement of compliance with the policy and all Waluguru taxpayers were required to construct terraces three days per week. Throughout 1954 the number of court prosecutions for burning fields and failing to construct terraces rose rapidly.[11]

Finally, in the summer of 1955 the Waluguru began to protest publicly. Government public meetings, rarely attended in the past, filled with angry Waluguru brandishing sticks and knives. The Provincial Commissioner feared that the level of discontent had risen to dangerous levels. In Dar es Salaam, the government decided the matter should be discussed on 13 July in two meetings, one at Mkuyuni in the morning and one at Matombo in the afternoon. Because of the threat of violence, extra police were brought from Nairobi. The meeting at Mkuyuni broke down as the Waluguru chanted 'We don't want terraces! Bring us back our old ways.' The British called upon local leaders to disband the group, but they were greeted at Matombo in much the same manner, although this time the protesters would not disperse. A full-scale riot developed as the Waluguru threw sticks and stones and the British hurled smoke bombs. The Provincial Commissioner attempted to read the Riot Act but could not be heard above the noise. In the confusion, a British officer shot a demonstrator, John Mahenge. The convoy of colonial officials quickly returned to Morogoro after a stop at the local Catholic mission. For a time at least, the Waluguru had won.

The list of problems with ULUS which provoked these protests was long and varied. Both the monograph by Roland Young and Henry Fosbrooke and the departmental inquiry into the riots by the government described these problems in great detail.[12] The Waluguru themselves had four often-repeated complaints about the colonial implementation of forced terracing: it was hard work, it brought hunger by destroying the soil and lowering yields, it forced men and women to labour together and it caused their Native Authorities to betray them. Although these complaints can be interpreted as arising out of the specific experience of terracing, I would suggest that we can broaden them out to view them as complaints against the increased pauperization of their society and their loss of power.

The major complaint cited by Young and Fosbrooke and the government inquiry as well as by the Waluguru with whom I spoke was the hard work required, for terracing requires many hours of back-breaking labour, and is particularly arduous when using shovels without shoes and when one must often walk a good way up and down steep slopes to the work site. Yet anyone who has lived in a rural African area knows that life in the village is characterized by hard work. Hard work is something that people will engage in when they can see a worthwhile result. Indeed, terracing has been practised on the western side of the mountains since at least the early 1900s, for, while residents of the area recognize that terracing is hard work, they can also easily perceive its benefits.

Residents of the Mgeta area follow a mixture of agricultural strategies, which show that they are not categorically opposed to terracing. Crops grown on the steep, denuded mountain slopes in this area are grown on narrow step terraces constructed each season for this purpose. Grass borders planted along the outer edge of the terrace serve to hold back soil, and eventually the grass is mulched in to act as a fertilizer. Rain-fed corn and kidney beans have been grown this way for almost a hundred years. Different explanations for the origins of this type of terracing – which cite missionary influence, early European settler influence and indigenous invention – circulate in Mgeta. All explanations agree that the technique spread rapidly, particularly as soil erosion reached crisis proportions in this high, dry area prior to the First World War. In addition to these rain-fed terracing systems, the farmers of Mgeta also practise various forms of bench terracing and soil ridging on the lower slopes of the Mgeta valley. On these terraces European vegetables, such as cabbage, onions, carrots and potatoes, are grown, using water from irrigation channels cut from the Mgeta river. Because these fields are often located close to the houses of their owners they are often manured with goat dung and mulched with vegetable refuse. Vegetables are grown during the dry season and thus can earn high prices at market. Vegetable growing was introduced to the area early in the British period by a British administrator of the mica mine in the area, Thomas Bain. Once his monopoly of vegetable seeds and marketing routes was broken, the terracing of vegetable gardens spread rapidly despite the hard work required. Thus the benefits of terracing on the western side of the mountains were evident because farmers were able to find a place for themselves in the colonial economy through the production of highly valued foodstuffs. In contrast, the Waluguru on the eastern side of the mountains did not see any benefits from terracing because their environment was not suitable for vegetable production.

Indeed, the colonial economy did not bring development to most of Morogoro, and thus could not guarantee that Waluguru farmers would be compensated for the work of terracing, for the colonial government would provide infrastructural support only for those areas capable of producing an export crop. Initially, the export crop chosen by colonial officials for Morogoro Region as a whole was cotton. Under German rule and early in the British period, Morogoro was considered the ideal site both for settler plantations and for native African production of the crop, because cotton could be grown on the lowland slopes and plains below the mountains. The British hoped to induce the Waluguru to move down from the mountains and grow cotton on the plains, and in the late 1920s it appeared that their hopes would be realized as Morogoro broke all previous records for cotton production. However, a series of poor climatic years and Depression prices caused marketed cotton amounts to drop rapidly. British officials responded with the 'Plant More Crops Campaign' of the 1930s, which did little to address the problems facing African producers. The failure of African farmers to respond by increasing production caused colonial officials to label Morogoro as a stagnant backwater and to abandon efforts to develop the region.

While cotton could not be grown profitably in most parts of the mountains, some Waluguru found a niche by developing production of foodstuffs for export to Dar es Salaam and surrounding areas. Yet this production was not supported by the colonial government and was not very profitable. On the western side, the Waluguru were able to find a market for European vegetables both locally and in Dar es Salaam, which provided them with slightly higher prices, in part because they faced little competition from other areas because of their ability to time their vegetable harvest. As a result, for them terracing was a worthwhile effort. On the eastern side, people increasingly turned to the planting of tropical fruit trees, oranges, mangoes and coconut around their houses to supplement their incomes, while continuing to plant hill rice, corn and millet to feed their families. However, profits from these fruit crops were often low because of competition in urban markets with several other major orange-growing areas. Thus the Waluguru on the eastern side found it increasingly difficult to make ends meet. As their population grew, land shortages became acute and crop yields were often inadequate. The 'hungry months' before harvest increased as grain harvests dwindled. Most Waluguru to whom I spoke do not remember selling much of their agricultural produce in the colonial era. They sold crops only to 'solve problems'; and when they did so they ate more cassava, a crop with bulk calories but low nutritional value.

Out of this crisis situation a new gender division of labour, which also contributed to making terracing unrewarding, was emerging. Men were able to earn more money for their labour from sources other than farming. They took paid labour as turnboys on the major transport routes that pass through Morogoro, on the sisal estates and in the colonial administration. The practice of young men engaging in paid labour away from their homes was described to me as a common occurrence, almost as a 'rite of passage' into adulthood. Although some men would eventually return to farming, many would continue to engage in wage labour until their retirement, when they would return home. It is universally recognized throughout the mountains that the consequence of men seeking out paid labour was greater workloads for women. Throughout the colonial period men on the eastern side became less and less involved in agricultural production and less willing to invest their labour in it. Therefore, during the most coercive years of ULUS, the power of the government in the form of agricultural instructors and compliant headmen reached out to women, often pulling them from under the bed where they were hiding and forcing them to construct terraces. Some women told me how they had feigned sickness only to be dragged out of bed and forced to work. They switched their tactics to hiding under the beds and leaving early to work in their own fields, but Native Authorities sought them out there, too. In this way, the government was able to get the mandatory yardage of terracing completed, but every hour spent terracing prevented women from growing the crops necessary to feed their families. Thus, because terraced fields brought lower yields, hunger increased exponentially. It is to this issue that we now turn.

The second frequently voiced concern of the Waluguru about terracing was the hunger which resulted. Many Waluguru to whom I spoke referred to the period of terracing as a time of *njaa*, or famine, and would equate it with past famines in which many people were said to have died. They associated the famine with what they saw as the destructive nature of terracing. In this they were right, for the way bench terracing was conducted by agricultural department personnel was destructive.

Rajabu Kazimia Kwanzi described the potential for soil conservation measures to promote erosion in his description of the introduction of terracing in the Matombo area:[13]

> One Bwana Shamba [agricultural instructor] came to show us how to do terraces one day at the area of Matombo which is now called Kiswira. We dug terraces and planted *kas kas* grass that same day. That night heavy rains came and washed away all the *kas kas* and soil. So the next morning when the people saw all the *kas kas* washed away they were very angry. They told the Bwana Shamba that terraces were no good as they cause the good soil to wash away. The Bwana Shamba didn't listen, he said, 'We will just continue until we succeed.'

Several Agricultural Officers and D.C. Gower recognized that topsoil within the mountains was too thin for the construction of bench terraces without composting. However, composting was viewed by officers in the field as too difficult to put into effect. As a result yields from terraced land were often below those of unterraced land, as Mikael Saleh Gugulu, a former local agricultural instructor in Matombo told me:[14]

> When I was an instructor I found the work tiresome. You had to dig deep and it took off all the fertile soil and crops could not grow well. Bwana Clarke knew that terracing was not good but the force was coming from the government who believed the work was necessary, so there was nothing Bwana Clarke or I, as an instructor, could do. We had to do the work.

Today, many people, including Ramadhani Saidi Simba, blame their persisting problems with soil erosion on the destructiveness of terracing. While pointing out his cassava patch on a nearby hill, he said:[15]

> On this small hill you can see I made terraces and the rain washed them away and even to this day I don't get a good yield. I have planted it with cassava and it is not doing well.

Mzee Simba's comment indicates the danger of ill-conceived and improperly implemented soil conservation policy. The procedure itself can destroy the soil and bring hunger. Most important, without the support of the people, it can come to be viewed as a destructive method.

The third complaint of the Waluguru about terracing, which ultimately stemmed from British misconceptions about the communal nature of Waluguru society, centred on the composition of the work parties sent to build terraces. Men and women complained that they were made to work alongside each other. They told me that it was acceptable for husbands and wives to work together but not for communal groups of men and women to do so. This complaint can be understood in part as a reaction to the increasing gender polarization of labour into farm labour and wage labour. However, it was most often an expression of frustration with the inability or unwillingness of the British to understand the 'ways of the Waluguru'. It indicates that the day when 'groups of related people working together', as the British termed the practice, had long since passed, if it had existed at all. Most important, it was linked with other concerns about land and labour control. These concerns were what divided the Waluguru by gender, age and kin status and what divided patrons and clients. The Waluguru wanted to know who would do the labour of terracing and who would control the terraced land. However, complaints about land and labour allocation could not be voiced in unison because land and labour were not held in unison. Moreover, the Waluguru could find no mediation from the British. In fact, they could not find recognition in British policy that struggles over land and labour existed, because British policy followed a strictly communal conception of land and labour allocation. Their policy was based on the erroneous ideas that the Waluguru were organized by matrilineal clans; that each clan communally controlled the allocation of land and labour within the group; that terraces would be constructed by clan groups organized under headmen; and that terracing would benefit the entire group.

The Waluguru do speak idealistically about a system of communal clan trusteeship of land and how it was in the 'old days before Independence' in 1961. Individuals trace rights of inheritance and identification to matriclans and pay respect to their *mjomba*, their maternal uncle, or the eldest male in the matriclan. Such statements led British officials to believe that land was owned communally by the clan and that the *mjomba* distributed this land to the children of the clan. Yet, in tracing their life histories, I encountered few people who, in fact, obtained clan land from their *mjomba*. The allocation of land in the mountains was far more complicated than British conceptions of it.

Nevertheless, the British, following a tribal perception of Waluguru society, did not recognize individual rights of ownership in land and for the most part ignored individual use-rights to land. Yet the pattern of the distribution of land among the Waluguru indicates that use-rights were a crucial consideration. With the increasing shortage of land and its concomitant commoditization, individual Waluguru struggled to transform these use rights to individual ownership rights. Yet they faced competition from clan heads, who, bolstered by indirect rule, struggled to retain a measure of control over land identified as 'clan land'. As the land shortage worsened, many people found themselves without any access to land. In the east, a few clan heads charged rent to non-clan member clients.

The lines of struggle over land solidified around at least five separate groups: clan members with clan land, clan heads not recognized by the British, clan heads recognized by the British, individuals with freehold or purchased land and those without land. Lines of struggle developed between clan heads and clan members, but not all clan heads in Morogoro were recognized by the colonial government as 'headmen' with the right to control large tracts of clan land. In areas without powerful headmen, clan members struggled successfully to retain control of their own land and began to pass it on to their children. Throughout the colonial period, parents tried to give a portion of their land to their male and female children at the time of their marriage or just prior to it.

However, many parents could not supply sufficient land for their children. If neither set of parents could supply land, the young person or his parents would canvas other relatives on both the mother's and the father's sides in an attempt to find plots of land. Individuals or a young couple could migrate down to the plains and foothills in search of freehold land, perhaps following another relative who had moved down earlier. They could either find an unclaimed piece of bush land or take a portion of the bush land previously claimed by a relative. Increasingly, throughout the British period, the Waluguru purchased land, or purchased trees as a way of claiming ownership of a parcel which they desired.

Another option for obtaining land was pursued by those individuals who had no money to purchase land but who wanted to live in one of the older, more populous areas of the mountains. They would go to one of the individuals recognized by the British as an headman to 'beg' land.[16] In return for land, the 'renter' would be required to submit a portion of the harvest, called *ngoto,* to the landowner every year or season, depending on the agreement, thus setting up a patron–client relationship. According to the Waluguru, the payment of *ngoto* was a very old practice by which the head of the clan received baskets of produce from non-clan individuals living on clan land.[17] The tribute received was supposed to be stored for use as seed and famine reserve by the clan. Under British rule, however, the nature of *ngoto* changed dramatically as patrons, buttressed by indirect rule took on large numbers of clients. Headmen recognized by the British were referred to as clan heads but their position was usually more complicated than that. In fact, although the idiom of kinship was used to refer to their power, they were often men who obtained power outside of any kin hierarchy. They may have obtained power in the slave trade, under the Germans, or through their ability to bring rain or make prophecies. These were people the Waluguru referred to as having 'names'. Gradually having a 'name' extended to power over land. This power was solidified by the policy of indirect rule when they were selected in the 1920s as clan heads. With their selection, these individuals gained the right to determine the distribution of land among a large number of individuals, both kin and non-kin. While actual clan heads found their power waning throughout the colonial period as kin members sought to retain their own land, 'clan heads' acting as patrons found their power growing as land shortage worsened.

In 1942 the British were shocked to discover that many patrons were receiving *ngoto* from large numbers of people, in some cases well over 100. The area with the highest number of *ngoto* payers per *ngoto* recipients in British estimates was Matombo. The British abolished the practice of paying *ngoto* arguing that the original intention of the practice had become perverted by greedy elders.[18] This ruling had little effect on the payment of *ngoto*, however, except to drive it underground, for it is still paid throughout the mountains today. Although Independence swept away most of the patrons in the area, today rental of land is often couched in terms of *ngoto*.

The complications of land ownership in the mountains and the various struggles for the land paralysed the terracing scheme. Clan heads, whether they were patrons or not, could not possibly do the work themselves and had no intention of doing so. Clients and clan members were not about to engage in terracing without assurance that the land would be theirs. Some clan members and even non-clan member clients tried to argue that they should be able to claim land on which they had made improvements but no confirmation of this position was to be found in colonial policy. Nevertheless, clan heads, uncertain what it meant for their power, became wary of terracing. The eventual solution, as we have seen, was to force women to terrace. Thus the uncertainties of land ownership throughout the colonial period and into the present day have prevented any voluntary investment of labour in improving the land on the eastern side of the mountains.[19]

The fourth complaint of the Waluguru about terracing was voiced loudly at the meetings held in June of 1955 but had been discussed among the Waluguru for some time prior to the riots. This complaint was summed up by the Waluguru when they chanted at Sultan Sabu bin Sabu, their Native Authority chief, 'Where is the money?', meaning, as at least one Mluguru said to me, 'What were you paid to sell your own country out?' Although, according to the ideology of indirect rule, appointed chiefs were to be indigenous leaders or repositories of 'tribal culture', who were to guide their people into the modern world, the riot indicates how far that vision was from reality. In the final years of ULUS, British colonial officials began to turn over responsibility for terracing quotas to local Native Authorities. The British believed that the Waluguru would willingly respond to the wishes of their 'tribal' leaders, but there were several reasons why the Waluguru resented this practice. Any 'tribal' leaders in Morogoro had only limited spheres of influence. Ritual clan heads had limited rights over their own clan members and virtually none over members of other clans. Native Authority chiefs, subchiefs and government headmen were viewed as representatives of government. Most Waluguru I spoke with were sympathetic with what they recognized as a Native Authority's duty to carry out colonial policy, but, at the same time, the Waluguru had no other representatives and they felt Native Authorities should protect their own people from unreasonable demands.

While dissatisfaction with Native Authorities extended to all levels, the case of Sultan Sabu illustrates how far this dissatisfaction had extended in Matombo. Sultan Sabu started out as a railway clerk and slowly worked his way up the colonial hierarchy. When he was chosen to take the position of Native Authority chief and assume the title of 'Sultan', he was Mtawala of Mkuyuni. The British chose his name to be submitted to public referendum because there were many candidates with strong local power bases, a situation the British felt would be chaotic and potentially threatening. They chose Sabu bin Sabu as the candidate most likely to be the least objectionable to all. Yet, during the meeting at Matombo, the remarks of Sultan Sabu angered the Waluguru and they attacked him, ripping his clothes and trying to strike him. Mohammed Fundi Kimbengere, who was present at the riot, described the sequence of events to me:[20]

> We were told of this meeting and were thinking this meeting could solve the problem of this terracing. So when the Sultan had finished his announcement people responded in chorus 'We don't want this problem of terracing. We don't want it!' The white bwana shamba stood up and said, 'No, don't reject terracing totally, you could at least dig one terrace a day rather than stopping.' D.C. Gower tried to help in convincing the people. The people continued shouting and objecting. The Sultan said, 'Even if you object you will keep on digging terraces even until the time of your grandchildren.' People became very angry and they even wanted to beat the Sultan. The head of the police ordered his men to fire smoke bombs. People ran away from the meeting place and came back with stones. The Sultan immediately wanted to run away and the *wazungu* [Europeans] tried to help the Sultan get into one of the cars. People started to throw stones at the car and the Sultan. Meanwhile, smoke bombs were being thrown at the people.

Mzee Kimbengere's description corresponds with that of many others who were present at the riot. There had been many rumours that the Sultan had been paid a great deal of money to 'sell out' his people and his harsh words at the meeting only seemed to confirm people's suspicions.

Amidst the changes which were going on in the life of the Waluguru, the Waluguru were exploring new forms of political expression. Nowhere is this more evident than in Kiswira Village. Kiswira is the new village name for the former Matombo Mission of the Holy Ghost Fathers. The mission took over a large area of land in the late 1800s and rented it out to the Waluguru by charging them *ngoto*, first in the form of crops and later in money. Clients living on mission land were subject to a special set of rules devised by the Fathers. Most mission inhabitants found these rules to be onerous and the mission itself to be unhelpful, and yet their circumstances did create a cohesion among them which proved useful under ULUS. When I spoke to them, they told me of the ways they banded together to solve the 'problems of terracing'.

The first step they took was to conduct a general meeting at which they selected a representative to travel to Mgeta, the area on the western side where terracing had occurred for many years. Their representative, Rafael Ngulali, carried an ear of their corn from a terraced field to compare it in size with the corn grown on terraces in Mgeta. He found the corn in Matombo to be significantly smaller. They concluded that while terraces might be useful in the high, dry areas of Mgeta it was not suitable for the wetter slopes of the east. The Tanganyika African Association (precursor to TANU) had been recruiting in the area and the people of Kiswira embraced the organization, joining in the election of representatives to speak on behalf of the Waluguru. These representatives were later present at the fateful meeting at Matombo, but the villagers of Kiswira say that only one of them had a chance to speak that day.[21] Besides the villagers of Kiswira, residents of Mkuyuni and Mtamba (which was known to the British as Matombo) were able to list the names of the four representatives chosen by the people to speak that day. While their connection with TANU was only mentioned by the people of Kiswira, villagers in all three areas stressed that these four men were chosen by the people to be 'their voice'. Thus, neither the old kinship relations nor their bastardized sons, the Native Authorities, were able to satisfy their need for political representation.

In examining the four major complaints of the Waluguru against ULUS, I have tried to demonstrate how dissatisfaction did not merely arise from the scheme itself. The Waluguru as a people were dissatisfied with colonialism and the policies of ULUS crystallized that dissatisfaction. Under ULUS, the Waluguru found their common voice. The hard work required of the Waluguru provided little reward and little hope for the future. The hunger that the scheme produced only magnified the hunger they faced every day and threatened to further destroy their soil. The arrangement of their work parties was a caricature of a past reality which ignored the intensely complex nature of land and labour relations in the mountains. Indeed, the Waluguru were not in fact 'the Waluguru', but rather a collection of groups of people, cross-cut by age, gender, kin status and economic and political position, each with different motivations; many struggled against each other. These disparate groups would only come together under one common threat, the threat to their land and livelihood posed by ULUS. Finally, Native Authorities provided no outlet for the people's growing frustrations with a colonial power unwilling to assist them in fulfilling their potential. Hence ULUS became the object towards which the Waluguru directed their discontent.

Pamela A. Maack

The riot and the euphoric time which followed as ULUS was disbanded were marked by the rallying cry 'Give us back our old ways.' But this was not a backward-looking cry. In the aftermath of the riots, the British investigated the role of TANU at Matombo and the continued rebellion of the Waluguru. They concluded that:[22]

> The association of the name TANU with the movement introduced a new element, a cry for 'Freedom'. This apparently meant freedom from irksome soil conservation measures and from restrictions on entering forest reserves . . . Progressively there followed claims for freedom from marketing restrictions, i.e., to close the produce markets, from the duty of porterage [sic], and from the payment of *ngoma* licences. There was general talk of a return to the 'good old days', and of a departure from governmental authority and services: exceptions were those of medicine (but not education) and roads.

Rejecting the burdens the colonial government sought to foist on them, the Waluguru experienced a transcendental moment of unity. The call for freedom from hunger and the power of colonialism could only be expressed in the vaguest terms of rejection of the present and the return to an earlier time. Yet beneath the unity of a call to return to the 'good old days' lay the reality of differentiation in the mountains and a differing conception of what was meant by those 'old days'.

Notes

1. David M. Anderson, 'Depression, Dust Bowl, Demography, and Drought: The Colonial State and Soil Conservation in East Africa During the 1930s', *African Affairs*, 83 (1984), pp. 321–43; and John Iliffe, *A Modern History of Tanganyika* (Cambridge, 1979), pp. 348–50.

2. Steven Feierman, *Peasant Intellectuals: Anthropology and History in Tanzania* (Madison, 1990).

3. Iliffe, *Modern History*, pp. 475–6.

4. Morogoro District Books, 'Native District Census'; *Morogoro Region Five Year Development Plan* (1984), p. 12.

5. TNA 61/378/5/ vol. 3.

6. Interview with Saidi Ramadhani Ming'walu, Melela, 16 June 1987.

7. P.C. Brett to the Secretariat, TNA 12978 excerpted from 10074/15, no specific date but written as a follow-up to a memo of 15 June 1927.

8. 'ULUS report up to May, 1952', J.S. Harris, TNA 26/5/6, ULUS 1/2 Year and Annual Reports.

9. This information was drawn from TNA 26/5/6, ULUS 1/2 Year and Annual Reports.

10. Morogoro District Book, P.C. Duff, 'Uluguru Land Usage Scheme (ULUS)', 1960.

11. Public Record Office (PRO) CO 822/807 'Departmental Enquiry into the Disturbed Situation in the Uluguru Chiefdom, Morogoro District, June–September, 1955'.

12. See Roland Young and Henry Fosbrooke, *Smoke in the Hills: Political Tension in the Morogoro District of Tanganyika* (Evanston, 1960); and 'Departmental Enquiry', Public

Record Office, CO 822/807. Henry Fosbrooke was Senior Sociologist for the colonial government at the time of ULUS. He filed numerous reports on the progress of the scheme, and evaluated its failure after its demise.

13. Interview with Rajabu Kazimia Kwanzi, Mtamba, 30 June 1987.

14. Interview with Mikael Saleh Gugulu, Mtamba, 1 July 1987.

15. Interview with Ramadhani Saidi Simba, Mtamba, 30 June 1987.

16. I never heard of a woman negotiating with a landowner.

17. The Waluguru have several designations for the clan head. When they want to stress his role as the solver of problems for the clan, they refer to him as maternal uncle or head of the clan; when they wish to refer to his right to control land, they call him landowner or owner of the country.

18. TNA 61/556/1.

19. For a discussion of why land ownership did not prevent land development on the western side of the mountains, see Pamela A. Maack, 'The Waluguru Are Not Sleeping': Poverty, Culture, and Social Differentiation in Morogoro, Tanzania' (Ph.D. Dissertation, Northwestern University, Evanston, 1992), chapter 6.

20. Interview with Mohammed Fundi Kimbengere, Kiloka, 25 June 1987.

21. It should be mentioned that TANU also apparently joined forces with the heir of a deposed Native Authority chief and prominent rain-maker, as well as his cousin, Ali Kingalu, who according to the British were seeking to foment discord among the Waluguru in an attempt at reinstatement. The British blamed the actions of this pair for much of the trouble in Morogoro. Nevertheless, not one of the Waluguru I spoke to mentioned the role of Ali Kingalu and his cousin. In fact, when I told them the British said he had been trying to cause trouble in order to be made Sultan, they laughed and pointed out to me that the former Sultan was deposed in the 1920s and in fact was not a Sultan but a rain-maker. They said that Ali Kingalu was chosen as a TANU representative because he spoke well and had volunteered. They were adamant in their assertion that the problems with ULUS were real and did not need to be blamed on the actions of one man.

22. 'Departmental Enquiry', Secret Report, p. 30, Public Record Office CO 822/807.

Part Four

Environment

&

Morality

The chapters in this part mark a particularly innovative turn in the tradition of Tanzanian environmental history. They deal with subjects which are vital for an understanding of ecological change, but which nevertheless have been only rarely included in discussions of African environmental change. Michelle Wagner, Thomas Spear and Jamie Monson examine the thought and institutions which created a morality of resource use. They situate their studies in three very different environments, the Buha savannah of Kigoma, Mount Meru and the Kilombero Valley. Wagner devotes most of her attention to precolonial Ha culture. In contrast, Spear and Monson concentrate on the colonial period, and explore the clash of very different European and African understandings of moral resource use.

Michele Wagner offers a history of earth spirits and the priests who mediate with them. The Ha people, she says, have long identified closely with small environmental niches and with the earth spirits who inhabit them. The priests guide the use of micro-environments, teaching farmers where to plant, where to draw water and what places must be avoided. She shows that although there is great continuity in the institutions and beliefs which govern the utilization of the environment, they have passed through at least four phases. Before the eighteenth century, the priests apparently enjoyed unrivalled authority in Buha. When kingship took root in Buha during the sixteenth or seventeenth centuries, however, the priests began to share both their authority and the supervision of sites of spirit veneration with kings and their ritual specialists. Thus a close association seems to have developed between precolonial political authority and environmental control, just as it did in regions of eastern Tanzania such as Usambara, Handeni and Uluguru. The nineteenth century, argues Wagner, brought caravan trade from the Indian Ocean coast (Ujiji, the great caravan terminus on Lake Tanganyika, was located in southern Buha) and greatly inflated the value of economic knowledge. 'Access to nature spirits', she argues, became 'a new kind of economic asset'. Priests took tribute in inflated amounts from coastal merchants who wanted their authorization to build trading stations, and from Ha farmers who sought security from famine, pestilence and other calamities which might expose them to enslavement. Under colonial rule, priests often obtained positions as subchiefs in the British administration.

Wagner's work shows that there were long-lasting institutions and beliefs in Ha culture which upheld concepts of proper resource use. When people transgressed such norms, the earth spirits withheld their gifts, and relations with them had to be restored by offering sacrifices through the mediation of the priests. The secretiveness with which people made their way to ritual sites suggests that frequently they may have been driven to make sacrifices by moral doubt and guilt. Nevertheless, like Conte, who acknowledges the possibility of precolonial environmental degradation, Wagner's account does not permit us a romantic view of an environmental morality impervious to corruption. In certain economic and political circumstances, environmental knowledge could become, writes Wagner, 'a means to economic advantage'. One guesses that the priests' intimate connection with political authority may sometimes have cast their legitimacy into doubt, particularly in the colonial period, when they served as tax collectors. Should they have suffered some loss of authority, their situation would indeed have been similar to that of chiefs, in Usambara, Uluguru and elsewhere in eastern Tanzania, who ceased to 'heal the land'.

Thomas Spear, whose stated purpose is to integrate ideology into a history of environment and political economy, explores the circumstances which led to perhaps the most famous episode involving environmental issues in colonial Tanzania: the Meru Land Case of the early 1950s. Spear vividly contrasts the very different European and African conceptions of land which provoked political and moral crisis in the Arusha and Meru communities of Mount Meru. Land became a burning issue on Mount Meru because German and British colonial regimes limited African access to land by demarcating forest reserves on the upper slopes of the mountain and by extending an 'iron ring' of alienated land around the mountain's base. Squeezed between forest reserves above them and settler farms below them, rapidly growing Arusha and Meru communities resorted to parcelling of plots and increasingly intensive forms of land use.

Europeans restricted Arusha and Meru access to mountain lands because they felt that African methods of land use were both harmful and inefficient, because they believed that their own methods of conservation were superior, because they perceived that their duty to protect Mount Meru for the benefit of the entire colony overrode parochial Arusha and Meru interests, because they wanted to protect European coffee growers from African competition and because settlers found land to be an irresistibly tempting object of speculation and marker of élite status. For the Arusha and Meru, however, their land on Mount Meru was associated with quite different moral values. It was home, the burial place of ancestors, the site of nourishing banana plots and, writes Spear, 'the central focus of people's lives'. These considerations inspired an ethic of conservation among the Arusha and Meru, who, using the techniques of agricultural intensification described by Kimambo in Part II, carefully intercropped, hedged and manured their land to prevent erosion and soil exhaustion. This commitment to conservation forced upon the Arusha and Meru a protracted political struggle which lasted through the entire period of German and British rule and culminated in the Meru Land Case. Ultimately they were successful, because while erosion, soil degradation and overgrazing were not unknown on Mount Meru, the mountain people were able to protect enough of their land to create a remarkably productive and soil-protecting agronomic system. In the course of their long struggle, argues Spear, the Arusha and Meru became convinced of the 'immorality of the wider colonial order'. Thus just as controversies over land and conservation led the Luguru people described by Pamela Maack to oppose colonialism and their appointed chiefs, so too on Mount Meru the moral and political crisis over land persuaded farmers to join the nationalist movement.

Although Jamie Monson studies a very different environment, the marshy and seasonally flooded Kilombero Valley, she too discovers a moral struggle over resource use which resembles the conflict over land on Mount Meru. In the Kilombero Valley, the resource at issue was timber. Monson shows that the creation of forest reserves revealed a contrast between very different ethics of conservation. She explains that British officials drew upon a complex ideology of conservation in order to justify their decision to exclude Africans from extensive forest reserves. They were primarily interested in protecting commercially valuable species of timber for exploitation by European timber concerns. However, their determination to do so was strengthened by their faith in 'scientific' assessment of resource use, by their conviction that African timber use was wasteful, by their belief that Africans must be protected from the corrupting influence of commerce (even though they expected all Africans to make a contribution to the prosperity of the colony) and by their confidence that 'subsistence' activities could be readily distinguished from 'commercial' undertakings. All these considerations led British foresters to prohibit residents of the Kilombero Valley from felling trees for the construction of large canoes used to take rice to market.

The canoe-builders, however, inhabited a quite different moral universe. Their choice of timber for canoe-building was dictated by their own understanding of conservation, for they chose tree species which produced the most durable canoes. Moreover, their use of canoes was governed by complex social and moral considerations which the British simply failed to fathom. Rather than owning canoes as individuals, they used canoes in groups of *walongo*, that is, people who were bound together by intricate patterns of reciprocal cooperation. *Walongo* worked together to fell timber, build canoes and crew them, but they also did various other kinds of work together, including agricultural tasks. Hence British efforts to ban the building of large canoes threatened to prevent them from fulfilling their obligations to cooperate with fellow *walongo*. As Monson says, conservationists and canoe-builders held entirely different views about what constituted 'wise' and moral use of forest resources. The canoe building *walongo* wanted to make frugal use of timber to transport and sell their rice crops for the benefit of themselves, their communities and their kin. They were frustrated in their effort to live morally, however, by both forestry policies and colonial economic structures which, as we have seen in the situations discussed by Giblin, Maack and Spear, limited African opportunities to participate in trade.

Seven

Environment, Community & History
'Nature in the Mind'

In Nineteenth- & Early Twentieth-Century
Buha, Tanzania

MICHELE WAGNER

At twilight after a bustling market day in the western Tanzanian town of Kasulu, an elderly woman sagging under a cluster of *ibitoke* beer-bananas approaches the Bogwe River. She takes a deep breath, pulls her *kitenge* cloth closer to her chest and then pushes her foot into the swirling stream, eyes set firmly on the opposite shore. Carefully she treads, one bare foot before the other, her gaze never breaking from the distant shoreline, never looking down. All of her life she has lived together with the Bogwe, but in deep mistrust. She has known the river, infested as it is with nature spirits, to be a capricious neighbour.

The history of this uneasy coexistence between a woman and a river – her distrust of the river, her fear of its spirits, her reluctance to approach it and the defensiveness of her traverse – is ecological history. Ecological history, the study of the ever-changing relationship of human groups to their physical environment, not only addresses the physical and material, but also deals with the conceptual. The knowledge system that people use to define and interact with their environment is an important component of ecological history, since this knowledge has a direct bearing on their techniques for managing, changing and adapting to the environment.

This chapter deals with ecological history in the Buha cultural region of western Tanzania. It examines the relationship between Ha communities and their physical environment in the late nineteenth and early twentieth centuries. By linking this relationship to its changing historical context, and by demonstrating how the conceptualization of it changed as well, the chapter seeks to establish the historical character of 'nature in the mind', or conceptual ecology. In doing so, it seeks

175

to contribute to the growing body of knowledge comprising Tanzanian intellectual history.

Like many bodies of specialized knowledge, the Ha have left the deeper inner workings and crucial interstices of the ecological–spiritual framework to experts. The ecological knowledge of the layperson is in many cases limited to what is 'obvious' – that is, what is obvious from a Ha point of view – without penetrating the deeper levels of how and why. Those deeper and more nuanced aspects of the basic formulation remain privileged information. They are left to the experts – the *bateko* or earth priests, and to the *banyamulagula* 'diviners' and *bapfumu*, the specialists of human dysfunctions. They remain today, as they have been for generations, quite secret.

In contemporary times, these ways of knowing about the environment are under siege – or this is the sense of elders. Science, particularly as it has been disseminated by agricultural extension workers, and religion, as it has been taught by Tanzanian priests, catechists and Islamic teachers, have introduced alternative ways of thinking about the human–environmental symbiosis. *Bateko* don't defend themselves, since the cornerstones of their arguments remain secret. And so, in a sense, this 'siege' remains unaddressed. But, even as self-identified 'modernists' look askance at their neighbours who continue to trot down to the river to offer beer to the nature spirits, they do so from the secure vantage point of sitting under the family's sacred *mulinzi* tree.

Buha

Buha is a cultural region of western Tanzania which stretches from Lake Tanganyika on the west to the edges of Tabora Region on the east. In the north it follows along the Burundi border, and at its northeastern corner reaches about 50 miles north of Kibondo. To the south, it is bordered by Uvinza. These have been approximately its boundaries for the last century and a half.

Buha of the nineteenth century comprised at least six political regions or kingdoms: Nkalinzi (also known as Bujiji), Bushingo (later called Heru-Ushingo), Kunkanda, Muhambwe and Buyungu. Another political region, Rukalanga, may also be considered among these.[2] The characterization of these units as kingdoms is based on the translation of the word *mwami* (pl. *bami*), the title of the highest political authority in each of these entities, as 'king'. This has been the convention in the neighbouring kingdoms of Rwanda and Burundi. Buha, unlike its neighbours, appears never to have been a single, unified kingdom. It remains a 'culture region' or cultural block, which upon close scrutiny demonstrates internal complexity and diversity from a historical and even a cultural standpoint.

To regard the human population of Buha simply in terms of affiliation to a kingdom or in terms of ethnicity, following the Hutu–Tutsi ethnic paradigm of the Great Lakes region, is to miss certain significant elements of Ha identity. For example, even within the kingdoms of Buha, people defined others and themselves, at least in part, by their residential habitat. Throughout Buha the majority of the population occupied lowland areas and lowlanders of all kingdoms tended to be referred to as 'Baha'. They clearly distinguished themselves from hill people whom they tended to call 'Batutsi'. What were these labels, Baha and Batutsi? At one level, they were occupational terms referring to lowland farmers and highland cattle keepers. At another level, they were historical terms which contrasted the 'indigenous' mainstream with newcomer 'others'. At yet another level, they were social class terms referring to ordinary people (Baha) and to those with an unusual 'pedigree' (Batutsi). Yet, in all their polysemy, the two terms none the less refer, at a simple, everyday level, to lowlanders and highlanders. Thus environment has long been an important element of human and community identity.

Several other, much smaller, human communities occupied different environmental and social niches in Buha. These include forest/savannah dwellers (known as Batwa), riverain peoples (known as Bayanga, Bakiko or Banyahoza), swamp inhabitants and lake dwellers. They were identified especially closely with their residential habitats because these habitats were not the conventional ones and tended to separate them from ordinary Baha.

The viability, or perhaps basic pragmatism, of considering ecological niche as an element of identification for human communities in Buha is surprisingly supported by European travellers such as Sir Richard Burton and Henry M. Stanley who otherwise seemed fixated on 'discovering' 'tribes'. Burton wrote of lakeshore dwellers whom he encountered at Ujiji, Buha:[3] 'The lakists are an almost amphibious race, excellent divers, strong swimmers and fisherman, and vigorous . . . ichthyophagists all.' Reiterating this awareness of environment in community definition, colonial administrator J.E.S. Griffiths identified Baha as 'plainsmen' and 'hillmen', even though the established trend among his peers, particularly among the Belgians in neighbouring Urundi, was to regard the natives as either Tutsi or Hutu.[4] Griffiths' notes in the Kigoma District Books show that he was certainly influenced by a 'tribalist' approach to Africans – in his era he could hardly have been otherwise – but even so, writing of Buha in 1936, he emphasized the role of environment:[5]

Uha can, like Gaul, be divided into three very definite parts: the Uha of the high grasslands in the south – the altitude ranging between five and six thousand feet – the Uha of the high bush country to the north, and the

Uha of the low bush country ... The houses of the bush-dwellers are simple and consist of rough beehive shaped structures, thatched more or less carefully with grass. Hamlets in the lowland country are generally built round waterholes but as these are rare, very large areas of the country are left uninhabited and useless.

The customs and ceremonies of the bush native are of the simplest and there appears to be very little which helps to bind him to society ... Among the cattle-keeping hillmen life is more complicated. The people live closer together, see more of each other and the presence of cattle seems to complicate all ceremonial. . .This is in direct contrast to the people of the bush who are of a roving disposition and move their villages on the slightest provocation.

The inaccessibility of the plainsman was very marked in the recent sleeping sickness epidemic which swept through the country. Fortunately, it was not among the cattle-keeping section of the people that the disease was found but among the more unstable people of the plains.

Griffiths' concern for the well-being of cattle keepers, and his marked lack of interest in the condition of plains dwellers, come out rather strongly in the final sentence of his statement. This attitude was consistent with the general wisdom of colonial administrators that among the Baha and their neighbours, Batutsi were more worthy of attention. Nevertheless, colonial administrators had some interest in Buha's smaller communities, even if only for curiosity's sake. In his 1940 article, 'Water Gipsies of the Malagarasi', C. Macquarie described a Buha riverain community as 'a small tribe of the most retiring habits, living among the lagoons and swamps of the Malagarasi water system'.[6]

The characterization of communities in a highly localized sense as pockets of 'water gipsies' or villages of 'lakists' runs counter to the dominant colonial theme of 'tribes'. Yet even the colonial officials who administered a political structure based on 'tribes' nevertheless identified water gipsies and hillmen. All of these varied communities resided in the single cultural space of Buha and, according to their particular needs and experiences, knew its physical environment in different ways.

Bisigo and Mashinga

Although they varied in their choices of environmental niches and their strategies for exploiting them, many of Buha's communities shared basic concepts about the constitution of the physical environment, its internal dynamics and its interconnections with humans.[7] By the nineteenth century, most highland and lowland dwellers, and those lakist and riverain peoples who had assimilated the basic structure of the ecological belief systems of their sedentary neighbours (for example, those fisherfolk who identified as having been incorporated into a Ha kingdom), conceived of an ecological system animated by nature spirits. The specific characteristics of these nature spirits, such as their individual names and traits, their preferred mediums and abodes and the particular meteorological and socio-medical phenomena with which they were associated, had originated from disparate sources. In each local setting, particular spirits were identified, their characteristics were 'discovered' or 'revealed', and they developed as elements of local history. Information about nature spirits filtered in on the winds of gossip, or during afternoon chats around the beerpot by traders and travellers, hunters and salt-makers. Plausible bits of information which elucidated the inclinations of familiar spirits were added to the local store of knowledge.

Over the years, a general frame of reference for nature spirits was transmitted back and forth across the Buha cultural region. Within this general framework there existed many local, and even regional, peculiarities and inconsistencies. At the beginning of the colonial period, for example, knowledge about nature spirits varied distinctly by region, with a clear division between eastern and western Buha. Regional variation remained the norm until about the 1940s, when the standardization of the Ha 'tribal' custom became formalized in ethnographic writing and transmitted though church and school, and widespread labour migration dramatically increased inter-regional contacts. Currently, the most marked variation follows generational lines. The oldest elders recall individual names for and the details about nature spirits, which often include unusual references and internal inconsistencies that they cannot explain. Many of the 'younger elders', in contrast, offer internally consistent, 'smooth' accounts which correspond closely with 'Croyances et Coutumes des Baha', a manuscript written by a missionary who spent much of his long career as a priest and bishop in Buha collecting, preaching on and distributing to other priests information about the customs of the region.

The most widespread and oldest category of Ha nature spirits is the *gisigo* (pl. *bisigo*).[8] The word reappears throughout Buha, although in western Buha, formerly the kingdoms of Nkalinzi and Heru Juu, it is the single predominant term for nature spirit, whereas in the eastern regions of Bushingo, Muhambwe, and Buyungu, elders recognize bisigo, but say that they are being forgotten. In these latter regions, the most widespread and current category of nature spirits is *ishinga* (pl. *mashinga*). In Muhambwe, interestingly, *mashinga* and *bisigo* currently exist side by side in a dual system which differs significantly from the western Buha one. The facts that multiple categories of nature spirits exist, and that their distribution, at least in contemporary times, is non-uniform, show that they were dynamic and subject to historical change.[9]

In western Buha, where *bisigo* have existed as the dominant, and by present evidence the exclusive, general category of nature spirits, a sense of boundary – of separateness – between humans and nature spirits was and is very strong. *Bisigo* were dangerous and all abodes, animals and phenomena associated with them were fastidiously avoided.[10] When humans had to approach the abode of a known *gisigo*, they politely warned the spirits of their presence with a cough or a whistle. A special whistle called *urwamira* was made by traditional healers and amulet-craftsmen for this purpose. Among themselves, people warned their visitors, and often repeated to their children '*Harahuma*' – 'there's a *gisigo* there'.[11]

Dangerous as they were, the properties and domains of *bisigo* were only loosely defined. For the most part – and most dangerously – *bisigo* remained invisible. But when they did appear, they could manifest a number of different perceptible properties and forms, ranging in form from physical phenomena such as whirlwinds to animals or humans. As physical phenomena, *bisigo* travelled especially in whirlwinds. Even the most foot-weary traveller, when sighting a whirlwind ahead, would be inclined to throw down his or her load, drop to her knees, and greet the *gisigo* respectfully with the wish '*Biheko, ushike amahoro y'uja*' – 'oh, bearer of luck, may you arrive where you are going in peace'.[12] *Bisigo* were also said to travel in fog, in angry storm-clouds, in fire spreading across a mountainside and in shadows or mirages passing over the savannah in the distance. These transient *bisigo* were sometimes called *mahembe*.[13] Transient *bisigo* also moved about in the forms of animals. Typically, they manifested themselves as sacred snakes such as the python or the spitting cobra. Embodied as animals they had forces that actual creatures did not have, such as the ability to vanish and reappear. In human form, *bisigo* could be recognized by their supernatural physical features, such as arms that stretched indefinitely, mist-like skin or eyes arranged vertically instead of horizontally or located on the back of the head. Other *bisigo* were more rooted, preferring to dwell in a specific habitat. These stationary spirits especially favoured ponds and rivers. They also liked to live in fragrant trees, especially kapok, mango and *minyinya*.[14]

As assiduously as humans tried to avoid *bisigo*, at times individuals had unfortunate encounters with them. Many Buha elders claim first-hand knowledge of such incidents. In one instance, Mama M, a resident of Kasulu near Heru Juu, collided with a *gisigo* in the Bogwe River, where she went to wash off some millet grains which were irritating her skin.[15] The spirit accused: 'You fell on me! You stepped on my children!' Mama M reported that she then slipped into a kind of a trance during which she was taken to the *gisigo*'s abode. Ultimately, she returned to the human world where she was found huddled on the riverbank, in a semi-conscious state, mumbling unintelligible phrases.

Most *gisigo* victims have never reported what happened to them because they were rendered mute or emotionally disturbed by the experience. Many of the victims were attacked physically as well. A traditional doctor (*mupfumu*) from Muhambwe says that broken limbs, full or partial paralysis, and blindness were (and continue to be) caused by *bisigo*.[16] *Bisigo* could attack unborn children, causing birth defects. They could even kill people. No one was exempt from the attack of *bisigo*. Even the *mwami* (king) of Heru Juu feared the *bisigo* of the Bogwe River. He avoided crossing or even looking at that river.[17]

The danger of *bisigo* and the boundaries in western Buha between people and nature spirits were mitigated in eastern Buha by the existence of another category of nature spirits, *mashinga*. In contrast to *bisigo*, which commanded the potential for danger and insecurity in the physical environment, *mashinga* controlled an environment's resources. 'They show us where wealth is found' explained a Muhambwe elder. 'They can point out where a well is.'[18] From the perspective of eastern Buha, *bisigo* always attacked people, but *mashinga* sometimes left them gifts. Therefore, encounters with *mashinga* were welcomed as well as feared. But fear always entered into the encounter because, like *bisigo*, *mashinga* could possess people and torment them with illnesses. Moreover, the bestowal of a gift by an *ishinga* entailed obligations, especially the obligation to keep it secret. 'If you believed and were shown, you took your share, but you did not reveal anything about the place or the spirit, or else it would punish you. You could not bear children.'[19] Baha also believed that the spirits wished to be shown respect and appreciation. To demonstrate their gratitude for the blessings of an *ishinga*, recipients reciprocated with gifts such as beer, honey, a chicken or cooked food.

More predictable in their choice of abodes than *bisigo*, and less mobile, *mashinga* lived in undisturbed environments: lakes, rivers, ponds, hills, anthills, trees, groves, large stones . . . In Muhambwe, elders say that these spirits preferred to live in hills.[20] If they lived along a shoreline, they sought proximity to a tree called a *munyabagana*.[21]

Western Baha regarded *mashinga* as 'approachable' spirits, beneficent but in a qualified, fickle way, not unlike powerful humans such as chiefs and family elders. But it was nevertheless a risk to approach them. Therefore, in most cases they believed it best to solicit the assistance of a *muteko*, or earth-priest, to communicate with nature spirits on their behalf.

The Muteko

Although the members of each Buha community – be they of the highland, lowland, swamp or savannah – had working knowledge of their particular habitats, the expert on environmental issues in each habitat was the local *muteko* (pl. *bateko*). The *muteko*, or earth-priest, whose authority derived from claims that his or her family were primordial residents of the region, prevailed in all matters pertaining to the environment.[22] Yet primordialism was a relative concept in Buha. *Bateko* primogenitors were not always the first persons to live in a region – oral traditions recall ancient others, such as transient fisherfolk or hunters. But the ancestors of the *muteko* were the first to settle permanently in a particular place and to attempt a rapport with the nature spirits they found there. Success in rapport-building meant that the family could stay and establish their roots there, but failure meant death and emigration.

The relationship between the pioneering *muteko* and the local nature spirits served as a pact as well as a vehicle connecting humans and the physical environment. As a pact, the relationship served as a kind of promise: the *muteko* could serve the spirits, perform rituals for them and direct the human community in environmental matters. The spirits would maintain an environment of security for humans unless humans engaged in activities that jeopardized themselves. The process of communicating with nature spirits, of performing rituals for them, and of perceiving the terms of the human–nature spirit relationship was described in the Kiha language as 'cooling' (*quhoza*) and as 'blessing' (*qutelekeza* or *quhezaqira*). As a vehicle, the *muteko* became the 'enabler' who made it possible for humans to reside in that locale. The *muteko* became an 'enabler' in a much more practical way too, for those who wished to join the settlement had to solicit the permission of the *muteko*. In controlling entrance into the community, the *muteko* became a social authority as well as a spiritual one. *Bateko* also exercised authority in boundary conflicts and disputes over resources. The special relationship, or pact, with the local nature spirits was passed on through the *muteko*'s family to the most receptive child, male or female. Thus the institution of *buteko*, the task of mediating between nature spirits and the human community, was transmitted from parent to child, in a single family.

Historical accounts of *bateko*

Although Baha *bateko* appear in written literature at least as early as the 1850s, with specific references to them occurring in explorer Richard F. Burton's *The Lake Regions of Central Africa* and later in the writings of traveller Verney Lovett Cameron and missionary Edward Hore,[23] one of the most vivid portraits of an individual who appears to have been a *muteko* is given by the German military Captain A. Leue, who in August 1895 led a 'pacification' expedition across Buha to Ujiji.[24]

In his written account of this journey, the German officer mentions making the acquaintance of a certain Gamhollo, whom he describes as a 'mysterious medicine man'. Leue writes of Gamhollo: 'He was on intimate terms with Kigongo, the patron saint of the country.' The spirit Kigongo, according to Leue, 'lived at the top of a tall tree' which he identified as a fig tree. With no small amount of coaxing to entice Gamhollo to present himself, Leue found the man to be 'a little mysterious fellow, nearly fifty years of age, with bold face and eyes. Quiet and reserved, he did not reveal anything, and to my eager questions he gave only an evasive reply or an embarrassed smile.' The quizzical-faced ritualist avoided the German captain, who lamented that 'all my friendly words were in vain'.

A fuller portrait of a *muteko* is given by the current *muteko* of Kayumpu (Buyumpu) hill, in the district Kibondo, western Tanzania. In presenting his own self-portrait, this *muteko* began, as many elders do, with an oral tradition which establishes his family's arrival in the region of Buha:[25]

> Kalazi, my ancestor, came from Nkoma [Burundi]. He and his brother came, they were two: Kalazi and Chungilizi. They came as hunters, and they reached Kunuyumpu, nearby here.
>
> It so happened that the animal they had been pursuing crossed over from Burundi to Kibondo, passing here at Kumuyumpu. When the animal came this way, another one crossed its track. There were two sets of tracks and they went in different directions. The two brothers couldn't figure out which set of tracks to follow. So they decided to pass the night there together. Here, at that time, there was no *mwami*, no *muteko*, nothing at all. People were just living any way at all, all scattered about, without order. Their main goal was to steal each other's lands and even to kill each other.
>
> So they passed the night there, the brothers. Kalinzi began to prepare food, using millet flour and beans. And the other prepared a shelter in which to sleep. It was late in the evening . . .
>
> As he cooked, the elder brother watched the younger and thought to himself, 'I am doing this work and I haven't even finished cooking yet, but this young one has already set up the sleeping shelter.'
>
> Then the elder brother, who was stirring the porridge, said to the younger, 'In order to find out which set of animal tracks is ours, let's put a piece of porridge into each animal's path and when we wake up tomorrow if we find that there is no food in one of the sets of tracks, then we will know that one is not our animal – it is the other one. The track in which we find our food, we will know that this track belongs to our animal.'
>
> They went to sleep. In the morning they checked the animal tracks and found the porridge [on one track] missing. The animal that they had been following all the way from Burundi had gone inside that hill: and this is where I bring [the sacrifice of] a cow every year.
>
> The food [on the other track] was there. They said, 'That one, that is our animal.' It was a bushbuck. When they climbed down the hill on to the flat land below they found the animal lying there dead. The one brother said,

'Do you see? Didn't I tell you?' And the younger brother replied, 'Ah! You as my elder brother, you can do such a thing! Can porridge walk? Does it have legs like human beings? You have played a trick on me!'

The elder said, 'You too have played a trick on me. And you, being younger, why did you do that? Why did you finish building the sleeping house even before I had finished preparing the food? From now on, you will be known as Gihumbi and you will build houses for all people. You will be a chief of all the people who will come . . . But I shall never touch your house. If I touch it, let it burn.'

The younger brother responded, 'And you, let you be known as Kalazi because you left the food and we found it and the animal was also found. If you are not there, nobody will rule. My child will not rule unless your child has given him that chance.'

And from that day on, Kalazi became the *muteko*. They separated and Kalazi became the *muteko* of this place because he was the elder brother. And Gihumbi [the *mwami*] is Chungilizi.

This oral tradition of origin establishes that the right of *buteko* (the abstract term for the institution of earth priesthood) came to Kalazi, as is the conventional pattern, because he was the first to 'take' the region. But the tradition goes beyond the usual 'first-comer' pattern by delving into the relationship between the *muteko* and the king, or *mwami*.

In claiming ancientness of authority in particular regions, *bateko* families run up against the claims of the ruling dynasties whose genealogies reach back many generations – current historical research places their roots in the seventeenth century[26] – but who cannot make the case for primordial origin. *Bateko* claim that their families were primordial and that their ancestors governed small territories before the arrival of kings. They relate that later, as kingship developed (or when kings 'arrived'), *bateko* maintained their local spiritual authority, and lent support and participation in rituals which enabled a *mwami* to govern.

In this tale, *buteko* came to Kayumpu hill amidst a background of both brotherly solidarity and also competitiveness and trickery between the two future leaders. Kalazi's threat to burn and destroy the *mwami*'s house and Chungilizi's acknowledgement that his heirs might not govern without the consent of Kalazi's people reflect the relationship between the institutions of *buteko* and *bwami* (kingship) – although quite clearly from a *muteko*'s point of view. That is, since a *muteko* had a hand in causing or preventing certain kinds of physical disaster in a *mwami*'s territory, a *mwami* had to acknowledge the *muteko*'s authority. However, the *muteko* exercised this authority in particular domains, specifically in issues regarding the earth, ideological empowerment of the *mwami* and human-environment interaction.

The consensus reached by the two leaders in this oral tradition is important for understanding how pre-*bami* leadership systems and *bwami* coalesced into one political ideological system, in which the consent of *bateko* was fundamental to maintaining the power of the *mwami*. In contrast to a struggle-focused view in which militaristic and materialistic *bami* overpowered, appropriated the resources of and ultimately supplanted the spirit-focused *bateko*, this oral tradition shows that *bateko* and *bami* developed a consensus but maintained authority in separate realms. It also points out that *bami* depended on *bateko* for their legitimacy to rule. Nature spirits remained stronger than either of the two: both the *mwami* and the *muteko* regarded spirits with fear and respect.

Another point that develops from this oral tradition is that particular locations – in this case the hill in which the bushbuck hid – had special significance for the *muteko*'s family. This auspicious location varied among *bateko*. For some it was a certain place in a river. For others, it was a spring or pond. Places such as particular rocks, caves, waterfalls and anthills also served as locations for *bateko* activities. Nearly all of these places existed in association with a grove of trees, *kibira*, which the *muteko* regarded as a sacred shrine and a permanent home to his or her particular nature spirits.[27] It was also the home of python snakes, which were linked to spirits, perhaps as their embodiment.

The sacred grove of the narrator above sits on the hill where the bushbuck once hid. During his visits to this hill, which occur at least once a year at the beginning of the dry season, he greets his nature spirits (*mashinga*) by name. He offers them gifts, including the cow which he mentioned, and he performs rituals, such as the ceremonious presentation of fragrant grasses or leaves, of which his nature spirits are particularly fond. His knowledge of the correct comportment to use with them comes from the accumulated experience of his forebears. These details were transmitted to him by his father, who, shortly before his death, introduced him to the family's spirits and demonstrated how to exercise diplomacy with them. A conventional formula for addressing nature spirits employed by many *bateko* is the following: 'If you are truly [name of spirit], if you are truly the spirit who knew my father and grandfather, if I am truly the son of X and the grandson of Y, then hear my request . . .'

Bateko used drums when communicating with earth spirits. This is highly significant because, just as they were throughout the Great Lakes, drums were objects of power in Buha and were associated with *bami* and with regional governors, the *batwale*. The drums of *bateko* differed from those of the *bami* in terms of the wood, hides used on the drum face, shape of the drum and mode of playing.[28]

The importance of the drum, and the implications of its misuse, are illustrated in the following tale told by the *muteko* of Buyumpu:[29]

The son of our deceased younger brother, when the father died, the son became a habitual drunkard. And he took to playing a certain drum, which we call 'Mulinga', whenever he was drunk. Well, then lions came and invaded and they killed people. Whenever people went to hunt them, they came up with cats or baboons, but as soon as the hunters gave up, another person would be killed. Finally, they sent a word to me here. I went to the hill and spoke my words. And I told the drunk man, 'Take this drum and keep it to yourself.' Now that region is in peace, people even sleep outside and there are no more lions.

The misuse of instruments reserved for communication with spirits, the violation of taboos: these breaches of conduct were causes of ecological and social disequilibrium according to the models at the core of *ubuteko*. It was the job of the *muteko* to prevent disequilibrium, or at least to manage it, by knowing the taboos and how to re-establish order when a taboo was broken. The *muteko*'s role was both preventive and curative. Preventively, *bateko* reinforced the boundaries set by nature spirits by distributing land and indicating where humans could not pass. They showed people where to live, where to plant, where to draw water, where to leave sacrifices and so forth. Curatively, *bateko* indicated the course of action to be taken when the human community was ailing because a boundary or taboo had been transgressed. Although their duties touched on both the prevention and the curing of environmental stress, *bateko* could not stop change from occurring. Their job was to interpose a human element in environmental issues, to ensure that humans and their environment remained interconnected and to exert whatever influence was possible from the human side to re-establish a working ecological order.

Historicity of the human–environment relationship: the case of Mwadye

The re-establishment of order by performing blessing ceremonies (*qutelekela* and *quhezagira*) was the ongoing task of the *muteko*: it was a method of addressing change. The ceremonies enabled a *muteko* to exert a measure of human control in a transforming situation. By appealing to a more powerful ally, humans through the *muteko* dealt as best they could with all manner of change, including regular, seasonal modulations as well as sporadic or unique incidents. Premised as it was on change, the Ha formulation of human–environmental interaction was historical in character. Moreover, the formulation itself was subject to historical change.

Direct evidence of historical change in this formulation exists in almost imperceptible bits and pieces, sometimes taking the form of inconsistencies which tumble into view in the puzzled pauses when elders find that their line of reasoning through a historical narrative somehow fails to make sense. Such is often the case with the oral history of Mwadye, a hill in Buha's Muhambwe region which was (and is) a dwelling-place for a well-known *ishinga*. Mwadye, one of a cluster of stone- and boulder-covered mountains rising from the savannah in Muhambwe, provides a particularly fascinating example of the historical nature of human–nature spirit interaction because the site has assumed multiple functions over time. Mwadye is best known for being the site of a major *ishinga*, but it later became a ritual site associated with the *mwami* of Muhambwe.

The site itself is stone-strewn mountainside where an enormous boulder, approximately 70 feet high, obscures the entrance to a cave. Perching atop the boulder is an unusually large and prominent tree, a '*bamba*' or false cotton (*Bombax*) tree, which a visitor in 1923 estimated to be 20 feet wide.[30] The cave can be entered by passing through a vertical fracture in the rock which is about 15 feet high and wide enough to permit a person to squeeze through shoulders first. Inside, one encounters a large, naturally lit antechamber, which leads into at least two other darker inner rooms.[31] The names 'Shumbuka' and 'Mastinga' were recorded by a European visitor as being associated with these interior chambers. Shumbuka is a causative verbal form related to the Kiha root -*shumb*- (peace, to receive congratulations).[32] Mastinga, not a typical (or possible) Kiha phoneme, was likely to have been misrecorded; perhaps it was a miswriting of *mashinga*.

Outside the cave, the gifts of the nature spirit, particularly hard sandstone stones which were well suited to use as grinding stones, lay scattered across the mountain.[33] Grinding stones from Mwadye are still considered to be of the highest quality.[34] Since a grinding stone is a vital piece of household equipment, these particularly hard specimens were no small gift. At the foot of Mwadye is a plain, called Kinywa, where there are said to be two springs which never run dry.[35] These, too, were regarded as gifts of the spirit of Mwadye.

A unique site in the dry and relatively uniform scrub-covered central Buha savannah, Mwadye held a sacred place in the world view of eastern Buha inhabitants. From pre-*mwami* times, it was watched over by *bateko*, who guided visitors to the site and kept its *ishinga* in balance. In the eighteenth century, as the influence of *bwami* crept southward across Muhambwe from what oral traditions identify as a regional nucleus in Buyungu, Mwadye became associated with kingship as well. The important role it played in the pre-existing cosmological framework was 'borrowed' by *bwami* and pulled into the set of symbols of royal power. As a sacred place in the royal ideological structure, Mwadye became home to a group of the *mwami*'s ritualists. Among them were royal burial ritualists who claimed that the remains of two *bami*, Ruhaga and Nkanza, were entombed in the cave.[36] The *bateko* from the pre-existing ideological system, however, continued in their function of blessing the nature spirit.

A varied set of guardians were keeping the site when C.J. Bagenal visited it in 1923.[37] Bagenal wrote that in addition to the ritualist Mihanga, who guided him, he was also accompanied by Luniheleza, a co-guardian, and the subchief Ndawe whose ritual connection to the site became apparent when he declined to approach closer than 100 feet of it. Bagenal also noted that Ndawe was not permitted to be seen by the *mwami*, a taboo consistent with the role of certain royal ritualists, particularly those conducting the burial.

Mihanga, whose ritual title Bagenal recorded as *warwirwa mwenyi mwariye* (possibly a Swahili-influenced writing of the Kiha expression *umwigwirwa mwene mwadye*, which incorporates the ideas of being in abundance and having a strong bond to Mwadye), recited a genealogy of the forefathers who had guarded the cave before him that reached back five generations. Curiously, even by his own account, the genealogy extended back at least a generation prior to that of the earliest *mwami* whose body was said to rest in the cave. This priority, in combination with the differences in the comportment of Mihanga and Ndawe *vis-à-vis* the cave, suggests that they were two different kinds of ritualists. Ndawe was possibly a burial ritualist and Mihanga may have been a *muteko*. Mihanga pressed Bagenal for a gift, making the claim that it was his traditional right to receive honey in exchange for giving outsiders access to Mwadye, a claim consistent with that of *bateko*.

The oral testimony of elders, although conflicting, tends to support the conjecture that Mwadye remained sacred and connected to different ideological systems at the same time. One elder recalled Mihanga as a royal ritualist who performed spiritual rites for the mwami at Mwadye.[38] The *mwami* could not cast his eyes on Mihanga, said this elder, because tradition dictated that the *mwami* avoid Mwadye and Mihanga was the ritualist of this forbidden site. This testimony would suggest that Mihanga was a burial ritualist. But the same elder also recalled that Mihanga's son Richard used to visit Mwadye several times a year to perform blessing ceremonies, particularly when the people in the region were troubled by wild animal attack or other disasters. This testimony brings to mind the role of *bateko*. The elder, not being of the specific family empowered with keeping Mwadye, did not have the authority to know what Mihanga and his son were doing. And Mwadye being such a sacred site, he wouldn't have ventured to find out – or to tell the researcher – but the general wisdom of eastern Buha is that Mwadye functioned as a sacred site for two institutions, *buteko* and *bwami*, the former being older.

Another elder, naming two *bateko* of Mwadye, Lunihiliza (evidently

Bagenal's Luniheleza) and Butotela, recalled that the hill played a role in his community's 'first fruits' ceremony:[39]

> [Mwadye was] our hill which we used to go to worship, where our elders gathered seed, such as during this season. He [Lunihiliza] went and spent a full week there. They collected liquor and sent it to Lunihiliza on the mountain. Seeds were collected from every subchief and all the seeds were sent to Mwadye to be blessed. Then the seeds were returned and people took them to sow.

In a conversation with his neighbours, this same elder described the link between Lunihiliza and Mwadye:[40]

> q: So where did this person [Lunihiliza] come from? This person who was known as a *muteko*?
> r1: He was chosen by the *mashinga* we have told you were inhabiting this country.
> r2: If the *ishinga* liked you, it chose you.
> r1: He was taken to the mountain [of Mwadye]. He couldn't be found anywhere. Then, when he returned, he was asked where he had been. And the father of Lunihiliza, who was called Butotela, said: 'I was at the mountain. So bring me liquor so that I may guide you to the place where I was.' That is what the mountain does.
> q: So the *muteko* got *buteko* from *mashinga*?
> r1: From those of Mwadye.

Mwadye, as the dwelling-place of an important *ishinga*, was clearly so sacred that its importance carried through from one ideological/cosmological system to another, and the site became associated with the history of the bami of Muhambwe. Although the particular historical association shifted from one political–historical era to the other, the location of Mwadye as a focal point in ideological-cum-geographical space and the 'knowledge' that Mwadye was somehow vital in the human–environmental relationship were passed on.

Nineteenth-century commercial expansion and the *muteko*

Mwadye, so meaningful to the world view of Muhambwe inhabitants of the pre-*bami* period, continued to hold special significance after the implementation of the *bwami* system, but the matrix of ideas linked to Mwadye in the earlier framework weakened. With new royal ritualists resident at Mwadye and a new *mwami*-focused explanation of the site's significance, the 'common-knowledge' memory of pre-*bami* Mwadye became more uncertain over time. The older ideas and explanations that had been associated with the site became a source of confusion and began falling out of common knowledge. As is often the case, complex ideas collapsed into fragments: an image, some words and notions of avoidance remained.

A similar process took place in the next century with regard to the role of *bateko* and nature spirits. During the late nineteenth and early twentieth centuries, commercial expansion created a new climate of materialism in Buha, which transformed many aspects of Ha societies. In the wave of materialism, the gifts of nature spirits, and even *buteko* itself, took on economic dimensions which had never existed before. In one of the more flagrant examples of this new materialism, individuals, including some *bateko*, sought to transform access to nature spirits into a new kind of economic asset.

In the 1830s and 1840s, long distance trade centring on the East African coast expanded westward to Lake Tanganyika, passing through southern Buha. Its western terminus was located on the Tanganyika lakeshore in a zone over which the Ha kingdom of Nkalinzi prevailed. The establishment of the caravan route and the lakeshore trade centre known as Ujiji depended on ongoing negotiation with Ha authorities, which took place throughout the second half of the nineteenth century. At many stages of the lengthy process, Ha authorities had the ability to thwart these developments, because the traders were only a tiny 'guest' community clinging to a toehold on the lake's edge. Key participants in the negotiation were certain Ujiji *bateko*. They mediated not only between humans and nature spirits, but also between established communities and newcomers. Moreover, when the newcomers included Arabs and Arabized Africans (*wangwana*), their job of mediation became complex cross-cultural power-brokering. Richard Burton's derisive description of the political process at Ujiji, written by the explorer in 1857, points out the centrality of the *bateko*:[41]

> The affairs of the nation are settled by the mwami, the chief, in a general council of lieges, the wateko (in the singular mteko) or elders presiding. Their intellects, never of the brightest, are invariably fuddled with toddy, and, after bawling for hours together and coming apparently to the most satisfactory conclusion, the word of a boy or an old woman will necessitate another lengthy palaver.

In their role as granters of access to land for settlement, Ujiji *bateko* found their authority and economic power increasing. Since alien traders had to solicit permission from them at each step in the expansion from temporary camps to permanent shops, lakist *bateko* became 'enablers' of Arab trade expansion into Buha. To ensure that they were indeed 'enabled', traders presented gifts to the *bateko*, as well as to the *mwami* and to village and regional leaders (*batwale*). The *bateko*, for their part, were accustomed to receiving tribute, and some of the more well-placed *bateko* at Ujiji demanded it aggressively. In the atmosphere of growing materialism, the custom of paying tribute continued and intensified, a point well documented by the explorers.[42]

As settlement around Ujiji grew denser at the end of the nineteenth century, the local *bateko* continued to benefit. With a denser population, their role in allocating land, settling land disputes and ensuring agricultural success became all the more crucial. Increasing activity on the lake also enhanced the importance of the lakist *bateko*, whose ritual role extended to calming the spirits of the lake and blessing lake-going vessels.[43] The intensification of trade on Lake Tanganyika led to the building of more canoes and boats, which required a ceremony similar to a baptism at the first launching. Piloting these vessels were more fishermen, more sailors and more traders and travellers than ever before, all of whom aspired to voyage in safety. As the sole arbitrators who could coax lake spirits into maintaining calm conditions, lakist *bateko* probably enjoyed an augmentation of their duties and their popular authority.

Bateko authority over lake travellers extended to European travellers, who found that in order to recruit oarsmen they too had to pay tribute. A frustrated V.L. Cameron wrote of some particularly wily *bateko* he encountered at Ujiji in 1874:[44]

> It now became necessary to engage men from whom I might learn the names of the different places round the lake, and to point out the nightly camps and act as interpreters. Two who had gone to the north end with Livingstone and Stanley were brought to me. But in the weighty matter of engaging them, the mutwale and wateko of course had a finger, and charged more for their fees than the men received as hire.

Nineteenth-century trade expansion certainly contributed to both the complexity and the lucrativeness of the role of the *muteko*, but, in addition to this expanded logistical role, the Islamic faith of many of the traders also contributed to the *muteko*'s spiritual authority. In the cosmological framework of the Arab and Swahili-*wangwana* newcomers to Ujiji, nature spirits had been prominent features long before they encountered the *bisigo* and *mashinga* of Buha. Arabs believed in *djinns* (genies), and Swahili-ized Africans identified *majini*, which resembled them with Ha ideas of nature spirits. Thus, the Muslim newcomers readily incorporated *mashinga* as the local form of *majini*, and all evil spirits, including *bisigo*, were referred to in the Swahili language as *mashetani* (devils).[45] In this way, the religious beliefs of the newcomers bolstered a major component of the ideological framework that legitimized *bateko*.

Inland, along the trade routes, *bateko* found their roles expanded as well. The *bateko* whose authority extended into territories on the trade routes became major beneficiaries of the developing system of *hongo*, a toll paid by caravan traders to the leaders through whose territories they passed. It was paid in kind, often in trade goods, after a lengthy negotiation process. In Buha, political and religious authorities ranging from the *mwami* to regional leaders *batwale* to *bateko* all had rights to claim tribute. Cameron found certain inland *bateko* to be equally as sly as their lakist counterparts:[46]

> We again turned our attention to the knotty question of the amount to be paid for crossing the river. And knotty it was, for no sooner had I settled one demand than others were brought forward. The people must have exercised their ingenuity to the utmost, for I received claims from the following officials, their wives and relations: first, the mutwale; second, his wife; third, head muteko or councilor; fourth, his wife . . .

Knowledge about environment – its boundaries, its dangers, its resources – became, in the commercialized climate of the late nineteenth century, a means to economic advantage. However, not all *bateko* sought this advantage. Those living far from the beaten caravan path or at a distance from the royal courts carried on their activities much as before, without the same degree of attention to economic gain paid by their eager, more advantageously placed counterparts. But their attitude toward these changes, and even their very presence are not documented in written records since they did not present themselves to travellers. Travel records preserve an image of the greedy Baha, from whose extortionate toll system explorer Henry Stanley literally fled under cover of darkness.

Bateko, 'traditional authority' and the British colonial establishment

During the changes that had taken place in Ha society prior to the onset of British colonial administration – including the expansions into Buha of *bwami* kingship and the East African coastal trade – *bateko* as a group had straddled the changes precisely because they were not a group. Some *bateko* had participated in the new systems, sometimes wielding special authority as the *mwami*'s official *bateko* ritualists or as the *bateko* who administered the land of Ujiji town. Others had remained attached to spirit shrines on the periphery of the trade centres and royal capitals. However, regardless of an individual *muteko*'s location in the overall political and economic structure, each *muteko* played a crucial role in his or her local arena. And locally, each *muteko* family retained its primordial authority. If this authority slipped, as in the case of the drunken *muteko* who had inappropriately played the sacred drum, help came from another family member or *muteko*. The errant individual was brought into line, without negative implications for the system. Indeed, the system was not significantly challenged even by larger problems, such as the rinderpest epidemic of the 1890s and the subsequent tsetse infestation after the turn of the century. These forms of adversity increased the community's reliance on their *muteko*. Because *bateko* as a group maintained their authority – even in the face of epidemiological and environmental crises – several of the British administrators posted in Buha in the 1920s and 1930s developed the opinion that they might fruitfully be used as 'native authorities' for the administration of indirect rule.

In the 1920s, when the British, replacing the German and Belgian regimes, began to administer Buha, they found that *bateko* commanded strong popular respect and authority. The *bateko*'s credibility with ordinary people contrasted sharply with that of many Ha political leaders (the *bami* and *batware*) whose stature had suffered under the European regimes. The resisters among them had been exiled or otherwise displaced from their positions. The collaborators among them, particularly those who had relied on European military force to carry out unpopular programmes, had watched their European partners depart and their authority falter. *Bateko* had remained outside the political calculations (and hence manipulations) of the first two regimes, however, because they had not appeared to serve European interests.

The administrators who governed in Buha disagreed about the possibility of incorporating *bateko* into the native administration. Some administrators emphasized the 'true' traditional legitimacy of *bateko*, whose political authority preceded that of the *bami*, and recommended their resurrection as colonial 'native authorities'. Other officials acknowledged that *bateko* were influential, but recommended working with the conventional political authorities, the kings, chiefs and subchiefs. In the early years of British administration, these two positions waxed and waned, depending on the perspective of the particular administrator and the nature of his relationship with the chiefs and subchiefs.

The position that *bateko* could be incorporated into the administrative structure as subchiefs was implied in a 1922 note written in the Kigoma District Book by F. Longland:[47]

> There are two classes of Sub-chiefs under the Paramount Chief or Mwami. These are known as Mteko (Wateko) and Mtwale (Watwale). Of these two the latter now are reckoned the more important although originally they were in degree below the former.

From Longland's perspective, *bateko*, being 'originally' more important, were the ideal candidates for leadership in the 'tradition-based' system of indirect rule.

In contrast with Longland's point of view, an assessment of the influence of *bateko* written by the Kigoma District Officer in 1931 offered the ironical argument that the *bateko*'s importance to local people made it unnecessary to incorporate them into the political structure:[48]

Wateko are the intermediaries between the people and the spirits of the ancestors, and their power is regarded as being beyond the control of their temporal rulers. The invaders [referring to Batutsi chiefs] have of course retained the Wateko, for thesepeople cannot imagine a state in which they do not exist. Whether the Government recognize the Wateko or not is of no concern to the people, for the natives imbued with a sense of the spiritual world will still look to the Wateko for their spiritual needs.

As administrators conducted inquiries into Ha 'tribal traditions' and debated the usefulness of incorporating *bateko*, some of the shrewder *bateko* resurrected themselves as subchiefs in the colonial sense of the role. These individuals grafted themselves on to the colonial establishment as subchiefs and headmen. How did they accomplish this? *Bateko* were well placed to vie for subchief positions which were allocated by the *mwami*. As recipients of tribute, they commanded the material resources needed to attract the *mwami*'s attention. They also commanded unquestioned popular authority over a territory. In addition, those *bateko* whose forebears had been drawn into *bwami* as royal ritualists had close, long-term relations with the royal family. These social and material assets gave *bateko* an advantage in the competition for political appointments at court.

Once exclusively mediators between their community members and nature spirits, certain *bateko* became in the colonial period mediators between Baha people and colonial policy. That many *bateko* survived and even flourished in colonial roles has been demonstrated by elderly *bateko* who are retired subchiefs and who continue to earn community respect.[49] These individuals also appear in the colonial record as successful administrators.

One piece of evidence testifying to the success of a ritualist-turned-administrator comes from Mwadye. During a 1932 anti-sleeping sickness campaign, the District Officer and his assistants attempted to remove Baha from fly-infested areas such as the bush surrounding Mwadye. Although they tried to disseminate information about the tsetse fly and the necessity for resettlement, Baha resisted, for from their point of view, such a disease was caused by earth spirits:[50]

It would be idle to pretend that any of them wanted to leave their homes for concentration. I found that few, if any, believed that sleeping sickness was caused by fly; they had always lived amongst fly and the disease had only recently appeared. As our chief argument in favour of concentration was that it would stop sleeping sickness by protecting them from fly, their disbelief, which was quite sincere, made our plans seem unreasonable, and many said emphatically that they greatly preferred to take their chance in their homes. The Waha are reputed to be wild and undisciplined people, and it was anticipated that it would be difficult to get them to move.

In the difficult task of removing Baha from their homes, one subchief stood out: Subchief Ndawe of Mwadye moved his people with a remarkable degree of popular compliance.[51] Ndawe, clearly having consulted the *ishinga* of Mwadye, had greater authority backing his request. But in other locations, administrators dared not remove *bateko* or ritualists from their sacred locations. Griffiths described his policy toward *bateko*:[52]

> These sacred places were in the charge of priests and could not be abandoned by them; where they occurred in areas which had to be evacuated, the priest had to be left in charge.

Nature spirits and risk-taking

During the evacuations carried out to combat sleeping sickness *bateko* remained behind to tend to the nature spirits because, according to the local system for tackling ecological problems, nature spirits were the means to a resolution. Nature spirits were also seen as the means to finding a solution for other kinds of problems faced by individuals and families. By the turn of the twentieth century, individuals were seeking out nature spirits with increasing frequency, hoping to find solutions to a variety of dilemmas, many of which were economic. In previous generations, ordinary people had regarded contact with nature spirits as risky and best left to the *muteko*. But, as the colonial system took hold, forcing unprecedented economic obligations on to ordinary people in the form of fines and taxes, and as the creation of markets which introduced new consumer goods created a general atmosphere of increased materialism, ordinary people opted to take greater risks for material gain. Nature spirits were a potential source for material assets and, accordingly, stealthy visits paid to spirit abodes became part of the childhood experiences of many people who were born at the turn of the century.

Although it passed through lion country, the path to Mwadye was marked by the footprints of many bare feet. Many travelled to the mountain seeking grinding stones to sell. Others went seeking favours from the spirits. But, of the latter group, most didn't tell their tales, for the quest for personal advantage was very private. Instead, the majority of tales of spirits' gifts focus upon those who went to collect stones and unwittingly stumbled across greater gifts. Such was the case of a certain Zihabandi, remembered at Busunzu village for finding money given by *mashinga*.[53] As the tale goes, Zihabandi was digging a grinding stone out of the ground at Mwadye when he found a cache of money hidden underneath it. Unfortunately, he announced his good luck to others and, as a result, he disappeared. Zihabandi's fate underlines the imperative of keeping a gift from *mashinga* secret.

Therefore, it is not surprising that there are almost no accounts of those who have sought a spirit's gift. Instead, the accounts of *mashinga* recalled the failure of those who, like Zihabandi, violated their relationship with an earth spirit.

Although the tales of encounters with earth spirits tended to emphasize failure, Baha saw concrete proof of the assistance of *mashinga* in the examples of those who became successful with no obvious explanation. They must have had supernatural help, onlookers reasoned. And if one's neighbour received help, why shouldn't one try it oneself?[54]

> There were people who knew that a certain person achieved something after praying to *mashinga*. [And they thought] 'So if he got something, why not me? I will go and pray to *mashinga* and see if I get that thing,' you see.

One account of a person who did seek help from a *shinga* comes from an elder who was a small child when his father took him to Nyamasanza to visit an earth spirit:[55]

> There is a kind of stone which was very famous. People from far-away places went to worship it. They called it Nyamasanza. It was a mere stone in the wilderness, it was roundish, about this thickness . . . very small, only about this size, but despite its small size, people used to go before it and pray to it: Nyamasanza, I would like to marry . . .
> I witnessed this done by my late father. I don't know what he was praying for, but after he had achieved what he had wanted, he took me, my sister, my mother and a neighbour to the middle of the wilderness where the stone was . . . there were bones of animals and a lot of pieces of broken beer-pots. Hm! I watched my father hurry there, carrying his sheep. He brought it there and he hit it hard, and he left it there while the blood drained out of its body near the stone. Then we retreated for a while and when we approached the stone again, we came on our knees presenting grass . . .

The probability that such sacrifices to *mashinga* were commonplace is supported by the numerous broken bones and potsherds in evidence at the site. Similar debris was in evidence at Mwadye a generation later, when a European visited the site in 1950 or 1951:[56]

> There were signs that many people had visited Mwaliye [*sic*] recently, as a small tree, at the entrance to the cave, was adorned with about twenty grass head-rings such as are used to carry pots of beer. People go there to invoke Mwaliye's aid and later they return, if their request has been granted, to drink beer and also, preferably, slaughter a sheep.

This utilitarian interest in earth spirits, which focused selectively on *mashinga* rather than *bisigo*, led in time to a general trend of focusing primarily on *mashinga* when recalling the generic category of earth spirits. This trend can be gauged chronologically through the narratives of elders. The very oldest elders, born just after the turn of the century, discuss *bisigo* to a much greater extent than their less aged cohorts, who focus largely on *mashinga*. In fact, when queried about the two categories of spirits, elders of the oldest group have expressed the conviction that *bisigo* are an older form of earth spirit.[57] Does this mean that *gisigo* as a conceptual category is older, or simply that the attention given to *mashinga* is newer? Why did the residents of eastern Muhambwe develop such an interest in *mashinga* while those of western Muhambwe continued to regard all earth spirits as *bisigo*? Was this based exclusively on ideological patterns that predated commercialism, or was it influenced also by the distribution of markets, economic demands and sources of income throughout Buha? Although questions persist, what seems to be taking place is that, in a way similar to the case of Mwadye which experienced a 'loosening' of its former connections to earth spirits when the *mwami* 'borrowed' the site, information about earth spirits began to wane in regard to *bisigo* and wax in terms of *mashinga*.

Conclusion

Just as their forebears had served as vital intermediaries in the changing circumstances of the past, *bateko* of the colonial period continued to mediate between their communities and changing environments, both physical and political. Regardless of their choice of strategy, whether they mediated from a position within the administration or outside it, *bateko* generally continued to honour and care for the nature spirits whose stewardship they had inherited.

Nature spirits and *bateko* are crucial components of Buha's ecological history. Indeed, it would be difficult to examine a Ha community's attitude or behaviour *vis-à-vis* its ecological system without including them. It is hoped that this study of the historical implications of Ha nature spirits will alert others to the sources of Tanzanian intellectual and ecological history which are literally embedded in the landscape and which await scholarly recognition.

Notes

1. Special acknowledgement is given to Jan Vansina for making possible the research for this chapter, which was conducted in Kigoma Region, Tanzania, September–December 1991 and July–December 1992. Much appreciation is also given to Joseph Mowiliza, Abdul Sheriff, Pamphilius Chubwa, John Mulishi, James Siedle, Xavier Pejuan, Kasulu Teachers Training College and the Tanzanian Ministry of Science and Technology. The phrase 'nature in the mind' comes from discussions with Jan Vansina; it is his usage.

2. Written documents from the late nineteenth century in combination with oral

testimony from 1991–2 field research have led me to believe that Rukalanga may be included among the kingdoms of the Buha cultural block.

3. Richard F. Burton, *The Lake Regions of Central Africa* (New York, 1860), p. 321.

4. J.E.S. Griffiths, 'The Aba-Ha of the Tanganyika Territory – Some Aspects of Their Tribal Organizations and Sleeping Sickness Concentrations', *Tanganyika Notes and Records* 2 (October 1936): 72.

5. Ibid.

6. C. Macquarie, 'Water Gipsies of the Malagarasi', *Tanganyika Notes and Records* 9 (June 1940): 61.

7. The qualifier 'many' is used here because it seems unlikely that all Banyahoza river-dwelling communities shared similar ideas about water spirits with farmers and herders who lived inland.

8. The majority of the words of the Kiha language begin with an initial vowel prefix, for example *i-gisigo*. In this paper, these initial prefixes (sometimes referred to as pre-prefixes because another prefix always precedes the root, for example *-gi-* as in *i-gi-sigo*) have been systematically dropped.

9. Johannes Van Sambeek, *Croyances et Coutumes des Baha*, vol. 1 (Kabanga, 1949); p. 87. Van Sambeek made similar observations about changes in the distribution of *bisigo*, referring to this historical process as one of 'recent importation' and 'substitution'.

10. Aldolofu Gataga Bavumye (10 December 1991, Matyazo), pp. 62–5 English text.

11. Van Sambeek, *Croyances* Vol. 1: pp. 97–8.

12. Van Sambeek, *Croyances* Vol. 1: p. 88. People did not believe that *bisigo* were bearers of luck. In fact, they believed quite the opposite. Addressing them with the flattering term *biheko* was intended to please them and keep them calm, so that they would pass by and leave the person in peace.

13. Wazee of Kibondo (interview 1, 1 November 1991, Kibondo), p. 33 English text.

14. Salum Nsumiye (interview 1, 1 November 1991, Kibondo), p. 21 English text.

15. Petro Shengero Ndilahomba (interview 1, 22 October 1991, Kasulu), pp. 41–8 English text.

16. Salum Nsumiye (interview 1, 1 November 1991), p. 19 English text.

17. Petro Shengero Ndilahomba (interview 1, 22 October 1991, Kasulu), pp. 43–4 English text.

18. Salum Nsumiye (interview 1, 1 November 1991), p. 18 English text.

19. Ibid.

20. Salum Nsumiye (interview 1, 1 November 1991), pp. 21–2 English text.

21. Salum Nsumiye (interview 1, 1 November 1991), p. 21 English text.

22. Another term for a *muteko* which expressed this sense of having been established in a place first was *musangwa*, 'the one who was found there (since the beginning)' or 'the one who has been present there'. It may be noted that persons of either gender could be selected as *bateko*. Indeed, many *bateko* were women.

23. Burton, *The Lake Regions*, p. 324. Verney Lovett Cameron, *Across Africa* (New York, 1877), pp. 165, 175. James B. Wolf, *Missionary to Tanganyika, 1877–88: The Writings of Edward Coode Hore, Master Mariner* (London, 1970), p. 142.

24. A. Leue, 'Uha (Deutsch-Ostafrika): Die Ebene bis zum Malagarasi' *Globus* 79 (1901): 76–8. This translation appears in the unpublished manuscript G.C.K. Gwassa, 'History of Buha through Tunze Papers' (Dar es Salaam: University College, 1967), pp. 23–4.

25. Salum Nsumiye (interview 1, 3 November 1991, Kibondo), pp. 2–6 English text.

26. Emile Mworoha *et al.*, *Histoire du Burundi* (Paris, 1987), pp. 114–20. The chronology of the development of kingdoms has been less thoroughly examined for Buha than for Burundi, but because the two cultural regions were closely related and because Buha is mentioned prominently in an important variant of Burundi's oral traditions of dynastic origin, a conservative estimate that *bwami* developed in Buha during the sixteenth and seventeenth centuries, which would be in line with current Burundi scholarship, is reasonable.

27. Van Sambeek, *Croyances* vol. 1, p. 88.
28. Petro Shengero Ndilahomba (interview 1, 22 October 1991, Kasulu), pp. 12–13 English text. Joachim Sigaye (12 December 1991, Matyazo), pp. 17–8, 27–8 English text.
29. Salum Nsumiye (interview 1, 3 November 1991, Kibondo), p. 8 English text.
30. C.J. Bagenal, 'Mwariye: A Sacred Mountain of Tanganyika', *Tanganyika Notes and Records* 26 (January 1954): 61–3.
31. Wazee of Busunzu (4 October 1992, Busunzu); Mulazi Kagori (4 October 1992, Busunzu).
32. Bagenal, 'Mwariye' p. 61.
33. Ibid.
34. James Mwilima (interview 7, 28 August 1992, Kasulu).
35. Ibid.
36. Wazee of Kibura (interview 1, 8 November 1991, Kibura), p. 59 English text. Wazee of Kibondo (interview 3, 7 November 1991, Kibondo), pp. 65–8. Bagenal, pp. 58–63.
37. Bagenal, 'Mwariye' pp. 58–63.
38. James Mwilima (interview 7, 28 August 1992).
39. Wazee of Kifura (interview 1, 8 November 1991, Kifura).
40. Ibid.
41. Burton, *The Lake Regions*, p. 324.
42. Burton, *The Lake Regions* pp. 320, 323–4.
43. J.M.M. van der Burgt, *Dictionnaire Français–Kirundi* (Bois-le-Duc, Holland, 1903), p. 66, includes a description of a canoe-blessing ceremony under 'barque'. Henry M. Stanley, *How I Found Livingstone: Travels, Adventures and Discoveries in Central Africa* (London: 1872), p. 553.
44. Cameron, *Across Africa*, p. 178.
45. Van Sambeek, *Croyances*, vol. 1, p. 88.
46. Cameron, *Across Africa*, p. 163.
47. Kigoma District Book, 'Tribal Government' section, notes on 'Mjiji Tribe', F. Longland, 1922.
48. Kigoma District Book, 'Native Administration' section, notes on 'The Wajiji', K.F.W., 13 July 1931.
49. James Mwilima (interview 7, 29 August 1992, Kasulu).
50. Gwassa, 'Tunze Papers', pp. 45–6.
51. Gwassa, 'Tunze Papers', p. 47.
52. Griffiths, 'The Aba-Ha', p. 73.
53. Wazee of Busunzu (4 October 1992, Busunzu).
54. James Mwilima (interview 7, 29 August 1992, Kasulu).
55. Ibid.
56. Bagenal, 'Mwariye', p. 63.
57. Wazee of Kibondo (interview 1, 1 November 1991), p. 22 English text.

Eight

Canoe-Building
under Colonialism

Forestry & Food Policies
in the Inner Kilombero Valley
1920–40[1]

JAMIE MONSON

In early November 1937, a team of forestry officials toured the wooded slopes of the eastern Uzungwa escarpment in southern Tanzania. In a small clearing in the heart of the Matundu forest, they came upon what they had been looking for: a small group of men engaged in hollowing out large trunks of the *mwawa* tree (*Khaya nyasica*, a mahogany) for canoes. The foresters found seventeen finished *mwawa* canoes and several others in various stages of completion. The canoes ranged from 33 to 58 feet in length, and from 7 to 10 feet in girth. A canoe of this size was capable of carrying a load of rice weighing 3 tons, with a crew of six to eight men.[2]

The foresters were alarmed by what they saw. They decried the 'wasteful destruction' of valuable hardwood timber by the Africans, declaring the need to 'instil in the native mind that this timber is valuable and the supplies not inexhaustible'.[3] All of the downed trees had been felled within ten minutes' walking distance of the canoe site, and one of the canoes had been abandoned half-finished, left to rot and 'riddled with borer'.[4] In the eyes of the foresters, the great size of the canoes represented an ignorant and wanton attack on old-growth timber. They doubted whether the average fisherman required 'a forty foot canoe for fishing, visiting his friends, and in the course of his everyday life'.[5]

The forestry department had found the evidence it needed to implement stricter regulation of African access to forest resources. Although each of the canoe-builders possessed a legal permit to fell trees and was therefore within the limits of existing law, the foresters saw the Matundu case as proof that district forestry legislation was too weak, for it allowed excessive exploitation of valuable species. The foresters successfully argued their case for stronger legislation at the district and provincial levels in terms of use rights to individual tree species. Limitations on what constituted 'proper' or 'economic' usage, imposition of fines and royalties, and the demarcation of forest reserves were all used to restrict tree cutting by local peoples.

The encounter in the Matundu Forest between the canoe builders and the forestry officials represents in microcosm a process which was going on throughout forested areas of Tanganyika, indeed throughout colonial eastern and southern Africa, during the 1920s and 1930s. These decades have been termed the 'conservationist era' because of the widespread attention paid to soil erosion and deforestation.[6] The struggle over rights to individual tree species grew out of a fundamental difference between colonial and African notions of what constituted 'wise' use of natural resources. The perceived wastefulness of African tree usage was seen as inimical to the 'gospel of efficiency' doctrine which had infused the forestry profession. Just like their American counterparts, conservationists in Tanganyika viewed 'primitive' exploitation practices as their nemesis. The rhetoric of the Tanganyikan foresters was invoked not to maintain the forest in its pristine or natural state, but to develop a more rational and 'scientific' exploitation of tropical hardwoods. This was to be accomplished by granting concessionary monopolies to European timber interests.

Yet there was more at stake for colonial powers than the curtailment of what they perceived as the irrational destruction of natural resources. Conservationism dovetailed neatly with agricultural policy, in particular with the 'grow more crops' campaigns of the Depression years. The resulting plethora of regulatory measures affected African agriculture, timber extraction and marketing. Indeed, the conflicts over canoe building in the Kilombero valley exemplify the complex inter-relationship between conservationism and agricultural policy, because canoes linked the forest to the farm and the farm to the market. The forestry policies of the 'conservationist era' were related in several ways to agricultural policies of the same period. The distinctions drawn by the foresters between 'subsistence' and 'commercial' usage of trees paralleled the language of agriculturalists, who distinguished 'food' from 'cash' or 'economic' crops.[7] Moreover, while foresters complained that the unbridled economic activity of canoe-builders was wreaking havoc on timber supplies, district agriculture officials were scrambling to limit grain exports from the region. Thus, restrictions on access to the forest were accompanied by (and related to) restrictions on the selling and shipment of rice.

The administrative imperative of the 1930s was to establish economic stability while at the same time maximizing revenues. This dual mandate of extraction and control created a 'rubric of regulation' which imposed and elaborated artificial distinctions between the cash and subsistence sectors.[8] Yet neither canoes nor the rice they carried fitted very neatly into these categories. Despite the existing commerce in grain, foodstuffs were not considered to be 'economic' crops under the new definitions.[9] Officials warned that the buoyant rice trade would imperil district food supplies, and tax-paying Kilombero farmers were instructed to plant cotton instead of rice as the district cash crop.[10]

Although the canoes played a part in the subsistence economy, colonial officials were primarily concerned about their commercial functions in the Kilombero economy. Mistakenly imagining that canoes were owned and operated by private individuals, the foresters argued that their commercial use justified the imposition of fines and royalties. Higher levels of the state bureaucracy were willing to support the curtailment of canoe construction if it would help to limit the sale of grain. These official stances reflect the opposition within the Tanganyikan territorial bureaucracy to uncontrolled accumulation in the rural sector. In the Kilombero case, governing officials were concerned about the economic and political impact of the rice trade, which allowed prominent farmers to bypass state structures in the appropriation of wealth and status.[11] They therefore raised the twin spectres of deforestation and famine in their efforts to stem the flow of rice-bearing canoes downstream.

The foresters who explored the Matundu escarpment did not explicitly address these issues in their report. If anything, they appear to have underestimated or misunderstood the extent to which the early colonial grain trade had created a differentiated rural economy in the Kilombero. Their references to ordinary and 'personal' use of canoes suggest a model of self-contained, subsistence agrarian enterprise. Yet the evidence they cite in their own reports testifies to the existence of a large-scale trade in grain between the flood plains of the inner Kilombero and the Indian trading houses of Ifakara.

The Matundu forest, along with other forested slopes of the inner Kilombero Valley, provided the arena in which these disputes were played out. The Matundu forest is an area along the northern side of the Kilombero River, on the lower foothills of the Uzungwa escarpment (see Map 6). These foothills are uniquely situated in a fertile forest area sandwiched between the highland plateaux of Iringa and the rice-producing lowlands of the Kilombero. Access to the river is provided by a series of navigable tributaries such as the Mnyera and Ruipa rivers. In this valley and its surrounding mountains farmers have grown rice, fished, kept small livestock, hunted and collected food for their livelihood for at least the past several hundred years.[12]

Trade in rice, grain and dried fish from the inner Kilombero rose steadily in the decade following the First World War and increased

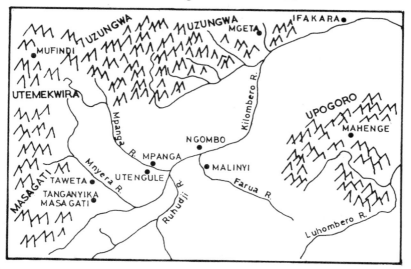

Map 6 *The Inner Kilombero Valley*

canoe traffic on the river from the upper Kilombero and its tributaries down to the market centre at Ifakara. Most of this traffic was conducted by agents of large Indian trading firms at Ifakara and Kilosa, who leased canoes with full crews in the valley to transport their rice.[13] Rice was transported overland from Ifakara to the Kilosa railway station, *en route* to any number of destinations in the territory. Between the years 1927 and 1929 alone, rice exports along the Kilosa route more than tripled, from 350 tons to 1144 tons.[14] The increased traffic in rice on the Kilombero, especially following the construction of a road between Ifakara and Kilosa, resulted in greater demand for the very large trees such as *mvule* and *mwawa* which were needed for the construction of canoes capable of transporting rice by the ton along with a large crew.[15] The *mvule* tree was the first choice of Wandamba fishing communities for the dugout canoes they called *wato* (Kindamba) or *mitumbwi* (Kiswahili). *Mvule* was particularly valued because of its durability, its resistance to rot, and its size.[16]

Yet the same trees which were most prized by the Wandamba for canoe-building – *mvule, mwawa, mtumbati (Pterocarpus bussei)* and *mfulu (Vitex cienkowskii)* – were also the most valued by the forestry department because of the potential revenue to be gained by granting timber concessions to European export enterprises. African hardwoods, and mahogany in particular, brought high prices in British and American markets. While Tanganyikan timber deliveries comprised a small percentage of total imports to Liverpool and London from British Africa, there was much room for an expansion of supply.[17] Mahogany was prized by British cabinet-makers and in the chair and couch trades, and was also used for veneers, railway carriages, shipbuilding and in construction.[18] Recognizing the value of timber in Ulanga, the Conservator of Forests reported:[19]

> Our recent tour of the Ulanga District has shown that it contains considerable quantities of valuable timbers of various species. The proportion of *mvule* of exploitable size is however not great and if the more accessible *mvule* was cut out during the next few years the value of a timber concession, which may be given out in the future, would be much reduced.

He proposed that consideration be given to constructing a sawmill 'situated at some convenient point on the Kilombero', to which timber could be floated down the river's wider tributaries, such as the Ruipa.[20] The Forest Department had already begun to grant timber concessions elsewhere. In Morogoro District, a concession at Turiani had already been granted to Messrs Kaiser Brothers, who were authorized as the sole harvesters of *mvule* within their concession area. In Iringa District, on the upper Uzungwa escarpment, Messrs Acker and Mieth had a concession to cut timber in 1938.[21] The Forestry Department was eager to establish similar concessions in other forest reserves, but worried about maintaining adequate supplies, just as the Conservator of Forests worried about long-term prospects in Ulanga.[22]

The royalties paid for logging within the Kilombero forest reserves were a good source of revenue within the district. In 1934, the royalties earned from harvesting *mvule* trees in Mahenge and Kiberege divisions alone amounted to over 1000 pounds sterling.[23] In 1937 for the tree species *mwahe* (*Pterocarpus holstii*) and *mlilangoko* (*Entandrophragma* spp.) the fee was Shs 23/- for each tree.[24] By 1949, the fee for cutting an *mvule* tree had reached Shs 130/-.[25] Revenue alone, however, does not account for the zeal with which the Conservator of Forests, with the support of the Provincial Commissioner in Morogoro, approached the conservation of timber.[26] The granting of monopoly control to timber concessions was designed to centralize the marketing and taxation of forest products, to stabilize and secure prices and to guarantee long-term supplies. No longer would the canoe-builders and the rice traders who purchased their products be allowed to circumvent the official points of exchange at which revenues were extracted.

Although the Provincial Commissioner supported the wishes of the Conservator of Forests in 1935, he did so over the objections of

Mahenge District Officer A.T. Culwick. Officials at the district level disagreed about the direction of future economic development in the Kilombero region. Culwick – ethnographer, agriculturalist and District Officer – was a proponent in the late 1920s and 1930s of an agricultural economy based upon export rice production. Culwick opposed cash crop production schemes along with the concessionary marketing monopolies which accompanied them.[27] Repeatedly, Culwick defended the African canoe-building industry as an essential foundation of the highly remunerative Kilombero rice trade. As an ethnographer, Culwick had an in-depth knowledge of the canoe economy, and understood the importance of canoes for local subsistence needs as well as their essential role in exports:[28]

> The recent floods have demonstrated conclusively how disastrous would be any policy which deprived the natives of the Ulanga valley of adequate timber for the construction of canoes. During the last few months the only means of transport over large areas has been canoes, without which there would certainly have been great hardship and loss of life from drowning and starvation.

He understood that there were risks to local communities when canoes were in short supply.

Culwick's defence of canoe-making was continually at odds with the interests of the Forest Department at Morogoro. There is even some evidence of collusion in the illegal cutting of *mvule* on the part of Culwick himself. An outraged Conservator of Forests alleged in April 1936 that Culwick had authorized the chief of Merera 'to cut a number of *mvule* trees for the preparation of canoes for the transport of crops from the upper waters of the Kilombero for marketing at Ifakara'.[29] These charges were denied by Culwick in a subsequent letter,[30] but do not seem entirely implausible given Culwick's often emotional commitment to the canoe transportation economy.

The Forest Department put forward two main arguments to justify their restrictive policies on access to hardwoods. The first of these arguments was an attack on the commercial use of canoes. Foresters argued that the very large canoes discovered at Matundu were constructed for the purpose of transporting grain, rather than to meet subsistence needs, and therefore should be taxed and licensed. Only one of seventeen canoes discovered in the Matundu Forest Reserve was small enough to be considered 'a suitable size for a man's personal use.'[31] According to the forestry officials, the Matundu canoes were being made by professional canoe-builders, who then sold them to 'the Wandamba who are the true river people.'[32] 'There can be no doubt', the foresters concluded in their report, 'that the large Mwawa canoes are used and desired principally for the transport of rice, and [since they are] being used for purposes of trade the trees should not be given free.'[33]

Jamie Monson

Photo 10 *Canoe-making in the Kilombero Valley.* (Jamie Monson)

The artificial distinction made by forestry officials between commercial and subsistence use did not reflect the socio-economic relationships surrounding canoe ownership and use-rights. The forest officials wrongly thought in terms of individualized canoe ownership, believing that a canoe intended 'for a man's personal use' was distinct from the larger canoes used for commerce. For the 'ordinary use' of the fisherman, 'he would in my opinion find a small canoe more convenient', stated Conservator Fraser in his 1937 report.[34] Yet canoe-building and canoe use-rights were not individualized in the Inner Kilombero Valley, and the idea that one man would 'own' one canoe for his private use was the creation of misinformed British observers. The building and crewing of *mitumbwi* was a task which involved several persons, who normally included an individual canoe 'captain' along with a group of his kinsmen, called *walongo*. In Kilombero societies, members of the extended family, or *walongo*, included not only maternal and paternal relations but also connections by marriage and by blood brotherhood (*lusale*, Kindamba). Walongo called upon each other in times of hardship such as sickness or food shortage.[35] During periods of heavy labour such as land-clearing, tilling and harvesting, *walongo*

206

members were expected to help one another. *Walongo* also joined together to build and crew canoes.

Culwick describes two ways in which an individual could acquire a canoe: he could build it himself, with the aid of his *walongo*, or he could contract with a canoe expert, who would in turn call upon his kinsmen for aid. In either case, a canoe of any size required a crew of two to eight polers, who become bound together by debts of mutual obligation.[36] According to Culwick:[37]

> They enter into a special relationship with the maker of the canoe and each other, a relationship which lasts as long as the canoe is in use or until it passes from the hands of its maker, either at his death or, in rare instances, by transfer.

According to informants from Ngalimila, non-kin workers were often recruited during the initial stages of canoe construction, when a tree was felled, shaped and then moved through the forest to the location where it underwent the final carving and shaping. A work party would be called out and compensated for their labour with rice beer brewed for the occasion.[38] Yet, even when a man contracted out with an expert to acquire a canoe, he still had to rely on the mutual-aid relationships of his crew members in order to use it. A crew was essential for the successful manoeuvring of a large craft in the fast-moving and sometimes dangerous waters of the Kilombero and its tributaries. Crewmen were entitled to a share in the profits when the canoe was hired out for transport or to a portion of the harvest after a fishing expedition. At the same time, members were expected to contribute labour to non-commercial activities, such as collecting rushes or firewood. Each crewman also had the right to use the canoe and the labour of other polers for his own purposes from time to time, according to informal customary arrangements.[39] In this way, canoes were shared out within and among the various villages and extended communities of the Kilombero.

The conception of the Forest Department, therefore, that any large canoe was by definition a 'commercial' craft and subject to steep royalty payments, did not reflect the complex web of social relationships within which canoes were created and utilized. Nevertheless, the mistaken idea that the Wandamba who lived along the river could be best served by having individually owned, small craft for their 'ordinary use' and its corollary idea that any large canoe was hollowed out purely as a profit-making venture were promoted energetically by the foresters as they imposed high royalties and ultimately prohibitions on the cutting of trees. The royalty of Shs 98/- proposed in 1937 far exceeded the going rate for a finished canoe, however, which was cited at Shs 60/- for a large craft.[40] The royalty, more than 30 per cent higher than the selling price of the product, was clearly designed to affect forest use and not simply to bring in revenues. Royalties and licensing were imposed in this case to eliminate the harvesting of particular tree species by the canoe-builders, as the foresters acknowledged in arguing that the levying of such fees was done 'with the chief object of preventing wastage [by which they meant commercial exploitation]'.[41]

The second argument used by Forest Department officials to support their policies was that African populations were ignorant of the true value of the natural resources at their disposal, and that they were wasteful, destructive and interested only in short-term gain. The Culwicks contradict this assumption most effectively in their ethnography, *Ubena of the Rivers*. They demonstrates that Kilombero communities were not wasteful users of timber; in fact, canoes were kept in circulation for as long as possible before being put out of commission. It was their long-range vision, not their short-sightedness, which caused local people to seek out *mvule* and *mwawa*, the timbers which best withstood the daily stress of canoeing:[42]

> Now a canoe is expensive, the task of hollowing it exceedingly laborious, and its conveyance from the forest to the nearest river arduous. Nothing could be further from the truth than the common idea that the native will fell valuable trees for canoes unnecessarily and without thought . . . no one is wealthy enough to commission any [timber] that are not really needed.

Yet even mwawa was not as highly favoured as *mvule* for canoes because *mwawa* would be 'gradually nibbled away by small fish'.[43] The canoe builders thus had a keen sense of the value of timber.

Moreover, there is reason to believe that the foresters overestimated the extent of timber use for canoe construction. The forestry officials used the number of canoes they found in the Matundu forest – a total of seventeen within a radius of a 10-minute walk – in order to quantify an estimated rate of loss of *mvule* trees on the Uzungwa escarpment. Yet there are several reasons why the Matundu canoe industry was not representative of forest use as a whole in the inner Kilombero. The situation on the Matundu escarpment was not indicative of tree-felling patterns within the entire Uzungwa forest because areas farther away from the river were much less likely to be cleared. Both the canoe builders and the European timber concessionaires were primarily interested in that part of the forest which was interlaced by the Kilombero's tributaries and had direct access to downstream transport routes. This is where their activities were most concentrated and where evidence of tree exploitation was most acute. The perceived 'wasteful destruction' of valuable timber was thus spatially as well as contextually specific.

The foresters themselves realized that *mvule* trees close to the rivers were most vulnerable to felling. As they stated in their report:[44]

The fact that an enumeration of mvule along the Ruaha–Kiberege road has revealed the presence of 4,000 tons of this timber has no real bearing on the case as these areas are not readily accessible to waterways down which a canoe could be floated.

Thus the concept of exploitation, or rather of overexploitation, was a relative one for colonial officials. They were not concerned so much with overall timber use but with timber use within a spatially specific forest zone, a zone which had special value because of its proximity to the Kilombero's tributaries. The waterways, which were so vital to the canoe trade were equally vital to the value of a potential concession with its sawmill.[45]

Time was as important a variable as space in determining the rate of forest exploitation, for the felling of trees for canoe construction had important temporal aspects. During the First World War, many canoes were lost or damaged as the British and Germans battled in Mahenge and Iringa Districts. The majority of these canoes were replaced between 1919 and 1921, bringing the total number of canoes in the valley to 233 in the year 1933.[46] Yet by the year 1935, Culwick predicted, these postwar canoes would begin to wear out, leading to a 'boom' in canoe-making in the late 1930s, although he believed that the expense of canoe ownership, the distribution of wealth and the crewing requirements of each craft would impose a ceiling on the number of canoes which could be made operational in the valley at any time.[47] In 1937, the year of the Matundu forest encounter, this boom may have been taking place, as one 'generation' of vessels was replaced by another. While it cannot be denied that a steady increase in the rice trade must have caused an upward movement in the demand for canoes, Culwick's point seems well taken. On average, Culwick determined that only 74.5 trees were felled each year to replace discarded or disintegrated craft.

Thus the exploitation of the forest was temporally as well as spatially specific. The attempt by colonial officials to extrapolate data such as tree censuses on the basis of single visits to localized sites must therefore be held up to careful scrutiny. Their motives in outlawing African use of individual species have already been stated. Their claim to 'scientific' assessment of forest destruction must be examined in light of those motives.[48]

The complex issues raised in this study of canoe-building in southern Tanganyika illustrate the importance of bringing an historical perspective to recurring debates over 'efficient' or 'economic' uses of the natural environment throughout eastern and southern Africa. For the local communities of the inner Kilombero, the 'conservationist era' brought about external regulation of the economy along with restricted access to the natural resources which had been a source of livelihood for generations. Yet it is very difficult from the existing sources to evaluate the long-term effects of regional forestry policies on local agricultural and forest ecosystems. Similarly, it has also been difficult to obtain information about the perceptions of the Kilombero residents most affected by these policies, and the role African resistance may have played in determining the course and outcome of regulation. Both of these topics are deserving of further study and will be essential components of a more complete history of the 'conservationist era' in the Kilombero Valley.

Despite the limitations of existing data, however, it is possible to draw some very preliminary conclusions, beginning with peasant response. It appears that non-cooperation was common, from the level of the Native Authority courts to that of the farmer. Enforcement of forestry policy was carried out through the Native Authority court system, but Native Authorities were often outspoken opponents of forest regulation and refused in some cases to enforce forest rules. It was not easy for forest guards to police the activities of the canoe-builders. Ordinances were frequently ignored and the illegal felling of trees continuing unabated. In 1930 seventy-five individuals were convicted at Mufindi and Dabaga for violating forestry rules on the escarpment.[49] Mufindi courts in the same year tried and convicted sixteen persons for cutting a total of 356 trees. In 1938, sixty-one offenders were fined 778/- for forest clearing in the Uzungwa region.[50] These cases and others indicate that the local population opposed the Forestry Department's regulations and were willing to risk apprehension, fines and even imprisonment in order to continue utilizing forest resources.

The long-term environmental consequences of the forestry policies can also be provisionally outlined. The overall function of forest regulation has been to concentrate deforestation activities in the Kilombero, leading to soil erosion and land degradation in the valley flood plain, because forest reserves and other set-aside strategies have increased the level of timber exploitation in non-regulated areas. Some slopes have been so overharvested that they had been largely denuded of their original forest cover by the 1960s. Thus government forestry policy appears to have created, or at least accelerated, the destruction of the very natural resources which it purported to protect. While these government impositions were intended to prevent 'wastage' and 'wanton destruction', they were part of an economic strategy that did not seek to end the exploitation of the forest but simply to change its form. In the final analysis, they failed to meet either of these ends. The proposed sawmill on the Kilombero River was never built, and the Forest Department's vision of a future timber concession on the lower Uzungwa was never realized. Restrictions on African tree use have continued, however, into more recent decades.

Notes

1. I am grateful to Steven Davis for his editorial assistance, and to Jim Giblin and Gregory Maddox for their initiative and patience in putting together this volume.

2. Ulanga District Books, Morogoro Forest Department, 'Safari Report, Ulanga District', Assistant Conservator of Forests under H. Fraser, 11 November 1937, p. 14; A.T. and G.M. Culwick, in *Ubena of the Rivers* (London, 1935), reported that a large canoe would carry one ton of rice or more (p. 269).

3. 'Safari Report, Ulanga District', Assistant Conservator of Forests under H. Fraser, November 11, 1937, p. 15.

4. Ibid.

5. Ibid.

6. On this topic, see David Anderson and R. Grove, eds., *Conservation in Africa: Peoples, Policies and Practice* (Cambridge, 1987); William Beinart, 'Soil Erosion, Conservationism, and Ideas About Development in Southern Africa', *Journal of Southern African Studies* 11, 2 (1984): 52–83; Steven Feierman, *Peasant Intellectuals: Anthropology and History in Tanzania* (Madison, 1990), especially pp. 181–204; A. Rapp, L. Berry and P. Temple, eds, *Studies of Soil Erosion and Sedimentation in Tanzania*, BRALUP Monograph No. 1 (Dar es Salaam, 1973); L. Berry and J. Townshend, 'Soil Conservation Practices in Tanzania: An Historical Perspective', *Geografiska Annaler* 54A (1972): 241–53; John Iliffe, *A Modern History of Tanganyika* (Cambridge, 1979), pp. 348–51 and 473–5.

7. D.M.P. McCarthy, *Colonial Bureaucracy and Creating Underdevelopment: Tanganyika, 1919–1940* (Ames, IA, 1982), pp. 79–80.

8. McCarthy, *Colonial Bureaucracy*, pp. 5–7.

9. For a more detailed analysis of the relationship between food and cash cropping in the Kilombero, see Jamie Monson, 'Rice and Cotton, Ritual and Resistance: Cash Cropping in Colonial Tanganyika, 1920–1940', in Isaacman and Roberts, eds, *The Social History of Cotton in Colonial Africa* (Heinemann forthcoming, 1994).

10. Ibid.

11. A more extensive discussion of the relationship between marketing structures and rural capitalism can be found in ibid., pp. 7–8, 22–23.

12. A detailed history of agrarian change in the Kilombero is given in Jamie Monson, 'An Agricultural History of the Inner Kilombero Valley of Tanzania, 1840-1940', (Ph.D. Dissertation, University of California, Los Angeles, 1991).

13. Ibid.

14. Mkeli Mbosa, 'Colonial Production and Underdevelopment in Ulanga District, 1894-1950' (MA Thesis, University of Dar es Salaam, 1988), p. 126.

15. Culwick and Culwick, *Ubena of the Rivers*, p. 269.

16. Ibid., pp. 271–2; TNA 461/7A/ vol. III, Mahenge District: Forestry, Report from A.T. Culwick to P.C. Eastern Province, 15 November 1935.

17. In the year 1929, imports to Liverpool from Lagos totalled 99 906 cubic feet, compared with East African deliveries which totalled only 381 cubic feet. In the early 1930s, East African timber imports averaged roughly one-tenth of West African imports: James P. Fraser, 'Tracking Down Mahogany', *Timber Trades Journal and Sawmill Advertiser* 120 (4 January 1930): 11–12, and attached monthly import schedules, 1930-32.

18. R.H. Weston, 'The Hardwoods We Handle: Market Value and Chief Features of a Few of Them', *Timber Trades Journal and Sawmill Advertiser* 120 (26 March 1932): 867.

19. TNA 461/7A/vol. III, Mahenge District: Forestry, Letter to D.O., Ulanga District from H. Fraser, Conservator of Forests, Morogoro, 10 November 1937.

20. Ulanga District Books, Morogoro Forest Department, 'Safari Report, Ulanga District', Assistant Conservator of Forests (Fraser), 4 December 1937, p. 4.

21. Iringa District Books, Forestry Reports and Notes on Minor Forest Produce Contributed by E.D. Maber, Forester, 1938.

22. Ibid.

23. TNA 461/7A/vol. III, Mahenge District: Forestry, Letter from D.O. (Culwick) to Conservator of Forests (Fraser), Morogoro, 25 October 1934. In comparison, district hut and poll tax collection that year amounted to a total of Shs 55 407.50/- roughly 2770 pounds sterling: TNA MF 7, 'Hut and Poll Tax Collections 1934-1935, Mahenge District'.

24. TNA 461/7A/vol. III, Mahenge District: Forestry, 'Tree Specimens', 20 August 1937.

25. Mahenge Diocese Archive (Kwiro), Boma Angelegenheiten mit der englischen Regierung, 1933-1960, Taweta, Letter to Taweta Mission from Forest Guard Paul Nalondo, Mahenge, 3 December 1952.

26. TNA 461/7A/vol. III, Mahenge District, Forestry, Report to A.D.O. Kiberege (Culwick) from Provincial Commissioner, Eastern Province, 15 November 1935.

27. TNA 461/2D/I: Mahenge District, Agriculture: Cotton Prices; Letter from Provincial Commissioner, Eastern Province to Assistant District Officer, Kiberege.

28. TNA 461/7A/vol. III, Mahenge District: Forestry, Letter to Provincial Commissioner, Eastern Province from Culwick, 28 May 1936.

29. TNA 461/7A/vol. III, Mahenge District: Forestry, Letter from Conservator of Forests, Morogoro to D.O. Ulanga (Culwick), 4 April 1936.

30. TNA 461/7A/vol. III, Mahenge District: Forestry, Letter from D.O. (Culwick) to Assistant Conservator of Forests, Mufindi, 22 April 1936.

31. TNA 461/7A/vol. II/171, Forest Department, Morogoro, Safari Report, Ulanga District, 4 December 1937, p. 15.

32. Ibid.

33. Ibid.

34. Ibid.

35. Culwick and Culwick, *Ubena of the Rivers*, pp. 26, 300 and 381; interviews in Mfiriga, Madeke, Ngalimila and Mpanga.

36. Culwick and Culwick, *Ubena of the Rivers*, p. 265.

37. Ibid.

38. Interview with Joseph Ngongela and Peregrine Mpinge, Ngalimila, 11-2-89.

39. Culwick and Culwick, *Ubena of the Rivers*, p. 266.

40. TNA 461/7A/vol. II/171, Forest Department, Morogoro, Safari Report, Ulanga District, 4 December 1937, p. 15.

41. Ibid.

42. Culwick and Culwick, *Ubena of the Rivers*, p. 268.

43. Ibid., p. 270.

44. 'Safari Report, Ulanga District', Assistant Conservator of Forests, 11 November 1937.

45. It has been shown that perceptions of land degradation and the destruction of natural resources are both culturally relative and contextually determined: Piers Blaikie and Harold Brookfield, *Land Degradation and Society* (London, 1987); Jamie Monson, 'Perceiving the Forest: British Forestry Policy and Land Degradation in the Kilombero Valley of Tanzania', paper presented to the Annual Meeting of the African Studies Association, 26 November 1991.

46. Culwick and Culwick, *Ubena of the Rivers*, p. 271.

47. Culwick and Culwick, *Ubena of the Rivers*, p. 272.

48. Kate Showers also describes the spatial biases in the observations of colonial authorities who attempted to document gullying and sheet erosion. See Kate Showers, 'Soil Erosion in the Kingdom Of Lesotho: Origins and Colonial Response, 1830s–1950', *Journal of Southern African Studies* 15, 2 (1989): 263–86.

49. TNA 461/19/4, Iringa District Forestry: Reports and Notes on Minor Forest Produce, E.D. Maber, forester, 1938, p. 3.

50. Ibid.

Nine

Struggles for the Land

The Political & Moral Economies
of Land on Mount Meru

THOMAS SPEAR

Recent surveys of environmental history, including the Introduction to this volume, have been at pains to point out what a complex, multi-faceted reality the environment is, comprising as it does the natural order, the economic means by which people exploit that order and the social and political means by which they organize that exploitation.[1] Given that all of these elements are socially constructed – not least ideas concerning 'nature', 'order' and 'economy' – they are also deeply embedded in cultural values and beliefs which, in turn, make them appear 'natural'. Nature, political economy and ideology are thus the necessary bedrocks of any study of environmental change, but while historians have been relatively successful in integrating ecology and political economy, ideology has largely been treated on its own when it has been explored at all.[2] This is not surprising, given the multiple layers of relationships and meanings involved in such a complex exercise, but one means of engaging them all is to focus on a particular environmental category, such as land, that cuts across all the elements and then to explore it in a multidimensional way.

Land encapsulates all these diverse elements in a particularly elegant way. Land as soil has particular physical properties that change as climates, ecosystems and patterns of human exploitation change. Land also is what people divide, occupy and assert rights to – socially and politically – in order to exploit it economically by investing labour and capital in it to transform it and its products. And land is home, its landscapes evoked in art, poetry and song to convey a sense of identity to the people who occupy it. Land thus has very distinctive and different meanings for different peoples, as becomes readily apparent

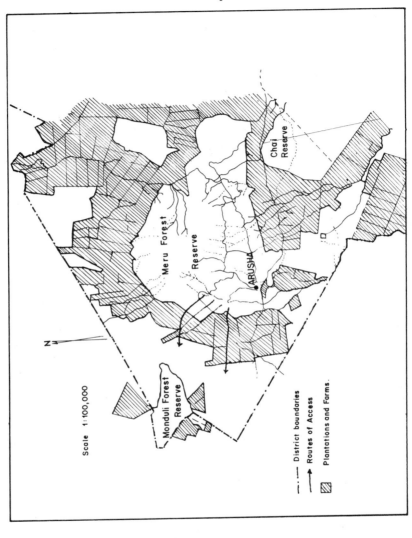

Scale 1:100,000

Meru Forest Reserve

Chai Reserve

ARUSHA

Monduli Forest Reserve

N

— · — District boundaries
———► Routes of Access
▨ Plantations and Farms.

Map 7 *Plantations and Farms in Arusha District*

214

when they vie with one another to occupy, live on and exploit the same area.

Mount Meru in northeastern Tanzania has long been such a contested area, and struggles over land on the fertile, well-watered southern slopes of the mountain have featured strongly in its recent history. During the early nineteenth century land was plentiful, and Arusha and Meru settlers expanded rapidly up its slopes. By the end of the century, however, Meru and Arusha had reached the upper limits of cultivation and came increasingly into conflict with one another as they fought over the vacant areas between them. And, in the early twentieth century, land on the mountain was drastically constricted by the Germans, who alienated an 'iron ring' of land around its base to settlers and created a forest reserve above 5300 feet, thereby foreclosing future expansion by Arusha or Meru. Population densities rose dramatically as a result, forcing individual Meru and Arusha to come to terms with ever decreasing amounts of land. They responded by first intensifying their agricultural productivity and later expanding on to the surrounding plains, but land was the focal point of Arusha and Meru resistance to colonial rule from the very beginning, when Meru and Arusha warriors murdered the first German missionaries to settle on Meru, to the end, when Meru challenged the British Empire before the United Nations in the famous Meru Land Case, and it continues to be a critical issue in national and local politics today.

It is one of the great ironies of Meru and Arusha history that all their rulers – German, British and Tanzanian – claimed to support peasant interests over those of settlers and yet all ultimately sustained the settlers' uneconomic claims to large tracts of land. The Germans, contrary to general government policy, made Mount Meru one of their few settlement areas in Tanzania, alienated large tracts of land to settlers and placed Arusha town in the middle of one of the most densely settled parts of Arusha. While the British expelled the German settlers in 1916, were well aware that Arusha and Meru needed the land and generally favoured peasant production, they reallocated the German estates to other settlers, alienated vast new tracts themselves and continually expanded the boundaries of the town. Finally, the settler farms on Mount Meru were among the few such farms not nationalized by the independent Tanzanian government.

Meru and Arusha expressed their need for land relentlessly throughout the colonial period. Because scarcely any year went by without a major incident of squatting or trespassing on settler land, of protesting the expansion of town boundaries, of contesting land allocations by the Native Authorities or of principled refusal to comply with colonial authorities, the area rapidly gained the reputation for being ungovernable. Given that all three authorities recognized the need for land and were generally sympathetic to Arusha/Meru interests, why did none of them act to remedy the situation and so remove this political thorn from its side?

That is our central question here. The answer is not a simple one, but it involves the very different conceptions of land and land use held by the main participants, and ultimately how Arusha and Meru were continually able to employ their detailed knowledge of their environment to manage and develop their productive resources in spite of government policies that threatened their economic survival.

For land, as any farmer knows, is not simply an inert economic resource. Land has economic potential, but that potential can only be realized by farmers who understand it and invest their labour accordingly, developing in the process ongoing, dynamic relationships with the land and with their fellow farmers who work it. These ecological, social and political relationships, in turn, become embodied in a moral order that validates them and gives them meaning. The struggles for the land on Mount Meru were not simply economic, then, but embraced competing social and moral orders, as different peoples on Mount Meru each sought to transform the land in its own fashion and vied with one another for supremacy. To get at the roots of the issue, we have to go back to the days before colonial rule when Arusha and Meru's relations with the land, and with each other, were forged.

Pioneers and the open frontier

In the long history of northern Tanzania, Arusha and Meru are relative newcomers. Meru were Chagga-speakers who first migrated to Mount Meru from western Kilimanjaro sometime in the seventeenth century. These early pioneers rapidly established their farms on the lower reaches of the mountain and as time went on, others joined them clearing and settling the forest in an arc stretching around the southeastern slopes that received the most favourable rainfall.[3]

Each settler established his own homestead by clearing the virgin forest, building his house and surrounding it with a dense stand of bananas that, mulched with clippings and household refuse and irrigated by means of a system of ditches dug across the slopes above the farm, yielded year after year. Such land was known as *kihamba* (pl. *vihamba*), beyond which people cleared annual fields in which crops such as eleusine, beans, maize and various vegetables were raised and rotated periodically with pasture for livestock.

As families grew and sons established their own homes adjacent to those of their fathers, homesteads became densely settled clusters of descendants of the pioneer who first cleared the forest and established claim to the land. One's *kihamba*, then, lay at the centre of one's world, socially as well as economically, the locus of the most important crops as well as of the family spawned by the pioneer who first settled on Meru, tamed its forests, learned its mysteries, and oversaw his family's development. His position, influence and powers devolved on his eldest son at his death, who then became responsible for maintaining the shrine to his father located on his *kihamba* and otherwise looking after the economic and social welfare of the family. Power was thus exercised by homestead elders by virtue of their status as pioneers. A family's *kihamba* was theirs to allocate among their wives and children. They also owned the family's livestock and exchanged cattle with other elders to marry their daughters. They then allocated portions of their *vihamba*, open fields and herds to their wives to support themselves and their children.

As individual homesteads expanded over time and sons proliferated and fell out with one another, older sons leapfrogged over their neighbours to pioneer new farms higher on the mountain. They remained linked socially and ritually with their fathers and brothers below, however, so that extended lineages and clans ran up the mountain parallel to the rivers that raced down it. It was these extended lineages and clans that bound individual Meru together, and it was the vertical slices of the mountain that they occupied with neighbouring clans which became the main administrative districts, overseen loosely by clan elders who met to mediate disputes among the members of different homesteads. Such leadership was more a function of status and respect than real power, but the leader of one clan, the Kaaya, was acknowledged as *primus inter pares* by virtue of the fact that Kaaya was the leader of the first Meru to settle from Kilimanjaro and hence became the first Mangi of all Meru.

Meru were well established on the mountain when the first Arusha settled there in the 1830s. Arusha were Maa-speakers who lost their cattle during the tumultuous wars then being fought among Maasai for control of pastoral resources on the plains and so were forced to become farmers. They first settled at Arusha Chini (lower Arusha), south of Mount Kilimanjaro, and later moved to Arusha Juu (upper Arusha), where they settled on the fringe of the plains and commenced to expand up the southwestern slopes of the mountain, much as Meru had done on the southeastern ones previously. Pioneers cleared the forest to establish their own homesteads and banana groves, called *engisaka* in Maa, and surrounded them with open fields for annual crops and pasture.[4]

Unlike Meru, however, Arusha were Maasai and associated closely with pastoral Kisongo Maasai on the plains. Arusha established a market at Arusha Juu, where they supplied pastoral Maasai with agricultural foodstuffs in exchange for livestock, milk, meat and skins. They also gave refuge to pastoralists who lost their stock to capture or disease, intermarried with Kisongo, herded stock with them, consulted with the Kisongo ritual leader (*loibon*) and initiated their young men into the same age-sets. Once initiated, Arusha warriors (*murran*) raided Meru and Chagga for cattle and women. Arusha population grew rapidly as a result, largely at the expense of Meru, and they soon overtook Meru in their rate of expansion up the mountain. After serving their period as *murran*, Arusha men married and settled down to farm with their age-mates. Arusha social organization thus developed differently from Meru. As members of successive age-sets cleared and settled higher reaches of the mountain, local sections of the age-sets, rather than clans, came to form the basis for local social organization and age-set spokesmen (*laigwenak*) spoke on behalf of their members and mediated local disputes.

Closure: 1896–1920

Arusha and Meru had cleared and settled most of the southern slopes of Meru from 4000 to 5300 feet by the 1880s, when a series of disasters swept across northern Tanzania. Bovine pleuropneumonia and rinderpest devastated the herds of pastoral Maasai, driving them into the mountains to seek refuge; smallpox spread rapidly along the trade routes recently forged up the Pangani Valley; and drought and killing famine blanketed the area, especially during the years 1883–6, 1891–2 and 1897–1900, when one natural disaster piled on another in numbing succession.

As people and livestock everywhere died in catastrophic numbers, survivors began to lose collective faith in their ability to manage their environment, and social upheaval followed. Pastoral Maasai entered into a series of brutal civil wars over cattle and who would succeed Mbatiany as their ritual protector (*loibon*), while German troops swept brutally through the Pangani Valley to put down coastal rebellions and establish their dominance over northern Tanzania. Arusha and Meru warriors sought to arrest the precipitous decline in their natural and social orders by a systematic crusade to restore moral order that culminated in the murder of the first two missionaries to settle on Meru in 1896.[5]

Brutal German punitive expeditions followed, during the course of which large numbers of Arusha and Meru were killed, their cattle confiscated, banana groves burnt down and Chagga wives repatriated to Kilimanjaro. Shortly thereafter the Germans granted huge blocks of land on north Meru to a hundred Afrikaner families newly arrived from South Africa, and they subsequently alienated a solid block of land across the southern slopes to German settlers, thereby blocking future Meru or Arusha access to the plains. At the same time, the Germans declared the area above 5300 feet a protected forest reserve, foreclosing further Arusha and Meru expansion up the mountain as well.

While Arusha and Meru had survived the natural disasters of the closing decades of the nineteenth century remarkably well, protected from diseases by their isolation and from drought by irrigation, the impact of the German conquest was devastating. In the aftermath, men and women alike were conscripted to build roads and the German *boma* and young men sought wage labour to buy food and cattle for their families, while everyone struggled to re-establish their banana groves, recover their herds and rebuild their families. After years of hardship, a bumper harvest in 1907 marked their recovery and, for the first time in years, elders competed with one another to see who could slaughter the most oxen during public feasts following the harvest.[6]

As their domestic economy recovered, Arusha and Meru withdrew from wage labour and again began to expand. With the frontier now closed, however, they were forced to turn inward, planting boundary areas between holdings or steep hillsides and riverbanks previously regarded as too difficult to work or irrigate. Arusha also continued to extend cultivation around the western side of Meru and east from Arusha town into former pastoral districts. And when British troops seized the area in 1916 and colonial authority collapsed, both Meru and Arusha resumed upward expansion, rapidly clearing and planting up to 5800 feet before the British were able to reimpose a forest zone above that in 1920.[7]

The British expelled the German settlers and confiscated their farms, but then reallocated them to Greek and British settlers, rather than providing relief to Arusha and Meru. Like the previous German authorities, the British were generally opposed to settler agriculture. They felt that the soils, labour supplies and transport were all insufficient to make it viable, but they were also concerned that existing commercial production be maintained. In the end they went much further than the Germans, however, opening up new lands south of the Arusha–Moshi road for sisal production that increased the amount of alienated land around Meru by 81 per cent.[8]

The British were also aware of the shortage of land available for Meru and Arusha farmers, but they saw this as a problem of insufficient pastures for cattle on the mountain and a shortage of stock routes through the alienated farms to the plains below. In 1920, therefore, they allocated six farms to Arusha and two to Meru to provide greater access to the plains. All were on the lower drier reaches of the mountain, which were unsuitable for banana cultivation. The British were to remain fixated on cattle as the source of the land problem on Meru throughout the colonial period, for reasons we shall explore later, and all future attempts at relief would take a similar approach.[9]

With no additional land for farming, many Arusha and Meru took to squatting on European farms. Most alienated land was poorly surveyed and remained undeveloped for long periods of time. Meru and Arusha thus had plenty of time to establish their *kihamba* and *engisaka*, thereby establishing a claim to the land, and many settlers in the throes of debt rented farming, grazing and water rights to their African neighbours. Both situations led to endemic land disputes when settlers later tried to reclaim their land, and the administration was often forced to accept Arusha/Meru occupation as a *fait accompli*.

Intensification and expansion: 1920–1950

With the recovery of Arusha and Meru agriculture, their populations also started to recover from the depredations of the late nineteenth century and German conquest. Population only increased slowly through the 1920s, but it more than doubled between 1928 and 1948 and continued to expand at high rates thereafter. With further territorial expansion limited, average population densities on the mountain began to rise, from 37/km^2 in Meru and 70/km^2 in Arusha in 1928 to 58/km^2 and 149/km^2, respectively, in 1948, while densities in individual districts climbed as high as 220/km^2. One of the people's initial responses was to shift from the older, more densely populated districts in the middle of the southern slopes of the mountain to less densely populated areas to the east and west. While this tended to level densities across the mountain, such redistribution had only a limited impact, as densities everywhere soon began to strain the potential of existing Meru and Arusha agricultural practice.[10]

Arusha and Meru agriculture produced a steady stream of diverse foods throughout the year. Their main crop was bananas, which produced consistently high yields year after year on the fertile, well-watered mountain soils. Bananas required little work to maintain, and yields could easily be improved by increasing the density of planting, mulching with cuttings, fertilizing with animal manure and irrigation. Meru and Arusha also raised a range of annual crops, including maize, beans, cocoyams and sweet potatoes, which they intercropped with each other or planted in succession to preserve soil fertility and produce a range of crops through the year. They rotated annual crops with pasture, allowing livestock to graze on crop residues between plantings and fertilize the soil with their manure, or converting fields periodically to pasture for longer fallows. Cattle and goats were thus carefully integrated into the overall crop routine and provided milk and meat to balance the high-carbohydrate banana diet.[11]

Each household was careful to maintain different kinds of fields in different areas: *kihamba* or *engisaka* for bananas on the middle slopes and a variety of open fields for annual crops and pasture elsewhere

where micro-environmental differences produced different growing cycles. Most fields were irrigated by means of simple ditches dug across the slopes above the fields. All those living along a major channel cooperated in its upkeep and shared its water in an established rotation. Given the variety of crops and activities, work was spread throughout the year and divided fairly evenly between men and women. Men generally cared for the bananas and cleared and cultivated the open fields, while women tended the annual crops, milked the cattle and prepared all the foods as well as caring for and raising the children.[12]

As population densities rose in the 1930s and 1940s, however, Arusha and Meru had to increase their production further on shrinking plots of land. They did so by planting former pastures in annual crops, stall-feeding their cattle and using their manure as fertilizer, extending banana cultivation into areas previously planted in annual crops and raising cash crops for sale.

As plot sizes shrank, farmers began to reduce the fallow periods when livestock were allowed to graze on open fields, thus enabling them to plant more annual crops. Forced to reduce the number of stock they kept on the mountain as a result, they split their herds, keeping milch cows and goats on the mountain while shifting dry stock to the plains where they were herded by neighbourhood boys or pastoral Maasai kin and age-mates. They stalled the remaining stock on the mountain, feeding them with banana refuse or grass carried up from the plains, and applied their manure to their fields to enrich the soil and increase their yields.[13]

At the same time, areas lower on the mountain and on the adjacent plains previously used exclusively for grazing were planted in maize and beans, while new grazing areas were established further out into the plains. As pastures and nearby grazing territories became planted in annual crops, fields previously devoted to annual crops on the middle slopes were planted in bananas, slowly extending the banana belt across the slopes and into their lower and higher reaches. Over time, then, there was a steady outward expansion of the banana belt, as bananas replaced beans and maize, beans and maize replaced pasture and grazing was extended into new areas on the plains.[14]

In addition to increasing their crop yields and overall production, Meru and Arusha also began to increase the amount of crops grown for sale. Arusha had long traded their agricultural surpluses to pastoral Maasai and others. By the 1930s Meru and Arusha were already producing enough maize to feed the migrant workers engaged on the estates in the area, and by the late 1940s they were selling an average of 829 tons of maize and 412 tons of beans annually. Their marketed output of maize and beans rose to 2820 and 549 tons respectively in the early 1950s. Onions and bananas also became major cash crops, with marketed production of onions rising from 29 tons annually in the early 1930s to 1297 tons by the late 1940s, producing net annual returns of 100/- to 160/- per grower.[15]

Maize, beans, bananas, and onions remained the preferred cash crops for many because they were easily integrated into local production routines, they could either be consumed locally or sold depending on need, and they fetched high prices on the estates and in the markets of Arusha town. Eventually, however, coffee became the most lucrative and important cash crop. Planted initially in the 1920s, overall production and the number of people growing coffee grew only slowly through the 1930s and early 1940s owing to depressed prices, but then picked up substantially in the 1950s and 1960s with rising prices and returns.[16] Meru and Arusha expanded coffee production because it was highly compatible with bananas and came to provide high rates of return on land and labour. They grew coffee interspersed with bananas, allowing the bananas to provide needed shade for the new trees, and mulched and irrigated it at the same time as bananas. It thus required little additional land or labour. Moreover, the combination of coffee and bananas supplied their needs for cash and food and provided higher rates of return than if either crop had been grown separately.[17]

Increasing banana and annual crop production, stall-feeding cattle and raising cash crops all greatly increased yields per acre, while widespread adoption of iron hoes and later ox ploughs also increased the productivity of labour. As densities rose over 100/km^2 during the 1930s in Arusha and 1950s in Meru, however, people began to leave the mountain in search of land elsewhere. Arusha first expanded west in the 1930s and 1940s along the spur to Monduli, where the cool highlands were ideal for raising cattle, maize and wheat, and they subsequently continued down the spur and onto the adjacent Kisongo plains in the 1950s. With the wheat boom of the 1940s, many began large-scale wheat production with ox ploughs, tractors and combine harvesters, but, when the boom collapsed in the early 1950s, they switched back to maize. Densities in Meru lagged ten to twenty years behind those in Arusha, but by the late 1940s they too were moving out into the northeastern highlands and southeastern plains to herd cattle and raise maize and beans.[18]

The decision to abandon the comfortable security of the mountain was a difficult one, and few made it rashly. Both peoples had long been reluctant to abandon secure ancestral *kihamba* and *engisaka* for the hot malarial and tsetse-infested plains where one was dependent on uncertain rainfall to raise one's crops. The move, when it came, was gradual, and most retained their stake in ancestral land on the mountain whenever they could. The first Arusha to leave were probably herdsmen, who often planted small plots of maize and beans to supplement their diet while they were herding cattle on the plains. As more stock were herded on the plains for longer periods, such plots became more permanent, but they rarely supplanted the family's fields on the mountain. Rather, expansion on to the plains was a further development of the mountain economy, as annual crops and grazing pushed out on to the plains even though they remained integrated into the expanding household economies on the mountain.[19]

The land problem and its solutions

In spite of Arusha and Meru success in providing for their expanding population, shortage of land has remained the most critical issue throughout the twentieth century. Members of the British government were aware from the very beginning of their administration of the dire shortage of land for Meru and Arusha on Mount Meru. The annual report for the district in 1919–20 emphasized: 'All land not already occupied is required for expansion of the two native tribes mentioned'.[20] At the peak of land alienation in 1928, the Provincial Commissioner, G.F. Webster, noted: 'serious congestion does . . . exist and is a factor in the alienation of land . . . to non-natives'. The following year he added that Arusha and Meru 'have felt land shortage acutely during 1929, especially so on account of the drought and consequent lack of grazing. There was a considerable amount of inter-racial friction owing to native cattle going on to European farms'. As many settlers exploited the situation to charge rent to Arusha and Meru for grazing and water, Webster further warned that very little more land could be recommended for alienation.[21]

Webster's warnings prompted the Assistant Secretary for Native Affairs, A.E. Kitching, to investigate the situation.[22] Kitching had first served as an Assistant District Officer in Arusha in 1920–21 and later as District Officer in 1926–8, prior to becoming Assistant Secretary. He thus knew the area well, and summed up the impact of German land alienation on the Meru and Arusha so incisively and so dramatically that it is worth quoting at length:

> The two tribes were relatively small units when the German Government entered their lives, but they were well placed. They were secure from molestation by other tribes. They occupied land almost unexampled by its fertility and their irrigation channels placed them beyond the vagaries of seasonal rains. Immense plains were at the disposal of their cattle and there was an abundance of agricultural land available for further expansion.
>
> These fair prospects were quickly brought to nought by the German Government. An extensive system of land alienation to non-natives was inaugurated and proceeded in the most reckless manner. The station site was carved out of native holdings and in the vicinity of the station other holdings were allocated to the native levies who had accompanied the

German forces. A township was allowed to spring up around the station and made further sequestration necessary. Two large mission stations and several small sites for mission schools and two small farms were alienated in the heart of the native area and a belt of farms was carried right around the mountain. In the south the boundaries of these farms ran cheek by jowl with native cultivation, and entailed the expropriation of many natives.

The German Government, realizing too late the effects of its land policy, ultimately decreed that no more Crown land should be alienated . . . but the damage had been done and when British Officers took over the district they found the Arusha and Meru cramped and penned within an area which was barely adequate for their immediate needs and practically incapable of extension to meet future requirements.

. . . In every quarter, normal tribal expansion . . . had been hopelessly compromised.

While the British provided some amelioration of the situation, Kitching continued, they had not known the full extent of the problem before they re-alienated most of the German farms themselves:

The straits in which the Meru and Arusha tribesmen had been left by the German Government were not fully apparent when the district was taken over in 1916. There were no survey maps or other means of identifying accurately land which had been alienated and many European farms were derelict and unoccupied and were used at will by the tribesmen. Notwithstanding these handicaps, the situation was quickly appreciated and when the question of the liquidation of enemy properties was raised in 1920, the requirements of the two tribes received special consideration with the result that [eight] farm[s] . . . were retained for native use.

The aim of granting Meru and Arusha the eight farms on the edges of the plains had not been to increase the amount of arable land available on the mountain, however, but to provide access for their cattle to the plains below.

Despite the fact that he felt the 'conditions of congestion of population . . . are probably without parallel in East Africa', however, Kitching was not prepared to recommend correcting earlier oversights by restoring land to Arusha and Meru:

It is clear . . . that a remedy will not be found by further purchases of alienated land . . . for the purpose of providing additional pastoral or agricultural land. The acquisition of farms with this view benefits only the few natives who are sufficiently fortunate to acquire holdings . . . and the needs of the population are too large and land too expensive for any substantial relief to be found in this fashion.

He also considered agricultural expansion on to the plains hopeless, as they were too dry, barren and infested with tsetse, the only possible exception being west along the ridge towards Monduli, where some Arusha were already expanding. He therefore recommended that more farms be acquired to give Arusha and Meru cattle greater access to the plains, just as the government had done in 1920.

Kitching's memo established the pattern of administration analysis for years to come and prompted the Governor to request that the Land Settlement Officer, Bagshawe, conduct a comprehensive survey of land distribution and use on Mount Meru. After months of further study, Bagshawe adopted Kitching's recommendations almost verbatim. He argued that Meru and Arusha had plenty of land overall; the problem was that most of it was on the plains without easy access through the ring of European farms. He therefore recommended acquiring seven more farms as corridors that would allow people to move their cattle between the mountain and the plains.[23] The administration accepted Bagshawe's proposal and requested that the British government pay to acquire the farms, arguing that Arusha and Meru should not be required to pay for land that 'was taken from the tribes by the German Government and alienated to European settlers without justification and without proper regard for the future'. London approved the purchase, but denied the financing, forcing the administration to turn to the Meru and Arusha Native Authorities to finance the purchases themselves by levying a surtax of Shs 2/- per person per year. In addition, the Arusha were required to relinquish a 50-yard strip along the township border.[24]

The land problem was far from solved, however. By 1938 a new study of the land problem in Meru by the Agricultural Officer, B.J. Hartley, praised the Meru as 'industrious cultivators', stressed their critical need for more land and recommended that they be given 60,000 additional highland acres immediately as well as any settler farms that might revert to the government in the future.[25] Arusha and Meru themselves were refusing to pay the surtax, noting that the government had taken the land without compensation in the first place and then burdened them with a supertax to reclaim it. The Provincial Commissioner, F.C. Hallier, was sympathetic to their cause. Noting that the mountain was badly congested and that people were being forced to rent land and water from settlers that was once theirs, Hallier continued:[26]

No matter how we might argue, the native feels that we took away his land (it matters not to him whether we did it or the Germans) and that it is nothing short of rank injustice to expect him to buy it back while we continue to draw revenue from land that was once his. We should not allow the above problem to rest or drift; early and vigorous action is required, otherwise I see trouble, real trouble, such as is evident in other parts of our Colonial Empire.

The government should forgive the loan, Hallier concluded, and it would be fully compensated by the greater production that would take place.[27]

The loan was remitted eventually, but by then both Meru and Arusha had become embroiled in further land disputes with settlers and the government. Meru had earlier purchased a leasehold farm on their own; the lease was expiring and they could not afford to convert it to freehold.[28] Meru were also threatened with further alienations north of Mount Meru, while Arusha were being evicted from their farms in town and faced the potential loss of another 2000 acres south of the town.[29] In response, Hallier was already petitioning the government to provide more land for Arusha and Meru. He proposed moving pastoral Maasai from northern Maasailand to southern Maasailand and granting the land east of the Rift to Arusha and Meru, thus allowing the government to alienate yet more Arusha/Meru land south of the railway.[30] When the government finally addressed the land problem again in the Report of the Arusha–Moshi Lands Commission in 1947, however, it fell back on the old expedient of providing more cattle corridors to the plains while alienating Meru land in Engare Nanyuki to settlers, thus provoking the famous Meru Land Case, in which Meru protested against the evictions to the United Nations. Their protest was unsuccessful, but the event provided a major impetus to the development of the nationalist movement that led Tanzania to independence a decade later.

Land use

The mere availability of land was not the only issue, however. There were also deep disputes over how land was used, including the relative merits of growing cash crops vs food crops, the role of cattle in agricultural production, and conservation. Settlers continually sought to restrict African production of coffee. While they complained publicly that poor disease control and theft by Meru and Arusha farmers threatened their own crop, privately they were more concerned over price competition and ensuring local supplies of labour.[31] They were able to persuade the administration to restrict further expansion of African cultivation in 1927, but Meru and Arusha continued to plant regardless, and the administration was forced to remove the restrictions in 1933 following the collapse of settler production during the Depression and in view of the demonstrated vitality of African production. To continue restrictions, the Chief Secretary noted, would convey the impression to Africans that the administration did not wish them to prosper and would be impolitic, given the profits people were making.[32]

While administrators reluctantly supported African production thereafter, the perennial problem of land shortage was never far from their minds, and many felt that Meru and Arusha risked their well being by growing cash crops instead of food. The District Agricultural Officer, A.E. Haarer, strongly supported the 1927 restrictions on coffee and worked hard to persuade Meru to forgo planting it in favour of food crops, but he acknowledged that they had doubled their plantings despite his best efforts to the contrary. He was even more disturbed by increased cultivation of eleusine: 'It is well known that Mbeke [eleusine] is not used as a food, but for fermenting banana juice and producing a strong alcoholic drink. Hence ... the increased use of Mbeke means that more bananas are used for producing drink than for food'.[33]

Not everyone was so concerned. The Chief Secretary noted that coffee was too profitable and popular with growers to restrict and that eleusine was merely a mild beer drunk by all, 'just like British country people'. If the Chief Secretary was less than impressed by Haarer's arguments, Kitching, then District Commissioner in Arusha, was enraged by them:

1. The general impression conveyed by the report ... is that the Meru tribesmen have taken leave of their senses and on account of the reckless exploitation of coffee and eleusine are in imminent danger of famine. Nothing could be further from the truth.
2. There has been an increase in the cultivation of coffee during the past three years ... but the area that has been planted is still an insignificant proportion of the cultivable land. The crop is not and never will be a menace to the cultivation of foodstuffs.
3. The Meru tribesmen have always been expert cultivators of eleusine. ... The crop is a very valuable commodity and is sold all over the district. ... It is used for making ordinary native beer. ...
4. The whole of the Meru area is intensively cultivated and the Meru are assiduous agriculturalists. They sell annually hundreds of tons of maize and beans and thousands of bunches of bananas in the settled areas and elsewhere.
5. Mr. Haarer was camped in the Meru area for ten full days only. In this period he visited eighteen European farms ... found time to visit my office on at least two occasions and opened an experimental seed station in Meru. He certainly had no time left to make an adequate inspection of the Meru area and as a result of inquiries which I have made I say explicitly that he did not do so. ... His report is rubbish.

The Provincial Commissioner forwarded Kitching's response to the Chief Secretary 'with complete confidence'.[34]

While Kitching summed up the Meru position rather well, the debate was by no means ended. Kitching's successor as District Officer, R.A. Pelham, feared that, while it was probably necessary to plant lucrative crops such as coffee and eleusine when land was so sparse and while Meru might even be encouraged to buy their maize from settlers, increasing population and cultivation would continue to impoverish the land.[35] The District Agricultural Officer banned further planting of coffee in 1937 to 'ensure . . . no further limitation of the land required for essential food production or grazing'.[36] And D.S. Troup, the District Officer in 1947, argued that the land shortage on Meru resulted from 'the maldistribution of the land which is supporting inedible cash crops at the expense of food crops, thereby precluding the maintenance of the population increase'.[37]

They need not have worried. Meru and Arusha were well aware of the land problem, put high premiums on soil conservation and food security and integrated cash crops in their agricultural routine precisely because they provided greater returns on land and labour than either food crops or cash crops would have provided alone. They expanded coffee production because it was highly compatible with bananas and because it provided high rates of return on land and labour. They also steadfastly rejected segregating coffee and bananas, as the agriculture department advocated, because in combination bananas and coffee produced a greater total yield than either grown separately, a fact the administration did not recognize until the late 1950s.[38] Together the two also ensured an adequate food supply as well as a cash income, a virtue underlined for Arusha and Meru by the low prices for coffee in the 1930s. Meru and Arusha never lacked sufficient food supplies for themselves. They continued to market surplus foodstuffs in large quantities, and they remained capable of supplying victims of drought on the plains during even the worst years.

While the administration would have preferred that settlers produce the cash crops and Arusha and Meru provide the labour, Meru and Arusha steadfastly refused to work for the settlers and persisted in expanding cash crop production. Given the poor wages paid by the plantations (as low as Shs 5/- per *kipande* in the Depression and never more than Shs 20/-), raising cash crops provided a far better return on labour than working for wages. Arusha and Meru could meet their needs for taxes, school fees and consumer goods far more easily and produce their own food at the same time. Individual farmers realized Shs 100–160/- annually raising onions in the early 1940s, while the average annual net returns of coffee rose from Shs 70/- in the 1930s to Shs 1500/- in the 1950s.[39] The combination of low costs, rising returns and compatibility with banana culture elevated coffee to the pre-eminent cash crop, although onion, banana, maize and bean sales all expanded apace.[40]

Many in the administration also felt that Arusha and Meru kept too many cattle on the mountain, extravagantly wasting valuable agricultural resources for the sake of prestige. Meru and Arusha carefully integrated cattle and small stock into their agricultural routines, however, feeding them nutritious banana cuttings and using their manure for fertilizer to increase crop yields. They also carefully managed their herds to maximize milk and meat production, while minimizing labour by retaining only milch cows on the mountain and herding dry stock on the plains. Taken together, the combination of crop and stock management was 'an extraordinary system of intensive mixed farming', producing a balanced diet of bananas, milk and meat for human consumption, while providing cattle with highly digestible banana fodder that was high in carbohydrates and minerals and had a productive value greater than hay, silage or mature grass.[41]

Some administrators also found fault with Arusha and Meru agricultural practices. Their practices of intensive permanent cultivation, intercropping, raising of cash crops and cultivation of steep hillsides were all blamed for poor yields, soil deterioration and erosion. In keeping with trends throughout Tanzania, the Agriculture Department initiated a major conservation campaign in 1948, but the effort soon collapsed as Meru and Arusha refused to cooperate, the administration lacked the will to provoke further unrest and conservation officers belatedly discovered that intercropping, hedges planted across the slopes, manuring and other local practices were as effective in maintaining fertility and preventing soil erosion as their cherished, but laboriously constructed bench terraces.[42]

Thus, through a judicious balancing of crops, fields, labour and investments, Arusha and Meru were able to increase the productivity of both their land and their labour to more than meet the needs of their expanding population, increasing their own standard of living as they did so. Contrary to administration policies designed to maximize production of food crops on shrinking plots, Meru and Arusha successfully optimized their overall production to provide for all their needs.[43]

Political and moral economies of land

Thus, while the administration seemed to respond to Meru and Arusha needs with a genuine sense of the injustices they had suffered, it continued to misjudge their responses and do nothing about their increasing need for arable land on the mountain. It focused on cattle and agricultural practices instead, in spite of the fact that Bagshawe's and Hartley's figures showed that Arusha and Meru had little more than one acre of cultivable land per person. That it continued to respond in this way resulted more from its conflicts with settlers than from the merits of the Meru and Arusha case. Settlers constantly complained to the administration about Arusha and Meru cattle trespassing on their farms as they were taken to and from the plains, and the repeated attempts to provide wider cattle corridors were explicitly intended to forestall such complaints. In addition, most of the land thus acquired was undeveloped semi-arid land on the plains that had little appeal to the majority of settlers raising coffee and mixed crops on the lower slopes of the mountain.

The administration's responsiveness to pressure from settlers was reflected in other ways as well. In 1935 the government issued a Confidential Circular clarifying its responsibilities regarding land. The government pledged to retain as much 'native' land as possible, while considering alienation to 'non-natives' only when broader territorial interests were served. This seemingly straightforward commitment to African rights was quickly qualified, however:

> While we seek to safeguard native rights, no one simply by virtue of being a native, has the right to land which neither he nor the community to which he belongs has occupied continuously in recent times. . . . Where there is congestion of native population in one area and ample room for expansion in another, there is a moral though not a legal obligation resting upon Government to all such expansion; but it must be strictly controlled, for otherwise Government will lose the power, which is its duty to maintain, of utilizing selected portions of the unoccupied land for the benefit of others whose claims are equally worthy of consideration on public grounds. If, for example, area A is thickly populated by an agricultural community of natives and area B is lightly populated and suitable for the growing of valuable crops, a native of A has no more right, legal or moral, than a good settler to occupy the best land in B.[44]

The administration thus quickly closed the door on Arusha–Meru aspirations it had so recently nudged open.

The constraints on protecting Africans' rights were further tightened in 1937 when Hallier enquired if the administration was bound to allow settlers to convert ex-German leaseholds to freehold in view of the likely need of Meru and Arusha for the land in the future. Under the terms of the original German leases, leaseholders could apply for the right to purchase their land freehold if they made certain improvements to it, and settlers were attempting to hold the administration to the original terms. The Land Officer responded that the government was 'morally bound', if not legally bound, to issue freehold rights of occupancy on ex-German leaseholds without regard to 'extrinsic factors such as congestion of native population, or need of land for future expansion, which in the case of an ordinary application for a Right of Occupancy would probably determine, *per se*, . . . that the Right of Occupancy could not be granted'.[45]

The administration's sense of its moral obligation to the settlers contrasted oddly with its legal obligations under the terms of the League Mandate to protect African interests and its own oft-stated preference for peasant agriculture. Few people in the administration even liked settlers. Clement Gillman, a British engineer in Tanzania for some 20 years, was a seasoned and critical agricultural observer. He much admired the skills of both Maasai pastoralists and Arusha–Meru farmers, but was scathing in his criticism of the settlers. Noting that little of their huge farms was cleared or developed, Gillman called Lower Nduruma 'an other [sic] very good example of how the term "settlement" is used by the Kenya-type shouters as a suitable disguise for their land-speculation schemes. The area is semi-desert of the worst'. Settlers were apparently not very attractive people either:

> I met the Usa Gang in a two hours' talk: General Boyd Moss, the gentleman 'settler' from high up the mountain, who produces nothing. Russell his shouting A.D.C., a few ugly looking penniless youngsters, a few innocent Greeks, dragged in to fill the room, ... and a German or two to make a background.

Afrikaner farms in Engare Nanyuki consisted of '10 or 12 ramshackle and incredibly filthy farms with litters of children'. Only one farmer impressed Gillman: he had built a stone barn for his horses while he was content to live in a thatched house himself.[46] Those in the district administration were more tactful, if no less critical:[47]

> The task of administering the tribes in the neighbourhood of Arusha proper is not made any easier by the presence of between four and five hundred European settlers, many of whom seem to regard Tanganyika as the happy hunting ground of Empire builders and to lose sight of the fact that the greater part of the Territory is held in trust for the native and not for the benefit of his would be exploiter.

Settlers, on the other hand, had political clout and were used to getting their way, especially with Africans.[48] They depended on the administration to recruit labour for them, both directly by the district officers, chiefs and labour officers and indirectly by setting tax and wage rates. They also sought to protect their markets and labour supplies through restrictions on African production, including the ban on extending African production of coffee in 1927; control of marketing and prices to maintain a two-tier pricing system that favoured European growers; and restrictions on the crops Africans could grow, ostensibly in the interests of controlling disease and theft.[49] Nor were they above acting directly if their appeals to the government failed. They conspired with one another in land auctions to keep rents low and when Asians bid against them, they either bribed the Asians to withdraw or beat them up.[50] They fought constantly with Africans and with each other over water rights, claiming expansive water rights against other users and arbitrarily blocking furrows to others' farms to get water for themselves.[51]

While the central administration thus often acceded to political pressures from settlers in the interests of political harmony and 'broader territorial interest', the district administration was forced to deal with the daily consequences of implementing policy, and those were usually not good. Meru and Arusha generally resisted any actions by settlers or the administration that intruded on their economic autonomy, leading them to become characterized in administration circles as especially 'truculent', 'intractable', 'arrogant' and 'undisciplined' peoples.[52] Colonial labour demands constantly provoked resistance. Few Meru or Arusha were willing to work for settlers, especially in poorly paid seasonal labour, and they generally refused to show up for corvée unless they supported the project for which it was used.[53] They also resisted colonial attempts to control their labour on their own fields. They rejected administration claims that the land problem on Meru was caused by people growing coffee at the expense of food crops. Such claims were not unrelated, of course, to settler demands to restrict African production of coffee in order to limit competition and make African labour more readily available to themselves. Instead, the Meru and Arusha continued to expand coffee production because it provided better returns on their labour than either producing food crops exclusively or working for settlers.[54]

Land and water, however, provided the enduring foci of Arusha and Meru resistance, from the time they killed the first two Europeans whom they felt threatened their land at the onset of colonization, to the time when Meru took their case against expropriation to the United Nations near its close. Meru and Arusha zealously guarded their water rights against settler intrusions and since they commanded the upper rivers and furrows above the settler farms and had legal precedent, they usually won. Arusha and Meru occupied undeveloped portions of settlers' estates and, when settlers sought to evict them, they claimed the land as their own by virtue of their having cleared and planted it with permanent crops, forcing either the settlers to accede to a *fait accompli* or the administration to acquire the land for them.[55]

Similarly, Arusha living within the town boundaries tenaciously resisted expropriation of their farms on the basis, usually correct, that they had cleared the land and established their farms before the town was even established and, when forced to leave, they insisted on being granted comparable land elsewhere in addition to compensation for their houses and crops. Since the British authorities ultimately came to recognize the legal validity of their claim and no comparable land was available elsewhere, subsequent attempts to extend the town resulted in prolonged political and legal disputes which the administration could only resolve by claiming that African farms were unhygienic and therefore had to be cleared for health reasons. Or, as in the case of the Bagshawe Report, the government simply insisted that Arusha give up town land as a quid pro quo for receiving land elsewhere.[56] Meru and Arusha used almost any excuse to present appeals for more land to the administration, and rarely a year went by when their appeals went unnoted in the annual district reports.

It was not simply the short supply of land and water that fueled Arusha and Meru resistance, however. They were the crux of Meru and Arusha moral economy, and both were severely threatened by colonialism. Both Meru and Arusha held that everyone had the right to as much land as he or she needed and, if such land was not available at home, then one had the right to clear forest land. As population increased during the latter half of the nineteenth century, the boundaries of Arusha and Meru cultivation had been pushed inexorably up the mountainsides, until by the turn of the century they were approaching the upper limits for bananas and annual crops. Expansion had been slowed, or maybe even reversed, during the 1890s by disease, drought and conquest, and local economies did not recover until 1907, as, we have seen. It was precisely during this period of retrenchment in the local economy, as in so many areas of East Africa, that the German authorities alienated vast tracts to settlers. Unlike Kilimanjaro and Usambara, little of the alienated land was on the mountain itself, and most had probably not been previously cultivated by Meru or Arusha, but its closure drastically restricted access to the plains for cattle, for raising annual crops and for future expansion. By the 1920s, Arusha and Meru economies had recovered, their populations were growing rapidly and confined by the 'iron ring' of alienated lands below and the forest reserve above, 'conditions of congestion . . . without parallel in East Africa' developed that were readily apparent to most observers.

Land shortage produced a sense of economic, political and moral crisis in Meru and Arusha societies not unlike that of the 1890s. Economically, people were forced to intensify production to maintain their standard of living. They enclosed and planted mountain pastures, pushed the limits of cultivation up steep hillsides and down river banks and began to grow crops such as coffee that provided higher returns on their labour. The shortage of land also produced political tensions between government chiefs, who sought to assert their right to distribute new lands; wealthy elders, who were often the beneficiaries of their largesse; and those who found themselves with insufficient land for their families. It caused tensions between the generations as well, especially between those who had benefited from the free-wheeling expansion of the 1880s, who continued to dominate land and cattle as the ruling elders of the 1920s, and their sons and grandsons, who became increasingly dependent on them for cattle and land in order to marry and settle. And, finally, it exacerbated tensions between educated Christians active in the new churches, schools and cooperatives and those who retained more traditional allegiances, as well as between men and women over access to land and produce.[57]

Thus shortage of land on the mountain contributed to a growing moral crisis in Arusha and Meru societies, for not only did each Meru or Arusha have a generalized right to land, he or she specifically had the right to *kihamba* or *engisaka*, well-watered land on the central slopes suitable for raising bananas. One built one's house in *kihamba / engisaka*, raised one's family there and surrounded it with the dense groves of bananas that sustained life. It was the central focus of people's lives.[58] One's right to *kihamba* or *engisaka* was thus fundamental to the social contract. If access to *kihamba / engisaka* was not available to all, sons would fight their fathers, brothers and age-mates would fall out among themselves and wives would leave their husbands. Individuals would starve and the social order would disintegrate.

As land became increasingly scarce, however, it was just such land that was threatened. Bananas would not grow readily on the higher slopes or on the plains. Thus, even if one got land in other areas, one could not realize a full economic or social life there. As suitable forest land and pastures on the mountain disappeared, each *kihamba / engisaka* shrank in size until it could no longer accommodate all the family claimants to it. At the same time, rights to *kihamba / engisaka* became increasingly individualized, as people sought to protect what land they had, even at the expense of their relatives. For those excluded from *kihamba / engisaka*, the social contract was broken. Some abandoned their homes to join the local Lutheran mission, which had land and a society of its own. Others left to squat on Afrikaner farms in north Meru, where they were shielded by distance from the shame of being landless and having to work for others.[59] *Kihamba / engisaka* bound people together; its absence threatened to tear them apart.

The moral crisis within Meru and Arusha societies was reflected in what they felt was the immorality of the wider colonial order. Settlers owned vast tracts of land, far more than they developed and used, but like the proverbial dog in the manger, they zealously prevented anyone else from using it. While Arusha and Meru themselves acknowledged private ownership, one could scarcely refuse to share one's land with others if it was more than one needed. It was a moral obligation that transcended any right to property. But, when settlers agreed to share land or water, which they possessed in overabundance, with others who had none, they charged for them. Similarly, the government had taken land without paying compensation, but it insisted that Meru or Arusha pay to use it or reacquire it. In spite of frequent government claims that it was making every effort to find more land, it continued to hold vacant numerous settler estates that had been abandoned by their lessees. It felt 'morally bound' to sell estates to European leaseholders, regardless of Arusha or Meru need, without feeling similarly morally obligated to help Meru or Arusha reclaim farms when they came on the market. And somehow it was continually able to find more land to alienate without being able to locate more land for Arusha or Meru.[60]

The reasons for the irony noted earlier – that, despite their claimed preference for African farmers, all the outside authorities involved on

Meru promoted settlers' interests at the expense of African ones – thus lay in contradictions inherent within colonialism itself. A distinguished group of colonial servants – Webster, Kitching, Gillman, Hartley and Hallier – spoke understandingly and eloquently on behalf of Meru and Arusha needs, but their recommendations were often ignored or sidetracked. Their failure was partly due to differences in perspective between district and central administrators. District administrators daily confronted the negative impact which land policy had on Arusha and Meru societies and on the administration's deteriorating relations with them, as evidenced by Hallier's fear of 'real trouble' developing if 'vigorous action' was not taken to address their grievances. The district authorities were right. Nothing was done, relations were perpetually bad, and real trouble did develop in the aftermath of the Lands Commission report. Dar es Salaam and London, on the other hand, were far removed from such tensions and more readily appreciated issues of territorial production, finance and the welfare of Europeans than those which were raised by disgruntled 'natives'.

But it was not simply a matter of different perspectives; it was an issue of power and of the different significance land had for the different participants. For members of the government land was essentially a political and an economic issue. They continued to believe that European settlers were required to develop commercial production, in spite of abundant evidence to the contrary, and settlers had more clout than African peasants, even if they were seen as *déclassés* by the Oxbridge men in the administration. The complaints of the settlers were heard in the European clubs, and they were acted on so long as they did not threaten to upset the uneasy colonial order between Africans and Europeans. Grievances of the Meru and Arusha were not acted upon, however, unless they threatened that order. Thus, while the administration normally acceded to settler demands, it blocked those it knew would excite African opposition, such as enforced labour or alienating still more land; and it reversed policies, such as the ban on African coffee, that threatened to undermine its authority.[61] The political initiative, however, lay with the Europeans; Africans could only protest and resist, while resolutely pursuing their own interests.

Settlers saw the significance of land differently from the administration. For them, land was primarily an economic commodity in which they could either speculate, as many of them did, or use in production, but it also had social and political dimensions. Being a European settler in the colonies was to belong to a certain economic class, a petty aristocracy, whose boorish behaviour and pursed-lip racism still oddly fascinates people today in novels and films. It was a life that had largely ceased to exist in Europe, at least for those who became settlers, and it could only be sustained by maintaining an illusion of wealth based on racial supremacy and cheap labour, despite the fact that most settlers were perpetually beholden to their banks and brokers. Their social superiority and economic status rested on maintaining the artificial distinctions – based on race, land and alleged productive superiority – that separated 'them' from 'us'. While the myth of race was rarely questioned, settlers had to fight for land and market advantages if they were to maintain their competitive advantages over African producers.

Arusha and Meru sustained more subtle and complex ideas about land than either the administration or the settlers. Land did, of course, have singular economic significance for people who relied on it to produce virtually all of their economic needs, alimentary as well as social. Land was the source not only of food, but also of wealth in disposable food surpluses, beer and the cattle who grazed on it; and wealth was the source of social influence and political power. Given the centrality of land in Meru and Arusha economic, social and political life, it could not help but have had great moral significance as well, as we have seen. Land, specifically *kihamba* and *engisaka*, lay at the core of people's moral being and differences over the moral significance of land lay at the base of their opposition to colonialism.

The centrality of land to Arusha and Meru life put them in fundamental opposition to settlers who threatened their land and to the administration that backed them, and meant that the administration could not meet Meru and Arusha demands without dismantling colonialism itself. That was something they were not prepared to do at the time, and Arusha and Meru did not yet have the power to force them to do so. That would change by 1951, when the eviction of Meru from North Meru erupted in the Meru Land Case and rang the death knell for colonialism in Tanzania.

Notes

1. This chapter is drawn from a manuscript I am currently completing on Arusha and Meru agriculture, tentatively entitled *Mountain Farmers* (London, forthcoming) and was first presented at the African Studies Association meeting in Seattle in 1992. It is based on research conducted in Tanzania in 1988 and 1991 under the auspices of the Tanzania Commission for Science and Technology and the Department of History of the University of Dar es Salaam, and was supported by grants from the National Endowment for the Humanities and Williams College. I am grateful to them all, and to the many individuals who facilitated my research, including Prof. Abdul Sheriff, Dr N.N. Luanda, Mr Wolfgang Alpelt, Mr Chikote, Mr J. David Simonson, Reverend Mesiaki Kilevo, Reverend Erasto Ngira and the Arusha and Meru elders who kindly shared their knowledge with me. I am also grateful to Richard Waller, James Giblin and Greg Maddox for their thoughtful comments on the manuscript.

2. J. Giblin and G. Maddox, in the Introduction to this volume; W.Cronon, 'Modes of Prophecy and Production: Placing Nature in History', *Journal of American History* 76, 4 (1990), 1122–31.

3. The early history of Meru is detailed in Spear, *Mountain Farmers*, chapter 3.

4. T. Spear, ' "Being Maasai" but not "People of Cattle" ': Arusha Agricultural Maasai in the 19th century', in T. Spear and R. Waller, eds, *Being Maasai* (London, 1992); P.H. Gulliver, *Social Control in an African Society* (London, 1963).

5. The missionaries entered Meru on the heels of the disasters of the 1890s, prompting Arusha and Meru *murran* to murder them as harbingers of moral disorder who threatened to seize their land and force them to work, as developed in Spear, *Mountain Farmers*, chapter 5, 'Blood on Our Land'.

6. Anton Lukas Kaaya, MHT 1; Kirilo Japhet Ayo, MHT 2; Yohanes ole Kauwenara, AHT 2; Lodenaga Lotisia, AHT 3; Fickert, *ELMB* 58 (1903): 41; Krause, *ELMB* 58 (1903): 94, 98; Ittameier, *ELMB* 62 (1907): 561.

7. P.H. Gulliver, 'The Population of the Arusha Chiefdom: A High Density Area in East Africa', *Rhodes–Livingstone Journal* 28 (1960): 12, and *Report on Land and Population in the Arusha Chiefdom* (Tanganyika Provincial Administration, 1957), p. 19.

8. N.N. Luanda, 'European Commercial Farming and Its Impact on the Meru and Arusha Peoples of Tanzania, 1920–1955' (Ph.D. Thesis, Cambridge, 1986), pp. 10, 53, 80–89, 195–209; Arusha District, Annual Reports, 1920–27, TNA 1733; LO to DC/AD, 3 Jan. 1929 (TNA: 472/LAN/13); LO to Chief CS/DSM, 19 Nov. 1929 (TNA; 10079/IV); A.E. Kitching, 'Memorandum on Native Land in Arusha District', 3 Dec. 1930 (TNA: 26257, also 25369); 'Land Development Survey: II: Acquisition of Land by Natives', 1930 (TNA: 26257).

9. Luanda, 'Commercial Farming', pp. 272–8.

10. Gulliver, *Land and Population*, pp. 20–23. Population densities were calculated from the 1928 and 1948 censuses after Wilfred Mlay, 'Population Pressure in Arumeru District' (Arusha, 1982). See Spear, *Mountain Farmers*, chapter 9 for details.

11. AO/AD to Sr. AO, 11 April 1931 (TNA: 9/17/1); Northern Province Native Agriculture, 1945 (TNA: 9/6/5); R.E.D. Baker and N.W. Simmonds, 'Bananas in East Africa', *Empire Journal of Experimental Agriculture*, 19 (1951): 283–90, 20 (1952): 66–76; K. Shephard, 'Banana Cultivars in East Africa', *Tropical Agriculture (Trinidad)*, 34 (1957): 277–86; N.W. Simmonds, *Bananas* (London, 1959), pp. 129–83, 252–71; J.D. Acland, *East African Crops* (London, 1971); Fokken, *ELMB*, 60 (1905): 38–9; A.E. Haarer, 2 July 1925 (TNA: 9/6/5); B.J. Hartley, 'A Brief Note on the Meru People with Special Reference to their Expansion Problem,' 25 March 1938 (TNA: 69/45/9); Hans Cory, 'Arusha Land Tenure', UDSM: Hans Cory Papers, 38, 23–25; Gulliver, *Land and Population*, pp. 65–6.

12. DO/AD to PC/NP, 12 Feb. 1926 (TNA: 69/233); Cory, 'Arusha Land Tenure', pp. 23–5; Louise Fortmann, 'Development Prospects in Arumeru District', USAID/Tanzania, 1977; Ngole ole Njololoi AHT 4; AO/AD, Monthly Reports, 1955 (TNA: 472/-); Mesiaki Kilevo, pers. comm.

13. A.E. Haarer, 2 July 1925; DO/AD to PC/NP, 16 Sept. 1930 (TNA: 69/45/9); Hartley, 'Brief Note on the Meru'; Notes by N.R. Reid, Arusha District Book; Veterinary Officer, Northern Province to DO/AD, 10 June 1939 (TNA: 9/6/5); Northern Province Native Agriculture, 1945; 1949 Cattle Census, District Note Book (TNA: 9/6/5); Gulliver, *Land and Population*, pp. 65–6; Cory, 'Arusha Land Tenure', pp. 23–4; Yohanes ole Kauwenara (AHT 2).

14. Chief Conservation Officer/Tengeru in his letter to AO/AD, 30 Jun. 1952 (TNA: 9/ADM/9). See also Hartley, 'Brief Note on the Meru'; Northern Province Native Agriculture, 1945; Clement Gillman, Tanganyika Diaries, XVIII/97h/29.5.36, 9 (Rhodes House: MSS. Afr. s.1175). Arusha District, Annual Report, 1952 (TNA: 472/ANR/1); Fortmann, 'Development Prospects', p. 245.

15. Spear, *Mountain Farmers*, chapter 9. No comparable figures for banana sales are available, although they were commonly sold on the estates and in the markets in town.

16. Spear, *Mountain Farmers*, chapter 9.

17. Simon Mbilinyi, *The Economics of Peasant Coffee Production: The Case of Tanzania* (Nairobi, 1976), p. 35, 90–4; PC/NP to CS/DSM, 23 July 1928 (TNA: 11160);

Northern Province Native Agriculture, 1945; Agriculture Department, Annual Report, 1945 (TNA: 472/-).

18. Gulliver, *Land and Population*, pp. 17-19; Agriculture Department, Annual Report, 1945 (TNA: 472/-); Northern Province, Annual Reports, 1957-58 (TNA: 471: R.3/2); AO/AD, Monthly Reports, 1953-55 (TNA: 9/4/2; 9/4/2/II; and 472/-); Northern Province, Annual Report, 1956 (TNA: 471/R.3/2).

19. Northern Province, Native Agriculture, 1945; Ngole ole Njololoi (AHT 4); Eliyahu Lujas Meiliari (AHT 8); Gillman, Diaries, XII/#95/15.12.34; Hans Cory, 'Arusha Law and Custom', (UDSM: Hans Cory Papers, 39) p. 21; Moffett to Wilson, 22 Oct. 1946 (RH: Wilson Papers); Chief Soil Conservation Officer to AO/AD, 30 June 1952 (TNA: 9/ADM/9); Gulliver, *Land and Population*, pp. 21, 43-6; Hans Cory, 'Memoranda on the Arusha Chiefdom; Arusha Chiefdom Population, 1948-57', (UDSM: Hans Cory Papers, 277) pp. 17-19; Cory 'The Arusha: Economic and Social Change', in P. Bohannan and G. Dalton, eds, *Markets in Africa* (New York, 1965), pp. 263-4; Fortmann, 'Development Prospects', pp. 24-5. AO/AD, Monthly Report, Dec. 1953 (TNA: 472/-).

20. Arusha District, Annual Report, 1919-20 (TNA: 1733/1).

21. Northern Province, Annual Reports, 1928 and 1929 (TNA: 11681).

22. Kitching, 'Memorandum on Native Land'.

23. 'Land Settlement Survey; II: Acquisition of Land by Natives' [Dec 1930]; LDO to PC/NP, 28 Dec. 1930; LDO to CS/DSM, 28 Dec. 1930; PC/NP to CS/DSM 7 Jan. 1931; Governor to Secretary of State for Colonies, 29 Jan. 1931 (all in TNA: 25369).

24. Governor to Secretary of State, 29 Jan. 1931, and reply 7 April 1931 (TNA: 25369); Notes, 27 July 1932 (TNA: 69/602); Minutes, 23 Nov. 1932 (TNA: 19449); P.E. Mitchell, 'Purchase of Land in Arusha District', 2 Mar 1933; Governor to Secretary of State, 21 Apr. 1933 and reply, 30 May 1933; CS/DSM to LO, 6 July 1933; PC/NP to Treasurer, 13 Jan. 1934; Financial Arrangements, 22 Sept. 1938; The Question of Title, 22 Sept. 1938 (all in TNA: 25369); Agreement between H.R. Gilbert, District Officer of Arusha, and Arusha Elders, 5 Jan. 1934 (TNA: 69/602).

25. Hartley; 'Brief Note on the Meru People'.

26. F.C. Hallier, 'Political and Economic Problems of the Moshi and Arusha Districts', 2 Aug. 1938 (TNA: 69/602).

27. Hallier, 'Political and Economic Problems', 'Memorandum on the Purchase of Farms 134, 187, 208, 209, 210, 173 and 328 for the Arusha and Meru Tribes', 12 Aug. 1938 (TNA: 25369, also 69/602). See also P.E. Mitchell, 'Memo on purchase of farms', 29 Aug. 1938 (TNA: 25369). Petition by the Wa-Arusha and Wameru, 13 Aug. 1938; Notes on a speech by the Governor, 13 Aug. 1938; Minutes by Financial Secretary, 31 Dec. 1938; Governor to Secretary of State, 19 Jan. 1939 and reply, 14 Feb. 1939; Governor's Speech to Arusha, 20 Feb. 1939 (all in TNA: 25369).

28. Asst. LO/NP to LO/DSM, 9 Oct. 1934 (TNA: 22519).

29. LO/DSM to CS/DSM, 24 Jan. 1935, two letters (TNA: 13017); Northern Province, Annual Report, 1927 (TNA: 11681); Dep. PC/NP to PC/NP, 9 May 1930 (TNA: 26147); DO/AD to LO/DSM, 24 Sept. 1930 (TNA: 69/AR/II); DO/AD to PC/NP, 17 Jan. 1931 (TNA: 12516); PC/NP to CS/DSM, 8 June 1934 and reply, 20 Oct. 1934 (TNA: 12516); DO/AD to PC/NP, 17 Aug. 1934 (TNA: 12516/II); PC/NP to CS/DSM, 1 Oct. 1934 (TNA: 12516/II); Northern Province, Annual Report, 1934 (TNA: 11681); PC/NP to CS/DSM, 8 Jul. 1938 (TNA: 69/602).

30. CS/DSM, Minutes of a meeting with Capt. Hallier, 21 Oct. 1937 (TNA: 25369, also 69/602).

31. 'Memorandum by the Chairman of the Board of Coffee', 6 July 1927, et seq. (TNA: 11160); 'Memo by Combined Association of Arusha', 27 July 1929, et seq. (TNA: 11908/I); Dir. of Agriculture to CS/DSM, 17 April 1930 (TNA: 12968/I).

32. Director of Agriculture to CS/DSM, 13 July 1928, citing report by the District Agricultural Officer, A.E. Haarer, 3 July 1928; DC/AD to PC/NP, 1 August 1928 and PC/NP to CS/DSM, 4 August 1928 (all in TNA: 11908/I); Circular Nos. 77 of 1927 and

3 of 1933 and related correspondence (TNA: 11160); D. Sturdy, 'Native Coffee on Meru,' in AO/AD to Sr AO, 15 May 1931 (TNA: 9/12/13); Northern Province, Annual Report, 1934 (TNA: 11681). See below for further discussion of this issue.

33. A.E. Haarer, report dated 3 July 1928, cited in Director of Agriculture to CS/DSM, 13 July 1928 (TNA: 11908/I).

34. DC/AD to PC/NP, 1 Aug. 1928, and PC/NP to CS/DSM, 4 Aug. 1928 (TNA: 11908/I).

35. DO/AD to PC/NP, 16 Sept. 1930 (TNA: 69/45/9).

36. T.C. Cairns, 'Native Coffee Growing,' 1940 (TNA: 9/6/5).

37. DC/AD to PC/NP, 4 Nov 1947 (TNA: 9/NA/1).

38. Commenting on the intercropping of coffee and bananas, the Northern Province Annual Report for 1959 commented: 'The indications are that the small farmer has evolved a pattern of cultivation that gives him maximum production and is best suited to his way of life and that pure stands of coffee are perhaps only advisable on the larger holdings.' (TNA: 471/R.3/2); James Lewton Brain, pers. comm.

39. Spear, *Mountain Farmers*, Chapter 10; Northern Province Native Agriculture, 1945 (TNA: 9/6/5).

40. Mbilinyi, *Economics*, p. 35.

41. Simmonds, *Bananas*, p. 271.

42. Department of Agriculture, Monthly Reports, 1948–51 (TNA: 472/-).

43. For an excellent discussion of the concepts of 'maximization' and 'optimization', see Fortmann, 'Development Prospects'.

44. Confidential Circular No. 13945/155, 20 Nov 1935 (TNA: 13401/II).

45. LO to PC/NP, 18 Nov. 1937 (TNA: 472/LAN/13).

46. Gillman, Diaries, X/78/9–22.10.28, pp. 75–78.

47. Annual Report, Arusha District, 1925 (TNA: 1733/36).

48. There was, for example, a rowdy attempt made by Arusha settlers to join Kenya in 1928 that put the administration on warning regarding their handling of settlers. Northern Province, Half-Yearly Report, 1928 (TNA: 10902).

49. For the restriction on African coffee growing, see Circular No. 77 of 1927, 20 Dec. 1927 and related correspondence (TNA: 11160). For arguments relating to controlling disease and theft, Dir. of Ag. to CS/DSM 17 April 1930 (TNA: 12968/I); misc. correspondence (TNA: 9/12/14); Dir. of Ag. to CS/DSM, 30 Feb. 1934; PC/NP to CS/DSM, 24 March 1934; PC/NP to Sr. AO/Moshi, 13 July 1934 (TNA: 11908/II).

50. DO/AD to PC/NP, 4 April 1928; K.C. Patel to PC/NP, n.d. and reply, 20 April 1928; PC/NP to LO/DSM, 20 April 1928; CS/DSM to PC/NP, 11 May 1928 (all in TNA: 69/205/AR).

51. See, for example, the numerous cases in TNA: 69/246/6, 472/112, and 472/WAT/25.

52. These are all words one finds with disarming frequency in the colonial files.

53. Minutes, District Meeting, 6 Oct 1949 (TNA: 9/ADM/11).

54. DO/AD to PC/NP, 16 Sept 1930 (TNA: 69/45/9). James L. Brain, pers. comm.

55. Arusha District, Annual Report, 1954 (TNA: 472/ANR/1).

56. The fact that individual Arusha displaced from town were rarely the ones who benefited from the land grants on the plains shifted the conflict from one between the British authorities and Arusha to one between wealthy Arusha cattlemen, often the chief and his allies, who would benefit from such transfers, and poorer Arusha farmers, who would not.

57. See Spear, *Mountain Farmers*, chapter 12, for discussion of the political and social tensions engendered by land shortage among Meru and Arusha.

58. Gulliver, *Land and Population*, p. 27.

59. The paradox of landless Arusha and Meru preferring to squat on Afrikaner farms perplexed me when I was doing field work. In view of Afrikaners' reputation for exploiting squatters, both Africans and other Afrikaners, I could only attribute it to

the fact that they also provided landless Meru and Arusha with land, oxen and ploughs, thus enabling them to farm on their own while working for their landlords. Mesiaki Kilevo, with whom I was sharing my field work, sharply contested this interpretation, however, claiming that Arusha preferred to work for Afrikaners because their farms were far from home, and thus Arusha going there were not exposed to the indignity of being landless and having to work for others in front of their peers. His comment forced me to take the moral crisis provoked by conquest, colonization, and land shortage much more seriously, and I now find it thoroughly convincing.

60. Gulliver, *Land and Population*, p. 27.

61. 'Memo of Combined Association of Arusha to His Excellency, the Governor', 25 July 1929 (TNA: 13417).

Conclusion

ISARIA N. KIMAMBO

The essays included in this volume have focused on the continuous interaction between humanity and the environment in the struggle for survival. This is timely for two reasons. First, as pointed out in the Introduction, historians of Tanzania have tended to avoid environmental concerns as part of their enquiry and analysis. To be sure, environmental discussions have appeared as background information to many studies, without featuring much in the main analysis. It is hoped that the case-studies in this volume have demonstrated the value of making environmental concerns a major part of analysis. Secondly, it is timely in the sense that the people of Tanzania now realize the importance of environmental concerns. In many ways communities face the consequences of the way their past activities have degraded their environments, and they have begun to search for remedies. Tree planting, for example, has become a common community activity in many parts of the country as people search for ways to restore soil fertility and increase supplies of fuel. Certainly, an analysis of past human activities will indicate that, in their interaction with the environment, people have continuously affected it, while at the same time changing their own ways of life. It is through such struggles that human beings have been able to make progress.

As long as human societies continue to act in their environments, there will be no time when this process of adaptation can cease. Even in the so-called developed world (where progress in development has been acknowledged), environmental issues continue to worry communities as the negative impact of human activities increases. The fact is that adaptation and control of environment are concerns of all human

Conclusion

communities. The problem for historians comes when considering rural communities of less developed countries like Tanzania. The tendency here has been to assume that people in such societies depended more on nature and did little to shape it.

James C. McCann tells us that this situation has arisen because 'historians have focused on agriculture as a sub-field of political economy [rather] than as an agenda for the study of field systems, technology and cropping patterns'.[1] By focusing on communities and their environments, the essays in this volume have redressed this imbalance to an extent. But, as we shall see in this chapter, environmental concern does not mean brushing aside the political picture. In his essay on Handeni District, James Giblin has made a strong case that 'politics was the foundation of environmental control'. However, this does not negate McCann's statement. In fact, in the introductory chapter of this volume, Giblin and Maddox have argued that for a successful understanding of the African past what is needed is not a history of agriculture instead of political economy, but a greater awareness of 'the interrelationship between social and political structures and the course of agricultural change in African history'.

The exclusion of environmental concerns from Tanzanian historiography has had the effect of blurring changes which resulted from continuous social adaptation to environmental conditions. The static and unchanging picture of society found in colonial literature represents an extreme example of this. As discussed later in this chapter, nationalist historiography in the 1960s attacked Eurocentric history in order to create an Afrocentric history, but the debates of nationalist historians failed to accommodate the full picture of economic and social transformations. Since the 1970s, nationalist historiography has been criticized by those using Marxist tools of analysis, basically for failing to see the process of exploitation in human relationships. But as we shall see later, even at this stage of debate, failure to perceive environmental adaptation in its historical perspective has tended to obscure the continuity of social struggles for survival in the face of changes in power arrangements. Nevertheless, it can be argued that environmental adaptation and control are the bases upon which the structures debated by both nationalist and Marxist historians have been erected. Thus, rather than seeing rural communities as inert masses which were merely the objects of capitalist transformation, historians should see them as dynamic, for they were always attempting to control environmental forces and adapt to changes in structures of power. The essays in this volume have given some illustrations of this process, as will be shown later in this chapter.

The nine case studies in the volume concentrate on varied ecological zones and different historical periods from the beginning of the nineteenth century to the end of colonialism. The four essays on the

Pangani Valley by Giblin, Conte, Kimambo and Spear demonstrate the ecological contrast between mountains and plains and show how environmental control involved not only mastery of mountain environments, but also cooperation with communities on the plains. Similarly, Monson's example of the Kilombero Valley demonstrates interaction between 'upland rain-fed shifting cultivation' and 'valley-bottom wetland farming'.[2] Residents of this kind of environment managed two ecological zones in order to survive. Further west, we have two other interesting examples. First, as Maddox shows, Ugogo in central Tanzania has a more arid environment where people were able to survive by combining pastoralism with agriculture. Secondly, in the extreme west, Michele Wagner's example demonstrates how a cultural unit known as Buha was built around varying ecological belts, with the bulk of the population (the Baha) living in the lowland as cultivators, while pastoralists (the Batutsi) occupied the grassy hillsides. The importance of environmental factors in these communities is illustrated by the identities (like those of the bateko) which were maintained even after new power arrangements had been established by the Batutsi pastoralists. The remaining two case studies help to relate population trends to the environmental picture. Juhani Koponen's essay outlines demographic trends from the late nineteenth century to the colonial period, while Pamela Maack's case study of the Uluguru Mountains in Morogoro examines population pressures in a mountain region which is surrounded by less attractive agricultural land.

The main theoretical issues discussed in these essays have been raised in the Introduction. Hence this concluding chapter will try to relate the study of environmental change to the historiography of Tanzania which has developed in the Department of History at the University of Dar es Salaam. Since the middle of the 1960s the Department has tended to focus attention on historiographical discussions. Such concerns were stimulated in the 1960s not only by the birth in 1961 of a new nation, originally called Tanganyika and later Tanzania following the union of Tanganyika and Zanzibar in 1964, but also by continuing struggles to define national independence.

Colonial historiography

In most newly independent African countries, historians of the 1960s faced a problem of how to interpret historical information written during the colonial period. This was so because colonial historiography tended to justify colonial domination. Such historiography had already begun to be questioned after the Second World War, just as nationalist movements were beginning to challenge that domination. Tanzania, however, had little written colonial history to be discussed in the early

1960s. Therefore, when the Department of History was established at the University of Dar es Salaam historians had to work fast to produce a national history. When T.O. Ranger, the first Professor of the Department, gave his 'Professorial Inaugural Lecture',[3] he claimed that within a short time the erroneous history created during the colonial period had been demolished, but at the same time he had to confess that it was necessary to create a 'straw man' representing colonial historiography by collecting pieces of information from colonial school textbooks which indicated the views which the colonizers had held about the history of Tanzania.

The lack of professional history did not mean that nothing had been written during the colonial period. Anthropologists (some of them working as government sociologists) had produced a number of publications on individual ethnic groups, many in the form of unpublished reports submitted to the colonial government, which were used to implement the structure known as 'indirect rule'. School textbooks were based on such information. They often assumed that because Africans had no history of their own before the coming of Europeans, history began with the coming of Europeans as explorers, missionaries and colonizers. Some European publications on East Africa had recognized the existence of some history before the arrival of Europeans, but basically they considered this to have been the history of 'invaders' from outside rather than the history of indigenous people themselves.[4]

Many historians today will see no reason to continue to comment on the weakness of colonial historiography since it is a position which has long been discredited. The 'nationalist' historiography of the 1960s effectively demolished it and made a case for the existence of a history of the Africans in their own right. Nevertheless, historical studies continue to confront the kinds of attitudes that were reflected in colonial historiography. For example, Jamie Monson's essay on the creation of forest resources in the inner Kilombero Valley indicates how British officials viewed African agriculture. Reports of the Forestry Department, she says, show that forestry policy was based on 'European rather than African perceptions of forest use'. British officials saw forests as valuable economic resources needing protection from 'shortsighted' local populations, but failed to establish a beneficial policy because they did not value the experience of a local population which had controlled and exploited the environment of the inner Kilombero Valley for centuries. That was the kind of position the nationalist historians were critizing, but, as we shall see below, insufficient attention to environmental issues prevented nationalist historiography from appreciating the complexity of local ecological knowledge described by Monson.

Conclusion

Nationalist historiography

The term 'nationalist historiography', which A. Temu and B. Swai call 'Africanist' historiography,[5] does not refer to history written by politicians. It was history inspired by the success of nationalism in giving birth to new African nations and was full of enthusiasm about possibilities for development in these new nations. It was this history to which the research efforts of the Department of History and associated researchers from Europe and America contributed. Before the end of the 1960s, one could even read *A History of Tanzania*[6] which traced the existence of the Tanzanian nation from the archaeological finds of Olduvai Gorge. This historiography held not only that the Tanzanian peoples had their own history, but also that they were in control of their development. Thus, the theme pursued by the nationalist historians of 'discovering people's initiatives' was aimed at changing the European image of the African past from one 'which never changed' to one which was dynamic and full of changes initiated by the people themselves. Yet, as has already been mentioned above, nationalist historiography concentrated not on environmental issues, to which it paid little attention, but instead on political changes, especially those which involved states and state-related institutions.

It did not take long before this kind of historiography came under fire. There were two phases of criticism of the nationalist historiography. Nationalist historians were themselves the first to recognize weaknesses in interpretation and research strategy. Denoon and Kuper, for example, were worried about the political implication of an interpretation that showed too much commitment to the 'political philosophy of current African nationalism'.[7] In 1968 I myself expressed worries about the concentration on political issues that subordinated economic issues. This is how I put it:[8]

> All the existing area studies share a preoccupation with politics. This was to be expected in 1961, but such studies are increasingly anachronistic. From the viewpoint of the administrator, social scientist, or teacher, what is most needed from the historian of modern Tanzania is painstaking and detailed economic history at the regional or district level, that is, a transfer of energy from area politics to area economics, similar to the transfer from national to area politics that took place soon after independence.

My concern was triggered by the massive nationalizations of economic institutions and private business after the Arusha Declaration in 1967, but my proposal to undertake 'parcels' of economic history research was unlikely to shed light on what was happening. Similarly, the criticism concerning commitment to nationalist political philosophy would introduce neither new research methodology nor different philosophical outlooks. In fact, it might be argued that the nationalists' lack of attention to local systems of environmental knowledge hindered their effort to show that Tanzania was 'full of changes initiated by the people themselves'. Meanwhile, Tanzania made a political commitment to Ujamaa, or a traditional socialist path of development, in 1967. This political change encouraged deeper discussion of nationalist historiography.

Beyond the nationalist historiography

The second phase of criticism, therefore, involved looking at both the methodology of research and the philosophy directing its interpretation. The enthusiasm of the 1960s was fading away by the end of the decade because of a significant reality: the anticipated fast development of the new nation had not taken place. The political situation in Tanzania had changed radically because of this realization, particularly with the Arusha Declaration, which was promulgated in 1967 specifically because of the failure of plans inherited from the colonial period. The Arusha Declaration expressed the intent of building a socialist society base on Ujamaa, the traditional principles of working together and sharing. For the Dar es Salaam historians, this was a new challenge because the earlier emphasis on political initiatives had not produced an understanding of the history of economic struggles that allowed societies to survive over centuries. It had in fact falsely suggested that in the colonial period people were still in control of their development. If that were the case, what then had gone wrong so soon after independence?

The discussions and debates initiated in the Department of History at Dar es Salaam by the Arusha Declaration in 1967 are still continuing. At first they were informed by 'underdevelopment theory'. Throughout the 1970s research concentrated on the economic system brought by colonialism. Rather than showing local initiatives, it suggested that precapitalist economies were powerless to resist capitalist penetration and that colonial capitalism was structured to serve metropolitan accumulation. Historians increasingly concentrated on the colonial period in order to understand the impact of capitalism under imperialism and to prove that, as a peripheral part of the capitalist system, colonial economies were underdeveloped instead of developing.[9] Furthermore, they argued that African precapitalist economies had not developed sufficiently to compete with the European economic system and used the example of long-distance trade in the nineteenth century (perhaps the only economic topic adequately handled by the nationalist historians[10]) to show how nationalist historians failed to see the destructive impact of capitalism on less developed economies.

Yet underdevelopment theory had not equipped historians to

understand adequately the structure of precapitalist economies and what happened to them in peripheral capitalism. Were they transformed into capitalism or were they simply participating in a capitalist system while retaining their precapitalist forms? Thus since the second half of the 1970s, Dar es Salaam historians have emphasized the political economy approach, which concentrates upon relations of production and consumption, differentiation and class structure, particularly in their histories of rural communities. Unfortunately for Tanzanian history, however, the concentration on colonial history has magnified the dichotomy between colonial and precolonial periods, and has failed to produce a clear understanding of the options which were open even to communities which faced the forces of imperialism.[11] Thus, it might also be argued that, like its nationalist predecessor, post-nationalist historiography has also had difficulty in identifying local initiatives because it has paid little attention to environmental issues.

The position of this volume

The essays in this volume have been informed by these discussions. We shall try to demonstrate this by looking at selected examples. The four essays on the Pangani Valley by Giblin, Kimambo, Conte and Spear concentrate on the environmental and economic interaction of agricultural production and exchange. The existence of mountains and plains environments together made the interdependence of the economies in the entire region spectacular. Yet, this interdependence co-existed with a low level of the forces of production in these economies. The multiplicity of crops, efforts in intensification and maintenance of a regional exchange system are all striking, especially in the highland areas with good rainfall and high fertility. Clearly the struggle for survival was continuous, for on the mountains, the level of production could not prevent worries about availability of food from day to day, while on the plains, as Giblin's example of Handeni District indicates, worries were not only about day-to-day dearth, but also about famine.

Societies which needed to control animal diseases, intensify agricultural production and maintain good relations with neighbours in order to exchange their products all required a political system that would make these things possible. Recognizing this emphasis on politics, however, does not return us to the same perspective that was found in nationalist historiography, for, rather than considering politics as paramount, here we are placing politics within relations of production and exchange. In order to do this it is necessary, just as McCann suggests, to understand the complexity and constraints of agricultural systems. This will enable us to see why the political system took the form it did in particular regions. In the case of Handeni, where the ecology was different from that of the neighbouring mountains because well-watered places were few, agriculture had to be concentrated in certain areas where vector-borne diseases were controlled and livestock could survive. The need to guarantee food supplies for the population in these permanent settlements led to the prominence of patron/client relationships. Although considered a to be stateless or non-centralized society, the Zigua had a class that controlled resources, productive land and cattle, and attracted the labour of clients who cultivated the land. Some of the produce was accumulated by the patron for redistribution during periods of drought and in this way the communities remained together and maintained a disease-free environment.

On the mountains, on the other hand, there were larger political units. Why was this the case? Agricultural intensification did not, of course, require kings and chiefs. From Usambara to Kilimanjaro, irrigation systems were controlled by the communities that used them. As indicated in Spear's chapter, the Arusha who settled on Mount Meru in the nineteenth century maintained the non-centralized structure of their Maasai kin while on the other side of the same mountain the Meru developed a state system similar to that of their Chagga neighbours. Where a governing class came into being, it resolved conflicts in order to maintain a suitable environment for production and performed rituals which provided ideological justification for its dominance. In return, the productive system sustained the ruling class. Thus the scale of political organization was invariably related to the environment and its capacity to produce surplus. Political leadership, however, could take a leading role in agricultural intensification. Nineteenth-century agricultural innovations such as modification of range management and the spread of maize show how political authorities could take leadership in this area, especially in Ugweno and Kilimanjaro.

The second point illustrated by the nineteenth-century essays concerns exchange. The complicated local exchange networks on the mountains have been described in the recent studies of Sally Falk Moore on Kilimanjaro, Steven Feierman on Usambara and myself on Upare.[12] However, the emphasis on regional trading networks connecting all the communities of wider regions has not been made as strongly before now, although Edward Alpers' chapter in *A History of Tanzania* did indeed touch on trade networks in south and central Tanzania which predated caravan traffic from the coast.[13] However, it is now clear that a similar trade network was also important in the Pangani Valley, where it created a commercial system in which scarce items such as iron, pottery, salt and tobacco became commodities, and in which certain people specialized as traders. Similar developments are also known to have occurred in the Nyamwezi region of western Tanzania and the Yao region of southern Tanzania.

Conclusion

The expansion of long-distance trade in this area has to be recognized as the first stage of capitalist penetration,[14] for it involved the integration of rural economies into a world trading network controlled by European and American industries. Nationalist historiography had categorized this process of integration as 'enlargement of scale', a concept borrowed from social anthropology, and especially from Godfrey and Monica Wilson's *The Analysis of Social Change*.[15] It referred to the passage from small-scale society, with confined social relationships and closely integrated kin groups, to large-scale society, with communication extending all over the world. Nationalist historians saw the advantage of using the concept to explain the political change brought about by expansion of long-distance trade from the coast which integrated communities of the interior into a worldwide trading network. The theme of 'enlargement of scale' was adopted by the History Department of the University College, Dar es Salaam, as the theme for the University of East Africa Social Science Conference held in Dar es Salaam in January 1968. Papers by Kimambo on the Pare, Edward Alpers on the Yao, Andrew Roberts on the Nyamwezi and Steven Feierman on the Shambaa all focused on this theme. Roberts and Alpers were able to illustrate how the Nyamwezi and Yao were exposed to external pressures which enabled them to enlarge their political systems far beyond what existed before. On the other hand, Feierman and Kimambo argued that even though the people of the northeastern mountains of Tanzania experienced political fragmentation, the theme of enlargement still applied to them because they became part of a broader system of regional politics.[16]

Criticism of the nationalist historiography for emphasizing politics and neglecting economics has already been mentioned. The environmental focus in this volume has helped to highlight another weakness in the 'enlargement of scale' theme: the tendency to magnify the idea that the stimulus of external influences was a prerequisite for local social change. It is necessary, of course, to recognize the dynamism of the capitalist system, for it developed long-distance trade which enabled rural communities to exchange commodities such as ivory for manufactured commodities such as cloth, beads, bracelets and guns. The case studies help us, however, to see that rural communities took their own initiatives in response to the expansion of commerce, by struggling to control their environment and reorganize production to secure more exchangeable items. The concentration of population in patron-centred settlements of the Handeni lowlands described by Giblin, for example, made it possible to maintain a suitable environment for survival of people and their domestic animals.

Penetration of trade also led to the growth of a big provisioning business and a slave-trading system. Here the case-studies enable us to visualize the impact of the violence which was caused by the slave trade, and to re-evalute criticisms levelled against the demographic argument of Helge Kjekshus. Kjekshus, who had argued that population growth in the nineteenth century was disrupted only by colonial violence, has been criticized for romanticizing the nineteenth-century situation.[17] In general, we can agree with Kjekshus that the violence engendered by the nineteenth-century caravan trade could hardly have caused demographic decline on the same scale as the depopulation described by Juhani Koponen in this volume which followed the imperialist invasion. Nevertheless, the violence of the slave trade did disrupt environmental control. Although Giblin has reported expansion of cultivation in areas controlled by powerful patrons, the concentration of population around patrons meant abandonment of other areas to bush and thus the spread of animal diseases. In Upare, moreover, I have indicated that the violence disrupted agriculture and caused a severe famine.

The impact of colonial violence has also been recognized, but its demographic effect has not been adequately assessed. Kjekshus estimated that the population declined in the early colonial period by as much as 50 per cent, but others, as Maddox's essay indicates, have argued that although the reduction in population was initially smaller, it extended well into the colonial period. Yet the impact of colonialism was both violent and far-reaching, as John Iliffe reminds us in commenting that local economies were reordered into a 'colonial pattern, just as they had previously been re-ordered around trade with Zanzibar'.[18] For, whereas the growth of long-distance trade was part of the competitive stage of capitalist expansion which only partially transformed local economies, at the imperialist stage, colonial government more thoroughly reordered local economies as it created a colonial economy which was intended to increase accumulation.

The most important economic asset controlled by the colonial system was the labour power of the local population, but it required bloody wars before this control could be secured. Although there were a few areas where colonial economic control was scarcely felt before the end of the German period, colonial economic pressure had reached almost every corner of the country by the beginning of the First World War, because most adult men had to pay tax in money. In a sense, the economic trends of the era of long-distance trade continued, for German colonialism brought opportunities to earn money by continuing to produce for exchange. New crop varieties were introduced by missionaries and settlers, and in suitable environments farmers took the initiative in integrating them into their production systems. Coffee growing is a good example, because its spread into Usambara, Upare, Kilimanjaro and Meru/Arusha was not planned by the colonial regime, and in fact met opposition from colonialists who wished to protect European coffee-growers by discouraging peasant coffee production. But by the 1920s it was too late to stop coffee growing. This is an example of the sort of continuity that has been neglected by those who have seen a sharp division between precolonial and colonial African economies, for many qualities which existed in precolonial economies, such as willingness to accommodate new crops and production procedures, persisted.

The essays dealing with the colonial period in this volume demonstrate these forms of continuity very well. Maddox describes a semi-arid Ugogo environment in central Tanzania where in the nineteenth and early twentieth centuries there were a number of famines, including the catastrophic *Mtunya* of 1916–20. Although the population was greatly reduced by death and dispersal, during the 1920s ecological and economic recovery made rapid population increase possible. This was accomplished by cattle-wealthy individuals who were able to attract other people and use their labour to extend both cultivation and animal production. Nevertheless, recovery in Ugogo was disrupted by colonial policies which aimed to increase production during the Depression of the 1930s and the Second World War. The labour that had congregated around wealthy cattle owners was dispersed to settler farms and plantations in other parts of the country. Famines returned and population increase was halted until the 1950s.

Counter-productive economic policy was evident not only in Ugogo, but also in many other parts of the country. In the Pare Mountains, for example, the colonial government decided in the 1930s to substitute cotton for the coffee that the Pare had developed for themselves even though the two crops did not grow in the same ecological zone.[19] Thus just as the colonial regime made the Gogo give up agricultural production to become migrant labourers, so too it frustrated local initiative in Upare by deciding that the Pare should concentrate labour on cotton. Clearly the colonial economy was not shaped for the benefit of the rural population, but was intended to benefit the metropolitan economic system.

A second example of continuity and local initiative is provided by Monson's chapter on the inner Kilombero Valley. The policy of creating forest reserves without regard for the agricultural systems of the people who had been using the forests previously may now appear ridiculous, but it was quite consistent with colonial economic organization, because the forests were reserved for exploitation by the metropolitan economy. Hence, because farmers were confined to restricted areas which they had to farm without adequate fallow periods and without erosion control, reduced yields and silting resulted in the rice-growing areas of the valley. Colonial officials knew that certain activities of the local population, such as grazing and burning of the undergrowth, could have been beneficial for the forest reserve, but would not allow them. The contradictions of conservation policy were highlighted by restrictions on use of *mvule* for canoe-building, for, while colonial forestry officials saw *mvule* as exportable timber, the Wandamba needed them for canoe construction if they were to respond to opportunities for transporting rice and fish from the Kilombero Valley to Indian traders settled in Ifakara and Kilosa. The Indian traders who hired the canoes actually played an important part in making the colonial economy work, but forestry officials worried only about timber and the canoes, which they thought were too large for the Wandamba.

A similar conservationist policy has been described by Chris Conte in his contribution to this volume on ecological history in the plateau forests of West Usambara. Here the Wambugu had settled for centuries on the central plateau, where they developed a pastoral way of life which utilized grassland pastures at the edge of the forest and forest grazing during dry seasons. By the colonial period, however, changed circumstances had forced the Wambugu to turn to cultivation in order to be able to survive in their environment. Colonial conservationists in both the German and British periods saw the Wambugu as a threat to forest conservation policy and thus tried to exclude them from the forest reserve. The Usambara forest policy demonstrates that economic exploitation was at the heart of forest conservation policy, for it replaced slow-growing indigenous timber with fast-growing exotic species.

Both in the Kilombero Valley and in Usambara, previous environmental adaptations by the local population were ignored by European conservationists. Indeed, it is interesting to note the differences in opinion between the district officers, who were sympathetic to the local population, and the forest officials, who would not compromise their conservationist policy. Yet, as pointed out above, it should not be surprising that the forest conservation policy was accepted by the colonial government because, despite contradictions, it was consistent with the general direction of the development of a colonial economy.

Colonial rural development policies were indeed contradictory when assessed from the point of view of the needs of the local population. But one should remember that colonial regimes were managing labour for a peripheral economy serving the centre in the capitalist system. From the centre, labour migration and peasant production were but two sides of the same coin. Indirect rule during the British period created the impression that local politics could be managed through indigenous leaders, but the demands for tax, labour and cash crops altered the situation to such an extent that the so-called 'traditional leaders' were nothing more than a low level of colonial administration. This is illustrated by the essay by Pamela Maack on the Luguru revolt against soil conservation measures in the 1950s. As one of the colonial development schemes proposed after the Second World War, the Uluguru Land Usage Scheme was intended to arrest soil erosion in the overpopulated Uluguru Mountains. The problem was an old one, for even the 'Germans had noticed overpopulation and forest destruction in Uluguru in the 1890s'.[20] However, bench terraces reduced rather than increased yields, at least to begin with, and thus intensified worries about access to land in a country already overpopulated for many years. Local chiefs did not help the situation since they seemed to side with the British colonial officials rather than with their people. In this instance, their role in environmental matters was markedly different from that of precolonial political leadership.

The revolt against terracing in 1955 was therefore an instance of open resistance to the chiefs and overall policy of 'indirect rule'. Steven Feierman has described a similar reaction in West Usambara, where peasants opposed the Mlalo Land Rehabilitation Scheme, which included 'plans for labour intensive erosion control, for removing land from cultivation, and for moving people out of the mountains'.[21] Both plans emphasized erosion control at a time when overpopulation and land scarcity were looming threats to an impoverished peasantry. In both cases the rise of nationalism in Tanganyika seemed to give new hope to the people, for the Tanganyika African National Union (TANU) moved to exploit the grievances of the peasantry as part of the drive for independence. In supporting the nationalist movement, peasants anticipated the possibility of re-establishing control over their environments, but it can also be said that perhaps TANU was not sufficiently responsive to rural concerns about environmental problems.

All these examples indicate that we need to know the history of interaction between rural communities and their environments if we are to perceive properly the problems of development in postcolonial Africa, for otherwise we may face the same kinds of failures which occurred in the colonial period. We have referred earlier in this chapter to continuity between the late precolonial and colonial periods in the responses of rural communities to the need for environmental control. In fact, continuity can be seen with particular clarity when we examine responses to agricultural market opportunities. But in contrast, there was dramatic discontinuity in forms of political authority. In this volume we have tried to restore the 'sense for possibilities for change' which existed in the precolonial period and which also existed in a more restricted manner during the colonial period among rural communities. The problem in the colonial and postcolonial periods is not that Africans were reluctant to accept agricultural change, but rather that the pattern of colonial economy stifled their efforts to achieve meaningful change.

Conclusion
Notes

1. James C. McCann, 'Agriculture and African History', *Journal of African History*, 32,3 (1991): 507.

2. Jamie Monson. 'How the "Squeeze" Began: Ecology Control and the Sustainability of Agricultural Systems in the Inner Kilombero Valley of Tanzania, 1840-1890.' Paper presented at the Annual Meeting of the African Studies Association, November 1990.

3. Terence O. Ranger, *The Recovery of African Initiative in Tanzanian History* (Dar es Salaam, 1969).

4. See for example, Reginald Coupland, *East Africa and Its Invaders* (Oxford, 1938).

5. Arnold Temu and Bonaventure Swai, *Historians and Africanist History* (London, 1981).

6. I.N. Kimambo and A.J. Temu, eds, *A History of Tanzania* (Nairobi, 1969).

7. D. Denoon and A.A. Kuper, 'Nationalist Historians in Search of a Nation: The "New Historiography" in Dar es Salaam', *African Affairs* 69 (1970): 348.

8. I.N. Kimambo, 'Historical Research in Mainland Tanzania', in Gwendolen Carter and Ann Paden, eds, *Expanding Horizons in African Studies* (Evanston, 1969), p. 82.

9. Walter Rodney, *How Europe Underdeveloped Africa* (Washington, 1982) and Martin Kaniki, ed., *Tanzania Under Colonial Rule* (London, 1980).

10. See for example E.A. Alpers, 'The Coast and the Development of Caravan Trade', in Kimambo and Temu. eds, *A History of Tanzania*, pp. 35-56.

11. I.N. Kimambo, *Three Decades of Historical Research at Dar es Salaam* (Dar es Salaam, forthcoming).

12. Sally Falk Moore, *Social Facts and Fabrications* (Cambridge, 1981), Steven Feierman, *The Shambaa Kingdom* (Madison, 1974) and *Peasant Intellectuals* (Madison, 1990), and I.N. Kimambo, *A Political History of the Pare* (Nairobi, 1969) and *Penetration and Protest in Tanzania* (London, 1991).

13. Alpers, 'The Coast and the Development of the Caravan Trade'.

14. See Kimambo, *Penetration and Protest*, pp. 2-4.

15. Godfrey and Monica Wilson, *The Analysis of Social Change* (Cambridge, 1945).

16. Kimambo, 'Enlargement of Scale among the Pare, 1750-1890', Alpers, 'Enlargement of Scale among the Yao in the Nineteenth Century', Roberts, 'Enlargement of Scale among the Nyamwezi in the Nineteenth Century', and Feierman, 'Enlargement of Political Scale in Pre-Colonial Africa', Makerere Institute of Social Research Conference, Dar es Salaam, January 1968.

17. Helge Kjekshus, *Ecology Control and Economic Development in East African History: The Case of Tanganyika, 1850-1950* (London, 1977).

18. John Iliffe, *A Modern History of Tanganyika* (Cambridge, 1979), p. 123.

19. Kimambo, *Penetration and Protest*, pp. 80-2.

20. Iliffe, *Modern History*, p. 349.

21. See Feierman, *Peasant Intellectuals*, pp. 160-73.

Bibliography
of Non-Archival Sources

Compiled
with the assistance of
CHRISTINE SLOOK

Acland, J.D. *East African Crops*. Harlow, England: Longman, 1971.

Allan, William. *The African Husbandman*. Edinburgh and London: Oliver & Boyd, 1965.

Alpers, Edward. 'Enlargement of Scale among the Yao in the Nineteenth Century'. Makerere Institute of Social Research Conference, Dar es Salaam, January 1968.

——. 'The Coast and the Development of Caravan Trade'. In *A History of Tanzania*, edited by I.N. Kimambo and A.J. Temu, pp. 35–56. Nairobi: East Africa Publishing House, 1969.

——. *Ivory and Slaves in East Central Africa*. London: Heinemann, 1975.

Ambler, Charles. *Kenyan Communities in the Age of Imperialism: The Central Region in the Late Nineteenth Century*. New Haven: Yale University Press, 1988.

Ambrose, Stanley. 'Archaeological and Linguistic Reconstructions of History in East Africa'. In *The Archaeological and Linguistic Reconstruction of African History*, edited by Christopher Ehret and Merrick Posnansky, pp. 104–58. Berkeley: University of California Press, 1984.

Anderson, David M. 'Depression, Dust Bowl, Demography, and Drought: The Colonial State and Soil Conservation in East Africa During the 1930s'. *African Affairs* 83 (1984): 321–43.

——. 'Cultivating Pastoralists: Ecology and Economy Among the Il Chamus of Baringo, 1840–1980'. In *The Ecology of Survival: Case Studies from Northeast African History*, edited by Douglas H. Johnson and David M. Anderson, 241-60. Boulder: Westview Press, 1988.

Anderson, David and R. Grove, eds. *Conservation in Africa: Peoples, Policies and Practice*. Cambridge: Cambridge University Press, 1987.

Austen, Ralph. *African Economic History: Internal Development and External Dependency*. Portsmouth, NH: Heinemann, 1987.

Bachmann, Traugott. *Ich gab manchen Anstoss*. Edited by Hans-Windekilde Jannasch. Hamburg: L. Appel, [c. 1956].

Bagenal, C.J. 'Mwariye: A Sacred Mountain of Tanganyika'. *Tanganyika Notes and Records* 26 (Jan. 1954): 58–63.

Baker, R.E.D. and N.W. Simmonds. 'Bananas in East Africa'. *Empire Journal of Experimental Agriculture* 19 (1951): 283–90 and 20 (1952): 66–76.

Bald, Detlef. 'Afrikanischer Kampf gegen Koloniale Herrschaft: Der Maji-Maji Aufstand in Ostafrika'. *Militärgeschichtliche Mitteilungen* 1 (1976): 23–50.

Bantje, H. *The Rufiji Agriculture System: Impact of Rainfall, Floods and Settlement*. Dar es Salaam: BRALUP, 1979.

——. *Flood and Famines: A Study of Food Shortages in Rufiji District*. Dar es Salaam: BRALUP, 1980.

Barbour, K.M. and R.M. Prothero, eds. *Essays on African Population*. London: Routledge, 1961.

Baumann, Oscar. 'Usambara'. *Petermann's Geographische Mitteilungen* 2 (1889): 47–49.

——. *In Deutsch Ost-Afrika während des Aufstandes*. Vienna: Ölmutz, 1890.

——. *Usambara und seine Nachbargebiete*. Berlin: D. Reimer, 1891.

——. *Durch Massailand zur Nilquelle*. Berlin: D. Reimer, 1894.

Baur, Étienne. 'Lettre'. *Annales de la Oeuvre de la Sainte-Enfance, Paris* 35 (1884): 328–41.

——. 'Dans l'Oudoé et l'Ouzigoua'. In *À Travers le Zanguebar*, edited by Alexandre Le Roy and Étienne Baur, pp. 9–110. Tours: Mame Et Fils, 1893.

Becker, Alexander. 'Über Bahnbau in Deutsch-Ostafrika'. *DKB* (1899): 760–3.

Becker, Brüder. 'Die Wambugukinder.' *Nachrichten aus der ostafrikanischen Mission* 8 (1894): 98–102.

——. *Arbeiten aus dem kaiserlichen besundheits-Amt*, 1897.

Beinart, William. 'Soil Erosion, Conservationism, and Ideas About Development in Southern Africa'. *Journal of Southern African Studies* 11, 2 (1984): 52–83.

Berntsen, John. 'The Maasai and their Neighbors: Variables of Interaction'. *African Economic History* 2 (1976): 1–11.

Berry, L. and J. Townshend. 'Soil Conservation Practices in Tanzania: An Historical Perspective'. *Geografiska Annaler* 54A (1972): 241–53.

Berry, Sara S. 'The Food Crisis and Agrarian Change in Africa: A Review Essay'. *African Studies Review* 27 (1984): 59–112.

Blackburn, R.H. 'Honey in Okiek Personality, Culture and Society'. Ph.D. Dissertation, Michigan State University, 1971.

Blaikie, Piers and Harold Brookfield. *Land Degradation and Society*. London and New York: Methuen, 1987.

Boell, Ludwig. *Die Operationen in Ost-Afrika*. Hamburg: W. Dachert, 1951.

Bongaarts, John, Odile Frank and Ron Lesthaege. 'The Proximate Determinants of Fertility in Sub-Saharan Africa'. *PDR* 10 (1984): 511–37.

Boserup, Ester. *The Conditions of Agricultural Growth: the Economics of Agrarian Change Under Population Pressure*. New York: Aldine, 1965.

Boswell, John. *The Kindness of Strangers: The Abandonment of Children in Western Europe From Late Antiquity to the Renaissance*. New York: Vintage Books, 1988.

Brett, E.A. *Colonialism and Underdevelopment in East Africa: The Politics of Economic Change 1919-1939*. New York: NOK Publishers, 1973.

Brooke, Clarke. 'The Heritage of Famine in Central Tanzania'. *Tanzania Notes and Records* 67 (1967): 15–22.

Bryceson, Deborah Fahy. *Food Insecurity and the Social Division of Labor in Tanzania, 1919-1985*. New York: St Martin's Press, 1990.

Buchwald, Johannes. 'Westusambara, die Vegetation und der wirtschaftliche Werth des Landes'. *Zeitschrift für Tropische Landwirtschaft* 1 (1897): 82–5.

Buell, Raymond Leslie. *The Native Problem in Africa*. New York: Macmillan, 1928.

Burton, Richard. 'The Lake Regions of Central Equatorial Africa'. *Journal of the Royal Geographical Society* 29 (1859): 1–464.

——. *The Lake Regions of Central Africa*, 2 vols. London: Longman, 1860.

Busse, Walter. 'Forschungsreise durch den südlichen Teil von Deutsch-Ostafrika'. *Beihefte zum Tropenpflanzer* 3, 3 (1902): 93–119.

Caldwell, John C. and Pat Caldwell. 'The Cultural Context of High Fertility in Sub-Saharan Africa'. *PDR* 13 (1987): 409–37.

Cameron, Verney Lovett. *Across Africa*. New York: Harper and Brothers, 1877.

Clyde, David F. *History of the Medical Services of Tanganyika*. Dar es Salaam: Dar es Salaam Government Press, 1962.

——. *Malaria in Tanzania*. London: Oxford University Press, 1967.

Coale, Ansley. 'Fertility in Prerevolutionary China: Defence of a Reassessment'. *PDR* 10 (1984): 471–80.

Cohen, David William and E.S. Atieno Odhiambo. *Siaya: The Historical Anthropology of an African Landscape*. London: James Currey Publishers, 1989.

Collett, David Phillip. 'The Spread of Early Iron Producing Communities in Eastern and Southern Africa'. Ph.D. Dissertation, Cambridge University, 1985.

Collier, Paul, Samir Radwan and Samuel Wangwe. *Labour and Poverty in Rural Tanzania:*

Bibliography of Non-Archival Sources

Ujamaa and Rural Development in the United Republic of Tanzania. Oxford: Clarendon Press, 1990.

Cooper, Frederick. *Plantation Slavery on the East Coast of Africa*. New Haven: Yale University Press, 1977.

Copland, B.D. 'A Note on the Origin of the Mbugu with a Text'. *Zeitschrift für Eingeborenen-Sprachen* 24 (1933–34): 241–44.

Cordell, Dennis D. and Joel W. Gregory. 'Historical Demographic History in Africa'. *Canadian Journal of African Studies* 14, 3 (1980): 389–416.

——. 'Earlier African Historical Demographies'. *Canadian Journal of African Studies* 23, 1 (1989): 5–27.

Cordell, Dennis D., Joel W. Gregory and Victor Piché. 'African Historical Demography: The Search for a Theoretical Framework'. In *African Population and Capitalism: Historical Perspectives*, edited by Dennis Cordell and Joel Gregory, pp. 14–34. Boulder: Westview Press, 1987.

Cory, Hans. 'The Arusha: Economic and Social Change'. In *Markets in Africa*, edited by P. Bohannan and G. Dalton. Evanston, IL: Northwestern University Press, 1965.

Coulbois, François. 'Une Tournée dans le Vicariat Apostolique de Zanguebar, Oct.–Nov. 1884'. *Les Missions Catholiques* 17 (1885): 462–6, 485–9, 497–502, 512–15, 521–5, 536–8, 545–8.

Coulson, Andrew. *Tanzania: A Political Economy*. Oxford: Oxford University Press, 1982.

Coupland, Reginald. *East Africa and Its Invaders: From the Earliest Times to the Death of Seyyid Said in 1856*. Oxford: Oxford University Press, 1938.

Cronon, W. *Changes in the Land: Indians, Colonists, and the Ecology of New England*. New York: Hill and Wang, 1983.

——. 'Modes of Prophecy and Production: Placing Nature in History'. *Journal of American History* 76, 4 (1990): 1122–31.

Culwick, A.T. 'The Population Trend'. *Tanganyika Notes and Records* 11 (1941): 13–17.

Culwick, A.T. and G.M. Culwick. *Ubena of the Rivers*. London: G. Allen and Unwin Ltd., 1935.

——. 'A Study of Population in Ulanga, Tanganyika Territory, I and II'. *Sociological Review* 30 (1938): 365–79 and 31 (1939): 25–43.

Dannholz, J.J. 'Säuglingssterblichkeit in Mbaga'. *Die ärztliche Mission* 9 (1914): 123–7.

Dawson, Marc H. 'Smallpox in Kenya, 1880–1920'. *Social Science and Medicine* 13B (1979): 245–50.

——. 'Socio-economic and Epidemiological Change in Kenya, 1880-1925'. Ph.D. Dissertation, University of Wisconsin, Madison. 1983.

——. 'Health, Nutrition, and Population in Central Kenya, 1890–1945'. In *African Population and Capitalism: Historical Perspectives*, edited by Dennis Cordell and Joel Gregory, pp. 201–17. Boulder: Westview Press, 1987.

de Courmont, Raoul. 'Rapport'. *Annales Apostoliques de la Congrégation du Saint-Esprit et du Saint Coeur de Marie* 9 (1894): 81–96.

Denoon, D. and A. Kuper. 'Nationalist Historians in Search of a Nation: The "New Historiography" in Dar es Salaam'. *African Affairs* 69 (1970): 329–49.

de Waal, Alexander. *Famine that Kills: Darfur, Sudan, 1984–1985*. Oxford: Clarendon Press, 1989.

Dobson, E.B. 'Land Tenure of the Wasambaa'. *Tanganyika Notes and Records* 10 (1940): 15–20.

Dyson, Tim and Mike Murphy. 'The Onset of Fertility Transition'. *PDR* 11 (1985): 399–440.

Egerö, Bertil and Roushdi Henin. *The Population of Tanzania: An Analysis of the 1967 Population Census*. Dar es Salaam: UDSM, BRALUP, 1973.

Ehret, Christopher and Derek Nurse. 'The Taita Cushites'. *Sprache und Geschichte in Afrika* 3 (1981): 125–68.

Eick, E. 'Berichte über meine Reise ins Kwai- und Masumbailand (Usambara) vom 12. bis 16. März 1896'. *Mitteilungen aus dem Deutschen Schutzgebiet* 9 (1896): 184–8.

Engler, Adolph. 'Über die Flora des Gebirgslandes von Usambara, auf Grund der von Herrn Carl Holst daselbst gemachten Sammlungen'. *Botanische Jahrbücher für Systematik, Pflanzengeschichte und Pflanzengeographie* 17 (1893): 156–68.

——. 'Über die Gliederung der Vegetation von Usambara und der angrenzenden Gebiete'. *Abhandlungen der Koniglichen Akademie der Wissenschaften* (1894): 1–86.

——. 'Über die Vegetationsformationen Ost-Afrikas auf Grund einer Reise durch

Usambara zum Kilimandscharo'. *Zeitschrift der Gesellschaft für Erdkunde zu Berlin* 38 (1903): 254–79.

Ewbank, Douglas C. 'Fertility Estimation'. In The Demography of *Tanzania: An Analysis of the 1973 National Demographic Survey of Tanzania,* vol VI, edited by Roushdi A. Henin, pp. 70–92. Dar es Salaam Bureau of Statistics, United Republic of Tanzania 1973.

Farler, J.P. 'The Usambara Country in East Africa'. *Proceedings of the Royal Geographical Society* 1 (1879): 81–97.

Feierman, Steven. 'Concepts of Sovereignty Among the Shambaa and Their Relation to Political Action'. D. Phil Thesis, Oxford University. 1972.

——. *The Shambaa Kingdom: A History.* Madison, WI: University of Wisconsin Press, 1974.

——. *Peasant Intellectuals: Anthropology and History in Tanzania.* Madison, WI: University of Wisconsin Press, 1990.

Fetter, Bruce. 'Demography in the Reconstruction of African Colonial History'. In *Demography from Scanty Evidence: Central Africa in the Colonial Era,* edited Bruce Fetter, pp. 1–24. Boulder: Lynne Rienner, 1990.

Fiedler, Klaus. *Christentum und afrikanische Kultur: Konservative deutsche Missionare in Tanzania 1900–1940.* Gütersloh: Gütersloher Verlagshaus G. Mohm, 1983.

Fleuret, Patrick C. 'Farm and Market: A Study of Society and Agriculture in Tanzania'. Ph.D. Dissertation, University of California, Santa Barbara, 1978.

Flinn, Michael W. *The European Demographic System, 1500–1820.* Baltimore, MD: Johns Hopkins University Press, 1981.

Food and Agriculture Organization. *The Rufiji Basin, Tanganyika: Report to the Government of Tanganyika on the Preliminary Reconnaissance Survey of the Rufiji Basin.* Rome: FAO, 1961.

Ford, John. *The Role of the Trypanosomiases in African Ecology: A Study of the Tsetse Fly Problem.* Oxford: Clarendon Press, 1971.

Fortmann, Louise. 'Development Prospects in Arumeru District'. Unpublished paper, Dar es Salaam: USAID/Tanzania, 1977.

Fraser, James P. 'Tracking Down Mahogany'. *Timber Trades Journal and Sawmill Advertiser* 120 (4 January 1930): 11–12.

Gadgil, Madhav and Ramachandra Guha. *This Fissured Land: An Ecological History of India.* Berkeley and Los Angeles: University of California Press, 1992.

Giblin, James. 'Famine and Social Change During the Transition to Colonial Rule in Northeastern Tanzania 1880–1896'. *African Economic History* 15 (1986): 85–105.

——. 'Famine, Authority, and the Impact of Foreign Capital in Handeni District, Tanzania, 1840-1940'. Ph.D. Dissertation, University of Wisconsin, Madison. 1986.

——. 'East Coast Fever in Socio-Historical Context: A Case Study from Tanzania'. *International Journal of African Historical Studies* 23, 3 (1990): 401–21.

——. 'Trypanosomiasis Control in African History: An Evaded Issue?' *Journal of African History* 31, 1 (1990): 59–80.

——. *The Politics of Environmental Control in Northeastern Tanzania, 1840–1940.* Philadelphia: University of Pennsylvania Press, 1993.

Goodman, Morris. 'The Strange Case of Mbugu'. In *Pidginization and Creolization of Languages,* edited by Dell Hymes, pp. 243–54. Cambridge: Cambridge University Press, 1971.

Goody, Jack. *Technology, Tradition and the State in Africa.* London: Oxford University Press, 1971.

Grant, D.K.S. 'Forestry in Tanganyika'. *Empire Forestry Journal* 3, 1 (1924): 33–8.

Gray, Robert F. *The Sonjo of Tanganyika.* London: Oxford University Press, 1963.

Green, E.C. 'The Wambugu of Usambara (With Notes on Kimbugu)'. *Tanzania Notes and Records* 61 (1963): 175–89.

Griffiths, J.E.S. 'The Aba-Ha of the Tanganyika Territory – Some Aspects of Their Tribal Organizations and Sleeping Sickness Concentration'. *Tanganyika Notes and Records* 2 (Oct. 1936): 72–6.

Gulliver, P.H. *Report on Land and Population in the Arusha Chiefdom.* Arusha: Tanganyika Provisional Administration, 1957.

——. 'The Population of the Arusha Chiefdom: A High Density Area in East Africa'. *Rhodes-Livingstone Journal* 28 (1960): 21.

——. *Social Control in an African Society.* London and Boston: Boston University Press, 1963.

Gutmann, Bruno. *Das Recht der Dschagga.* Munich: Beck, 1926.

Guyer, Jane I. 'Household and Community in African Studies'. *African Studies Review* 24 (1981), pp. 87–137.

Bibliography of Non-Archival Sources

Gwassa, G.C.K. 'History of Buha through Tunze Papers'. Unpublished paper, Dar es Salaam: University College, 1967.

Gwassa, G.C.K. and John Iliffe, eds. *Records of the Maji Maji Uprising: Part One.* Nairobi: East Africa Literature Bureau, 1968.

Hakansson, Thomas. 'Social and Political Aspects of Intensive Agriculture in East Africa: Some Models from Cultural Anthropology'. *Azania* 24 (1989): 12–19.

Hammond-Tooke, W.D. 'Kinship Authority and Political Authority in Precolonial South Africa'. In *Tradition and Transition in Southern Africa*, edited by Andrew D. Spiegel and Patrick A. McAllister, pp. 185–199. New Brunswick and London: Transaction Publishers, 1991.

Harries, Lyndon. 'Bishop Lucas and the Masasi Experiment'. *International Review of Missions* 34 (1945): 389–96.

Hartwig, G.W. *The Art of Survival in East Africa: The Kerebe and Long-distance Trade, 1800-1895.* New York: Africana Publishing, 1976.

Henin, Roushdi A., Douglas C. Ewbank and Nicholas E. Oyo. 'Fertility Trends: Analysis of Fertility Histories'. In *The Demography of Tanzania: An Analysis of the 1973 National Demographic Survey of Tanzania VI*, edited by Roushdi A. Henin, pp. 94–109. Dar es Salaam Bureau of Statistics, United Republic of Tanzania 1973.

Hill, J.F.R. and J.P. Moffett, eds. *Tanganyika: A Review of Its Resources and Their Development.* Dar es Salaam: Government Printer, 1955.

Hinnebusch, Thomas H., Derek Nurse and Martin Mould. *Studies in the Classification of Eastern Bantu Languages.* Hamburg: Buske, 1981.

Hjort af Ornäs, Anders and M. A. Mohamed Salih, eds. *Ecology and Politics: Environmental Stress and Security in Africa.* Uppsala: Scandinavian Institute of African Studies, 1989.

Hogendorn, Jan S. and K.M. Scott. 'Very Large-Scale Agricultural Projects: The Lessons of the East African Groundnut Scheme'. In *Imperialism, Colonialism, and Hunger: East and Central Africa*, edited by Robert I. Rotberg, pp. 167–98. Lexington, MA: Lexington Books, 1983.

Hopkins, A.G. *An Economic History of West Africa.* New York and London: Columbia University Press and Longman, 1973.

Horner, Anton. 'L'Oukami (Afrique Orientale) I'. *Les Missions Catholiques* 5 (1873): 584–6.

——. 'L'Oukami (Afrique Orientale) VI'. *Les Missions Catholiques* 6 (1874): 20–1, 33–4, 44–5.

Hutley, Walter. *The Central African Diaries of Walter Hutley, 1877-1881.* Edited by James B. Wolf. Boston: African Studies Center, Boston University, 1976.

Hyden, Goran. *Beyond Ujamaa in Tanzania: Underdevelopment and an Uncaptured Peasantry.* Berkeley and London: University of California Press and Heinemann, 1980.

Iliffe, John. *Tanganyika Under German Rule, 1905-1912.* Cambridge: Cambridge University Press, 1969.

——. *Agricultural Change in Modern Tanganyika: An Outline History.* Nairobi: East Africa Publishing House, 1971.

——. 'Review of *Ecology Control and Economic Development in East African History*'. *Journal of African History* 19 (1978): 139–41.

——. *A Modern History of Tanganyika.* Cambridge: Cambridge University Press, 1979.

——. *The African Poor: A History.* Cambridge: Cambridge University Press, 1987.

Isaacman, Allen. 'Peasants and Rural Social Protest in Africa'. *African Studies Review* 33, 2 (September 1990): 1–120.

Ittameier, Carl. 'Die Erhaltung und Vermehrung der Eingeborenen-Bevölkerung'. *Hamburgische Universität, Abhandlungen aus dem Gebiet der Auslandskunde* 13, D/1 (1923): 1–82.

Jaeuber, I.B. *The Population of Tanganyika.* New York: United Nations, 1949.

Jatzold, Ralph and E. Baum. *The Kilombero Valley (Tanzania): Characteristic Features of the Economic Geography of a Semihumid East African Flood Plain and Its Margins.* Munich: Weltforum Verlag, 1968.

Johanssen, E. 'Die Mission unter den Wambugu'. *Nachrichten aus der ostafrikanischen Mission* 8 (1894): 24–6.

——. 'Missionsarbeit unter den Wambugu'. *Nachrichten aus der ostafrikanischen Mission* 11 (1897): 124–7.

Johnson, Douglas H. and David M. Anderson, eds. *The Ecology of Survival: Case Studies from Northeast African History.* Boulder: Westview Press, 1988.

Bibliography of Non-Archival Sources

Johnston, H.H. *The Kilimanjaro Expedition*. London: Kegan Paul, 1886.

Kaniki, Martin, ed. *Tanzania Under Colonial Rule*. London: Longman, 1980.

Kimambo, I.N. 'Enlargement of Scale among the Pare, 1750-1890.' Makerere Institute of Social Research Conference, Dar es Salaam, January 1968.

——. 'Historical Research in Mainland Tanzania'. In *Expanding Horizons in African Studies*, edited by Gwendolen Carter and Ann Paden pp. 75–90. Evanston: Northwestern University Press, 1969.

——. *A Political History of the Pare of Tanzania, c. 1500–1900*. Nairobi: East African Publishing House, 1969.

——. *Penetration and Protest in Tanzania: The Impact of the World Economy on the Pare, 1860–1960*. London: James Currey Publishers, and Athens: Ohio University Press, 1991

——. *Three Decades of Historical Research at Dar es Salaam*. Dar es Salaam: University of Dar es Salaam Press, forthcoming.

Kimambo, I. N. and A. J. Temu, eds. *A History of Tanzania*. Nairobi: East African Publishing House, 1969.

Kingdon, Jonathan. *Island Africa: The Evolution of Africa's Rare Animals and Plants*. Princeton: Collins, 1989.

Kisbey, W.H. 'A Journey in Ziguraland'. *Central Africa* 18 (1900): 172–5.

Kjekshus, Helge. *Ecology Control and Economic Development in East African History: The Case of Tanganyika, 1850–1950*. Berkeley and London: University of California Press and Heinemann, 1977. Second impression with new Introduction and Bibliography; London: James Currey, 1996.

Kleine, F. K. 'Die Schlafkrankheitsbekämpfung in Deutsch-Ostafrika vor und nach dem Krieg'. *Deutsche Tropenmedizinische Zeitschrift* 45 (1941): 23–9.

Kongola, E. *Historia Mfupi ya Mbeyu ya 'Wevunjiliza' toka 1688 mpaka 1986: 'Mbukwa Muhindi wa Cimambi'*. Dodoma: n.p., 1986.

Kootz-Kretschmer, Elise. 'Abriss einer Landesgeschichte von Usafwa in Ostafrika'. *Koloniale Rundschau* (1929): 124–31.

Koponen, Juhani. 'Population Growth in Historical Perspective: The Key Role of Changing Fertility'. In *Tanzania: Crisis and Struggle for Survival*, edited by Jannik Boesen, Kjell J. Havnevik, Juhani Koponen and Rie Odgaard, pp. 31–57. Uppsala: Scandinavian Institute for African Studies, 1986.

——. *People and Production in Late Precolonial Tanzania: History and Structures*. Uppsala, Sweden: Scandinavian Institute of African Studies, 1988.

——. 'War, Famine, and Pestilence in Late Precolonial Tanzania: A Case for a Heightened Mortality'. *International Journal of African Historical Studies* 21, 4 (1988): 637–76.

——. *German Colonial Policies in Mainland Tanzania, 1890–1914: Development for Exploitation*. forthcoming.

Krapf, J.L. *Travels, Researches and Missionary Labours During Eighteen Years' Residence in Eastern Africa*. London: Boston, Ticknor and Fields, 1860.

Kremer, Eduard. 'Die unperiodischen Schwankungen der Niederschläge und die Hungersnöte in Deutsch-Ost-Afrika'. *Aus dem Archiv der Deutschen Seewarte* 33 (1910).

Kuczynski, R.R. *Demographic Survey of the British Colonial Empire*: vol. II: *East Africa etc.*. Oxford: Oxford University Press, 1949.

Külz, L. 'Familien-Nachwuchsstatistik über die Eingeborenen von Deutsch-Ostafrika'. *DKB* (1914): 440–57.

——. 'Zur Biologie und Pathologie des Nachwuchses bei den Naturvölkern der deutschen Schutzgebiete'. *Beihefte zum Archiv für Schiffs- und Tropenhygiene* 3 (1919).

Lamphear, John. 'The Kamba and the Northern Mrima Coast'. In *Precolonial African Trade*, edited by Richard Gray and David Birmingham, pp. 75–101. London, New York and Nairobi: Oxford University Press, 1970.

Larson, Lorne. 'A History of the Mahenge (Ulanga) District, c. 1860–1957'. Ph.D. Thesis, University of Dar es Salaam. 1976.

Larsson, Brigitta. *Conversion to Greater Freedom?: Women, Church and Social Change in North-western Tanzania Under Colonial Rule*. Stockholm: Almqvist & Wiksell, 1991.

Latham, M.C. 'A Clinical Nutrition Survey of Certain Areas of the Dodoma and Kondoa Districts of Tanganyika'. *East African Medical Journal* 41 (1964): 69–77.

Le Roy, Alexandre. 'À la Découverte.' *Les Missions Catholiques* 19 (1887): 293–6, 308–12, 320–2, 330–4, 341–4, 353–6, 365–7, 381.

Bibliography of Non-Archival Sources

Leue, A. 'Uha (Deutsch-Ostafrika): Die Ebene bis zum Malagarasi'. *Globus* 79 (1901): 76-8.

Luanda, N.N. 'European Commercial Farming and Its Impact on the Meru and Arusha Peoples of Tanzania, 1920-1955'. Ph.D. Thesis, Cambridge University, 1986.

Lugard, Lord. *The Dual Mandate in British Tropical Africa*. London: W. Blackwood and Sons, 1922.

Lundgren, Björn. *Soil Conditions and Nutrient Cycling Under Natural and Plantation Forests in Tanganyikan Highlands*. Uppsala: Department of Forest Soils, Swedish Unversity of Agricultural Sciences, 1978.

Maack, Pamela A. ' "The Waluguru Are Not Sleeping": Poverty, Culture, and Social Differentiation in Morogoro, Tanzania'. Ph.D. Dissertation, Northwestern University, Evanston, 1992.

McAlpin, Michelle. *Subject to Famine: Food Crises and Economic Change in Western India, 1860-1920*. Princeton: Princeton University Press, 1983.

McCann, James C. *From Poverty to Famine in Northeast Ethiopia: A Rural History, 1900-1935*. Philadelphia: University of Pennsylvania Press, 1987.

———. 'Agriculture and African History: Review Article'. *Journal of African History* 32, 3 (1991): 507-13.

McCarthy, D.M.P. *Colonial Bureaucracy and Creating Underdevelopment: Tanganyika, 1919-1940*. Ames, IA: Iowa State University Press, 1982.

McNeill, William H. *Plagues and Peoples*. Garden City, NY: Anchor, 1976.

Macquarie, C. 'Water Gipsies of the Malagarasi'. *Tanganyika Notes and Records* 9 (June 1940): 61-7.

Maddox, Gregory. '*Njaa*: Food Shortages and Famines in Tanzania Between the Wars'. *International Journal of African Historical Studies* 19, 1 (1986): 17-34.

———. ' "Leave, Wagogo! You Have No Food!": Famine and Survival in Ugogo, Central Tanzania 1916-1961'. Ph.D. Dissertation, Northwestern University, Evanston, Illinois. 1988.

———. '*Mtunya*: Famine in Central Tanzania, 1917-1920'. *Journal of African History* 31, 2 (1990): 181-98.

———. 'Famine, Impoverishment and the Creation of a Labor Reserve in Central Tanzania'. *Disasters* 15, 1 (1991): 35-41.

Maddox, Gregory and Robert H. Jackson. 'The Creation of Identity: Colonial Society in Bolivia and Tanzania'. *Comparative Studies in Society and History* 35, 2 (1993): 263-84.

Malcolm, D.W. *Sukumaland*. London: Oxford University Press, 1953.

Mandala, Elias C. *Work and Control in a Peasant Economy: A History of the Lower Tchiri Valley in Malawi, 1859-1960*. Madison, WI: University of Wisconsin Press, 1990.

Martin, C.J. 'Some Estimates of the General Age Distribution, Fertility, and Rate of Natural Increase of the African Population of British East Africa,' *Population Studies* 7 (1953), pp. 181-99.

———. 'Estimates on Population Growth in East Africa, with Special Reference to Tanganyika and Zanzibar'. In *Essays on African Population*, edited by K.M. Barbour and R.M. Prothero, pp. 49-62. London: Routledge and Kegan Paul, 1961.

Mascarenhas, A.C. 'Aspects of Food Shortages in Tanganyika, 1925-1945'. *Journal of the Geographical Association of Tanzania* 3 (1968): 37-59.

Mbilinyi, Majorie. 'Agribusiness and Casual Labor in Tanzania'. *African Economic History* 15 (1986): 107-38.

Mbilinyi, Simon. *The Economics of Peasant Coffee Production: The Case of Tanzania*. Nairobi Kenya Literature Bureau, 1976.

Mbogoni, L.E.Y. 'Food Production and Ecological Crisis in Dodoma – 1920-1960: Colonial Efforts at Developing the Productive Forces in Peasant Agriculture'. MA Thesis, University of Dar es Salaam, 1981.

Mbosa, Mkeli. 'Colonial Production and Underdevelopment in Ulanga District, 1894-1950'. MA Thesis, University of Dar es Salaam. 1988.

Merker, Moritz. *Die Masai*. 2nd edn. Berlin: D Reimer, 1910.

Meyer, Hans. *Der Kilimandjaro*. Berlin: D. Reimer, 1900.

Mihanjo, Reginald P.A.N. 'Social and Biological Reproduction during Capitalist Transformation: The Historical Demography of the Lake Nyasa Region'. Paper presented to the Department of History Research Seminar. University of Dar es Salaam, 11 November 1993.

261

Bibliography of Non-Archival Sources

Mkomwa, Ernest L. and Godfrey Nkwileh. 'Jadi, Mila, Desturi na Historia ya Wazigua'. Unpublished Manuscript. Handeni, 1968.

Mlay, Wilfred. 'Population Pressure in Arumeru District.' Unpublished paper, Arusha, 1982.

Mnyampala, Mathias E. *The Gogo: History, Customs and Traditions.* Trans. and Introduced by Gregory Maddox. New York: M.E. Sharpe, 1995.

Mochiwa, Anthony. *Habari za Wazigua.* London: Macmillan, 1954.

Moesta, K. 'Die Einwirkung des Krieges auf die Eingeborenenbevölkerung in Deutsch-Ostafrika'. *Koloniale Rundschau* 11 (1919): 6–22.

Molnos, Angela, ed. *Cultural Source Materials for Population Planning in East Africa,* vols. I–III. Nairobi East African Publishing House, 1973.

Monson, Jamie. 'How the "Squeeze" Began: Ecology Control and the Sustainability of Agricultural Systems in the Inner Kilombero Valley of Tanzania, 1840–1890'. Paper presented at the Annual Meeting of the African Studies Association, November 1990.

——. 'An Agricultural History in the Inner Kilombero Valley of Tanzania, 1840–1940.' Ph.D. Dissertation, University of California Los Angeles, 1991.

——. 'Perceiving the Forest: British Forestry Policy and Land Degradation in the Kilombero Valley of Tanzania.' African Studies Association Meetings, St Louis, 26 November 1991.

——. 'Rice and Cotton, Ritual and Resistance: Cash Cropping in Colonial Tanganyika, 1920–1940'. In Allen Isaacman and Richard Roberts, eds. *The Social History of Cotton in Colonial Africa,* edited by Allen Isaacman and Richard Roberts. Portsmouth, NH: Heinemann, forthcoming, 1994.

Moore, Sally Falk. *Social Facts and Fabrications: 'Customary' Law on Kilimanjaro, 1880–1980.* Cambridge: Cambridge University Press, 1986.

Moore, Sally Falk and Paul Puritt. *The Chagga and the Meru of Tanzania.* London: International Africa Institute, 1977.

Moreau, R.E. 'A Synecological Study of Usambara, Tanganyika Territory, with Particular Reference to Birds'. *Journal of Ecology* 23 (1935): 1–43.

Mortimore, Michael. *Adapting to Drought: Farmers, Famines and Desertification in West Africa.* Cambridge: Cambridge University Press, 1989.

Musere, Jonathon. *African Sleeping Sickness: Political Ecology, Colonialism and Control in Uganda.* Lewiston, NY: E Mellen Press, 1990.

Muya, Mwalumwambo A.O.M. 'A Political Economy of Zigua Utani'. In *Utani Relationships,* edited by Stephen A. Lucas, pp. 187–248. Dar es Salaam: University of Dar es Salaam, 1975.

Mworoha, Emile, *et al. Histoire du Burundi.* Paris: Hatier, 1987.

Neubaur, Dr. 'Die Besiedelungsfähigkeit von Westusambara'. *Zeitschrift für Tropische Landwirtschaft* 6 (1902): 496–513.

Ngallaba, Sylvester A.M.M. 'Fertility Differentials in Tanzania with Special Reference to Four Regions'. MA Thesis, University of Dar es Salaam, 1972.

Nigmann, Ernst. *Geschichte der Kaiserlichen Schutztruppe für Deutsch-Ostafrika.* Berlin: Mittler, 1911.

Nurse, Derek. *Classification of Chaga Dialects.* Hamburg: Buske, 1979.

——. 'Bantu Expansion into East Africa: Linguistic Evidence' In *The Archaeological and Linguistic Reconstruction of African History,* edited by Christopher Ehret and Merrick Posnansky, pp. 199–223. Berkeley: University of California Press, 1984.

——. 'Extinct Southern Cushitic Communities in East Africa'. In *Cushitic–Omotic. Papers from the International Symposium on Cushitic and Omotic Languages, Cologne, 6–9 January 1986,* edited by Marianne Bechaus-Gerst and Fritz Serzisko, pp. 93–104. Hamburg: H. Buske, 1988.

Nyagava, S.I. 'History of the Bena to 1906'. Ph.D. Dissertation, University of Dar es Salaam, 1988.

Ohadike, Patrick O. 'Social and Organization Variables Affecting Central Africa Demography'. In *Demography from Scanty Evidence,* edited by Bruce Fetter, pp. 245–67. Boulder: Lynne Rienner, 1990.

Östberg, Wilhelm. *The Kondoa Transformation: Coming to Grips with Soil Erosion in Central Tanzania.* Research Report No. 76. Uppsala: Scandinavian Institute of African Studies, 1986.

Parker, Bishop. 'Letter'. *Church Missionary Intelligencer and Record* 12 (1887): 692–4.

Bibliography of Non-Archival Sources

Patton, Michael. *Dodoma Region, 1929-1959: A History of Famine*. BRALUP Research Report No. 44. Dar es Salaam: BRALUP, UDSM, 1971.

Peiper, Otto. 'Geburtenhäufigkeit, Säuglings- und Kinder-Sterblichkeit und Säuglingsernährung im früheren Deutsch-Ostafrika'. *Veröffentlichungen aus dem Gebiete der Medizinalverwaltung* 6, 9 (1920).

Peltola, Inkeri. *Uzaramu*. Helsinki, 1950.

Picarda, Cado. 'Autour de Mandera'. *Les Missions Catholiques* 18 (1886): 184-9, 197-201, 208-11, 225-8, 234-7, 246-9, 258-61, 269-74, 281-5, 294-7, 312-24, 332-4, 342-6, 356-7 and 365-9.

Pitt-Schenkel, C.J.W. 'Some Important Communities of Warm Temperate Rain Forest at Magamba, West Usambara, Tanganyika Territory'. *Journal of Ecology* 26 (1938): 50-81.

Pottier, Johan P. 'The Politics of Famine Prevention: Ecology, Regional Production and Food Complementarity in Western Rwanda'. *African Affairs* 85, 339 (April 1986): 207-37.

Ranger, T.O. *The Recovery of African Initiative in Tanzanian History*. Inaugural Lecture Series no. 2. Dar es Salaam: University College of Dar es Salaam, 1969.

——. 'Missionary Adaptation of African Religious Institutions: The Masasi Case'. In *The Historical Study of African Religion*, edited by Terence Ranger and Isaria N. Kimambo, pp. 221-51. London, Nairobi and Ibadan: Heinemann Educational, 1972.

Rapp, A., L. Berry and P. Temple, eds. *Studies of Soil Erosion and Sedimentation in Tanzania*. BRALUP Monograph No. 1. Dar es Salaam BRALUP, UDSM, 1973.

Raum, O.F. *Chaga Childhood*. London: Oxford University Press, 1940.

Richards, Audrey and Priscilla Reining. 'Report on Fertility Surveys in Buganda and Buhaya, 1952'. In *Culture and Human Fertility*, edited by Frank Lorimer. Paris, 1954.

Richards, Paul. 'Ecological Change and the Politics of African Land Use'. *African Studies Review* 26, 2 (June 1983): 1-73.

Rigby, Peter. *Cattle and Kinship Among the Gogo: A Semi-pastoral Society of Central Tanzania*. Ithaca: Cornell University Press, 1967.

——. *Persistent Pastoralists: Nomadic Societies in Transition*. London: Zed Press, 1985.

Roberts, A.D., 'Enlargement of Scale among the Nyamwezi in the Nineteenth Century.' Makerere Institute of Social Research Conference, Dar es Salaam, January 1968.

——. ed. *Tanzania Before 1900*. Nairobi: East African Publishing House, 1968.

Rodgers, W.A. and K.M. Homewood. 'Species Richness and Endemism in the Usambara Mountain Forests, Tanzania'. *Biological Journal of the Linnean Society* 18 (1982): 197-242.

Rodney, Walter. *World War II and the Tanzanian Economy*. Ithaca, NY: Africana Studies Research Center, Cornell University 1976.

——. *How Europe Underdeveloped Africa*. Washington, DC: Howard University Press, 1982.

Salim, A.I. 'The East African Coast and Hinterland, 1800-45'. In *UNESCO General History of Africa*, vol. VI: *Africa in the Nineteenth Century Until the 1880s*, edited by J.F. Ade Ajayi, pp. 211-33. Oxford and Berkeley, CA: Heinemann and University of California Press, 1989.

Schabel, Hans. 'Tanganyika Forestry under German Colonial Administration, 1891-1919'. *Forest and Conservation History* 34, 3 (1990): 130-141.

Schneider, Harold K. 'Traditional African Economics'. In *Africa*, 2nd edn, edited by Phyllis M. Martin and Patrick O'Meara, pp. 181-98. Bloomington, IN: Indiana University Press, 1986.

Seavoy, Ronald E. *Famine in East Africa: Food Production and Food Policies*. New York: Greenwood Press, 1989.

Sen, Amartya. *Poverty and Famines: An Essay on Entitlement and Deprivation*. Oxford: Clarendon Press, 1981.

Sender, John and Sheila Smith. *Poverty, Class and Gender in Rural Africa: A Tanzanian Case Study*. London: Routledge, 1990.

Shephard, K. 'Banana Cultivars in East Africa'. *Tropical Agriculture (Trinidad)* 34 (1957): 277-86.

Sheriff, Abdul. *Slaves, Spices and Ivory in Zanzibar*. London: James Currey, 1987.

Shivji, Issa G. *Law, State and the Working Class in Tanzania, 1920-1984*. London: James Currey, 1986.

Showers, Kate. 'Soil Erosion in the Kingdom of Lesotho: Origins and Colonial Response, 1830s-1950s'. *Journal of Southern African Studies* 15, 2 (1989): 263-86.

Siebenlist, Th. *Forstwirtschaft in Deutsch-Ostafrika*. Berlin: 1914.

Bibliography of Non-Archival Sources

Simmonds, N.W. *Bananas.* London: Longman, 1959.

Sissons, Carol Jane. 'Economic Prosperity in Ugogo, East Africa, 1860–1890'. Ph.D. Dissertation, University of Toronto. 1984.

Soper, Robert. 'Iron Age Sites in Northeastern Tanzania'. *Azania* 2 (1967): 19–36.

Spear, Thomas. *Zwangendaba's Ngoni, 1821-1890: A Political and Social History of a Migration.* Madison: African Studies Program, University of Wisconsin, 1972.

——. *The Kaya Complex: A History of the Mijikenda People of Kenya Coast to 1900.* Madison: University of Wisconsin Press, 1974.

——. *Kenya's Past: An Introduction to Historical Method.* London: Longman, 1981.

——. ' "Being Maasai" but not "People of Cattle": Arusha Agricultural Maasai in the 19th Century'. In *Being Maasai,* edited by Thomas Spear and Richard Waller, pp. 120–36. London: James Currey Publishers, 1992.

——. *Mountain Farmers.* London: James Currey Publishers, forthcoming.

Spear, Thomas and Derek Nurse. *The Swahili: Reconstructing the History and Language of an African Society, 800-1500.* Philadelphia: University of Pennsylvania Press, 1984.

Stahl, Kathleen. *History of the Chagga People of Kilimanjaro.* London: Mouton & Co., 1964.

Stanley, Henry M. *How I Found Livingstone: Travels, Adventures, and Discoveries in Central Africa.* London: Sampson, Marston, Low and Searle, 1872.

——. *In Darkest Africa,* vol. 2. New York: Scribner's Sons, 1890.

Steudel, Emil. 'Die Schlafkrankheit in Deutsch-Ostafrika vom Beginn bis Gegenwart'. *Mitteilungen aus den Deutschen Schutzgebieten* 28 (1928): 61–79.

——. 'Das Gesundheitswesen in Deutsch-Ostafrika'. In *Deutsch-Ostafrika,* edited by W. Arning, pp. 179–93. Berlin: D. Reimer, 1936.

Stuhlmann, Franz. 'Bericht über eine Reise durch Usegua und Unguu'. *Mitteilungen der Geographischen Gesellschaft in Hamburg* 10 (1887–8): 143–75.

——. *Mit Emin Pascha ins Herz von Africa.* Berlin: D. Reimer, 1894.

Sumra, Suleman Alarakhia. 'An Analysis of Environmental and Social Problems Affecting Agricultural Development in Handeni District'. MA Thesis, University of Dar es Salaam. 1975.

Supf, Karl. *Deutsche Kolonial-Baumwolle* Berlin, n.d.

Swantz, Lloyd W. 'The Role of the Medicine Man Among the Zaramo of Dar es Salaam'. Ph.D. Dissertation, University of Dar es Salaam, 1974.

Swantz, Marja-Liisa. *Ritual and Symbol in Transitional Zaramo Society with Special Reference to Women.* Uppsala: Scandinavian Institute of African Studies, 1970.

——. *Women in Development: A Creative Role Denied? The Case of Tanzania.* London: Hurst, 1985.

Swartz, Marc J. 'Some Cultural Influences on Family Size in Three East African Societies'. *Anthropological Quarterly* 42 (1969): 73–88.

Tanganyika. *Report on the Native Census, 1921.* Dar es Salaam: Government Printer, 1921.

——. *Census of the Native Population of Tanganyika Territory, 1931.* Dar es Salaam: Government Printer, 1932.

——. *Report of the Committee on Supply and Welfare of Native Labour in the Tanganyika Territory.* Dar es Salaam: Government Printer, 1938.

——. *A Ten-Year Development and Welfare Plan for Tanganyika Territory.* Dar es Salaam: Government Printer, 1946.

——. *African Census Report 1957.* Dar es Salaam: Government Printer, 1963.

——. *Forestry Department Report.* Dar es Salaam: Government Printer, years vary.

——. *Labour Department Annual Report.* Dar es Salaam: Goverment Printer, years vary.

——. *Medical Department Report.* Dar es Salaam: Government Printer, years vary.

——. *Provincial Commissioners' Annual Reports.* Dar es Salaam: Government Printer, years vary.

Telford, Alexander M. *Report on the Development of the Rufiji and Kilombero Valleys.* Dar es Salaam: Government Printer, 1929.

Temu, Arnold and Bonaventure Swai. *Historians and Africanist History: A Critique.* London: Zed Press, 1981.

Thiele, Graham. 'State Intervention and Commodity Production in Ugogo: A Historical Perspective'. *Africa* 54, 3 (1984): 92–107.

Troup, R.S. *Colonial Forest Administration.* Oxford: Oxford University Press, 1940.

Tschannerl, G. *et al. Handeni Water Supply: Preliminary Report and Design Criteria.* BRALUP Paper No. 22. Dar es Salaam: UDSM, 1971.

Tucker, A.N. and M.A. Bryan. 'The Mbugu Anomaly'. *Bulletin of the School of Oriental and African Studies* 37 (1974): 188–207.

Bibliography of Non-Archival Sources

Turshen, Meredeth. *The Political Ecology of Disease in Tanzania*. New Brunswick, NJ: Rutgers University Press, 1984.

——. 'Population Growth and the Deterioration of Health: Mainland Tanzania, 1920–1960'. In *African Population and Capitalism: Historical Perspectives*, edited by Dennis Cordell and Joel Gregory, pp. 187–200. Boulder: Westview Press, 1987.

United Nations. *Additional Information of the Population of Tanganyika*. New York United Nations Department of Social Affairs, Population Division, 1953.

van der Burgt, J.M.M. *Dictionnaire Français-Kirundi*. Bois-le-Duc, Holland, Société 'L'Illustration Catholique,' 1903.

Van Sambeek, Johannes. *Croyances et Coutumes des Baha*, vol. 1. Kabanga: Service d'information, Pères blancs, 1949.

Vansina, Jan. *The Children of Woot: A History of the Kuba Peoples*. Madison: University of Wisconsin Press, 1978.

——. *Paths in the Rainforests: Toward a History of Political Tradition in Equatorial Africa*. Madison: University of Wisconsin Press, 1990.

Volkens, Georg. *Der Kilimandscharo*. Berlin Geographische Verlagshandlung Dietrich Reimer, 1897.

von der Decken, C.C. *Reisen in Ost-Afrika*, 2 vols. Leipzig and Heidelberg: Winter'sche Verlagshandlung, 1869.

Von Freyhold, Michaela. *Case Studies from Handeni. Rural Development Through Ujamaa*, vol. 2. Dar es Salaam: USDM, unpublished, 1971.

Von Götzen, Adolf. *Deutsch-Ostafrika im Aufstand*. Berlin: D. Reimer, 1909.

Waller, Richard. 'Emutai: Crisis and Response in Maasailand, 1883–1902'. In *The Ecology of Survival: Case Studies from Northeast African History*, edited by Douglas Johnson and David Anderson, pp. 73–112. Boulder: Westview Press, 1988.

Warburg, O. 'Die Kulturpflanzen Usambaras'. *Mitteilungen aus den Deutschen Schutzgebieten* 7 (1894): 131–99.

Waters, Tony. 'A Cultural Analysis of the Economy of Affection and the Uncaptured Peasantry in Tanzania'. *Journal of Modern African Studies* 30, 1 (1992): 163–75.

Watts, Michael. ' "Good Try, Mr. Paul": Populism and the Politics of African Land Use'. *African Studies Review* 26, 2 (1983): 73–89.

——. *Silent Violence: Food, Famine and Peasantry in Northern Nigeria*. Berkeley: University of California Press, 1983.

Weston, R.H. 'The Hardwoods We Handle: Market Value and Chief Features of a Few of Them'. *Timber Trades Journal Sawmill Advertiser* 120 (26 March 1932): 867.

Wilson, Godfrey and Monica Wilson. *The Analysis of Social Change*. Cambridge: Cambridge University Press, 1945.

Wilson, Monica. *Rituals of Kinship Among the Nyakusa*. London: Oxford University Press, 1957.

——. *Communal Rituals of the Nyakusa*. London: Oxford University Press, 1959.

——. *Religion and the Transformation of Society: A Study of Social Change in Africa*. Cambridge: Cambridge University Press, 1971.

——. *For Men and Elders: Change in the Relations of Generations and of Men and Women among the Nyakusa-Ngonde People, 1875–1971*. London: International African Institute, 1977.

Winter, Edward H. and T.O. Beidelman. 'Tanganyika: A Study of an African Society at National and Local Levels'. In *Contemporary Change in Traditional Societies*, vol. 1, edited by Julian H. Steward, pp. 61–201. Urbana, Chicago, London: University of Illinois Press, 1967.

Wohltmann, F. 'Die Aussichten des Kaffeebaues in den Usambara-Bergen'. *Zeitschrift für Tropische Landwirtschaft* 1 (1897): 612–17.

Wolf, James B. *Missionary to Tanganyika, 1877–1888: The Writings of Edward Coode Hore, Master Mariner*. London: Frank Cass and Co., 1970.

Wright, Marcia. *German Missions in Tanganyika, 1891–1941*. London: Clarendon Press, 1971.

Wrigley, C.C. 'African Historical Demography'. *Journal of African History* 20 (1979): 127–31.

——. 'Aspects of Economic History'. In *The Colonial Moment in Africa: Essays on the Movement of Minds and Materials 1900–1940*, edited by A. D. Roberts, pp. 77–139. Cambridge: Cambridge University Press, 1990.

Wrigley, E.A. and R.S. Schofield. *The Population History of England, 1541–1871: A Reconstruction*. Cambridge, MA: Harvard University Press, 1981.

Young, Roland and Henry Fosbrooke. *Smoke in the Hills: Political Tension in the Morogoro District of Tanganyika*. Evanston, IL: Northwestern University Press, 1960.

Index

Prepared with the assistance of

ROSA A. CANALES

Index